THE SECOND GENERATION

THE SECOND GENERATION

A STUDY OF THE FAMILY AMONG URBANIZED BANTU IN EAST LONDON

B. A. PAUW

Published on behalf of the
Institute of Social and Economic Research
Rhodes University

CAPE TOWN
OXFORD UNIVERSITY PRESS
LONDON NEW YORK

Oxford University Press, Ely House, London W. 1

GLASGOW NEW YORK TORONTO MELBOURNE WELLINGTON
CAPE TOWN IBADAN NAIROBI DAR ES SALAAM LUSAKA ADDIS ABABA
DELHI BOMBAY CALCUTTA MADRAS KARACHI LAHORE DACCA
KUALA LUMPUR SINGAPORE HONG KONG TOKYO

Oxford University Press, Oxford House, Cape Town

First published - 1963
Second impression - 1964
Third impression - 1968
Fourth impression - 1969
Second edition - 1973

The first edition of this book formed Volume Three of *Xhosa in Town: Studies of the Bantu-speaking Population of East London, Cape Province*, edited by Philip Mayer, and was published on behalf of the Institute of Social and Economic Research, Rhodes University, by the Oxford University Press, Cape Town. The research and publication of the first edition were financed by the National Council for Social Research, but opinions expressed and conclusions reached are those of the author and are not to be regarded as representing the views of the Council or its successor, the Human Sciences Research Council.

ISBN 0 19 570028 7

PRINTED IN SOUTH AFRICA BY
CITADEL PRESS, LANSDOWNE, CAPE

CONTENTS

LIST OF TABLES

ADDITIONAL TABLES: APPENDIX I

LIST OF FIGURES

PREFACE TO THE FIRST EDITION

PHILIP MAYER

The present work brings to an end the trilogy *Xhosa in Town* which deals with the Bantu-speaking population of one industrial city in South Africa. This trilogy does not claim to be exhaustive, but I hope that its plan—for which I have been responsible—has given each contributor the opportunity to say something worth while, on topics which are important in the context of contemporary Africa.

I may perhaps explain how the link between this and the preceding volume, *Townsmen or Tribesmen*, is conceived.

Besides the peasant cultivators typical of Bantu Africa, there exists today in South Africa a large category of landless Bantu. Long before towns and industries rose to their present importance, many South African Bantu were living and working on white-owned farms, with no homes other than those provided for them by the farmer. The recent expansion of towns—it may be said—has merely added a new dimension to the phenomenon of the landless Bantu. Many of the present Bantu town-dwellers are migrating peasants, who have lands and homes in the reserves to which they can retire when their work in town is done; but some are landless men, who permanently depend on their town earnings, having nothing outside town to fall back on. These latter constitute an urban Bantu working class, together with a much smaller urban middle class. *The Second Generation* is about them.

As between the reserve peasant, tilling his own land in a community of independent kraal-owners, and the farm labourer, who owns no land and depends on an employer, there is obviously a sociological difference of a vital kind. Likewise, there is a vital difference between the town worker who can go 'home' to his kraal and the one who cannot. The latter has no land rights in town to set against the rural land rights of the former, since Bantu are not accorded freehold rights in South African towns. Yet the loss of the age-old share in the land—marking, as one would think, a decisive step in African social change—has received little attention in anthropological literature so far. The landed/landless categories, bisecting the rural/urban categories, give the four main types just indicated: peasant, rural labourer, migrant, and real townsman. Of these, the first has received the most attention, in tribal monographs; the second has been mostly neglected,[1] and the essential differences between the third and fourth have been hardly indicated in our all too few studies of South African urban communities.

The trilogy *Xhosa in Town* is partly an attempt to fill this scientific gap. Rather than tribal (ethnic or linguistic) categories, it has been designed around the sociological categories of migrant and real townsmen, as observed in the Bantu locations of the city of East London. Being tribally homogeneous (96 per cent Xhosa-speaking), the East London Bantu population has lent itself to the purpose specially well. The previous volume (*Townsmen or Tribesmen*) was devoted to the migrants. This present volume is, I think, the first study to be made specifically of permanent townsmen as such, at least in South Africa.

[1] The most notable exception is the section on the farms in Hunter, M., *Reaction to Conquest*. Cf. also Roberts, M., *Labour in a Farm Economy*, for a discussion of the economic position of the farm labourer in the eastern Cape Province.

Townsmen or Tribesmen showed how some Xhosa during the course of their East London careers undergo the transition from migrant to real townsman. It defined the process of urbanization primarily as the slackening of ties with the former rural home, carried to the point where the person no longer feels the pull of the hinterland. This is the point where a person's within-town ties, collectively considered, decisively predominate over his extra-town ties, as can be revealed by a study of his network of relations. The present volume is not so much concerned with these first-generation townsmen as with their children. By concentrating on the town-born second generation Dr. Pauw has kept his field rather small but ensured its precision. When a Xhosa has been born and reared in town we can safely assume for certain that complete town-centredness which, in the case of the first-generation immigrant, can only be established by careful individual checking. In the supposed 'immigrant', the desire to go back may reawaken after years of latency (cf. *Townsmen or Tribesmen*); but we know for certain that all of Dr. Pauw's second generation are fully urbanized, in the sense of having all their important personal ties bounded by the town; that they will live and die in town, having no major personal interests elsewhere, and nothing to go back to. We know that they are finally detached from the countryside of their forebears. One symptom is that they rarely do as so many migrants do—send their town-born children away to relatives in the country for upbringing and education.[2]

In East London, the second-generation townsmen are not a large proportion of the Bantu population—only 14 per cent of the adults. However, the reasons for devoting a separate volume to this minority hardly need explaining. The town-born Bantu, as a body, are generally assumed to be the most sophisticated and 'westernized'. It is worth while to investigate in which sense and to what extent this assumption is true, in one medium-sized South African city. Besides, town-born Bantu who have, as Dr. Pauw shows, few or no personal links in the rural areas may raise important political and administrative problems in the South African setting of today. From a wider point of view our findings here should provide significant parallels and contrasts for other parts of the African continent, as industrialization and urbanization approach the level already reached in South Africa. In short, there is every reason to want to know what these people are like. *The Second Generation* is an overdue exploration of a sociologically important field.

With only two years available for fieldwork and writing, it was thought better to select a few topics for intensive study rather than attempt a sketchy 'general picture' of the town-born generation. The terms of reference excluded, in the first place, the formal wage-earning activities in which the East London Xhosa spend most of their waking hours. Wage-earning as such had already been considered in the first volume of the trilogy (*The Black Man's Portion*), to which readers are referred for a picture of living and working conditions. In so far as nearly all Xhosa in East London are restricted to the same sorts of jobs, and all are debarred from trade unions proper, it seemed that the essential differences between migrant and proletarian life could not well be observed in the context of employment. Dr. Pauw's study, therefore, was to run parallel to *Townsmen or Tribesmen* in the sense of concentrating on domestic, personal and leisure-time relations and activities. Within these bounds further important limitations were set by shortness of time. In particular, Dr. Pauw has not been able to

[2] Cf. *Townsmen or Tribesmen*, chap. 17.

give detailed attention to either churches or schools, nor to the many and varied voluntary associations—religious, athletic, political, sociable—which are a notable feature of location life. His main themes are kinship, marriage and the family, and the individual life cycle.

Dr. Pauw's first chapter serves *inter alia* to support the contention made in *Townsmen or Tribesmen*, that the process of urbanization as defined above is greatly influenced by ideology. Among the rural Xhosa one finds two rival ideologies: that of the 'School' section who approve Christianity, formal education and westernization, and that of the 'Red' section who obstinately prefer 'real old Xhosa ways', including the pagan religion. The Red section figures so largely among migrants to East London that it merited the greater part of the previous volume to itself. But its ideology forbids its members to stay in town longer than is economically necessary, or to rear their children there. Thus the parents of the second generation are found to have been School people, in overwhelming proportion. The formal reason which their children allege for their parents' having settled permanently in town—i.e. land shortage in the country—is by no means untrue or unrealistic, but it does not tell the whole truth. Faced by the very same problem of land shortage, most Red families contrive to keep up homes in the rural setting, at whatever cost and inconvenience.[3]

For some readers, the most interesting question about Bantu townspeople will be their degree of 'westernization'. Dr. Pauw's work offers little satisfaction to anyone who may have been hoping to scratch a townsman and find a 'primitive savage'. 'In terms of the contrast between "Western" and "traditional" ' (to quote the final chapter) 'we may say that the culture of the urban Xhosa of East London is predominantly orientated to Western cultural patterns' (p. 194). It is important that the casual reader, particularly if he be a South African, should bear this in mind, so as not to be misled by the appearance in the body of the book of some material on ancestral sacrifice, initiation, witchcraft, and the like. Any study which, like this one, concentrates largely on African life within the four walls of the home, is bound to bring up a certain amount of 'un-Western' material. For the domestic aspects of life are without doubt those in which tribal traditions linger on longest. Indeed, in urban studies in the Rhodesian Copperbelt it seems to have been taken for granted that domestic relations are governed by tribal norms, though industrial relations are not.[4] In *The Second Generation* the 'tribal' details of life are seen, as it were, somewhat more than life size, because time did not allow them to be set in full perspective against their actual background—the background of ceaseless 'Western' activity in church, club, school, workshop, factory, office, and so forth. For example, a later investigation which we have been conducting into the football clubs affiliated in the powerful Gompo Union has brought out the thoroughly 'Western' nature of the organization and its activities.[5] Similarly, a study of one of the largest and most vigorous of the many Bantu churches in East London has failed to reveal anything significantly 'tribal'.[6]

The Second Generation is largely a study of normal domestic life, in a sense that *Townsmen or Tribesmen* could not be. Bantu born in town are entitled to have

[3] Cf. *Townsmen or Tribesmen*, pp. 211 ff.
[4] Epstein, E. G., *Politics in an Urban African Community*; Mitchell, *Tribalism and the Plural Society*.
[5] Moodie, D., unpublished material.
[6] Dubb, A. A., unpublished M.A. thesis (Rhodes University), 1962.

their wives and children with them, whereas those who come in from the country do not easily qualify (according to present South African law) for the same privilege if they want it.[7] Hence *Townsmen or Tribesmen* dealt with men and women who regard themselves as 'camping by the wayside'—people separated for the time being from their nearest kin, and mostly dependent for domestic companionship on age-mates, friends or irregular sexual partners. In *The Second Generation* Dr. Pauw's analysis of marriage, child-bearing and family life gives rise to many interesting points, which I do not propose to anticipate. But two of the tendencies he documents have perhaps a specially wide interest, namely the high incidence of 'illegitimate' birth, and the tendency towards what has been called the matrifocal family. Both are against Xhosa tradition. In the context of labour migrancy, which separates men and women from their spouses and closest kin, neither development is unexpected. In the context of the permanently town-settled second generation, they require more special comment.

In effect Dr. Pauw is showing us illegitimacy and matrifocality as two sides of the same coin. There is, perhaps, some material here which will be useful towards an eventual refining of the concept of matrifocality itself: for the matrifocality of Dr. Pauw's East Londoners differs in rather important respects from some previous examples. For example, R. T. Smith has described as matrifocal a type of family in British Guiana[8] which in the initial stages includes a resident husband/father. The husband/father was shown as gradually fading out of the picture, on account of his decreasing usefulness to the household group. The limits of his usefulness were shown to be set by the lowliness of the roles which these men play in the society at large. In Dr. Pauw's analysis, a similar connexion between intra- and extra-familial unimportance is suggested. The argument is interesting and can be studied with profit, provided we bear the critical differences in mind—that, in the East London case, the matrifocal 'family' (other than the widowed household) is one which dispenses with a husband/father from the very beginning; and that, side by side with it, there exists a family of very different type, in which the husband/father has a continuing important role to play at all stages. This other, patrifocal, type is both the moral and the statistical norm of the Xhosa, urban as well as 'tribal', from the white-collar down to the humble unskilled worker. What Dr. Pauw's evidence proves, therefore, is that urban Xhosa women can, if necessary, support children by their own efforts; that the price such households pay for the absence of a legitimate husband/father is loss of esteem, rather than actual loss of viability. While the role of the working-class Xhosa male in the society at large does not make him in the strictest sense an 'indispensable' member of every family group, nevertheless it is consistent with a quite high degree of patriarchal authority in 'normal' families. On the basis of the present material it would appear that the patriarchal or patrifocal ethic remains strongly ingrained among the urban Xhosa. It derives its strength, no doubt, from two sources: the patriarchal tradition of rural Xhosa society, and the European middle-class model to which the better-educated townsmen aspire. Clearly, the urban working-class Xhosa husband/father is something very different from the 'marginal' one of British Guiana.

[7] In East London, workers and their families may be let a house by the municipality after the husband has been a legal resident for five years. This is permissible according to section 23(*d*)(ii) of the Native (Urban Areas) Consolidation Act of 1945.

[8] Smith, *The Negro Family in British Guiana.*

Compared with most other African territories, South Africa is remarkable for the size and vigour of its Bantu *élite*—the middle and professional classes. It happens that many of the best-educated and most sophisticated residents of the East London locations are first-generation, and therefore not eligible for this study. Dr. Pauw is mostly concerned with the man in the street, and does not show the *élite* in full force. He does, however, provide some interesting material on the intermediate stratum of white-collar and better-educated families, showing their less frequent propensity to be influenced by anything that could be called 'tribal' norms. He makes it plain that 'Western' middle-class values are consciously fostered in the families of the better-educated; that witchcraft beliefs appear to play a much lesser role than among those with no or little education; that where educated people preserve some traditional Xhosa elements in wedding procedure, these are no longer conceived as ritually essential, but tend to become mere folk-lorist gestures. Thus, it appears, the choice of Western as against tribal modes of behaviour—in areas where there is free choice—is related to education and occupation. In terms of the old 'detribalization' concept (which, as I have argued elsewhere,[9] does not entirely deserve its present unpopularity in anthropological thinking), Dr. Pauw is confirming the faith in formal education and economic opportunity as agents of change. However, the second generation of Bantu East Londoners as a whole does not show any notable upward mobility as compared with its immigrant parents. In particular, the average standard of education is not significantly higher. Compared with rural Xhosa, the Xhosa in East London have enjoyed a wider choice of paid employment, and in some cases self-employment, but they have been subject to restrictions on social mobility—e.g. job reservation, influx control, limitations of land rights in town—as documented in the two previous volumes.[10]

This preface would not be complete without a tribute to the author's high qualities as a research worker, without which it would have been impossible to produce anything like this study in the time available. As the author of *Religion in a Tswana Chiefdom*, Dr. Pauw needs no introduction to the anthropological public. It is pleasant to be able to say that our association has now taken him back into his main field of interest—Bantu Christianity—as well as to record the willingness with which he temporarily switched over to this very different subject. We owe him thanks, too, for writing in a language which is not his mother tongue, though this would never be guessed from the admirable use to which he has put it.

[9] Cf. Mayer, Philip, 'Migrancy and the Study of Africans in Town', *American Anthropologist*. June 1962.

[10] Cf. *The Black Man's Portion*, *passim*; *Townsmen or Tribesmen*, chap. 3.

ACKNOWLEDGEMENTS – FIRST EDITION

The author wishes to make the following acknowledgements:

To the Chairman and members of the Board of Management of the Institute of Social and Economic Research at Rhodes University for enabling me to conduct the research and write up my material.

The late Professor H. R. Burrows and Mr. J. A. I. Agar-Hamilton (as Directors of the Institute) and Mr. E. T. Sherwood (as Secretary up to January 1959) took a keen interest in the work and were always anxious to make conditions as pleasant as possible.

To the National Council for Social Research for financing the research and publication of the material.

Mr. J. A. Chew, Secretary of the Buffalo Catchment Association, arranged for pleasant office accommodation, and he and members of his staff rendered practical assistance almost daily while I was in East London.

The East London City Council's Manager for Native Affairs (Mr. P. Venter) allowed us to conduct our research in the locations completely unhampered and was always ready to render assistance or provide information.

The General Mission Council of the Dutch Reformed Church (Cape) consented to my joining the research staff of the Institute temporarily, and agreed to regard the period of my association with the Institute as study leave, so that I was able to retain my status as minister of the Dutch Reformed Church.

To the clerical staff of the Institute under Mrs. H. S. Mostert, who efficiently took care of typing and administrative arrangements.

To Dr. D. W. Terry of Rhodes University for reading and commenting on an early draft of the manuscript, and to the Rev. Dr. P. J. du Plessis of East London, who read and commented on a draft of chapter 6.

To Dr. H. Linhart of the South African Wool Textile Research Institute, Rhodes University, for advice and assistance in connexion with statistical testing.

The research would hardly have been possible without the help of Bantu Assistants among whom I particularly mention Messrs. S. C. Mvalo and E. L. Xotyeni for faithful services.

It is needless to explain how much I owe to the many Xhosa informants, not only for willingness to provide information, but also for the friendly manner in which we were usually received.

In particular I wish to mention my association with Professor Philip Mayer who acted as my supervisor. I much appreciate his friendship, which is one of the gains that have come my way through work on this book.

It would not have been possible for me to undertake this work if my wife had not been willing for a second time to face a period of unsettled existence, this time with a family very conspicuously in its 'phase of expansion'. To this and to her continued encouragement the book owes a great deal.

B. A. PAUW

Institute of Social and Economic Research
Rhodes University, Grahamstown,
March 1962

PREFACE TO THE SECOND EDITION

This book comprises an unaltered version of the first edition, excepting a few corrections and reformulations, and an additional chapter (chapter 11) based on material collected twelve years after the original study. During the interval the greater part of East London's Bantu population has been resettled in Mdantsane, a completely new township outside the city, in which the system of administration, housing and other conditions of living differ significantly from those of the old East London 'locations'. East London itself still has a substantial Bantu population but all these people are expected to be resettled in Mdantsane within the near future. It has therefore been accepted that patterns now evident in Mdantsane reflect the future trend for the urban Bantu of the area, and the new factual material pertains largely to Mdantsane.

My teaching duties allowed only a short vacation, nine days during the latter part of September 1972, for new fieldwork. During the following months I could keep trace of political developments in the Ciskei through press reports. On account of the short time available I had to rely heavily on interviewing officials and leading residents of Mdantsane and extracting information from official records placed at my disposal. A few households were visited at random for observation and superficial interviewing, observations were made of the transfer of a group of East London residents to Mdantsane and I was allowed to attend three regular sessions of the Mdantsane Township Council's Housing Committee.

I am particularly indebted to Mr. A. M. J. van Rensburg, Manager of Mdantsane, who was extremely co-operative in granting extensive interviews, showing me around Mdantsane and assisting in various other ways, without trying to direct or limit my investigations. Several members of his staff also gave valuable assistance. I also wish to thank Mr. W. R. Hart, Acting Manager of the East London Municipality's Bantu Administration Department, residents of Mdantsane who provided information, and the Department of Bantu Administration and Development for permission to enter the Mdantsane area.

I sincerely appreciate the assistance of the Council of the University of South Africa in financing the fieldwork for the new chapter, and the stimulus received from discussions with my colleagues in the Department of Anthropology at the University.

To Messrs. Oxford University Press who have taken the initiative towards publication of this edition and Rhodes University's Institute of Social and Economic Research for allowing me to negotiate with the publishers independently I also owe a special word of thanks.

B. A. PAUW

University of South Africa
Pretoria
January 1973

INTRODUCTION

This book, which is the third in a trilogy[1] on the Bantu-speaking population of East London, South Africa, was planned to deal exclusively with those Bantu who have been born and bred in town. As research proceeded, it became clear that it would be extremely difficult to claim with certainty that all informants included in our samples or selected for special interviewing answered to this description. In a number of cases it emerged after lengthy interviews that an informant was, in fact, not town-born, but came to town with his or her parents in early youth. Others, again, may have been born in town but spent some of their formative years in the country. We may claim with confidence, however, that the majority of informants were, in fact, town-born, and that for those who were not, town had become their home many years ago. Virtually all who were in their early twenties or younger—and these account for a considerable proportion of our informants—may be regarded as truly town-born. We feel confident, therefore, that subject to the adequacy of our research methods and sampling,[2] the material presented is representative of the second generation of Bantu in town. The terms 'urban Bantu', 'urban Xhosa', or 'Xhosa (Bantu) townspeople' will be used to indicate the category of persons with which the present volume is concerned, that is, persons born and bred, or at least fully settled, in town, as distinct from the migrants.

East London has a population of over 100,000. Bantu in the city number over 65,000, of whom the great majority live in three urban locations.[3] A survey conducted in 1955 indicated that only 14 per cent of the adults (15 and over) in these locations claimed to have been born in East London.[4] More than 90 per cent of the town's Bantu population belonged to either the Xhosa or Mfengu (Fingo) ethnic group. The two groups are both Xhosa-speaking, and share a very similar cultural heritage. In this series the Bantu of East London are therefore treated as virtually consisting of Xhosa and Mfengu, and unless otherwise specified, the term 'Xhosa' is used as shorthand for 'Xhosa-speaking', embracing the Mfengu and the sprinkling of members of other Xhosa-speaking tribes represented in East London.[5]

The approach to this study was primarily one of fact-finding. My interest as a missionary prompted the desire for first-hand factual knowledge of the urban Bantu. Further this approach was suggested by the more practically orientated interests of local bodies, particularly the Buffalo Catchment Association, whose request for a comprehensive study of the Buffalo River catchment area prompted the undertaking of the Border Regional Survey of which the present

[1] The other two titles in the series (*Xhosa in Town*) are Reader, D. H., *The Black Man's Portion*, O.U.P., 1961, and Mayer, Philip, *Townsmen or Tribesmen*, O.U.P., 1961.

[2] See Appendix II.

[3] In terms of Southall's typology of African towns ('Introductory Summary' to Southall, A. (Ed.), *Social Change in Modern Africa*, O.U.P., 1961, pp. 6 ff.) the East London locations approximate to his type A ('old established, slowly growing towns') rather than to type B ('new populations of mushroom growth'). What is said of housing in type A towns applies almost word for word to most of the housing in East London. The town also has close links with near-by rural areas inhabited by the same homogeneous ethnic groups which make up the bulk of its population. It differs from the ideal type in that there is strict influx control. (For population growth and other demographic details, administration, housing, and occupational structure, see Reader, op. cit.)

[4] Reader, op. cit., p. 37.

[5] Reader, op. cit., chap. 3; cf. Mayer, op. cit., pp. xiii, 1–3.

study forms part. Nevertheless, an attempt has also been made to relate the material to some theoretical trends in social anthropology.

When one's aim is primarily that of a factual survey, it is difficult to relate all one's material to one central theme. We are concerned, of course, with the process of urbanization. For the category of persons with which we are dealing the process may in one sense be regarded as virtually completed. They are, as Professor Mayer has put it in his volume, 'fully "urban" or "urbanized" '.[6] Their main social ties and cultural interests are contained within the town. In another sense, however, they are still involved in a continuing process of urbanization. They belong to a community in which migrant labourers and persons in the process of becoming settled in town still predominate. Should the proportion of 'fully urbanized' (in the former sense) gradually increase, we may expect further changes in the culture and social structure of the settled urban Bantu population. In this sense the process of urbanization is incomplete, even for those who have been born and brought up in town. It seems reasonable, however, to suppose that the main trends in the process will be reflected most clearly among the latter category.

The main concern of this study, I would say, has been with the interplay of Western and traditional Xhosa culture, and urbanization. These factors cannot be separated, as if the interplay of the two distinct cultural traditions is confined to the cultural level, and the dynamics of urbanization to the structural level. Firstly, although it is useful to distinguish between cultural change and structural change from an analytical point of view, the two are so closely related that change at the one level is not isolated from change at the other level. Further, Western values and Christian teaching have had their effect on the social structure of the Xhosa, even in rural areas. Traditional customs and values, we shall see, have again retarded structural changes primarily related to urbanization, while urban living, besides its structural implications has also affected customs, interests, and patterns of behaviour. The factors of Western culture, traditional Xhosa culture, and urbanization should rather be seen as a triangle of forces exerting pressure on urban Bantu society with effects at both the structural and cultural levels.

The book roughly falls into three sections, dealing respectively with the background, culture, and social structure of the urban Xhosa, although, of course, these aspects cannot be strictly separated. Chapter 1 deals with the rural origins and certain characteristics of preceding generations and their migration to town, while in chapter 2 an attempt is made to convey something of the atmosphere of the urban location. Chapter 3 deals with different aspects of culture and attempts to distinguish different cultural types. Chapters 4 and 5 form a bridge between 'cultural' and 'structural' material, the former providing some case material, and the latter describing ceremonial and ritual associated with family and household. Chapters 6 to 8 are concerned with marriage, family, and household, and are followed by a chapter on the wider social universe.

[6] Op. cit., p. xv.

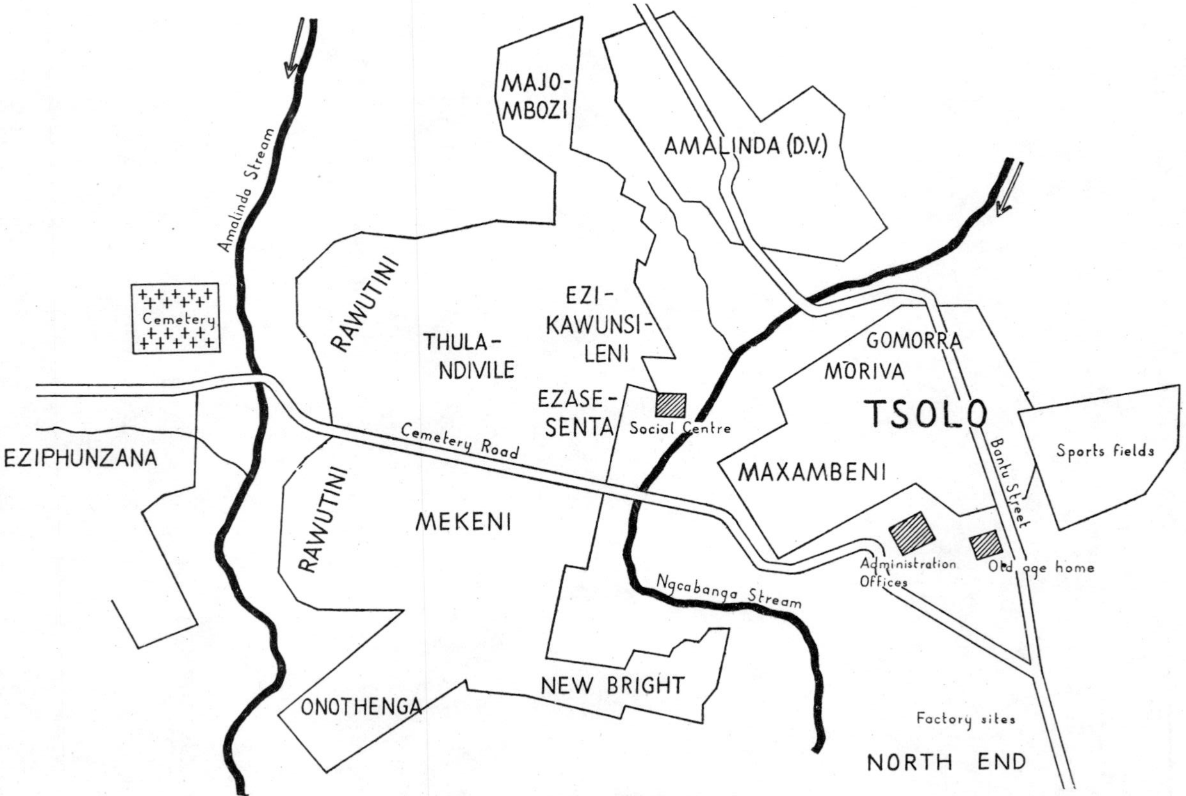

FIGURE I—*East Bank Location*

I

From Country to Town

Although it is a well-known fact that, in so far as a settled urban Bantu population exists, it is the result of a population movement from country to town, the nature of this movement does not seem to have been the same in every urban centre in South Africa. It is therefore important to have some details of this movement in respect of different towns.

What, then, are the origins and background of our East London urban Bantu?[1] Where did their families come from originally? Did those who settled in town come from places farther afield, or were they predominantly from the immediate neighbouring area of the Ciskei, as Reader has shown to be the case with the present Bantu population of East London, taken as a whole?[2] Did they have their homes in reserves, or on White-owned farms, either as servants or tenants? Were they the products of mission-school education, converted to Christianity, or were they pagans? Did proportionately more persons whose forebears had entered professional or skilled occupations migrate to town, or are present townsmen all the descendants of typical Xhosa peasants? What are the factors which caused them to settle in town? These are some of the questions we shall attempt to answer in this chapter.

COUNTRY ROOTS

In view of the predominance of patrilocal residence among the Xhosa and other South African Bantu, an investigation into the domicile of patrilineal ancestors should be sufficient to locate the country roots from which townsmen have sprung. An attempt was made, therefore, to retrace the places of domicile of fathers and paternal grandfathers of present townspeople, i.e. not complete details of their migratory careers[3] but the places where they actually 'sat down' (*ukuhlala*, to sit down, or stay).

In discussing these movements and the grandfathers' original homes, we distinguish the following geographical areas:

I. *Near Ciskei*, comprising the districts closest to East London (East London, Peddie, King William's Town, Komga, Middledrift, Keiskammahoek and Stutterheim).

II. *Farther Ciskei*, comprising other Ciskeian districts still relatively close to East London (Fort Beaufort, Stockenstrom (Seymour), Victoria East, Cathcart, Queenstown and Glen Grey).

III. *Near Transkei*, comprising the following districts bordering on the Ciskei: Tsomo, Nqamakwe, Butterworth and Kentani. These are a shorter distance from East London than most of the 'farther Ciskei' districts.

[1] See Introduction for the connotation of the term 'urban Bantu (Xhosa)'.

[2] Reader, D. H., *The Black Man's Portion* (*Xhosa in Town*), O.U.P., Cape Town, 1961, appendix I, table 7 (p. 154).

[3] Migratory careers of migrant labourers are discussed by Reader, op. cit., pp. 59–61.

IV. *Other Transkei*, comprising the rest of the United Transkeian Territories (outside the 'near Transkei' districts).

V. *Other Cape*, comprising the remainder of the Cape Province.

VI. *Other*, comprising places outside the Cape Province.

It is further useful to distinguish different types of places of domicile, namely (*a*) Bantu reserves, (*b*) farms owned by Whites, where Bantu could be domiciled as servants or tenants, (*c*) farms owned by Bantu, where Bantu could be owners, servants, or tenants, (*d*) other towns, and (*e*) the British Protectorates (Basutoland and Bechuanaland—there were no grandfathers from Swaziland; types (*a*) to (*d*) refer only to the Republic of South Africa). The original places of domicile of the paternal grandfathers in our sample are classified in terms of geographical area, and the types enumerated above, in table 1. The discrepancy between the total number in the table and the total in the sample (130) is accounted for by the fact that eight respondents had no legal fathers, two pairs of respondents had fathers and paternal grandfathers in common, so that each pair was counted as a single case, and in one case the father was a Coloured and in another a White man. The latter cases are, of course, significant in themselves, but were disregarded in the present tables, since they do not refer to the pattern of Bantu migration to East London.

TABLE 1

Grandfather's original place of domicile

GEOGRAPHICAL AREA	TYPE OF PLACE: Bantu reserve	White farm	Bantu farm	Other town	Protectorates	Unknown	TOTAL
I. Near Ciskei	43	4	2	—	—	—	49
II. Farther Ciskei	16	2	—	—	—	—	18
III. Near Transkei	17	—	—	—	—	—	17
IV. Other Transkei	12	—	—	1	—	—	13
V. Other Cape	—	2	—	1	—	—	3
VI. Other	—	—	—	1	3	—	4
Unknown	—	—	—	—	—	14	14
Total	88	8	2	3	3	14	118

It is obvious that the great majority of Bantu townspeople in East London trace their paternal family origins to the reserves, largely to the Ciskei reserves, but to some extent also to the Transkei. In any case, they have been drawn predominantly from reserves not too distant from East London (geographical areas I, II, and III). Altogether very few grandfathers came from outside the Ciskei or Transkei. It is also significant to note that only a small proportion came from White-owned farms.

According to Reader's figures 57 per cent of the town's Bantu population *born outside* East London were born in the Ciskei, and 35 per cent in the Transkei.[4] Broadly speaking, therefore, the town's settled population was drawn from much the same geographical areas as those from which it still draws its new immigrants and migrant labourers. It may be that the proportion coming from the Transkei is larger in the category not born in East London, than it is in the case of paternal grandfathers of townspeople, but in view of the large proportion of 'unknown' cases in our own sample, this cannot be claimed with certainty.

[4] Figures extracted from Reader, op. cit., appendix I, table 7, p. 154. (Pondoland, which is treated as a separate area in Reader's table, is part of the United Transkeian Territories, and therefore part of what I have distinguished as 'other Transkei'.)

Often enough the move to town was more or less direct, from a single place where the grandfather lived all his life and where the father was born and brought up. Even in such cases, however, the father's final acceptance of town as his only home usually came gradually. There are probably very few who did not come to town as migrants still regarding some rural kraal as their real home. Many fathers never even settled in town permanently. An East London-born young man of 23 living with his father, who is 58, says that 'the need of money is the main cause' for his father's coming to town. But 'he likes the country and keeps on visiting it. He is not settled in town, and still has a desire to return.' The father came to town as a young man from Ngculu in the Nqamakwe district of the Transkei, where his own father had lived all his life.

Not only has the uprooting[5] and 'replanting' in town tended to be a gradual process, but very often there have been multiple changes of domicile in the life of the two ascendant generations. This may be observed from table 2, where the different patterns of townward migration in terms of different types of places or areas are summarized. (By 'multiple reserve' is meant that the move to East London was preceded by domicile in more than one place in the reserves.)

TABLE 2

Patterns of townward migration

PATTERN OF MIGRATION	NUMBER OF CASES	
1. Reserve—East London:		
(*a*) Single move	47	
(*b*) Multiple reserve—East London	16	
(*c*) Variations on 1(*a*) and (*b*)	13	76
2. Reserve—farm—East London:		
(*a*) Reserve—White farm—East London	7	
(*b*) Reserve—Bantu farm—East London	1	
(*c*) Multiple reserve—Bantu farm—East London	1	9
3. (*a*) Reserve—other town—East London		9
(*b*) Variation on 3(*a*)		1
4. (*a*) White farm—East London (with variations)		11
(*b*) Bantu farm—East London (with variations)		3
5. Other town—East London (with variations)		3
6. Protectorate—East London (with variations)		3
Unknown		3[6]
Total		118

Judging from the numbers in our sample, migration to town had followed the pattern of a single move to town from the grandfather's original place of domicile in about half the cases (all in category 1(*a*), and some in categories 4(*a*), 4(*b*), 5, and 6). In the other half of the cases, one or more changes of domicile had preceded the move to East London during the life of father and grandfather. Usually not more than one or two such moves had taken place, but instances in which the preceding generations had experienced several changes of domicile were not uncommon.

The grandfather of an East London-born girl was born at Qamata in the Cofimvaba area (St. Mark's district) of the Transkei. He moved to Mncuncuzo,

[5] For the use of the term 'rootedness' as a structural concept, see Mayer, Philip, *Townsmen or Tribesmen* (*Xhosa in Town*), O.U.P., Cape Town, 1961, pp. 5 ff.

[6] The discrepancy between the number of 'unknown' cases in this table and table 1 results from the fact that in a number of cases in which the grandfather's original home was not known sufficient details about subsequent moves were given to allow for classification in terms of pattern of migration.

which is also near Cofimvaba, and later to a farm in the Cradock district, then to a farm near East London and finally to a reserve in the King William's Town district, where he died. Her father moved with the grandfather as far as the East London farm, but from there went to a farm at Tanga, in the Komga district, whence he came to East London. These men were tenants renting land for their own use on the White-owned farms where they were domiciled. Mr. X, who has grown-up town-born daughters, was born at Tyira in the Qumbu district of the Transkei. His own father had moved there from another place in the same district. Mr. X became a journalist, and since leaving the Transkei has lived in Orlando, Johannesburg, in East London, in Port Elizabeth, and again in East London. He still maintains his right to the kraal and lands at Tyira.

Where multiple moves took place, patterns in terms of types of places vary considerably. A substantial proportion involved one or two moves from one home in a reserve to another (in a different rural location or district, but still in a reserve) prior to the move to East London (table 2, category 1(*b*)). Sometimes the move from reserve to town was made via one or more White- or Bantu-owned farms where father or grandfather was domiciled for some time (2(*a*), (*b*), and (*c*)). In other cases another town intervened as place of domicile between the grandfather's original reserve home and East London (3(*a*)). Sometimes this was a smaller country town, but more often it was one of the larger urban centres like Johannesburg, Durban, Port Elizabeth, and particularly Cape Town. On these basic patterns of migration from reserve to town there are many variations (1(*c*) and 3(*b*)) of which only a few examples can be given.

A was born at Ngunduza in the Kentani district (Transkei, reserve) which was his father's lifelong home. After his father's death, A's mother, who was his father's second (polygynous) wife, returned to her own people at Qombolo in the same district. Later she decided to come to East London to work in order to be able to support the young A, while he was left at Qombolo under the care of his *umalume* (mother's brother). After his marriage, A and his wife also came to town. When later, after the death of his mother in town, his father's first wife came *ukukhuza* (to offer condolence), she suggested that A should go and stay with her in the King William's Town reserve, where she had also returned to her own people, to assist her, as she had no son of her own. After a stay of four years with her in the country, A returned to town where he is now settled. His eldest child, who was born in East London, is now a young girl of about 17. In this case the pattern was: reserve to East London to another reserve and back to East London.

Simon's[7] father, Mtule, was born in Mncotsho reserve location in the King William's Town district, which was the only home his father had known. After the death of his mother, who was his father's right-hand wife, he came to town as a young unmarried man 'because of ill-treatment, and because he disliked his father's wife of the great house'. Later in life he lived at Gonubie in the East London district for a short while, where he rented White-owned farm land, returning to East London after this brief interlude of country life. His town-born son is now a married man with children. (Reserve to East London to White farm and back to East London.) Other variations on the pattern of migration from reserve to East London are the following: reserve

[7] The names and initials of persons referred to in this chapter have been changed.

to East London to another town and back to East London; from reserve to another town to Basutoland to East London; from reserve to reserve to another town to East London to another town and back to East London.

Not many grandfathers of townsmen were born and brought up on White-owned farms, but for those who were the move from farm to town also varied, either directly to East London or via other farms, towns or reserves (4(*a*)). Samson's grandfather lived on a farm in the East London district, which was also the birthplace of his father, who for a time lived in Cradock town but later returned to the East London farm. Although neither his father nor his mother ever settled in East London, Samson, who is now a young man, maintains that he was born in East London. This may well be, as it is not unknown that mothers from the district sometimes give birth during a visit to town. Mary, a town-born woman of 38, says that her grandfather lived on a farm at Barties, near Port Alfred, but later moved to a reserve in the Peddie district. Her father was born at Barties, moved with her grandfather to Peddie, but came to East London soon after his marriage.

There are also examples of families who owned their own farms, whose descendants became townsmen (4(*b*)). Mr. Y has had a particularly interesting career. His father came from Alice to Ngwenkala, in the Komga district, where he rented a farm from a White man, but later acquired land of his own at Kwelega, and also where the East London suburb of Nahoon is now situated. In 1896 he also bought a house in the East Bank Location, which is the same wood-and-iron structure still inhabited by Mr. Y. The latter in his youth attended an American college for some years, and returned via England and Brazil, spending some months in each country. Back in South Africa he was married by Christian rites, but subsequently contracted polygynous marriages with three other women. His father's farms at Kwelega and Nahoon, as well as some properties in the location, were bequeathed to him by will and testament. He regards himself as having been an inhabitant of the location since 1896, but seems to have lived on each of the farms his father rented or owned at some or other stage. His four wives were first established at Ngwenkala, and when he had to give up the farm, his great wife went to live in King William's Town. The other three wives settled at Nahoon, and two ultimately moved to town, the one staying with her husband, the other on her own with her children. Mr. Y no longer owns any of the farms.

There does not seem to be any dominant geographical pattern in the movements to town. There are instances in which successive moves reveal a pattern of gradual approach to East London. In other cases, again, the grandfather's original home was not far from East London, but he or his son first moved away farther afield to Cape Town, for example, before, as it were, being drawn back to East London itself. Sometimes, after an initial move to East London, there followed a move elsewhere, after which the road again led back to East London. Very often the movements do not reveal any distinct geographical pattern, as the following examples show. A grandfather's only known place of domicile was in a reserve in the Stutterheim district (near Ciskei). He died when his son, Robert, the father of an East London-born woman, was still an infant, whereupon Robert's mother returned to her own relatives in the Kentani district (near Transkei), from where she later again moved to relatives of her late husband in a different place in the Stutterheim district (near Ciskei). Robert moved about with his mother, but ultimately came to East London.

Ganeko was a farm servant in the Seymour area (farther Ciskei). He was born on the farm which was also his father's only known place of domicile. From there Ganeko as a young man went to the towns, first to King William's Town (near Ciskei), where he got married, then to Queenstown (farther Ciskei), and ultimately to East London, where his son, now a young man, was born. Thus the variations in geographical patterns of movements could be multiplied. It is important to note, however, that the great majority of these moves were confined to the Ciskei and nearer Transkei.[8]

FATHERS AND LAND

As one might expect, the majority of town-born adults are the children of men who became permanently settled in town, regarding it as their only home. Occasionally the paternal grandfather had already made the move to town, but very few of the fathers' generation are themselves town-born. Broadly speaking, the definite move, the taking up of domicile in East London, took place during the fathers' generation. What, then, made the fathers settle in town?

It appears that land rights of the fathers, or more correctly, the absence of rights to arable land on their part, was an important factor contributing to their settling in town. From the point of view of land rights, there are three main categories of fathers:

A. Those who held land under secure conditions of tenure.

B. Those who held land under insecure conditions of tenure.

C. Those who neither owned their own land nor had any to cultivate for their own interest.

A. Of the fathers in our sample for whom details were available, roughly a quarter had during their lifetime exercised *tenurial rights* to arable land under conditions which could be regarded as relatively *secure*. Most of these held communal land in reserves in their own right, but several held reserve land under quitrent, while a few had freehold rights either to small farms, or to reserve land, or to other agricultural allotments such as those in the rural village of Macleantown, not far from East London. It is significant that most of these men were regarded, by informants, either as never really permanently settled in town, or as having maintained strong interests in the country, although they settled in town with their families. It is possible to distinguish three different types among these landowner fathers.

(1) How it is possible for a man to have town-born children, while he remains *completely country-orientated* all his life, is illustrated by the following case. James, a young man of 28, is the eldest of five East London-born children living with their widowed mother. Although family living was established in town, the mother developing strong business interests by letting rooms, offering board and lodging, and carrying on petty trade, the father lived in the country most of the time, 'with only short periods in East London'. On his death in 1947 the

[8] In terms of Ravenstein's theory of migrations (cf. e.g. Gist, Noel P., and Halbert, L. A., *Urban Society*, Crowell, New York, 1945, pp. 263 ff.) Bantu migration to East London—disregarding shorter spells of migrant labour—could be regarded as usually having taken the form of 'short-distance' moves. It is probable that long-distance moves would figure more prominently in the pattern of Bantu migration to urban areas such as those of the Witwatersrand. However, the conditions of Bantu townward migration are so different from those in Western countries that a superficial comparison of this kind does not seem to serve any purpose.

freehold land he owned in a King William's Town reserve was sold. Some town-born people with country parents explain that they were born when their mothers were visiting East London.

(2) A more common occurrence was for a man who owned land in the country to settle down to town life with his family, while maintaining a strong interest in the country. He became what Mayer has termed *the 'double-rooted' type*, genuinely taking root in town, without abandoning his country roots.[9] This would happen, for example, when the parents had business or professional interests in town. Mr. Z, the father of a town-born girl, has built up a stable trade as a general dealer in the East Bank Location. He has never abandoned his land in the Transkei, which is now occupied by his son. Occasionally he visits the country home, but finds it difficult to do so often, because of his age and failing health. Nevertheless, Mrs. Z is outspoken in her preference for town life. C.D. is a sophisticated young married man whose parents come from a near-Transkei district. They settled in town because his mother was appointed to a nursing post in East London. His father, however, still pays the local tax in respect of his land in the Transkei, land and kraal being occupied by the father's sister, an unmarried mother.

Double-rootedness could also find expression in polygyny or non-recognized forms of multiple sexual unions. Edward is a 41-year-old East London-born married man whose father already had two wives in the country when he 'married' Edward's mother who was working in town. He maintains that his mother only later discovered that his father already had two other wives. It was not made clear whether she ever lived with the other wives in the country, but disharmony between her and the others was given as the reason for her ultimately being 'driven away' by the father. Although he maintained his country kraal with the two wives, he found 'town life better than country life'. With properties both in East London and another city, 'he spent most of his time in town' and died and was buried there. One may well doubt whether any form of marriage took place in this case, and whether this is not also one of those instances of men who had their families in the country, but entered upon temporary liaisons in town, creating families without legal fathers.[10]

Another type of double-rootedness was found where a man worked and established his family in town, placing some relative, for example a widowed mother or sister, in charge of his land and kraal in the country, which he continued visiting regularly.

(3) There are, however, also cases of fathers who did own land, but nevertheless ultimately severed their connexions with the country home *and altogether settled in town*. Adversities such as droughts, illnesses or deaths—the latter two usually giving rise to fear of witchcraft—caused some of them to move to town, while a relative was left to occupy kraal and land to which the emigrant still maintained his rights. The 'caretaker occupant's' moving away or dying might then have caused the owner to abandon all rights and sever the ties with the country. In one case the second marriage of a country widower to a woman in town was the cause of his ultimately settling in town permanently, because his second wife preferred to stay in town and disliked the idea of living in the country with the first wife's children. The town-born daughter of a Xhosa who

[9] Op. cit., pp. 224–32.
[10] Mayer, op. cit., pp. 256–69.

had inherited a farm from his father, but now has only a town home, said: 'The farm was sold and he was forced to come to town. He lost his farm—he alone knows how he lost it.' But location gossip has it that he lost it 'through too great a liking for the bottle'.

B. A second category of fathers, smaller than the first, are *those who did cultivate land* for their own interest, but *without real security* of tenure. These would include farm servants who were allowed to cultivate a patch of land on the farm, usually White-owned, where they were employed, tenants renting farm or reserve land, sharecroppers, and the like.[11] With these may be included men who migrated to town from farms during their youth, without ever having cultivated land independently of their own fathers.

Dislike of their living conditions on the farms was generally given as the reason for farm servants' coming to town. 'There was too much poverty: the income was very little.' A father of several East London-born children left the farm area where his father had always been a servant, coming to East London as a young unmarried man. 'He disliked farm life because the farm owner made him work all day long in the farms for nothing.' He married a town-born woman and remained in East London for the rest of his life.[12]

Tenants came to town because they found living on rented land too uncertain, or because of inability to keep up the rent on the land. Mathozana's father, Jim, came from a White-owned Stutterheim farm where his father was a tenant. Jim 'broke away from his family' because of the uncertainty of tenure: 'any day you may get an order to vacate the farm', combining this motive with the desire to be able to set up his own home independently of his father. A town-born man states: 'My family, from the time of my grandfather, have always lived on farms, and never in the reserves.' His father rented land on a Bantu-owned farm, but 'became fed-up with farm life, because he found the rent too much'. Something else happened in the case of a farm-born father who had managed to rent an allotment in Macleantown village from another Xhosa. When residents were 'ordered to erect brick houses in the village' and 'mud houses' were no longer allowed, he was forced to quit and come to East London.

William, a sharecropper in a King William's Town reserve, was one of several sons whose kraals surrounded that of their father. He was not the eldest son, and for this reason regarded his chances of owning land of his own as very remote. His position as sharecropper was insecure, 'because next year the landowner for no reason wants another man', so that he preferred to migrate to town. Although his town-born daughter regarded him as having become completely settled in town, his body, on his death, was conveyed to the country for burial.

C. The third and largest category of fathers are those who *never owned land, nor cultivated any for their own interest*, excepting a few who later in life, after already having been in town for some time, managed to obtain land on a temporary basis. One father, for example, came to town as a young unmarried man and never held land at his reserve home. At one stage of his town career he rented land on a White-owned farm at Gonubie, near East London, but his

[11] For a discussion of land tenancy and sharecropping in a reserve, see Elton Mills, E. M., and Wilson, Monica, *Land Tenure*, Keiskammahoek Rural Survey, vol. IV, Shuter and Shooter, Pietermaritzburg, 1952, pp. 26–31.

[12] For farm servants' migration to town, see further Mayer, op. cit., pp. 169–71.

farming venture lasted only a year, after which he returned to town 'to run a general dealer's business'.

A few moved to East London or another town as young children with their own parents (grandparents' generation) or were born in town, but on the whole, the fathers who had never owned land were men from the reserves, most of whom embarked on town careers as young unmarried men. With few exceptions they became permanently settled in town.

Almost invariably the reasons given for their settling down to town life included a reference to adverse circumstances at the country end, and the two reasons most commonly mentioned in this connexion referred to conditions which made it difficult for them to acquire land and the other necessities for setting up independently as peasant farmers in the reserve.

First of all there are the cases where an eldest brother or another member of the family, such as a widowed mother or stepmother, held priority rights to the family estate. Some reference to inheritance among the Xhosa is necessary for an understanding of this factor. In the past, land and cattle were the major requirements for a man to get started in the peasant economy, while the possession of an own homestead (*umzi*) denoted the attainment of full independence. Inheritance has always been one of the most important means of acquiring these necessities, and, in respect of land, it has for some time been growing in importance with the increasing shortage of land.

Subject to the allocation of property to the different houses in a polygynous family, the eldest son inherits land, cattle and homestead, but a widow has the right to remain in the homestead and cultivate her late husband's land. She is nowadays usually also regarded as head of the homestead. Formerly elder sons sometimes received land by allocation during their fathers' lifetime, while the youngest son remained with the widowed mother and inherited the land and *umzi*, together with the mother's other property. For Keiskammahoek it is reported that 'as [communal] land became scarcer, however, and men took a share in cultivation, rights over fields came to be regarded as male property to be inherited by the eldest son, or, where polygyny survived, by the eldest son of each house'.[13] This seems to apply to the Ciskei generally, and also to parts of the Transkei.

Although the eldest son is by tradition expected to appropriate the estate in the interests of all his late father's sons and female dependants, and public opinion disapproves of any heir who 'eats up' the inheritance alone, informants say that in modern times junior members of the family can often expect little benefit from the estate of their late father. Under these circumstances it is to be understood that many younger sons foresaw a hard struggle to establish themselves in the country, and preferred to settle in town.[14] An elder brother 'at home', who would inherit or 'take over', was often mentioned as the reason for the father's settling in town. An East London-born youth said that his father had chosen to stay in town because he was the youngest son in the family and had 'no privileges' in the country home in Butterworth (Transkei). The grandfather's homestead, land and livestock were eventually inherited by his father's eldest brother.

It is, of course, not impossible for a younger brother to obtain land by allocation where communal tenure exists, but in most Ciskei reserves the allocation

[13] Elton Mills and Wilson, op. cit., p. 18.
[14] Cf. Mayer, op. cit., p. 211.

of new fields from virgin land has for many years virtually ceased, so that only existing fields which become vacant are available for allocation. These are not numerous, and competition for them is strong. There is little doubt that the scarcity of land began to make itself felt rather more than a generation ago, so that one may well understand why a father from a King William's Town reserve, where his eldest brother had inherited the family land, regarded his 'chances of owning land as very remote'.

Sometimes the rights of a widowed mother or stepmother to a late father's homestead and land prevented a man from getting started in the country and caused him to make his home in town, either as a temporary measure, or permanently. Sam, a man from the Mooiplaats reserve in the East London district, who has grown-up town-born children, stayed in town because he 'did not like' his stepmother, who is now widowed and occupying her late husband's land and homestead with her children. Although he is already 65 and receives a small pension, Sam is still 'waiting for the stepmother's death' when he hopes to return to the country. Another father from the Kentani district, whose widowed stepmother is also in the country home, does not contemplate returning, for fear of witchcraft, which he regards as being particularly prevalent in the location where he comes from.

In one case a grandfather had been living in his elder brother's homestead without any land or homestead of his own. The grandfather died while the father was quite a young man, and the fact that he had not inherited any land or homestead was cited as one reason for his settling in town.

Another type of father whose expectation of inheriting anything was limited was the father who had not grown up at his paternal home, usually because of his own father's death, or because of marital disharmony between the parents. It is customary among the Xhosa that when a man dies, leaving only young children, a close agnatic kinsman acts as guardian of the deceased man's property, which should be handed over to the eldest son of the deceased when he grows up. It is known, however, that conflicts often arise when the time comes for the heir to take possession, and current opinion has it that under conditions of contact with Western culture there is a growing tendency for guardians to take advantage of their position at the expense of the orphans. On the other hand, in respect of land rights the Administration has tended to take the view that a guardian who takes over the field of a dead man whose children are minors becomes the permanent owner of that field, and is not under an obligation ultimately to hand it over to the eldest son of the deceased.[15] Under modern conditions, therefore, a son who loses his father during his youth is often at a disadvantage.

This is even more so when he is not brought up in the late father's homestead or in that of the guardian of the estate. By tradition a widow who returned to her own people after the death of her husband, or a woman who left her husband or was sent away with the intention of terminating the marriage, could only take her child with her if it was still small, and it had to return to the father's place later. Nowadays the child often does not return, and a number of men intimated that they had grown up with their mother's people, to whom their mothers had returned from their fathers' homesteads. Theoretically such men would have had a right to land at the place where they had grown up (i.e. their mothers' homes of origin), but they had little hope of inheriting

[15] Elton Mills and Wilson, op. cit., p. 17.

anything, and could expect at least the same difficulties as men who were the younger sons of local fathers. Moreover, it seems as if they would find it even more difficult to obtain land by allocation than men who belonged to long-established lineages of the area.

The typical case is that of the man brought up in his mother's brother's homestead, where he had been taken after his father's death. Nontsikelelo said her father had no homestead or land in the country, because he had been brought up by his mother's brother in a Tsomo reserve after the death of both his parents. Her paternal grandfather's huts remained vacant and ultimately 'the walls fell to the ground' and his land was reallotted. Another father who was brought up by his mother's people said that his sister was now occupying his late father's land, but he would not claim it, for fear of being bewitched. Samuel, again, came from a polygynous household, being the youngest son of his father's third wife, whose house was the 'rafter' (*iqadi*) to the 'great house'. Because the great wife had no children, Samuel was 'put into the great house to be the son of the great wife'. After the death of his father and his own mother, the great wife left Idutywa, where they were staying, and returned to St. Luke's reserve near East London, taking Samuel with her. From here he later came to East London and settled here, 'because he realized that St. Luke's was not quite his home, so that he had no claim there, while he had forfeited his rights in Idutywa'.

In another case polygyny had given rise to disharmony which caused the departure of mother and son. Philemon, the father of an East London-born woman, was the son of his father's great wife, but his father 'had a right-hand wife whom he loved and respected more' than Philemon's mother, and he therefore 'drove her away'. She returned to her own people in Komga town location, taking Philemon, who was still a small child, with her. As a young man Philemon came to East London and settled here.

An orphan may be brought up by some other female relative, which also jeopardizes his chances of acquiring land. A town-born woman relates that her father's parents died when he was a baby in arms and he was brought up by his father's sister. Our subject said: 'I do not know what happened to my father's father's land and homestead, but my father went to Cape Town soon after marriage to work there, and finally came to East London.'

There are numerous minor causes which also prevented certain fathers from having their own land. Some predeceased their own fathers, or in any case died early. Henry, the father of an East London youth, did not regard himself as permanently settled in town. In the country he lived in his father's homestead and cultivated land belonging to his father. 'He died before he had asked for an axe'—asking for an axe being the traditional expression for asking permission to set up one's own homestead, because an axe was used for the erection of the huts. Another father was the son of a farm-owner, but on the grandfather's death the farm was sold and the proceeds shared by the children. A third father was a minister who had worked in many different places and never owned land.

The reasons for landlessness that have been discussed cover the great majority of fathers who had no land. For a small number no particular reason was revealed in the answers of informants other than that they had left home as unmarried men or shortly after marriage.

The mobility of many fathers and paternal grandfathers prior to the move to

East London was never mentioned by informants as a reason for the father's landlessness, but it does seem to have a bearing on the matter. Migrancy within the country areas is not uncommon among the Xhosa. In the Keiskammahoek reserve both emigration to other reserves and immigration of single families have taken place since the establishment of present villages.[16] 'The descendants of later arrivals are still referred to as wanderers [*amaranuga*], and are only slowly losing the stigma that attaches to such people' the longer their lineage becomes established in the village.[17] Not until he had lived with a member of the village for some time and the people had grown accustomed to him, could such a new-comer apply for land in a communal village. Although an immigrant's son brought up in the village could apply for land like any other member of the village, the tendency to allocate vacant land to a close agnatic kinsman of the previous owner must have handicapped the sons of immigrants in the competition for a vacant field.

Those fathers of our townspeople who had moved about, or whose fathers had moved about, prior to the move to East London, would undoubtedly have belonged to this class of wanderers in the country. As we have seen, they constitute a large proportion—probably about half—of the fathers of town-born East London Bantu. The indications are that although these migrant families are not uncommon in the rural areas, they constitute a smaller proportion of the rural population from which the townspeople have been drawn. This would mean that these wanderers have shown a greater tendency to take up their permanent domicile in town than the more settled rural population. This can easily be understood in view of the less favourable position of the wanderers vis-à-vis the 'old-timer' families, particularly in relation to land.

It is obvious, then, that owning land or not was a question of major importance in the process of fathers' settling down to town life. Of the fathers who owned land, the majority either remained men of the country, although their children were born in town and became townspeople, or they became double-rooted, becoming townsmen to a certain extent, but retaining their interests in the country. On the other hand most of the landless fathers whose children are townsmen in the full sense of the word, born and brought up in town, themselves came to regard East London as their only home.

'Having or not having' land, however, was by no means the sole deciding factor. This has already become apparent from the fact that even some of the 'haves' eventually severed their country ties and in some way or another abandoned or lost their land. It still remains to be seen how, on the other hand, some of the 'have nots', in spite of their landlessness, never regarded themselves as permanently settled in town, even though their children had been born and brought up there. A minority of landless fathers throughout their life retained the desire and the hope of some day returning to the country and settling there again.

That this hope could in fact materialize, is illustrated by what happened to one town woman's father. Because of dissatisfaction with farm life he had moved to town from the White-owned farm at Cove Rock in the East London district, where he was born and brought up. After some time in town he moved to the Ramnyiba reserve in the King William's Town district where he became a squatter in a vacant homestead. He failed to obtain land of his own, but

[16] Elton Mills and Wilson, op. cit., pp. 112–22.
[17] Ibid., p. 120.

managed to rent land from a friend, which he cultivated for seven years, until his death in 1940. The mother then returned to town.

There are, however, the more pathetic cases. There is the father who 'came to work here, his aim being to apply for his own homestead site, but death prevented him from doing this. He was never settled permanently in town, but was overtaken by death. He only returned home when he became seriously ill and death was nearing, and he died at his home. It was his last wish that he should die in the country and be buried alongside the graves of his relatives and ancestors. He returned all by himself, his wife and children remaining in town.' Another father, whose own father owned a farm in Keiskammahoek, had four elder brothers at home, and had come to town and married a town-born woman. 'He was never quite settled here and was only working to earn money. He returned to the farm to die, as his health was failing when he returned.' The retention of country ties occasionally also finds expression in the body of the father of a town family being taken to the country for burial after his death in town. There are also fathers still alive who express the intention of returning. One mentions his visiting the country home regularly, while the case has been quoted of one awaiting the death of his stepmother who occupies the homestead and land.

Various other factors besides the owning of land or not played a role in the move from country to town. Some of these have already been mentioned in the case of landowner fathers who became double-rooted or relinquished their interests in the country altogether.

In some cases stress and adversities of an economic nature can be diagnosed as cause for settling in town; landlessness itself is, of course, a form of economic stress, while the poverty and low wages of which former farm servants complained may also be related to their landlessness, the same as the heavy liability of rent in the case of tenants. Economic factors not related to landlessness have, however, also been playing their role. There is the farm-owner who landed in difficulties and 'had to sell'. Droughts have also taken their toll.

More often tensions of a psychological nature were mentioned as the reason for abandoning the country home. Adversities in the form of illnesses or deaths might have given rise to fear and uneasiness, usually coupled with the fear of witchcraft, which again reflects tensions in social relations.[18] An East London woman said of her father, who, as a young man, came to town from St. Mark's in the Transkei: 'He became sickly in St. Mark's as a result of witches. Here in town he was healthy and had children, and all was well.' In one case fear of witchcraft was mentioned without reference to any particular misfortune experienced. In another case a more rational explanation was given: a man living as a 'farm' servant on an agricultural allotment at Amalinda, now part of East London, contracted tuberculosis and had to move to the location, because the owner 'could not keep on his farm a sickly man who could not work'.

The particular areas of tension were sometimes mentioned. One man came to town as a young man after the death of his mother who was the right-hand wife of a polygynist. He disliked the great wife, and 'because of ill-treatment' decided to come to town. A father whose parents were farm servants came to town because he wished to have his own homestead—an expression denoting a desire for independence, not only from the White master, but also from his

[18] Similar motives were put forward by rural-born Red migrants for their avoiding 'incapsuation' by the home-group in town (Mayer, op. cit., pp. 162–5, 181–4).

own father. By tradition a man does not easily become 'emancipated' from his father's control early in life, while on a White-owned farm it could be even more difficult than in a reserve where communal tenure prevails.

It is important to note that psychological tensions often tie up with traditional culture (for example the belief in witchcraft) or social structure (the tensions arising from polygyny or from the strongly emphasized patriarchal organization of the extended family).

Some people were attracted to settle in town by what they regarded as the more favourable conditions of living there. They 'liked town better' or 'enjoyed town life'. A Sotho man said that he did not know what caused his father to settle in town, but he 'always remarked that East London was a better place than Quthing'—his home in Basutoland.

Specific economic reasons were sometimes put forward: 'he had a good job in town with the Railways', 'he accumulated money', 'town is better for business', and 'better opportunities to get rich here', are typical statements. A person with professional training might have to settle in town for the sake of following his or her profession.

People usually did not come to town with these views but gradually realized the possibilities and started exploiting them. Samson had 'found town a better place than the country' and discovered that there were 'chances of making money here. . . . Settling in town was not the original intention. He worked here, accumulated money, bought properties from which he collected rents, got used to town life, and finally decided it was much better than country life.' The acquisition of a house as the father's own property in the location was often mentioned as one of the factors leading to his complete acceptance of town as his only home.

Town was also sometimes preferred from the point of view of health. Those who had experienced illnesses or deaths in the family, or who had specifically fled from witchcraft, usually found that they were not troubled here in town, although the town location is by no means regarded as a refuge from all witchcraft. Some also positively valued town conditions from a health point of view. Mrs. Z, the wife of a successful shopowner who still maintains strong country ties, held that 'if we had remained in the country, surely we would have long been dead by now. My husband and I are both sickly, but doctors are quite near here and there is plenty of palatable food which you cannot get in the country.'

A man could also become town-rooted as a result of a marriage in town, particularly if he married a town-born woman whose own family was well established in town. A father who had come from Pondoland married a town-born woman who 'persuaded him to abandon the country home. . . . They lived much easier in town . . .', occupying a room free of charge in the wife's parents' house, and when she needed any money, her parents would assist her. A widower who had left his children in his homestead in the country remarried in town, and his second wife, although a country woman herself, 'caused him to stay in East London, because she did not like *isithembu*'—a word used of polygyny and polygynous marriages, in this case referring to the presence of children by a previous marriage in the country homestead.

There could, of course, be considerable interplay of different factors in any particular case. In discussing the reasons for her father's settling in town, Rachel mentioned the fact that he came to town as a young man who had not yet acquired any land of his own, while an elder brother was to inherit what his father had. There were also younger brothers at home. In town he settled down to a good job and eventually bought his own house in the location. Jane's father had quitrent land in the Butterworth district. He originally came to town with the idea of working and earning money, while his unmarried sister occupied his homestead. During the ploughing season he would return home to plough the land 'in order to maintain the sister and her children, and to bring some of the crop to town to feed his own family. His sister has since come to town with her children, leaving the homestead vacant, in consequence of which my father is no longer interested in ploughing, because nobody will look after the growing crop.' Moreover, he lost interest in country life when his father died: 'he suspected his father died as a result of witchcraft. There are many witches in Ngxalati.' Severe droughts in the country also influenced him. To crown all, he had married a town-born wife.

In the following example it is interesting to see how both the belief in witchcraft and the reliance on the efficacy of 'European' medical technique can play their role together. Town-born Rebecca said of her father: 'the belief was that his children would not survive in the country: they died in infancy as a result of witchcraft. The main idea in coming to town was to be nearer doctors and that a change of place might do them good, and in fact it did, because all children born here survived. Moreover, there were no longer intervals between the births of children necessitating treatment in order to be able to conceive.'

It seems as if troubles of the kind that have been discussed, at the country end, usually led to complete town-rootedness of fathers. In cases where landowners had no particular troubles in the country but were attracted by town conditions, double-rootedness more often resulted.

HOW MOTHERS SETTLED IN TOWN

The mothers of town-born adults may be grouped in three major categories. Firstly there are the mothers who were themselves born in East London. Of eighty-eight mothers in our sample for whom details were forthcoming,[19] thirteen were East London-born—a larger number than the fathers who were born in East London. With these may be grouped the mothers who found themselves in town because their parents had settled there. Of these there were five in the sample. Some belonging to this category became unmarried mothers, living on in town with their children, sometimes as part of their own families of origin. Most of them, however, were married, and were often the cause of their country-born husbands also settling down to town life. In one case a town-born mother accompanied her husband to the country 'when he retired home for health reasons', but after his death she returned to town.

Secondly there were the mothers who went to East London with their husbands, or to join them there, and of whom there were twenty-eight in the sample. On the whole they came to town and settled for the same reasons as the fathers did. A factor peculiar to women, however, is the notoriously difficult position of the daughter-in-law in Xhosa peasant society, particularly during the earlier part of her married life, when she is burdened with many duties and avoidance rules. In some cases this induced women to accompany or follow their husbands to town, and not to return to the country. Manini, mother and

[19] In twelve cases details were insufficient for classification. The mothers of thirty respondents who were not East London-born were not taken into consideration in this section. Very few of them settled in town.

grandmother in a large town family, said that she came to town with her husband because her mother-in-law and her husband's brother's wife ill-treated her in the country homestead. Another mother, the wife of a man whose father was a tenant on a farm, not only disliked farm life, but did not want to be 'ruled' by her husband's elder brothers' wives. Moreover, she came from a Christian home and disliked staying with her husband's pagan family.

The third and largest category are the mothers who came to town on their own, either as unmarried girls (30 in sample) or as widows, divorcees or deserted wives (11 in sample). Of those who came as girls the great majority were married in town. A few arrived in town as unmarried mothers and some more experienced pre-marital pregnancies after coming to town, but even some of these were eventually married.

Mothers who came to town in girlhood were said to have been motivated by factors such as the following: the death of parents resulting in economic stress and in tensions, as for instance between a girl and her stepmother, the inability of parents to provide in all their wants, particularly in the line of clothing, pre-marital pregnancy, and the example of friends and relatives who had gone to town. These motives are similar to those found among girls of the present generation migrating to town, as reported by Mayer,[20] and do not require further discussion here.

Widows again, as well as divorced and deserted women, whether they remained with their late husbands' people or returned to their own homes of origin, were often subject to social and economic stress from which migrating to town offered an avenue of escape.[21] Such women could be the mothers of town-born children either by having illegitimate children after coming to town, or by having given birth to children by their husbands during sojourns in East London prior to the husbands' deaths.

As regards parents' settling in town, respondents were asked whether town became the only home of father and mother respectively, and it is significant that more mothers than fathers were regarded as completely settled in town. This is not merely the result of the fact that a larger number of mothers were town-born. It also happened that country-born mothers became fully settled in town while their husbands always remained country-rooted or double-rooted. In most cases this may be explained by the fact that a mother was predeceased by a father who maintained country interests up to the time of his death. In such cases the death of the father was often the final reason for the mother's complete acceptance of town as her only home. A mother who became widowed or separated from her husband in town would turn her back on a rural home for the same reasons as those for which country women would come to town after losing their husbands. The following case illustrates, however, that a mother could completely settle down to town life, even during the lifetime of her country-rooted husband. Joseph's mother was permanently settled in town. 'She got to like town; she was very strong in business here; her business flourished and caused her to settle here.' Meanwhile the father spent most of his time in the country where he held freehold land.

FAMILY BACKGROUND: CULTURE AND OCCUPATION

The reaction of the Bantu of the eastern Cape and the Transkei to evangelistic and educational activities of missions has in the past tended to be either one

[20] Op. cit., pp. 237–41, 243–4.
[21] Cf. further Mayer, op. cit., pp. 241–2.

of acceptance of church, school, and many aspects of Western culture, or one of strongly conservative resistance. Mayer has described how these attitudes have become crystallized into a dichotomy of School people, the acceptors of Christianity, education, and Western ways, and Red people, the conservative, pagan resisters who preserve as much of their traditional culture as possible.[22]

To ascertain whether settling in town might have been related to this cultural dichotomy, town-born adults were asked to classify their parents and grandfathers in terms of these two recognized categories, and inquiries were made about their education and church connexions. The result of these inquiries is summarized below.

	Fathers	*Mothers*	*Fathers' fathers*	*Mothers' fathers*
Number in sample[23]	**88**	**98**	**88**	**97**
Church members or adherents[24]	74	89	52	75
Attended school	59	72	8	30
School people	68	86	44	72
Were Red, became School	10	7	10	4
Red or unknown	10	5	34	21

In spite of the fact that many persons were uncertain about some details, particularly those referring to the church connexions and education of grandfathers, it is obvious that already in the grandfathers' generation a majority of families were or became School people. It is true that only a minority of grandfathers were known to have received school education, but the number who were regarded as church people substantiates the classification in terms of the Red and School categories. Of the parents, the generation which in most cases was responsible for settling in town, almost all were School people, and the majority had, in fact, enjoyed school education, mostly beyond standard two.

One needs to compare this with the numerical relation of Red and School people in the Xhosa rural areas. Even today there is a substantial proportion of Red people in the rural areas from which the East London Bantu are drawn. In 1958–9 Mayer found that 85 per cent of peasant homesteads in the East London district and 45 per cent of those in the King William's Town district were Red. This did not take into account the servants on White-owned farms who are 'known to be predominantly Red'.[25] Further impressions suggest that about 40 per cent, if not more, of the Bantu in the rural areas of the Ciskei are Red. In the Transkei the proportion is probably larger. The inference seems justified that people of School culture settled in East London more readily than the Reds. In fact, hardly any of the fathers who were regarded as Red fully accepted town as their only home. This is consistent with what Mayer has found among present-day migrants, namely that settling in town permanently is incompatible with Red values.[26] This was clearly expressed by an informant who regarded her mother as having been a Red woman who had become School, not because she had been to school or had been converted to

[22] Op. cit., chapter 2.

[23] Only truly town-born respondents were taken into consideration. The discrepancy between the various totals and the total number of town-born respondents (100) is accounted for by a few respondents with a father or a mother in common, and by the elimination of fathers and paternal grandfathers of respondents who had no legal fathers, and of fathers or grandfathers who were White or Coloured. It was felt that the Red–School classification could not be applied to the latter.

[24] 'Adherents' in the sense of persons claiming allegiance to a church without necessarily being catechumens, members on trial or baptized persons.

[25] Op. cit., pp. 20–1.

[26] Op. cit., pp. 90–4.

Christianity, but 'because of settling permanently in town'. Her full acceptance of town life implied that she was no longer Red.

Not only were the parents who settled in town largely School people, but most of them came from School homes, so that it may be said that the real townspeople mostly have a two-generations-old tradition of School culture behind them.

The grandfathers were mostly peasant farmers. Between 10 and 20 per cent were in other occupations, ranging from ministers of religion to unskilled labourers. On the other hand, peasant farming was the main occupation of only a minority of fathers. Of non-peasant fathers who were known to have been employed, the majority were unskilled labourers, while about a third were white-collar or skilled workers, or shopkeepers. Of mothers who were employed in town the majority were either in domestic employment or self-employed as petty traders. Our sample does not give reason to suppose any preference for settling in town along occupational lines.

SUMMARY

From the material presented in this chapter we may attempt to answer the question: who 'got stuck' in town? The males were largely men who had no land of their own to cultivate in the country, and who had very little hope of obtaining any. Females were largely women who had come to town with their husbands, or who had come as unmarried girls, and were married in town, in both cases remaining in town because of their husbands' meagre prospects in the country. A minority of women came to town as a result of widowhood, while others who became widowed in town had less prospects of making a living in the country than before their husbands died. These immigrants came from East London's hinterland, the Ciskei and near Transkei, a culturally relatively homogeneous area as far as the Bantu are concerned.[27] However, those who settled in town were largely drawn from the School section of the rural population. It seems therefore that in the past Red values have had a retarding effect on urbanization, as, in fact, they continue to have up to the present.

Bantu urbanization is essentially a feature of contact with Whites and Western culture. The towns with their Western-orientated industrial and commercial activities exert a certain pull, but at the rural end the pressure on land exerts a push which seems to be more powerful. This push at the rural end is again related to the meeting of the two streams of migration in 'pre-urban' times—the Bantu from the north-east, and the Whites from the south-west—and the ensuing conflicts of the previous century.[28] However, the move to town has often been 'patterned' by factors inherent in the traditional culture and social structure, such as witchcraft beliefs, customs relating to widows and daughters-in-law, rules of inheritance, a patriarchal family organization, and polygyny. This often resulted in complex patterns of motivation in which the interplay of traditional and Western values and beliefs and systems of organization is unmistakable, but often these patterns cannot be classified in terms of one or the other culture, neither can the traditional and Western 'elements' be sorted out.

[27] For tribal composition of the urban sample, see p. 183.

[28] For a summary of these early conflicts, as a background to the study of the growth of the urban Bantu population in East London, see Reader, *The Black Man's Portion*, chapter 1.

2

The Location Scene

Although this study is mainly concerned with the Bantu of East London who have become completely urbanized in a structural sense, so that the city has become their only home, it is impossible to separate them from the rest of the population in a general description of a whole township or residential area such as a Bantu location. The location scene described in this chapter is that shared by widely differing types of urban Bantu with migrants from the country, including both School people of greatly varying educational levels and illiterate Red pagans.[1]

The origins and development of East London's three locations, the areas set aside to accommodate the Bantu population of the city, have been described in detail by Dr. D. H. Reader.[2] In the somewhat impressionistic description that follows, an attempt is made to convey something of the atmosphere of the East Bank Location, also known as Duncan Village, but often just *eLokesheni* to its inhabitants. This is where about two-thirds (45,000-odd) of the city's Bantu population are housed, while many of the domestic servants accommodated on employers' premises in town have close social contacts with the location.

LANDMARKS (see fig. 1, facing page 1)

About four-fifths of the location population are accommodated in the 'wood-and-iron' sections, where only the plots are rented from the City Council, and plot-holders have erected houses of timber and corrugated iron (plate I). The rest are housed in brick or cement-walled houses rented from the Municipality, varying in size from one to four rooms.[3] At the time of writing, the proportion in municipal houses is gradually increasing as some of the inhabitants of the wood-and-iron sections—mostly sub-tenants renting from the owners—are moving into the attractive latest addition to municipal housing schemes at Eziphunzana. New houses for about a thousand families have been completed, and hostel accommodation for five thousand single males is to be added. On all sides the location is separated from White and Coloured residential areas by strips of veld and bushes, but notices warning against unauthorized entry are the only indications of the boundaries of the proclaimed location area.

Of three road approaches, the most important leads to the location from the White business centre via North End with its mixed population and smaller shops. Beside the road there is an open-air unofficial market where traditional Bantu medicines, bead-work and mats are sold. It is nothing of a tourist attraction, and caters almost exclusively for the location people. After passing some factory sites one proceeds along the old road into Tsolo, the oldest part

[1] For a study of the migrants, see Mayer, Philip, *Townsmen or Tribesmen*. The relation of the location to the East London of the Whites is discussed by Mayer, op. cit., pp. 42–4.

[2] *The Black Man's Portion*, chapter 2.

[3] For more illustrations, see Mayer, op. cit., facing p. 48; Reader, op. cit., plates IX to XII.

of the location, within which different neighbourhoods are distinguished as Moriva, Gomorra, and Maxambeni. Following Bantu Street, the road passes below Gomorra, and after crossing the Ngcabanga stream, leads on into Amalinda Duncan Village, which is a municipal housing area.

Just beyond the factory sites mentioned above, a new road branches off to the left, and after passing the administrative buildings skirts the Tsolo wood-and-iron area to become Cemetery Road, which runs between the wood-and-iron area of Mekeni on its left, and Ezasesenta (municipal) and Thulandivile (wood-and-iron) on the right, and passes through Rawutini Duncan Village before crossing the picturesque Amalinda stream and leading on past the cemetery into the new Eziphunzana. To the north of Ezasesenta and Thulandivile lie Ezikawunsileni and Majombozi Duncan Village, both municipal housing projects. To the south of Mekeni there is New Bright (wood-and-iron), while Onothenga, the first home-ownership scheme, links up with Rawutini.[4]

Conditions of extreme congestion prevail in the wood-and-iron sections. Houses are often built within 2 or 3 feet of the kerbside. A small 10-by-12 feet yard or inner quadrangle is a luxury enjoyed by the few, the only spaces between the houses consisting of nothing more than a maze of narrow alleys in many parts. Very few may boast a fence separating one house from another.

Here is a typical house in Gomorra, which illustrates the cluttered atmosphere of the wood-and-iron sections (fig. 2).

FIGURE 2

Sketch-plan of house in Gomorra

On the street front there is a small veranda giving access to rooms 1, 2, and 3. On the sides and at the back narrow alleys, hardly more than 3 feet wide, separate it from neighbouring houses. A dark passage, dimly lit by a ray of light from a garret window, gives access to rooms 4, 5, 6, and 7. Rooms 8, 9, and 10 are under a low flat roof and are entered from the narrow alley at the back. The owner with his wife and child occupy only a small room of about 7 feet by 9 (1), while all the other rooms are let, each one to different tenants.

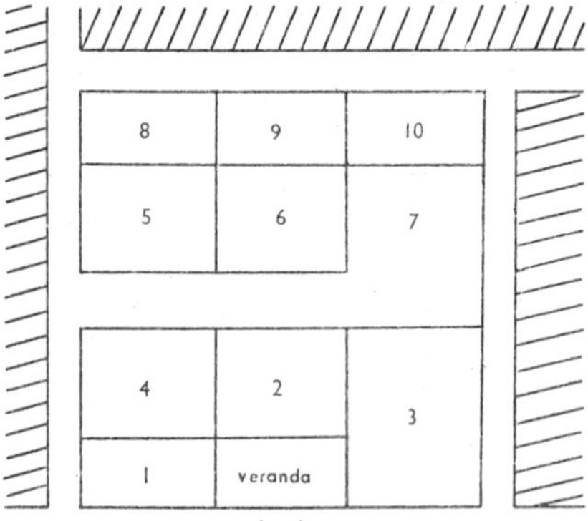

[4] The following are current explanations of these neighbourhood names: *Tsolo*—named after the district of Tsolo in the Transkei, local association unknown; *Moriva*—neighbourhood of Moravian Church; *Gomorra*—used to be a hotbed of vice; *Maxambeni*—from *amaxamba*, sugar-pockets, so called because long ago people used to hide pockets of stolen sugar in the bushes that were there at the time; *Amalinda*—neighbours on the White area of Amalinda; *Mekeni*—named after the 'first African police sergeant' in East London; *Ezasesenta*—the 'social centre' erected by the National War Memorial Health Foundation is in this area; *Thulandivile*—means 'quiet, I have heard', but local association unknown; *Rawutini*—name for the Witwatersrand, given to this area because the houses were built by a firm from the Witwatersrand and/or whose

[*Continued on opposite page*]

Most of the wood-and-iron houses are similar conglomerations of rooms. The back rooms, which are sometimes separated from the main building by a small yard or narrow alley, are usually referred to as 'kitchens'. In this jumble of planless building a few gaily painted little cottages are notable exceptions. There are also a few brick houses, some of them manses or 'mission houses'. Public taps and ablution blocks with toilet facilities are placed at regular intervals between the houses.

The relative spaciousness of the municipal housing areas, where every house stands on its own fenced plot, is in strong contrast with the wood-and-iron areas, where almost every available inch of space has been built upon. Most of the municipal houses are kept reasonably clean and tidy. The latest scheme at Eziphunzana consists of prim little houses built in a setting of green bush and veld and painted a variety of pastel shades, which sprawl over the hills in gracefully curved lines. Although monotonous in the uniformity of house design, the project as a whole makes an attractive appearance.

A few business and professional men have built their own well-sized brick houses on a single block of land in Majombozi. Two of these, particularly, are sumptuous by location standards, and stand comparison with very good houses in White middle-class residential areas, where their counterparts would cost about R8,000 (£4,000) to build (plate IV). They are furnished with complete sitting-room, dining-room and bedroom suites, electric stoves and refrigerators, and are equipped with American kitchens. The grounds, however, are developed only on a modest scale.

The location has no single business area, and shops are found in all neighbourhoods. The offices of the Municipal Native Affairs Department, with the municipal clinic, post office, police station, and home for aged persons, form a cluster of buildings at the approach from town. In a street in Mekeni there are a few shops close to each other, and female hawkers selling meat, vegetables, and used clothes line the street on both sides to display their goods. All the meat-sellers, and some of the others, trade illegally, and on the approach of police or officials they merely disappear with their goods, or if there is no time for this, leave the goods tended, perhaps, by children who deny all knowledge of the responsible persons when questioned. Similar hawkers displaying their goods by the roadside, on a doorstep, or on their verandas are found scattered throughout the location, but this is the only 'market' where they congregate.

Some business men have erected special shop buildings, and a few have attractive shop furnishings, but none of these shops is very large. The largest has a floor space of approximately 600 square feet. The majority of shops are run in small, ill-lit front rooms of wood-and-iron houses where goods, shop attendants and customers jostle together in the restricted space. A number of fresh-produce dealers, barbers and tailors follow their trade under similar conditions. There is at least one photographic studio, while other photographers of varying ability work in their houses. Dairies and butcheries are all housed

[*Note* 4 *continued*]

labourers came from there; *Eziphunzana*—local significance unknown, but there is a rural location in the King William's Town district by this name; *Ezikawunsileni*—'council' houses, an early municipal housing scheme of one-roomed houses; *Majombozi*—named after a well-known East London teacher, prominent some years ago; *New Bright* [*sic*]—after New Brighton Location in Port Elizabeth; *Onothenga*—from *thenga*, buy, being the Municipality's first home-ownership scheme.

in light and airy brick buildings and, being under strict supervision by municipal officers, are usually kept clean and tidy. A few tea-rooms are run in ordinary houses, and there is also a fish-and-chips 'saloon'. A Bantu-owned dry-cleaning business and a garage have lately been opened. The offices of two Bantu attorneys and a few Bantu doctors' surgeries are in different parts of the location.

A business may be run under the name of the owner or the neighbourhood. Others have chosen tribal names or names from the Xhosa hinterland, like Ndlambeland Butchery, Khaya Labathembu (Home of the Thembu) Store, Ngqika Store, and many have Xhosa names like Vukani Dry Cleaners (*vukani*: wake up), Dambisa Cash Store (*dambisa*: lessen), Salinga (we tried) Store, and Masizakhe (let us build ourselves) Store. Occasionally it is a fashionable international name, as in the case of Broadway Tailors. A new note is struck in the name Pan-African Motors.

A stroll through the streets provides evidence of still more trades and activities carried on in a more casual way. Outside a house there may be a notice such as the following: 'Music Studio', or 'Bachelor's Aid: Invisible Mending also Dress-making by Experts', while a third advertises photography and the repair of watches and gramophones. In a number of places one runs up against a collection of old battered cars parked in the street, an indication that someone who undertakes repair jobs lives near by. None of these 'mechanics' seem to work at their jobs permanently and steadily, however, and some of these cars remain stationary for months on end. One man repairs and sells second-hand paraffin stoves and displays them in front of his house on a box in the middle of the road which is used only by pedestrians. Many women sell fat-cakes, but this is usually done in the ordinary run of their household chores, and may hardly be noticed from the street.

The liquor trade is, of course, a major location activity, but because of its illicit nature it is conducted fairly surreptitiously.[4a] Often, however, one noticed a few tell-tale blackened drums used for brewing beer, or a number of four-gallon tins full of the porridge which is cooked in preparation for beer brewing. A drinking-place is commonly referred to as *isiroxo*, a word referring to a place which is hidden. The word 'shebeen' is sometimes used by more sophisticated people, but only of places where non-traditional liquor is always in abundant supply. Shebeens do not differ from other houses, except that the homes of a few very successful shebeen queens contrast with the neighbours through their better state of repair and fresh paint. Liquor customers are served in the owners' living-quarters, a dining- or sitting-room if there is one, but many beer-sellers occupy only one or two rooms with their families, and customers are served there in a family atmosphere. The customer of a woman selling European liquor drops in and sits down like a casual visitor, waiting till there is privacy enough to place the order, or, if the opportunity is not forthcoming, will intimate his wishes by recognized sign language when unobserved.

No Whites may occupy business or professional premises in the location, but delivery vans and carts, including ice-cream carts, of many East London White businesses are a common sight.

There are upwards of twenty church buildings in the location. The most important churches have well-built brick buildings of which only a few have steeples. Most of them are unimposing auditoriums or simple halls. The wood-and-iron churches cover a whole range, from the neatly constructed cruciform

[4a] But see Appendix IV, 'New Liquor Legislation'.

auditorium of the Bantu Presbyterian Church, down to the irregularly shaped shanty-like little hall of a small independent or 'separatist' church. All the churches built in municipal housing areas are on officially recognized church sites and are brick buildings. The enormous auditorium of the Rev. N. B. H. Bhengu's Assemblies of God, which seats 2,500 persons with ease, is quite unique in size among churches of the Bantu in South Africa, but the architectural design is unimposing.

There are three groups of school buildings, but many primary classes are conducted in churches or church halls, which often overflow into the church yards, so that classes conducted in the open air are a familiar location sight. Of the three well-sized public halls, one, erected by the National War Memorial Health Foundation and now controlled by the Municipal Native Affairs Department, serves as a 'social centre', where a regular crèche is run, and the municipal welfare officer organizes different forms of entertainment.[5] Films are shown regularly, and the hall is made available for concerts, dances, and indoor sporting events. Tennis courts and a swimming-bath have been added recently by the city council.

The cemetery is another place worth visiting. It is placed in a picturesque setting on a grassy slope near the Amalinda stream, but lacks the trees and neatly laid-out paths which many Whites associate with such places. On a few graves there are tombstones and paving, and some have simple wooden or metal crosses. Inscriptions in English or Xhosa follow the pattern of those in White cemeteries. On many graves, however, all kinds of used articles have been placed, such as plates, cups, glasses, and tea-pots, while there may be an occasional vase with flowers. Babies' drinking bottles and broken or used toys appear on some of the smaller graves.

A few major thoroughfares have tarred surfaces. The streets along the routes leading out of the location carry a heavy traffic, mostly of commercial vehicles, buses and taxis, some driven by Indian and Coloured men. Location drivers tend to drive with bravado, and show little consideration for other users of the road, using their hooters a great deal. In the narrow streets traffic easily gets entangled at peak hours. Huge buses have to edge their way around corners on the wrong side of the road, and when two of them meet at such a corner, some manoeuvring is needed to pass, the road meanwhile being completely blocked to impatiently hooting taxis. Most of the streets are badly eroded and therefore avoided by vehicular traffic. On the whole, streets are not clean, and in the wood-and-iron sections streams of dirty household water run along street gutters. In the municipal housing sections there are one or two playgrounds consisting of a few swings and see-saws on an unfenced open space.

The location would make a much more unpleasant impression but for the two small rivers, with strips of veld and bush, running through and around it, and the rise and fall of the hills over which it has spread. From some places one even has a pleasing view of the sea. A number of people keep animals, and there are upwards of forty cattle-kraals scattered around the fringes of the residential areas. It is nothing unusual for a lazy cow to delay traffic in the busy Cemetery Road. From the heights of New Bright there is a pleasing view across the valley of the Ngcabanga stream, and in the hollow between Tsolo and New Bright are neat school gardens.

[5] A new crèche building was opened while writing-up was in progress. On the other hand entertainment emanating from official sources seems to have petered out.

ACTIVITIES

In the wood-and-iron sections there are always many people about in the streets. From 6 a.m. onward the flow of traffic increases as workers queue up for buses, board taxis or proceed to work on foot. After 9 a.m. the rush is over, and people move about in a casual mood. Some women are busy with their household chores, and men do repair jobs, but at all times of the day many people, both men and women, can be seen sitting around outside. Here are a group of children at play with mealie stalks dressed up in rags, for dolls. There a boy of 15, wearing a beret, sits playing the guitar. A boy of 13 careers down a slope on a tyreless, chainless, saddleless bicycle. A woman hawker passes with a box of vegetables on her head. Many children of school-going age are about. You hear some penny-whistles, a radiogram blaring out a monotonous concertina tune in a shop round the corner, and a woman in a beer-brewer's yard humming the tune of a hymn. All day long women and girls come and go to fetch water from the public taps. Some people have their first meal of the day between ten and eleven.

In the early afternoon there is a restful atmosphere. Every day at about 1 p.m. a group assembles on the slopes below Gomorra, waiting for details of the progress of the daily fah-fee gambling game. From 2 p.m. onwards, children return home from school and women start returning from domestic service. Near the houses, on the fringe of Gomorra, a group of men and women lounge on the grass, one of the women combing another's hair. In front of a house, partly in the 'street', four men sit playing or watching a game of draughts. Elsewhere people are trying to separate two fighting men, and an informant remarks that when two young men fight, you may be sure it is about a girl. A mother is busy delousing her child's hair, while another woman sits on her doorstep reading *Imvo Zabantsundu*, a widely read Xhosa newspaper.

From 4.30 p.m. the streets grow steadily busier, but amid those hurrying home from work others stroll around with a casual air. Red women may dance around in the street here and there. Between 5 and 6 p.m. the workers stream home in their multitudes: labourers in dark blue overalls, nurses in their spotless white uniforms, smartly dressed messengers, women in factory overalls, and men wearing shabby coats and trousers. After sunset there are crowds of people about, and the small shops are packed with workers buying their daily provisions. In a less crowded street in a municipal housing area a party of schoolgirls may pass, singing a popular concert tune to which they march with rhythmic movements of the arms and body. This is the time of the day when location streets are at their busiest, while in the homes there is a great deal of pleasant conversation, casual visiting, and beer and tea drinking. Workers, however, are too tired to keep late nights and mostly go to bed from 8.30 p.m. onwards. Some even turn in immediately after returning from work. A Transkei man of about 45, who lives in one room with his wife and children, was found in bed at 6 p.m. and explained that it was his custom to go to bed early. 'This keeps me from the streets, and prevents my getting drunk and being assaulted.' Later in the evening some of the younger people may still be out on entertainment, but by 11 p.m. most streets are quiet.

In the municipal housing areas where there is much more space inside and outside the houses, there are the same stages in the daily rhythm, but they are much less pronounced than in the crowded wood-and-iron neighbourhoods.

The location street-scene is one of greatly varying activity. Dress (or undress) varies from the smart suit, working overalls, or tattered coat, to the occasional naked toddler. Many men like to carry brief-cases, not only the very smartly dressed ones—'just for show', some informants say. On a hot day one invariably passes several men carrying large black umbrellas or coloured sunshades. Red women with their beadwork, long dresses, bare shoulders, quaintly arranged doeks, and painted faces are always around. Someone points out a neatly painted wood-and-iron house which belongs to the most successful shebeen queen in the location, and the big car you see parked is hers. Round the corner you greet the minister passing in his not-quite-so-big car. In the same busy Main Street you pass the successful business man driving his latest model car, and the boy of 10 urinating in the gutter. Incidentally it is not unusual to see a man urinating on the outskirts of the residential areas within full view of the public.

Children play with half-broken shop-bought toys, with motor-cars fashioned of wires, and with bits of wood dressed as dolls in small remnants of material. They may build a little hut with saplings of wood, imitating those built for boys' initiation, or they may follow the hula-hoop craze. The groups of adolescent boys playing dice are very much part of the location scene, although some avoid spots where they are too much in the public eye.

Different weekdays are much the same in the location, but on Thursday afternoons the *manyano*-women of the different churches give a special atmosphere to the streets with their coloured uniforms. It is the afternoon when all these women's associations meet. The girls' associations meet on Wednesdays. Friday is pay-day, and there is even more activity than usual toward the late afternoon. Extra provisions are bought, including some meat, which only a few can afford every day. Many people like to prepare a special meal for Friday night. Migrants from the country hurry to catch buses taking them home for the week-end. Most workers have Saturday afternoon and Sunday free, and many have Saturday morning free as well. In the morning people attend to small jobs at home, go to see people on business, and go shopping or marketing, but on Saturday afternoon there is an atmosphere of relaxation as casually strolling young folk fill the streets, older people gossip, and men shave each other's hair beside the street. Some attend sporting events or visit the beach. But the street-venders carry on their business, and women who have been too busy during the week take the chance of doing their washing. There are usually a few funerals on a Saturday afternoon, because when a death has not taken place too early in the week, people like to postpone the funeral until Saturday afternoon, when most people are able to attend. Such family rituals as take place, for example, ritual slaughterings, and the opening and closing of boys' initiation ceremonies, usually also take place over the week-end. Faithful church people spend a large part of Sunday attending services and other church activities, the three o'clock service in the afternoon usually attracting the largest attendance. Other people spend the day paying visits and relaxing much as they do on a Saturday afternoon, while some young people attend the social 'get-togethers' held in one or two halls.

The location also has its festive occasions every year. Christmas is, perhaps, the most widely celebrated. There is a large exodus of migrants to their homes in the country, while some country people again visit relatives or friends living in town. During the weeks preceding Christmas some organizations hold Christmas-tree functions for the children, but family Christmas-trees are uncommon. On Christmas eve some families observe special thanksgiving prayers. It appears that thanksgiving for the blessings of the past year figure prominently in many people's ideas about Christmas. Some people specially slaughter animals for the feasting which they also associate with thanksgiving to God. Annually on Christmas eve a 'Hobo Dance' is held in one of the public halls. It has the reputation of being an occasion for extraordinary moral licence and of developing into somewhat of an orgy. The same applies to the Old Year's eve dance.

Children are usually given new clothes on Christmas morning, and many adults also try to provide themselves with something new to wear on Christmas day. Some attend the Christmas services in church and many try to have a special dinner in the middle of the day or in the evening. Others spend the day drinking and singing, making merry in a drunken way and asking for 'Christmas boxes' wherever they come. Some young people make it an occasion for tomfoolery—girls dressing up as boys and boys dressing in other quaint ways. Beach and other picnics have also become popular among young people of late.

Visits to town by tribal chiefs are sometimes marked by festivity. During 1959 the chieftainess of the Imiqhayi, a section of the Ngqika people, visited West Bank Location, and received an enthusiastic reception. She was escorted into town by a small commando of men on horseback, local Bantu Boy Scout troops, and a procession of cars. Besides speeches by officials and leading men of the East London Ngqika community, an official praiser (*imbongi*), dressed in fur cap and cloak, poured traditional praises into the microphone. The crowd of about six hundred or more included migrants, both Red and School, as well as town people. A town-born teacher living in West Bank Location, one of the leading Ngqika in East London, took an active part in organizing the reception.

Guy Fawkes is also commemorated in the location. Troops of children parade the streets, making their own private collections. The boys blacken their faces with soot and dress up in men's clothes and quaint hats. Girls stuff their figures to resemble adult women, and paint and dress up in Red fashion. They sing Xhosa songs begging for 'money for the Guy Fawkes'. The money is not used to buy crackers, but is given to the parents 'to buy clothes for us', or to be used at Christmas-time. There is some lighting of crackers in the evening.

Public holidays have the air of a Saturday afternoon, and are sometimes marked by visits of groups from the country, and by church bazaars and conferences. Conferences also take place over ordinary week-ends, and recently a conference of a 'Herbalists' Association' drew a gathering of over two hundred 'native' doctors from different parts of the Cape Province, many of them dressed in the traditional 'witchdoctor's' regalia.

This, then, is the material and social milieu in which our urban Bantu live. In the following chapter we shall try to give some idea of the culture of the town-born people as a separate category in the location.

3

Cultural Differentiations

A study of the culture and social structure of urban Bantu today is essentially a study in cultural and social change. We have seen that the life of the grandfathers of our urban Bantu had already been considerably influenced by missions and schools, to which one could add White government agencies and trading. During the fathers' and children's generations the influence of Western culture on the urban Bantu increased progressively, particularly in the economic sphere. Those who made their homes in town inevitably moved farther away from the ancestral way of life and experienced the impact of the White man's ways more intensively.

It has been stressed that the changes taking place in many African and other societies as a result of contact with Western peoples and cultures should not be regarded as a unique form of change. Certainly these changes should be studied within the framework of social and cultural change in general, but the fact cannot be overlooked that the changes with which we are dealing are more radical and more rapid than those which these societies experienced before contact with Western influence. Pre-contact changes 'occurred within the limits of a largely subsistence economy and a kin-bound social structure. . . . Social change within aboriginal Africa was on the whole change within systems of a certain type rather than change of systems, while there have often been most radical changes of system since the establishment of colonial rule.'[1] It is further obvious that contact with the Whites, at least in the case of the South African Bantu, provided the main impetus to this change.

Nevertheless one agrees with cautions against the use of the term 'westernization' in describing these changes, as if the Bantu and other African peoples are simply gradually exchanging their traditional institutions for Western ways and customs. 'What results from the contact between two cultures is, as Malinowski repeatedly stressed, neither a haphazard mixture of different elements nor an approximation to either of the two societies, but the growth of a new independent social tendency with its own cultural resources.'[2] However, it seems that as far as the urban Bantu are concerned, the new 'fabric' which we see emerging will in time be more akin to the Western way of living of the Whites in South Africa than to traditional Bantu culture. In this restricted and relative sense the process of change observed among urban Bantu may be termed 'westernization'. Thereby the continuity of traditional Bantu culture with their present and future way of living is not denied. Whereas the growth of new practices is 'the product of the choice of individuals subject to the pressure of the situation',[3] the indigenous cultural heritage remains an important influence

[1] Southall, Aidan, *Social Change in Modern Africa*, O.U.P., for International African Institute, 1961, p. 2.

[2] Banton, Michael, *West African City*, O.U.P., 1957, p. 220.

[3] Ibid.

in the minds of many urban Bantu in the choices they make, and plays its role in the growth of new patterns of behaviour.

The culture of urban Bantu is discussed here against the background of this hypothesis, that it represents a stage in the process of change towards greater affinity with Western culture, though the continuity with traditional Bantu culture is retained and the continued retention of a distinct identity from existing variations of Western culture is most probable. In this sense 'westernization' does not denote a peculiar type of social change, but is useful as a descriptive term in dealing with the concrete situation under consideration.

Although the change is unmistakable, it remains difficult to characterize the culture of the urban Bantu today. Hardly any clear patterns seem to have crystallized yet, and the variations in patterns of behaviour, values and beliefs, and the different combinations of these in different regions of the culture, seem to defy systematization. At this stage it is impossible to give a complete picture of the culture of the urban Bantu without a large amount of fieldwork involving detailed interviews on a wide range of topics with a large sample of informants. The present study did not allow for such an ambitious approach, but in this chapter a number of 'dips' into the life of the urban Xhosa in East London are taken, to indicate in as systematic a way as possible the cultural variations among them. From the outset, however, it was the aim of the present investigation not merely to indicate the existence of cultural diversity, but also to discern specific cultural types or categories. Since the economic diversity is so obvious, could be expected to have a bearing on other characteristics, and is measurable with greater approximation to accuracy than most other characteristics, economic level seems to be the most appropriate starting point for such a classification. We set out, therefore, by grouping households into a few economic categories on the basis of income and material culture, and by further comparing these categories in terms of occupational and educational level. Income and occupation, material culture, and education are then discussed separately and in greater detail. Further sections deal with religion, leisure activities, and traditional culture, and lead on to the formulation of a number of cultural types.

ECONOMIC CATEGORIES

Economic level is best discussed in terms of the household, since it is the important economic unit, being the group of persons 'who eat from one pot'. Although the wages are not necessarily pooled where there is more than one bread-winner in the household, part of the wages of each bread-winner is usually spent in the interests of the whole household in some way or another, for instance, by a contribution to the household head, by paying the rent, buying food independently, or buying furniture for the home. Material culture is also best discussed in terms of the household.

In assigning the households in our sample to different economic levels, only cash income was taken into consideration,[4] and a *per capita* income was calculated on the basis of the total income of all the members of the household. Members 'partially present' and temporarily absent (see chapter 8) were counted as members of the household for this purpose.

[4] Only cash income was recorded in our investigations. The extensive questioning that is usually necessary to ascertain details about the value of income in kind would have made our interviews too lengthy. Except in the case of domestic servants, income in kind does not figure prominently in urban Bantu households.

Although many households have several members enjoying cash income, household income is nevertheless low, the majority of households recording a *per capita* weekly income of less than R2 (20*s.*), a considerable proportion being less than R1. Of the households in our sample 12 per cent had an income of more than R4 (40*s.*) *per capita* per week, but this gives an exaggerated impression of the proportion of the town population living in relative comfort, since they represent less than 6 per cent of the total population of the households sampled, most of them being small households, and a few consisting of single persons.

It was argued that the highest income earned by a single member of the household should also be taken into consideration in deciding the economic level, since it was felt that a household solely dependent on the high income of a single bread-winner should be assigned a higher level than another which might have the same *per capita* income, but derives such income from several members earning low wages.

Personal observations and the perusal of all the details for households at the highest income levels led us to expect a concentration of a certain type of the most westernized households in an upper economic category. A minimum *per capita* weekly income of R2.50 (25*s.*) combined with an individual weekly income of R9.00 (90*s.*) or more proved an effective point of division to show up this type satisfactorily. There was nothing to give the impression that any distinct cultural type could be isolated by a further division at any particular income level, but the remaining households were nevertheless separated into middle and lower categories. Households with a *per capita* income of less than R1 (10*s.*) and of which the income of each individual member was less than R5.00 (50*s.*) per week formed the lower category, with the remaining ones making up the middle category.

A distinction was also introduced in terms of material culture. There is not much in material culture observed in the homes of urban Bantu which could be regarded as 'traditional', but there are many households of which the material culture is of a very simple nature, even though all the individual items might be factory-made. To distinguish between the very simple households and those that are more impressively furnished, a system of scoring was used, points being awarded according to whether the furniture in the main room comprised a complete suite, or only loose pieces, and whether the furniture was new and well cared for in appearance, in a reasonable 'in-between' condition, or definitely old and worn. Additional points were assigned for electric lights, radio, radiogram and electric stove (whether these were in the main room or not).

The sample households were divided into two categories—'well-furnished' and 'simple'—according to the points scored. A minimum of four, the equivalent of points awarded for a suite in reasonable condition without any of the other appliances mentioned, was taken as the minimum qualification for a 'well-furnished' household.[5] Nearly all the households classified as 'simple' by this

[5] Points were awarded as follows:

Complete suite of furniture. Appearing new and well cared for, 5; in-between, 4; old and worn, 2.

Loose pieces of furniture only: Appearing new and well cared for, 4; in-between, 2; old and worn, 1.

Electric stove, 6; *radiogram*, 4; *radio*, 2; *electric lights*, 2.

Madge (*The Tools of Social Science*, Longmans Green, London, 1953) criticizes the use by Chapin and others of a system of points for material possessions as an index of family social

[*Continued overleaf*]

criterion actually had only loose pieces of furniture in the main room, but there were a few with only old and worn suites. On the other hand, of those qualifying as 'well-furnished' there were three with only loose pieces of furniture, whose scores, however, were boosted by the fact that they had radios, and two of them also electric lights. All the other 'well-furnished' households had suites of furniture which offered at least a reasonable appearance (not old and worn).

The grouping of the 109 households in our sample resulting from the application of these criteria is shown in table 3. On the basis of income and material culture we have, then, four categories sufficiently numerous to allow further analysis, viz.

I an upper income category, well-furnished: 13 households;
II a middle income category, well-furnished: 23 households;
III a middle income category with simple furniture: 40 households;
IV a lower income category with simple furniture: 19 households.

The 'upper simple' and 'lower well-furnished' categories (two and six households respectively) are too small to justify further analysis.

TABLE 3

Economic categories (households)

Material culture	INCOME LEVEL Upper	Middle	Low	Unknown	Total
Well-furnished	13	23	6	4	46
Simple	2	40	19	2	63
Total	15	63	25	6	109

In order to ascertain whether there is any association between occupations and the economic categories in our sample, the occupations of employee members of the household were graded as white-collar, skilled, semi-skilled and unskilled work, and each household was accorded the level of the highest occupation represented in it. A problem arose where a household included persons who were completely self-employed. If a household had both employee and self-employed members, it was accorded a self-employed 'level'. The same happened, of course, if it was solely dependent on self-employment. Actually such households are not comparable to any of the levels mentioned above, because the self-employed persons vary from relatively well-to-do shopowners to hawkers and beer-brewers. However, in our major categories the number of households of self-employed level was negligible.

From table 4 where this grading of households by occupation has been made, we see that in all categories excepting the 'upper well-furnished' category (I), more than two-thirds are of the unskilled level. In category I only one out of thirteen is unskilled, while a distinct majority are of the white-collar level. We also note that all of white-collar occupational level are found in the 'upper

[*Note* 5 *continued*]
status, on the grounds that 'it too glibly assumes a stereotype of family trappings, which although possibly valid, remains somewhat uncongenial and unmistakably foreign' (op. cit., p. 140). My own use of points for furniture is not as a straightforward index of social status, but as an index of classification in terms of material culture, used in conjunction with other characteristics of the categories thus defined, to arrive at the formulation of more general cultural types. I do not assume these cultural categories to be synonymous with social classes, although the possibility that these categories are related to social status is not ruled out. (See further pp. 176 ff.)

well-furnished' category (I). In terms of occupational grading, therefore, the 'upper well-furnished' households in our sample tend to a higher level than the rest, but there does not seem to be any significant difference between the other three categories.[6]

For the sake of greater simplicity the 'upper well-furnished' category (I) is henceforth referred to as *white-collar*, the 'middle well-furnished' (II) as *intermediate*, the 'middle simple' (III) as *simple-A* and the 'lower-simple' (IV) as *simple-B*.

TABLE 4

Economic category by occupational level

	ECONOMIC CATEGORY					
Highest occupation in household	Upper well-furnished I	Middle well-furnished II	Middle simple III	Lower simple IV	Other V	Total
Employees						
White-collar	8	—	—	—	—	8
Skilled	3	4	5	—	—	12
Semi-skilled	—	1	2	1	—	4
Unskilled	1	15	30	14	8	68
Self-employed	1	2	1	1	6	11
Not employed	—	—	1	2	—	3
Unknown	—	—	2	1	—	3
Total	13	22	41	19	14	109

Our categories may also be compared in respect of the maximum educational qualifications attained by any one of its members, assuming that this gives a reasonable indication of a household's relation to education. This was expressed in terms of the number of years required to complete the courses that had been taken by the most highly educated member. Thus eight years are equivalent to standard six (Sub A plus B plus six standards), eleven years to Junior Certificate or the Native Primary Higher teacher's certificate. A qualified general nurse with a year's training in midwifery would score fifteen years if she had passed Junior Certificate and seventeen with Senior Certificate.

Table 5 shows that in the 'white-collar' households in our sample the maximum educational level was higher than standard six in all but one of the thirteen households, while in the intermediate category a smaller proportion, though still a majority of households, had advanced beyond standard six. In both simple categories only a minority go beyond standard six, while both have a substantial proportion that do not go beyond standard four. A more detailed analysis shows that the average maxima for the different categories are 12 years, 9·5 years, 7·3 years and 7·7 years respectively, while the medians are 11, 9, 8 and 7 years respectively. The general impression conveyed by these figures is that the white-collar category is superior in terms of maximum education to the intermediate category, and that the latter is superior to the other two, but we cannot claim a significant difference between the two simple categories.[7] Although the difference between the white-collar and intermediate

[6] If only the households of employees in columns I–IV (table 4) are considered, and 'white-collar' are lumped with 'skilled', and 'semi-skilled' with 'unskilled', I is found to differ significantly from (II+III+IV) (significant at a 1 per cent level), but the table II III IV is not significant. (See appendix II for details of statistical tests applied.)

[7] If only columns I–IV (table 5) are considered, and rows of figures are lumped (0–6 years with 7–8 years, and 9–13 years with 14+) the table (I+II) (III+IV) is significant at a 1 per cent level, but the tables I II and III IV respectively are not significant.

categories in our sample is not statistically significant, it seems likely that a larger sample may have proved them to be significantly different.

TABLE 5

Economic category by educational level

Maximum education in years	White-collar I	Inter-mediate II	Simple-A III	Simple-B IV	Other V	Total
	ECONOMIC CATEGORY					
0–6	—	1	10	6	3	20
7–8	1	6	20	9	5	41
9–13	7	14	11	3	4	39
14+	5	1	—	1	1	8
Unknown	—	—	—	—	1	1
Total	13	22	41	19	14	109

INCOME AND OCCUPATION OF INDIVIDUAL PERSONS

On the whole the occupations and income of Bantu who may be regarded as second generation townspeople do not show marked differences from those of the Bantu population of East London taken as a whole. The summary in terms of employment categories given below shows that in both cases the majority of males are in unskilled employment, although the proportion might be somewhat smaller for townspeople proper than for all Bantu. Further the proportions in other categories are relatively small in both cases. In either case roughly half of the females are employed, the majority also in unskilled employment.

CATEGORIES OF EMPLOYMENT

	Sample of 'second generation'[8] M	Sample of 'second generation'[8] F	Sample of all Bantu in town[9] M	Sample of all Bantu in town[9] F
Employees: white-collar	5	2	41	34
skilled and semi-skilled	8	9	218	52
unskilled	42	42	1,152	493
Self-employed and employers	6	11	70	145
Household duties, and diverse categories not employed	15	61	213	872
Unknown and employment unspecified	—	1	8	5
Total	76	126	1,702	1,601

A more detailed analysis of occupations (see notes below table 23) reveals one important difference between males in our own sample and those in the general sample, namely that occupations of the 'rough and heavy' type, such as unskilled labour in the building trade, seem to attract hardly any town males and are probably filled exclusively by migrants. (Reader found that 12 per cent of all Bantu male employees were unskilled workers in the building trade.[10])

Some males and females not in employment derive an income from rents. The majority of townspeople have only a single source of income, but sometimes wages are combined with the returns from self-employment or rents. It is suspected that our sample is deficient in the category of unemployed youths.

[8] Extracted from table 23 (appendix I).

[9] Extracted from Reader, op. cit., table on p. 64, and appendix I, table 14, on p. 158.

[10] Op. cit., table on p. 64.

The males in our sample show some tendency toward a higher income than is usual for the East London Bantu male population as a whole. For our town males in employment the median weekly income was somewhat over R6.00 (60*s*.), whereas for the whole employed male population it is R5.80 (58*s*.).[11] More than one-fifth of town men in employment were earning more than R8.00 (80*s*.) per week, while four men in the sample had an income in excess of R10 (£5). A teacher earning R76 (£38) per month (R19 or £9 10*s*. per week) had the highest income recorded, while a man in his late 60's, who sells milk, is employed casually as prisoners' escort, and derives some further income from rents, claimed a total income of R16 (£8) per week. A truck-driver and a clerk at the hospital both earned over R12 (£6) per week.

There is some occupational differentiation in terms of age. Younger men show a mild tendency toward factory labour and jobs as messengers while the self-employed males are mostly older men. Education has only a relative effect on the kind of employment taken up (table 24, appendix I). The majority of men in white-collar and skilled jobs have enjoyed at least a secondary school education, but there are also a number of the same educational level in unskilled employment.

Less than a quarter of the women who have an independent income earn more than R4 (40*s*.). Two nurses earning R44 (£22) per month (R11 or £5 10*s*. per week) were the only females in the sample with a weekly income of more than R8 (80*s*.). Two women in unskilled employment earning a total of more than R6 (60*s*.) supplemented their wages by means of petty trade and rents, while a woman trading in used clothes claimed an income of R6.40 (64*s*.) per week. Domestic employment (including washing and ironing) and factory work are the most common occupations for women, accounting for more than half of those in employment, but it appears that factory labour is more common, and domestic employment less so among town women than it is for the East London Bantu female population as a whole. In terms of cash wages, factory workers nearly all do better than domestic servants, some of them earning close to R6 (60*s*.) per week. Most domestic servants, however, have the advantage of being supplied with most of, or all, their meals at their places of employment.

The factory female workers are nearly all girls and young women under the age of 35. Domestic servants are fairly evenly spread over younger and older age groups. Self-employed women are mostly older than 35. Education seems to have even less connexion with the type of employment in which women find themselves than in the case of men. Professional employment, however, goes with at least secondary school education, while skilled and semi-skilled workers usually have at least an advanced primary education. On the other hand, a large proportion of females with secondary school education are in unskilled employment, and even more are unemployed.

MATERIAL CULTURE

Our discussion in this section is confined to a few aspects of housing, furniture and interior decoration of the homes of town Bantu. The survey questionnaire did not seek information on clothing, but some examples of different types of dress are given in chapter 4.

Housing conditions in the East London locations have been described in

[11] Reader, op. cit., p. 65.

detail by Dr. Reader, and he has given ample statistical evidence of the intensely overcrowded conditions, particularly in the wood-and-iron areas.[12] Townspeople share these conditions with the migrant population, and there is nothing to indicate that the former live under distinctly superior conditions. About a quarter of the town households in our sample, comprising 26 per cent of the total household population, lived in municipal housing areas where housing conditions are, on the whole, much better than in the wood-and-iron areas. This is somewhat more than the 19 per cent of the total population (10,290 out of 55,020).[13]

In terms of house tenure we may distinguish three types of households, namely owner-households, municipal tenants and room tenants. Owner-households are those of which the head or another member owns the house (but not the site) which they occupy. Such a house could be a wood-and-iron structure, occasionally a brick or semi-brick building in the wood-and-iron section of the location, or a brick house built under the Municipality's home-ownership scheme.[14] In the location as a whole the last two categories of owners constitute only a small minority, and all the owners in our sample owned wood-and-iron houses. Tenants of municipal houses are not allowed to sublet, but they do so occasionally. With only one exception the room-tenants in our sample were renting rooms in wood-and-iron houses.

Of the sample households living in wood-and-iron areas, just over half were owners. However, this seldom implied that they were more favourably housed than tenants, because most owner families crowd into one or two rooms in order to let as many rooms as possible.

Judging by our sample, nearly half of all town households occupy only one room, while less than a third occupy more than two rooms (table 25 (appendix I)). Those occupying four rooms are mostly tenants of the largest type of municipal houses. A household occupying more than four rooms is an exception, none occurring in our sample.[15] On the average there were 2·9 persons per room (table 26 (appendix I)), the median figure also being between two and three, but a density of three to six persons per room was quite common, seven or eight not unusual, and occasionally one found as many as ten or eleven occupying a single room.

In the wood-and-iron areas the different rooms occupied by one household hardly ever comprise a complete house, nor do they form a separate unit in the house, often enough not even being adjacent. A municipal house, however, is usually occupied by a single household.

When comparing our economic categories in terms of housing conditions (tables 25 and 26), we find that simple households on the average had fewer rooms at their disposal (less than two rooms per household) and more persons per room (three to four) than the white-collar and intermediate ones, the two simple categories being much the same. Although white-collar households do not appear to have more rooms at their disposal than intermediate ones (the averages being 2·3 and 2·4 respectively), the white-collar category had an average room density of only 1·9 persons compared to the 2·5 of the intermediate category.

[12] Op. cit., pp. 41–3, 103–9.
[13] Extracted from Reader, op. cit., appendix I, table 2, on p. 151.
[14] Cf. ibid., pp. 109–10.
[15] Kitchens have been included in the count of rooms. Even when a room primarily serves the function of kitchen, it often serves as bedroom for some members of the household at night.

House-owning households were fairly evenly spread over all four economic categories, and in all they showed a tendency to confine themselves to only one or two rooms in their houses. A majority of the simple owner-households occupied only one room. Since it is known that the houses owned are multi-roomed, it is obvious that all categories tend to let part of the houses they own, rather than allow themselves more living-space. Tenants of municipal houses, not being allowed to sublet, are the ones with the most rooms at their disposal. They were represented in all economic categories in our sample.

The furniture in the homes of town people shows a very wide range of variety (table 6). The majority of homes are very simply furnished: usually there are a table and a few chairs, a separate table with a single plate paraffin stove (mostly a pressure stove) and some cooking utensils, some form of cupboard, and one or more beds—but hardly ever a separate one for every member of the household. Occasionally one finds a home-made table or bench, but these homes are generally furnished with old, second-hand furniture, usually loose pieces, but occasionally comprising a suite. Some homes make a more sophisticated impression with dining- or sitting-room suites, which, although obviously not new, still make for quite a respectable appearance. Here one often finds a profuse display of ornamental and other crockery and glassware.

A substantial minority of homes have at least one suite of furniture appearing new and well cared for. In some of these homes one finds electric lights, a radio or occasional radiogram, and here and there an electric stove. There are homes in the location furnished with refrigerators, but none of those known to us could be regarded as long-established East London homes.

By our system of scoring, a small number of households in the sample scored from six to eight points, which implies that in addition to a suite of furniture they had either electric lights, a radio, or a radiogram. Six households scored more than eight points. For example, one had a new suite of furniture, electricity laid on, a radiogram and a separate radio. The most impressive household in the sample had the same items, besides an electric stove.

TABLE 6

Economic category by score for furniture

	ECONOMIC CATEGORY					
Score	White-collar I	Inter-mediate II	Simple-A III	Simple-B IV	Other V	Total
1	—	—	29	14	2	45
2	—	—	12	5	2	19
4	3	11	—	—	5	19
5	3	3	—	—	3	9
6	1	2	—	—	—	3
7	3	4	—	—	—	7
8	—	1	—	—	—	1
10	—	—	—	—	2	2
14	2	—	—	—	—	2
16	—	1	—	—	—	1
20	1	—	—	—	—	1
	13	22	41	19	14	109

Whereas some thirty years ago the furniture in the homes of the well-to-do smacked of 'Victorian England',[16] the better furnished homes of today are well

[16] Hunter, Monica, *Reaction to Conquest*, O.U.P. (Second Edition) 1961, London, p. 446.

abreast of the times. Many Bantu nowadays buy new, modern furniture, of the same design as one would find in many middle-class or working-class White homes. Much of this is bought on the hire-purchase system.

In terms of the criteria applied, it is not possible to discover any difference in respect of furniture between the two 'simple' categories. Well-furnished households, however, showed more differentiation, with scores ranging from four to twenty. From table 6 it appears that white-collar households could be more impressively furnished than the intermediate ones.[17] The majority in the white-collar category had an extra item in addition to a suite of furniture (six points or more), while the majority of intermediates scored four or five points, in most cases awarded for a suite of furniture without any additional items. Further, of the four most impressive households, three were white-collar.

Interior walls are mostly decorated with photographs of members of the family and friends, or with cheap religious pictures (table 27 (appendix I)). Calendars are common, and church or educational certificates are next in popularity, followed by pictures from books or magazines. Occasionally there is a photograph of a high church dignitary, such as Rev. Nicholas Bhengu or Lekhanyane—the latter in a Sotho home. A few homes in the sample displayed pictures of past generations of British royalty, and at least two had representations of the Xhosa prophet Ntsikana.[18] In wood-and-iron houses walls are often papered with pages from magazines, which may produce a decorative effect while still fresh. The homes lacking any mural decorations are usually also the ones most simply furnished.

We are now in a position to form a preliminary impression of the cultural significance of our economic categories. In all respects discussed so far, the white-collar category is superior to the other three: it represents, of course, the upper income level, and in terms of occupational level it is predominantly a category of the homes with white-collar workers; it tends to a higher educational level than the rest, and furniture is somewhat more impressive. In terms of housing it has the lowest number of persons per room, although it does not differ much from the intermediate category in respect of the number of rooms occupied.

Excepting occupational level and income, the intermediate category, again, is superior to the two simple ones. The latter two, however, seem to differ only in respect of income. We cannot claim superiority for the simple-A category in terms of occupational or educational level, furniture, or housing conditions. The distinction we make between simple-A and simple-B does not appear to have significance in terms of culture, therefore. In view of the fact that, except at the highest income levels, household income is often subject to considerable fluctuation, it is understandable that a distinction between medium and low income (the distinction between the two simple types) cannot be very meaningful. A household with a low income at the time of the survey might have moved up to a medium level a month or two later when a mother's or daughter's baby was old enough to enable her to take a job in a factory. Or a teenage son might tire of working, and the loss of his wages could cause a drop from medium to low income level. Similar fluctuations could also result from a change from one job to another.

[17] Students' t-tests for differences between I and II showed no significant differences, however. Differences between III and IV were also insignificant.

[18] See pp. 181–2.

We are left, then, with the impression of three major types more or less represented by our categories of white-collar, intermediate, and simple (middle and lower income levels combined). The first is essentially that of the better-educated white-collar workers. The intermediate and simple households do not differ much in terms of income level, but the educational level is higher for the intermediate than the simple type.

The question arises whether the difference between well-furnished and simply-furnished households reflects a difference in interests and aspirations, or whether households have a simple material culture only because they cannot afford to buy good furniture, or they find it impossible for some other reason. From table 3 it would appear that the distinction between well-furnished and simple could possibly be related to income. To some degree this is probably true, but it would be an over-simplification to say that the differences in material culture are merely the result of differences in income, thereby inferring that households have simple material culture only because they cannot afford expensive furniture. In this respect we should note that many households with a relatively good income have much simpler furniture than others which have the same or a lower income.

It could also be argued that on the whole the simple households have less living-space than the well-furnished ones, and that a family living in a single room, as the majority of simple households do, has very little room for much in the line of furniture. It could be argued further that the conditions of extreme congestion constitute a factor over which individual households have no control, that they have no other choice than living under such conditions, and that they would probably have had more and better furniture under less crowded conditions. This is probably true in some cases. Yet the fact that quite a number of households manage to put up a better appearance in spite of living in a single room, while there are about the same proportion of simple ones with three or four rooms to live in, precludes us from attaching an overriding importance to this factor. Moreover, as we have seen, many houseowners who could have more living-space if they chose to, prefer to let part of their houses, occupying only one or two rooms themselves. They are not forced to live as they do by the shortage of accommodation.

It appears that education is the most important single factor responsible for the difference between white-collar and intermediate homes on the one hand, and simple homes on the other. More than anything else we have been able to discern that a simple material culture tends to go with a lower educational level. Educational level also seems to constitute a distinction between white-collar and intermediate. To some extent it is linked with the distinction in terms of occupation, since the highest educational qualifications are required for the white-collar jobs.

EDUCATION

Attending school is universally accepted as a normal part of a child's career in town, and sending the child to school is an important responsibility on the part of the parent. Although a small proportion of town adults have enjoyed little or no education, the great majority of them have advanced beyond standard two, while the mean educational level is standard five to six. About a quarter have advanced beyond standard six, but only a few of these have more than Junior Certificate or another qualification entailing training of equal duration.

The results from our sample do not reveal significant variations in terms of sex and age, though a more detailed analysis than that undertaken in table 28 suggests that females may be a little better educated than males. The median educational qualification for males is standard five, for females standard six, while a smaller proportion of females than males have less than standard three, and a larger proportion have more than standard six.

Older townspeople are not markedly less educated than the younger ones. In the older age groups in our sample we find that on the whole the mean educational qualification drops slightly lower, the proportion with less than standard three increases, and with more than standard six decreases, but this trend is not evident consistently throughout all age groups. It seems, therefore, that the educational advancement of the town population has been at a relative standstill for several decades. This might be related to the fact that most of our townspeople have a school background of two generations or more, so that they represent that sector of the Bantu population which already some time ago reached a stage of educational development beyond which progress must necessarily be slower. Further, some informants maintain that town scholars leave school more easily than those in the country, because of numerous distractions in town.

Our figures also suggest that townspeople have terminated their schooling at any stage. Although standard six seems to be the minimum aimed at by townspeople, or by town families for their children, leaving school often does not take place at any particular standard, or on the completion of a certain curriculum. Instead, scholars leave school at any stage according to their own or their parents' whims, or on account of circumstances necessitating it. One might leave to take up employment, either on account of economic distress in the family, an offer of a job regarded as an opportunity which might not come one's way again, or the desire to be economically independent. Some leave school just because they disliked it, without taking up any employment. Many girls have to leave school because of pregnancy, and do not return.

RELIGION

The great majority of townspeople claim allegiance to one or other of the many churches in the location. Some of the largest congregations are those of older denominations established among the Bantu by White missionary activity, like the Methodists, Anglicans (Church of the Province of South Africa), Presbyterians and Roman Catholics, which are either integrated with the White membership of these churches, or closely connected with White churches or church leaders. East London also has a large congregation of the Order of Ethiopia, a one-time Bantu separatist movement which was later affiliated with the Church of the Province, while retaining its identity as a semi-independent body. Another semi-independent group is the section of the Assemblies of God under the leadership of Rev. Nicholas Bhengu, a Pentecostal movement which has made a very marked impact on the Bantu of East London during the last decade.[19]

Further there are a number of small congregations of 'mission' churches and still more of the Bantu independent or separatist movements, but the influence of the latter is limited.

[19] See Mayer, op. cit., pp. 193–205, and Dubb, A. A., *The Role of the Church in an Urban African Society*, unpublished M.A. thesis, Rhodes University, 1962.

Only twenty persons in our sample (10 per cent) did not claim allegiance to a church (table 7). Most of these were persons with a strong pagan background, belonging to the 'semi-Red' category which we shall discuss later. The Methodist Church is by far the strongest single denomination among townspeople: more than a third of the church people in our sample claimed to be Methodists. Next in numerical importance were the Anglicans (10 per cent), followed by the Assemblies of God, the Bantu Presbyterian Church and Roman Catholic Church. The great majority of church people (73·8 per cent) belong to the more 'orthodox' or historic branches of Protestantism.[20] Of these only a small number belong to semi-independent churches, or to the completely independent ones which have no official links with White churches. Altogether adherents of independent Bantu churches count for only 10·4 per cent of the church people in our sample. That the 'Zionist' type of independent churches, orientated to Pentecostalism,[21] is hardly represented is in keeping with the fact that they appear to be less significant in the Transkei and Ciskei than in some other parts of South Africa.

TABLE 7

Religious affiliation by household economic category

Type and denomination	HOUSEHOLD ECONOMIC CATEGORY White-collar I	Inter-mediate II	Simple-A III	Simple-B IV	Other V	Total
PROTESTANT						
A. Linked with White Churches						
Historic type						
Methodist	12	13	28	5	8	66
Anglican	5	2	6	4	2	19
Bantu Presbyterian	1	3	5	2	3	14
Other[1]	—	4	6	4	—	14
Non-historic type[2]	—	1	7	2	7	17
B. Semi-independent						
Historic type						
Order of Ethiopia	—	1	2	—	1	4
Non-historic type						
Assemblies of God	—	12	2	—	1	15
C. Independent						
Historic type[3]	5	7	2	—	3	17
Non-historic type[4]	—	—	3	—	—	3
ROMAN CATHOLIC	—	5	3	3	2	13
Total church people	23	48	64	20	27	182
Not church people	—	—	9	11	—	20
Total	23	48	73	31	27	202

[1] Congregational, Presbyterian, Moravian, Baptist, Church of Scotland, Dutch Reformed
[2] Apostolic Faith Mission, Old Apostolic, Full Gospel, Diverse 'Apostolics'.
[3] Presbyterian Church of Africa, 'Orthodox', Bantu Methodist, 'Ethiopian', Independent Congregational, 'Bantu'.
[4] Church of Christ, Zion Christ Church.

The numbers in our sample for most of the churches or types of churches are too small to claim a statistically significant tendency for any economic category to be associated with particular denominations or denominational types. It

[20] The semi-independent and independent churches, classified as 'historic', are themselves of relatively recent origin, but in patterns of worship and church organization they follow the examples of historic churches.

[21] It may be that a few who called themselves 'Apostolic' could have belonged to independent churches with Pentecostal leanings, but that would not have changed the picture substantially.

does seem important, however, that twelve out of fifteen adherents of the Assemblies of God came from intermediate households. This is in keeping with the stress that the Rev. Bhengu lays on economic advancement and investment among others, in good furniture.[22] It is in sharp contrast to the distribution of adherents of other non-historic churches (mostly Pentecostal), most of whom come from simple households. It is also worth noting that all persons from white-collar households claimed allegiance to churches of the historic type. It is possible that with a larger sample one would have been able to show a trend of the white-collar and intermediate types, particularly the former, to the historic churches, and of the people of simpler material culture to the Pentecostalists and other non-historic churches (excluding the Assemblies of God).

While the great majority claim allegiance to churches, many maintain only a nominal connexion. A differentiation was therefore made according to the degree of participation and interest in the church. Communicant members (colloquially referred to as 'full members') and catechumens attending church at least once a month have been graded as having a high degree of interest if they were also members of an association affiliated to the church, and 'steady' if they did not belong to such an association.[23] A 'medium' category includes full members and catechumens who attend church only occasionally (less than once a month), and persons who attend more regularly but are not full members or catechumens. Those who were neither full members nor catechumens and attended church only occasionally, as well as all who claimed to be church people but never attended, were graded 'low'. Admittedly our criteria give only an approximate indication of a person's interest in the church, but in every case the leisure activities a person mentioned were also considered, to see whether they revealed any interests seeming to conflict with the classification arrived at, or conditions which made it impossible for the person to attend church. We are confident, therefore, that our classification is accurate enough not to be misleading.

According to their own statements the church takes a significant place in the lives of many townspeople. About half of the church people in our sample qualify for a steady or high degree of interest (table 8). Just over 20 per cent exhibit a low degree of interest, and their church allegiance cannot be regarded as more than nominal. Our medium category includes members and catechumens who attend irregularly, so that probably some of them are also only nominal church people. It appears safe to estimate that a quarter to a third of those claiming to be church people are no more than nominal members or adherents.

When comparing the degree of interest in churches in terms of church affiliation (table 8) we find that the Methodist Church has a lower proportion of persons exhibiting a steady or high degree of interest than most other churches. It is, of course, not unusual for numerically strong churches or congregations to carry a higher proportion of relatively disinterested members than smaller ones. Churches and types with higher proportions in the high and steady categories are the Bantu Presbyterian Church, all those of the non-historic type combined, as well as the independent churches of the historic type.

[22] Mayer, op. cit., p. 200, and Dubb, A. A., op. cit.

[23] Admittedly our standard of attendance is not high enough to distinguish the core of really zealous church people, so that our 'high' category is still more inclusive than this type. It was felt that the application of a stricter standard of attendance might lead to false claims more easily than a lower one.

All these have small congregations, excepting the Bantu Presbyterian Church and the Assemblies of God. The latter constitutes a young and particularly virile church community in East London.

TABLE 8

Religious affiliation by degree of interest in church

Type and Denomination	DEGREE OF INTEREST High	Steady	Medium	Low	Total
PROTESTANT					
A. Linked with White churches					
Historic type					
Methodist	11	18	18	19	66
Anglican	4	7	5	3	19
Bantu Presbyterian	6	5	1	2	14
Other	3	4	3	4	14
Non-historic type	5	6	3	3	17
B. Semi-independent					
Historic type					
Order of Ethiopa	—	2	1	1	4
Non-Historic type					
Assemblies of God	9	1	3	2	15
C. Independent					
Historic type	9	1	5	2	17
Non-Historic type					
Zionist	1	1	1	—	3
ROMAN CATHOLIC	1	3	7	2	13
Total	49	48	47	38	182

Our sample does not exhibit marked differences between males and females, but males in the 15–24 age group seem to be less interested than the older ones (table 29). Among younger females there is possibly the same tendency, but less marked than among males.

TABLE 9

Degree of interest in church by economic category

Degree of interest	ECONOMIC CATEGORY White-collar I	Inter-mediate II	Simple-A III	Simple-B IV	Other V	Total
High and steady	18	22	35	9	13	97
Medium	4	15	15	7	6	47
Low	1	11	14	4	8	38
Nil	—	—	9	10	1	20
Total	23	48	73	30	28	202

There is a tendency toward a higher degree of interest in churches among the better educated persons than among the less educated ones (table 30). This would lead us to expect a trend toward decreasing interest from one economic category to the other. The proportion with little or no interest does increase in this order, white-collar, intermediate, simple-A and simple-B, and the proportion with a high or steady degree of interest is highest in the white-collar category and lowest in the simple-B, but in the simple-A category it is higher than in the intermediate one (table 9). Altogether it does seem as if the white-collar category tends to have a higher degree of interest in church than the others.[24]

[24] The elimination of column V (table 9) and the lumping of 'Medium', 'Low' and 'Nil' produce a table which is significant at a 1 per cent level.

A question which has to be discussed here is whether those of the urban Bantu showing little or no interest in the churches constitute a secularized type or whether they are to be regarded as pagans. We have already referred to the so-called 'Red' or 'red-blanketed' people who conservatively adhere to traditional cultural patterns, including pagan religious and magical beliefs. They constitute a considerable element among the migrants in East London and in the rural areas forming its hinterland, distinct from the so-called 'School' people who take a more positive attitude to Western ways (chapter 1). Among townspeople there are very few whom one could immediately pick out as 'Reds' in the way one could distinguish them among migrants. Permanent settling in town is, as we have already observed, not compatible with Red ideals. One does, however, find people who, in their ways of speaking and other manners, give evidence of still being closer to Red ways than most townspeople. These one could call 'semi-Reds'. To distinguish this type among the persons in our sample, we applied the criteria of no or little interest in church—to Red people conversion to Christianity means breaking away from Red ideals—and belonging to households of which the heads are regarded as still being Red, or as persons who were Red originally, but became School later in life. Twenty-two persons in our sample (just over 10 per cent) qualified as semi-Red by these criteria.[25] Some of them actually regarded themselves as Reds. The content of their religious beliefs still appears to be largely pagan, though it is often mixed with elements of Christian belief.

More than half of the persons with little or no interest in the church then still remain unaccounted for, and it may be that some of them represent a type whose outlook is largely secularized and materialistic. They would mostly be nominal church people with a School background.

No attempt has been made to form a general impression of the nature of the beliefs of church people,[26] but it is evident that many of them still adhere to traditional beliefs and customs relating to witchcraft and the ancestor spirits.

LEISURE ACTIVITIES

As an indication of the interests of the urban Bantu, associations and other leisure activities are of particular importance, since they enjoy a larger degree of choice here than, for example, in the field of employment or education. As yet an advanced education which opens the field to clerical and professional jobs or the best-paid skilled jobs is the privilege of a small minority. Many who might have wished to continue their education to such an advanced level are prevented by the lack of funds. The bulk, even of the urban Bantu, have no choice than to enter unskilled employment of some kind.

Our questionnaire for the urban sample included some open-ended questions on leisure activities. Respondents were asked what they did on Saturdays, Sundays and during their free time on other days. There were a few specific questions about drinking habits and an inquiry about membership of associations.

Some people spend much of their leisure at home, and it is very common for

[25] In the rest of this chapter we speak of cultural categories instead of economic categories wherever the semi-Reds figure separately.

[26] The author is now engaged on a separate study of Christianity among Xhosa-speaking people.

women who are in employment to be engaged in domestic work at home after working hours and over the week-end. About 11 per cent of the women in our sample mentioned needlework of some kind. Some men also spend their free time at home doing repair jobs, working in the garden, tending to cattle or fowls, or assisting with domestic work. Reading was mentioned by about 9 per cent, several persons specifically mentioning reading the Bible. Outside the home the most common activities are those in connexion with the churches and religious associations, visiting, sport, and drinking.

Church activities and religious associations. Nearly two-thirds of our sample (133 persons, table 10) mentioned church attendance as one of their Sunday activities (Saturday for a few Sabbatarians), and of these, fifty (25 per cent of the total sample) claimed to be members of a religious association such as the so-called *manyanos* and a temperance association. This tallies with the impression gained from our direct questioning on the churches, namely that many townsmen show a significant degree of interest in the churches. For about half of the fifty members of religious associations the church and religion appeared to be their main interest outside their homes, only a few of them mentioning other outside activities like membership of a school committee or burial society, or visiting. Most of them fall into our category of high interest in church and probably represent a type of particularly zealous church people. Some of them mentioned Bible reading and week-day church services among their leisure activities. The two sexes present much the same proportions in this category, and all age levels and economic categories are represented.

TABLE 10

Some leisure activities by cultural category and sex

Activity	CULTURAL CATEGORY: Non-Red: White-collar	Non-Red: Inter-mediate	Non-Red: Simple	Non-Red: Other	Semi-Red	Total
MALES						
(Total in sample)	**14**	**20**	**25**	**9**	**8**	**76**
Church activities	13	15	14	6	1	49
Drinking	4	5	13	3	7	32
Sport	11	12	10	5	3	41
Other typical town diversions*	10	9	6	3	1	29
Visiting	8	8	12	5	4	37
Political organizations	4	1	2	1	—	8
FEMALES						
(Total in sample)	**9**	**27**	**58**	**18**	**14**	**126**
Church activities	7	22	41	13	1	84
Drinking	—	3	10	2	10	25
Sport	1	4	8	3	—	16
Other typical town diversions*	4	6	8	6	2	26
Visiting	3	10	16	8	4	41
Political organizations	—	—	—	2	—	2
Masazane	1	2	5	3	1	12

* 'Other typical town diversions' include the following: films and concerts, visiting the beach, jiving, dancing, vocal groups, bands, community centre 'get together', and horse-races. The numbers opposite this item refer to persons who mentioned one of these among their leisure activities.

Most of the remaining twenty-four persons who were members of religious associations counted sport among their leisure interests, and about the same number were members of a political organization or of the women's organization known as *Masazane*. Some mentioned typical town forms of recreation such as dancing and attending films, and a few drinking. Excepting the very zealous church people, active participation in church activities therefore seems to be easily compatible with a variety of other interests. A married woman of 47 belonging to a simple household is a member of the Women's Association of the Methodist Church, of the *Masazane* association and of the Swallows Rugby Club. On Sundays she attends church and during her free time does sewing, knitting and crocheting. William, who is a married man of 30 employed as a packer in a factory, claims membership of the Methodist Young Men's Association, of the A.N.C. and the Black Lions Rugby Club. On Sundays he attends church; he plays rugby, cricket or tennis on Saturdays, and coaches cricket for the boys in his free time during the week. He drinks mostly 'kaffir beer', but sometimes has a drink at the hotel. He has passed standard six, and comes from a simple household. Mrs. F, who holds a teacher's qualification, is a member of her church *manyano*, of the church choir and *Masazane*. On Sunday she attends church and during her free time does sewing and knitting and visits the hospital and the graveyard.

Visiting figures prominently among leisure activities of all cultural categories (table 10). It is mostly of an informal nature, a casual dropping in to see one's friend after work or when there is a spare moment, without dressing for the occasion. On Saturday afternoons and Sundays many people do dress for going out, and visiting is often more deliberate, but in other respects it is still very informal. People visit their friends individually and in the company of one or two other friends of the same sex, sometimes in the company of a sweetheart in the case of unmarried people. Husbands and wives very seldom go visiting together, and family visiting hardly ever occurs.

Drinkers visiting each other might have a drink of kaffir beer or brandy together if there is some in store. Otherwise a point is usually made of serving tea to adult visitors, and if shortage of any commodity makes it impossible, the host apologizes for not offering anything to drink, explicitly mentioning the reason. The time is passed in conversation. A few might play draughts or a game of cards with their friends.

Sport. Interest in sport was expressed by the majority of men in our sample, more than half of these claiming to be players, the rest being club members and spectators. But only 12·7 per cent of the women mentioned sport, only about a third of them claiming to be players. This would represent a particularly high participation on the part of males, certainly higher than one would expect among urban Whites. On the other hand it is clear that Bantu women do not go in for sport on a large scale.

The proportion of our sample interested in sport is considerably higher among persons with an education level of standard five or higher than among those with less education (table 32). As one would expect, there is also more interest among persons younger than 35 than among older ones, although quite a number of older men still exhibit an interest in sport (table 31).

In terms of our cultural and economic categories it appears that male sporting enthusiasts are found in considerable proportions in all non-Red categories, while semi-Reds are also represented (table 10). The proportion does seem to decrease, however, from white-collar to intermediate and from the latter to the simple non-Reds and the semi-Reds combined. The numbers of females are too small to claim a clear tendency, but it is important to note that females interested in sport figured in every category excepting that of semi-Reds. Observation has also left the impression that sport does not fit into the sphere of interest of a semi-Red female, whereas it could in the case of a male.

Twenty-six males, about half of those expressing an interest in sport, mentioned rugby, and nearly all of them claimed to belong to clubs. A few women were also members of rugby clubs. Tennis was next in importance with five males and five females; boxing, golf and cricket are also of some importance among men, while a number of schoolgirls play netball or basketball. Other kinds of sport mentioned by males were 'body-building' and weight-lifting, soccer, table-tennis and baseball. Soccer and table-tennis also figured among females.

Other town diversions. No other typically town diversions such as attending film shows and concerts, dancing and jiving, the 'get-together' sessions at the community centre, participation in musical companies, or going to the beach or to horse-races are nearly as popular as sport, but considered as a single category it was found that one or other of these forms of recreation was mentioned by about 27 per cent of our sample. They figured in a higher proportion among males than females, but the disparity between the sexes is much less than in the case of sport. About 20 per cent of the females claimed participation in these activities.

Films are shown twice a week at the community centre, and daily in a cinema for non-Whites situated just outside the location. Although only a small proportion count films among their regular interests, it appears that many more, particularly of the younger set, attend the cinema occasionally. The film no doubt sets the pattern to many of these, particularly in the field of sex and gang activity. Groups of small boys chasing each other in mock gun-fights are a familiar sight in the location. An unemployed girl of 17 with standard six education, during an interview about week-end activities, mentioned going to the bioscope with her boy-friend, and spontaneously lingered on the topic: 'The pictures I like very much are those of lovers, because they are a lesson how to love each other, and I do everything that has been done there to my boy-friend. I always wonder why my grandmother never told me that there is something like a love-affair.'

The most common type of concert staged in the location takes the form of a variety show by a musical troupe. Mostly these shows are staged by one of a number of vocal groups or bands in the location, consisting mostly of town youths. Several young men and boys in our sample mentioned membership of such a group among their leisure activities. Some of them perform on a semi-professional basis. These groups perform under names such as 'Diamond Horseshoe Vocal Group', 'Havana Swingsters', 'Four Yanks', 'Bright Five', 'African Quavers', and 'Foundation Rhythm Swingsters Band'. The vocal groups are commonly referred to as 'Combos'.

The location is also frequently visited by groups from Port Elizabeth and other eastern Cape towns, and there are occasional visits by artists from the Rand. The latter are regarded as more polished than local entertainers. Generally, Johannesburg is looked upon as the ideal in the field of entertainment, with East London as something of a backwater. One person was of the opinion that 'East London lags behind by a hundred years' in comparison with Johannesburg. It is said that performances by Johannesburg artists draw larger attendances than those by the local groups, and that more of the 'decent' type of people attend these shows. Occasional school concerts take the form of variety programmes of choirs, 'sketches', and physical culture displays. The type of auction concert which is popular among School Bantu in the country is sometimes staged by country schools performing in town, but it is not common. School concerts as well as those by performing groups are often followed by general dancing for which a band is provided.

Besides formal dances organized by clubs and in aid of charity, dancing competitions are also held and there are a number of 'professional' dancing teachers. The proportion of our sample actively interested is small, and the prominence that dancing and some other forms of entertainment are given in the Bantu press seems to create an exaggerated impression of their importance in the social life of the Bantu. Going to the beach is popular mainly with younger folk. Such an outing is often associated with love-making more than with going for a swim. One girl told how she would first go for a swim while her boy-friend waited on the beach, and after that would come 'the time for romance'. Others mentioned love-making in the bushes near the beach. A small number of town Bantu are horse-racing enthusiasts. A few bus-loads attend the races at the turf club in Nahoon every Saturday. Only one or two persons in our sample mentioned horse-racing. Other forms of entertainment known to be of some importance but not figuring in any answers to the questionnaire are public farewell functions and receptions which usually take the form of a 'social gathering' with speeches and refreshments, or an occasional 'braaivleis'.

An unpleasant feature of town entertainment is that few functions can be conducted in an orderly fashion from beginning to end. Of a sophisticated reception for the delegates to the regional meeting of a certain body which included a sight-seeing trip and a braaivleis, it is reported that 'as usual there were a few altercations, and the behaviour of some gentlemen during the braaivleis was rather uncivil'.[27] A dance 'which maintained its air of dignity throughout' was regarded as quite an exception. This was only possible because 'well-known trouble-makers were refused entry'.

When considering these typical kinds of town entertainment as a single category it will be seen that for our sample the proportion of each cultural category claiming to participate decreases in the order white-collar (61 per cent), intermediate, simple (non-Red), and semi-Red (14 per cent) (table 10). This trend is more explicit among the males in our sample than among the females.

Drinking figures prominently as a pastime of town Bantu, particularly among men. Thus, 42 per cent of the males and 22 per cent of the females in our sample admitted drinking some form of liquor. Probably the proportion who do drink are still larger, because there is a tendency with some School Bantu to be secretive about drinking,[28] since many churches expect their members to abstain. In this connexion it is sometimes said that on the whole the Bantu cannot drink moderately, so that Bantu Christians should rather avoid drink altogether. The tendency towards secrecy is probably less among townspeople

[27] *Indaba Zasemonti* (East London News), Saturday, 9 November 1959.
[28] See Mayer, op. cit., pp. 117–18 and 222–3.

than in the rural school communities, but we must allow for a certain degree of bias in the answers to our questionnaire in this respect.

The confessed drinkers in our sample were spread over all educational levels among males, but no females of higher education than standard six admitted drinking. Male drinkers are also spread over all cultural categories. It is significant that nearly all semi-Red males admitted drinking. For the category of simple non-Reds the proportion was just over half, while for the intermediate and white-collar categories it dropped to below 30 per cent. Among non-Red females none of the white-collar category admitted drinking, a few of the intermediate category did, as well as a number of non-Reds from simple households, as against more than two-thirds of semi-Red women. It is obvious that drinking is a regular pastime among semi-Reds, and it figures prominently among simple non-Red males. Among other categories it appears to be less important, but it should be remembered that if there was unwillingness to admit drinking, it would probably have occurred among persons belonging to these categories more than the others.

Hardly any males with a high degree of interest in the church admitted drinking, whereas the majority with low interest did. But again the factor of secrecy may be responsible for some degree of bias. The proportion of drinkers was low among all categories of 'church' females.

Although liquor of Western origin is consumed on a large scale, the great majority of people still drink the traditional 'kaffir beer', many of them expressing a liking for both. Brandy is the most popular form of non-traditional liquor, but lately there has been a tendency for cheap wine, known as *umrara*, to take the place of brandy. Informants attribute this trend to increases in the prices of liquor. Most of the Western liquor consumed by location people is acquired in the location through illicit channels, prices being from two to three times as much as they are in bottle-stores in town.[28a] Of the small number who indulge in hotel drinking, some also consume other forms of non-traditional liquor. The violent types of home-brewed drinks which have emerged in the process of Bantu urbanization are also brewed in East London, but their popularity appears to be confined to a minority of drinkers. The brewing and drinking of this type of liquor are mostly confined to dens in the bushes in and around the location where it is difficult for the police to trace the owner of the brew.[29]

The most common pattern of drinking among townspeople is that of buying the liquor from one of the illicit brewers or dealers in the location, and consuming it at home, often in the company of friends. The regular group of drinking companions known as *iseti*, which is a feature of drinking among migrants in town,[30] is not common among townspeople, though a number of persons in our sample did say that they drink with *iseti*. What is more common is for small groups of two or three friends, who are often in each other's company, to enjoy most of their drinking together. Usually they pay for a drink jointly, each making a contribution known as *inkazathi* (collection). They do not necessarily patronize the same place, but often 'roam about the location looking for something to drink'. Those who do not drink at home enjoy their

[28a] Since the time of writing restrictions on the sale of non-traditional liquor to Bantu have been lifted. See Appendix IV, 'New Liquor Legislation'.

[29] Cf. further, Reader, op. cit., pp. 96, 121.

[30] See Mayer, op. cit., pp. 111–13.

drinks at the shebeen or the less sophisticated brewer's home, or else at the brewing dens in the bushes, where they join the company of any person they find there.

There is a licensed hotel for non-Whites in the North End situated midway between the location and the White business area, which is frequented by some of the more educated Bantu.[31] A quarter of the male drinkers in our sample mentioned hotel drinking, although some of them go there only occasionally. Although some people said that they always drink with closed doors or referred to privacy in other ways, there is no evidence that secrecy about drinking constitutes such a widely observed pattern as it does among country School people.

Apart from the fact that there are more males who drink than females, the only difference we have been able to establish in the drinking habits of men and women is that hotel drinking is so far confined only to males. One might expect that it is further confined to the most 'westernized' males, but although three of the four drinkers of white-collar type in our sample mentioned hotel drinking, there were also a number of men from simple homes with not more than standard five or six education. Informants further maintain that drinking 'in the bushes' is confined to a less respectable type of person. In the location it would appear that there is a tendency for the customers of a drinking-place to vary according to the type of brewer or dealer.[32] The 'progressive' shebeen queen living in a freshly painted house with modern furniture, and who owns a motor-car, would attract the white-collar type of customer, while a less-educated beer-brewer living in a simply furnished back room would mainly be patronized by simpler folk.

GAMBLING

Since public gambling is illicit, people do not easily talk openly about their gambling activities, and no persons in our sample volunteered such information in connexion with their leisure activities. We therefore have no statistical material on the incidence of gambling or its relative importance among different categories of people. It is well known, however, that certain forms of gambling are very extensively practised in the location, by townspeople and others. It also figured in responses to open-ended questionnaires applied by Bantu assistants.

Fah-fee, a form of gambling based on the drawing of numbers, is extremely popular. A large number of townspeople of varying types, including people from white-collar homes and regular church-goers, participate. A married woman of a white-collar household, who is a member of her church *manyano* and who claims to attend church services regularly, is known to be a sub-runner. It is obvious that many people are highly 'addicted' to fah-fee. Some keep records of the numbers drawn in each pool every day and study these before making their bets, and dreams are relied upon for an indication of lucky numbers.

Fah-fee is run exclusively by Chinese. There are said to be seventeen of them, each running a separate pool. Four of these have grouped together to form a jackpot. The Chinese live in town, but each has a Bantu runner in the

[31] Before restrictions on the sale of Western liquor to Bantu were lifted in 1962 only Bantu persons in possession of a standard four certificate qualified for a permit to buy such liquor for personal consumption.

[32] See Mayer, op. cit., p. 223.

location who is paid a weekly wage, said to be R6.00 (60*s*.). They are assisted by sub-runners who offer their services on a commission basis, the commission being subtracted from the amounts collected by the successful punters whose bets were collected by the sub-runner. Numbers are drawn twice daily: the first results are announced at about one or two o'clock at a place where fah-fee enthusiasts gather daily on an open space on the fringe of Gomorra. The second results usually come out shortly after dark.

There is an informal organization of fah-fee supporters with a permanent chairman, vice-chairman and secretary, who were elected 'long ago'. They seem to have some say in the appointment of runners, and complaints of punters are dealt with by them, in consultation with the runners.

Dice games known as *roqoroqo* and *roya* are played, mostly by young men and boys, particularly those of the *tsotsi* type (see p. 57ff.). *Roqoroqo* is an onomatopoeic word for a rattling noise, in this connexion the rattling of the dice. The numbers one to six are drawn on a board, and while the 'banker' rattles the dice underneath an upturned tin, bets are laid against the different numbers. In a game watched by the author the numbers had been drawn in ink on an old piece of cardboard and the banker kept his money in a good sailcloth bag. Out of a group of about ten or twelve men and boys, four or five persons laid a bet each time, the ages of players ranging from 11 or 12 to well over 20. Mostly only one or two pennies were risked at a time, but at four to one an older player once won 2*s*. (20c), and shortly after won another round with a bet of 3*s*. (30c), but this caused a 'bank broke' and he had to take over the bank. *Roya*, from the Afrikaans *gooi* (to throw), is played with two dice which are shaken in the hand before making a throw.

Among these youths gambling is usually associated with violence. 'When we go to gambling we are fully armed with our knives, because for the slightest mistake you make you are attacked with knives. If you have your friends with you it is better, because they will take sides with you.' 'In street gambling [mostly dice games] one is safer in the company of one's friends because of fighting. We all have knives there, and once you cheat you are a dead man. But if you have friends they will protect you.' Nowadays Mekeni is regarded as the hotbed of these vicious dice enthusiasts, but one comes across groups of boys playing dice in all parts of the location.

Yutoyi is also played at a certain house in Gomorra. An East London-born young man who is a regular player claims: 'It is one of the most popular games in the location where you find all classes of men such as teachers of high standing, one or two church stewards, clerks in offices, down to the real *tsotsi* and a few bush-dwellers who also come to try their luck. Here nobody feels the passage of time because the game is so amusing and thrilling. There is always something to cause laughter, while every man is concentrating on the money he has put on one or two of the six names on the board. The six names are called horses, and they are 'Scamp', 'Cysion', 'Golden', 'Yutoyi', 'Envoy' and 'Harrier'.'

Other forms of gambling mentioned by informants are Cassino, 'Flash', 'Cole Card', 'Three Cards' and *Thungathunga*. The last is a shell game in which small boxes are substituted for the nut-shells. The name *thungathunga* (from *ukuthunga*, to sew) perhaps originated with a variant of the game in which the operator lays a thread on a smooth surface, so that it makes a number of loops. The player puts his finger in any loop he chooses and the operator has to remove the thread by manipulating the two ends without changing hands.

Some gamblers are never employed and largely, if not exclusively, rely on gambling for a living. Mostly these are the younger males of the *tsotsi* type who also indulge in robbery and petty thieving, but these 'professional' gamblers also include some older men, and sometimes, as in the case we quote below, it is a case of 'like father like son'. An unemployed young man claims that he makes more money in gambling than any of his equals who are employed, and continues: 'My father is a rich man, and he has never been employed. I am copying his way of living. I do not want to rob any person of his own money, but I want to fish a person's money in a fair way, which is gambling. I help the fah-fee runners so that I get a bit of commission to have a stand for the gambling games in the late afternoon and evening. In the afternoons I always stay at the centres so as to make money. When I have no money for the start, I help my mother in selling vegetables at home so that she lends me money. She gives me freely, for she knows that I am never a big loser. Here at home there are gambling games every evening.' (Standard five, 23 years old.)

OTHER ASSOCIATIONS

The only other leisure activities of importance are those connected with political organizations and the women's *Masazane*.

In his study of the migrants, Professor Mayer has briefly indicated recent trends in the field of politics among the Bantu in East London: how the once active and widely representative Vigilance Association, which concerned itself mainly with local interests, was superseded by the African National Congress and its Youth League, and how, since the 1952 riots, interest in these organizations has greatly dwindled.[33] The results of our own investigation also support the conclusion that interest in political activity is at a low ebb at the moment. Thus, 10 per cent of the males and only two females in our sample claimed membership of the A.N.C. or the I.C.U.,[34] members of the former being in the majority. The small numbers in our sample do not suggest any particular trend in terms of cultural category, education or age.[35]

Nearly 10 per cent of the women in our sample claimed membership of the association known as *Masazane*, which is a kind of women's burial society, but besides being concerned with mutual aid in time of bereavement, it also provides recreation and avenues for settling disputes among its members. The women in our sample who claimed membership of *Masazane* constitute a fair cross-section of town females in terms of cultural category and education, but the majority were 40 years and older.

The Scout and Wayfarer (Girl Guides) movements have branches in the location, but very few youths and girls older than 15 are actively interested in these. Mention may also be made of the professional organizations of teachers and nurses, to which some members of the professions belong.[36]

TRADITIONAL CULTURE

Although it is true that the culture of the urban Bantu does not consist of selected 'elements' or 'traits' of traditional Bantu culture and Western culture

[33] Op. cit., pp. 52–4. See also Reader, op. cit., pp. 15–18, 25–30.
[34] The Industrial and Commercial Workers' Union which was particularly active in the Union and also in East London during the late twenties.
[35] For further reference to political interests, see chapter 9.
[36] For a further discussion of associations and clubs, see chapter 9.

respectively, which have been thrown together, it is nevertheless possible to discern certain patterns of behaviour which are obviously largely determined by the traditional indigenous culture of the Bantu. Not that these constitute unchanged elements of that culture, but we may say that, in the areas of activity referred to, present action is dominated by patterns of traditional culture.

Of some importance in this respect is the area of language. The languages represented among the Bantu population of East London are Xhosa, Southern Sotho, English and Afrikaans. Southern Sotho is virtually confined to a small minority of Southern Sotho persons, while the number with a knowledge of Afrikaans is small. It may safely be said that most town Xhosa are able to speak, read and write English, but among themselves they seldom speak anything else than Xhosa. One does sometimes hear English conversation between Xhosa persons, but this is the exception. More English is heard in meetings in which the more educated predominate, but it is extremely doubtful whether there are any Bantu persons in East London who in their homes and in their contacts with other Bantu speak more English or Afrikaans than a Bantu language.[37] The manner in which Xhosa has been influenced by English and Afrikaans, and even by other Bantu languages, is a study in itself, but it is essentially still Xhosa, except perhaps in the case of *Tsotsi* language, to which we shall refer later (p. 58). There is little reason to expect that in a town like East London Xhosa will 'capitulate' to a European language among the masses.

Traditional beliefs about the spirits of the dead (*izinyanya*) still play a role in the life of some townspeople,[38] and something of the ancestor cult does still persist. However it was not possible to investigate the extent to which such beliefs and ritual occur among townspeople. A small number of persons in our sample, representing all cultural categories, admitted having made sacrifices within the last two years, but a reliable indication of the significance of such beliefs needs much more careful investigation than a single question in a survey questionnaire.

We describe below a sacrifice which took place while fieldwork was in progress. Although sacrifices of this kind may not be very common in town, it is described at some length, since it is significant that in a long-established town family the ancestor cult could apparently lie dormant for a long time and then on occasion come to life with so much ritual detail and within its traditional kinship setting.

The family concerned centres upon an unmarried mother (X in the genealogy, fig. 3, p. 60) who is a successful beer-brewer and liquor trader. They use the name of her father's paternal grandfather (B) as surname. She and some of her children live with her aged widowed mother, an unmarried older brother (H), unemployed and depending on X for his living, and a younger brother (I) who is working. They occupy part of the house which belongs to the mother. The eldest brother (G) and his family live in a back room as a separate household, while some rooms are rented. The father (C) died in a Ciskei reserve in 1918, from where the family later came to town. X claims that all her children were born in East London, the eldest being about 30 years old.

[37] The use of English does not have as great a significance as a status symbol as it has among some other urban African populations. In Gwelo, for example, 'English is used by those who are able in all social encounters except those with immediate kin' (Schwab, W. B., 'Social Stratification in Gwelo', in Southall, op. cit., p. 140).

[38] For belief in spirits among the migrants to East London, see Mayer, op. cit., chapter 9.

Although there is some good furniture in the house and some members of the family claim to be church people, their ties with the church are slender, and most of them could be regarded as semi-Red.

Our Bantu assistant unexpectedly came across the ritual when it had already reached the feasting stage. H and X later described it to us in full.

Some time after C's death a beast was slaughtered to mourn his death and to 'accompany' him (*ukukhapha*). Of late there had 'been incidents at home . . . children misbehave, their pay just disappears without their doing something useful with it. . . . We came to the conclusion that the old man [C] must have a complaint, so that we decided to slaughter this beast.' This decision was reached at a meeting of members of the Maduna clan to which they belong. It was summoned by G, and he invited E, who also lives in the location, D who lives on the West Bank, two other kinsmen from the reserve who are also descended from A, and another member of the clan who teaches in the East London district and whose exact kinship relation could not be stated. At this meeting a date was decided upon. 'We wrote to all Maduna people we know in Johannesburg, Grahamstown and elsewhere to notify them.' D mentioned the names of the persons who should be notified and the letters were written by I. Instructions were also given by D about procuring a beast for the sacrifice and the preparation of beer and food. Since the family does not own a cattle-kraal, a small temporary enclosure of branches had to be made in the back yard as a substitute for the kraal where the meat of a sacrificial animal should be cooked. Although not the eldest, H was made responsible for the preparations, 'because he is the one who has time, not being employed'.

The beast was slaughtered on a Friday, as had been decided, in one of the cattle-kraals below Gomorra where the family live. All the Maduna who had come for the performance of the ceremony were present at the slaughtering. First D said a few words *ukunqula* (to call upon or worship (the ancestors)) in the following vein: 'I say to you, Maduna of our home [*Maduna akowethu*], that this work which we are doing, may proceed nicely . . . you of Maduna, of Gubevu, of Jiyana, of Nokhala, come back and help us.' From a beaker which he was holding, he sprinkled some *ubulawu*-medicine of the Maduna. The actual slaughtering was performed by F, who is younger in age than D, but he had to slaughter, 'because he is the greatest among us, because his father was the greatest among us'. He took a spear, moved it between the hind legs of the beast, over the belly, round the nape of the neck, and then back to the navel, where he gave small thrusts until the beast bellowed. Then he pierced it to death in the neck. When the beast bellowed, the Maduna people grew excited and D shouted: 'There it is, descendants of Maduna, the beast is bellowing; Camagu has agreed.' (*Nakoke, lusapho lakwa-Maduna, inkomo iyakhala; i-Camagu livumile.*) The meat was cooked in the special enclosure which had been prepared at home, where beer was also ready. The tasting (*ukushwama*), typical of Xhosa ritual slaughterings, was first performed: all the Maduna present had to take a bite from the portion known as *intsonyama* and a sip from a beaker of beer specially put aside for the purpose. After that all present could join in the feasting. The meat was served in plates, but in the plates were twigs of olive (*umnquma*) or sneeze-wood (*umthathi*). All the meat had to be consumed at home and the bones burnt in the cooking enclosure.

In one context D was referred to as being in charge of the activities, but then again X volunteered that the ritual was performed by G. It seemed as if no single person was regarded as solely in charge. X spontaneously communicated that 'my son who works at the —— Textile Mills (K) has been wasting his money, spending it on nothing. But since the custom [*isiko*] was performed, he now comes back and brings me his money to keep. He would come home the day after receiving his pay without a penny, dead drunk, but since then he is a proper person [*ubengumntu*], he is no longer a drunkard. This confirms that Xhosa customs are effective [*akhona*].' The ritual was referred to as *ukuguqula ubawo* (turning back or converting the father).

The fact that so many details of this traditional ritual were observed need not imply that the actual townspeople concerned are still very particular about these matters, but it may be the result of the fact that senior kinsmen who have had more experience of traditional ritual and who may possibly still have close ties with life in the reserves, were available. At another sacrifice which I attended personally there was much less ritual detail. It was performed by a family of School people from the country who had been in town for only about eight years. The man who took the initiative in having the ritual performed to mourn the death of his father had had no previous experience of making a ritual slaughtering, and the senior clan member who was supposed to direct the activities did not seem to know what was expected of him. It appears that the presence in town of many migrants who are still faithful observers of the ancestor cult, and the proximity of the reserves, from where kinsmen can easily be summoned, is an important factor in keeping traditional institutions alive. Observations of the initiation ceremonies in town also conveyed this impression.

It is further significant how, in the ritual described above, the traditionally important patrilineal kinship ties are thrown in relief on such an occasion. In this family's everyday life there is not much to remind one of these ties. It is a good example of a 'matrifocal' family (see chapter 8) in which the authority is passing from the widowed mother to the daughter. X has never been married, but formerly lived with a man who is the father of some of her children, and later she had a regular lover for many years, by whom she also had a few children. The unmarried elder brother, who could have been regarded as head of the 'main' household, is economically dependent on X, who shoulders the main responsibility for their means of livelihood. During the interview she did most of the talking, and at one stage she claimed that the house belonged to her. When they were questioned why the ceremony was performed in town and not in the country where the father was buried, the answer was that 'our home is here now; this is his daughter's place'. Question: 'Why at the daughter's place and not at the son's place, as Xhosa custom used to be?' X: 'The son has no home of his own.' G: 'Also, our mother is in this house.' X: 'As I am an unmarried mother the property really belongs to my mother.'

However, when steps had to be taken about the children's misbehaviour, it was the eldest brother who summoned the patrilineal kinsmen, and it was said that the ceremony was performed by him. The deceased father's 'brother' (D) played the most prominent part in the meeting and the ceremonial, while the most senior male relative by descent had to perform the killing. The important persons who had to be informed were members of the father's clan, and the clan ancestors were called upon in prayer.

Although the most detailed observance of the ancestor cult by townspeople probably occurs among the semi-Red type, it is by no means confined to them.

I quote one of the examples recorded for more westernized families. A married man who is a chauffeur, has a Junior Certificate, and whose mother is a teacher, told of a goat they had slaughtered the same year 'to let the people of my home come out of the forest and to acknowledge my responsibility to perform *izila* [the mourning ceremony] for my father' who died some two years before. 'Coming out of the forest' is a standard expression referring to the termination of certain mourning observances implying the return of the bereaved to normal life. This family has close ties with a well-known church.

An attempt was also made to test the attitudes of persons in our sample to the traditional belief in witchcraft and sorcery. Since the Xhosa do not distinguish between witchcraft and sorcery as separate categories of activity, and refer to performers of both as *amagqwira*,[39] the term 'witchcraft' is used here as an abbreviation of 'witchcraft and sorcery', unless it is otherwise specified. First respondents to the questionnaire were asked whether they had ever been harmed by a witch and, if so, in what manner. Then followed a question: 'Do you think witches can harm a person?' Less than half of the sample (eighty-three persons) explicitly expressed disbelief in witchcraft (negative attitude), twenty-three were undecided, and the remaining ninety-one took a positive attitude by either giving examples of the manner in which they had been harmed by witches or at least expressing their belief in the ability of witches to harm persons. The 'undecided' attitudes were mostly the 'do not know' cases, but also included: 'I cannot say, but hear so', 'it may be possible', 'I am told that witches can harm'. It is obvious therefore that the belief in witchcraft is still very common among townspeople.

From tables 11 and 12 it is clear that witchcraft beliefs occur among townspeople of all levels. A substantial proportion of better educated persons, even of persons of our white-collar category, expressed a positive attitude. However, the figures do suggest that witchcraft beliefs are less common among the better educated than the less educated, and among the white-collar and intermediate categories than among the simple and semi-Red ones. This is probably true to a certain extent, but there is evidence that people of this type sometimes deny the belief in witchcraft and the effectiveness of techniques of traditional doctors but in times of crisis consult these doctors and accept treatment which implies that they believe in the reality of witchcraft (cf. p. 88). It is obvious that among semi-Reds the belief in witchcraft is more openly and generally recognized than among any non-Red categories, even than among people of the simple category.

TABLE 11

Attitude to witchcraft beliefs by education

	EDUCATION				
Attitude	0–4 years	5–6 years	7–8 years	9 plus years	Total
Positive	15	27	34	15	91
Undecided	2	5	13	8	28
Negative	8	16	34	25	83
Total	25	48	81	48	202

[39] Not to be confused with *amagqira*, native doctors ('witch-doctors'). The verb referring to the performance of witchcraft is *ukuthakatha*.

TABLE 12

Attitude to witchcraft beliefs by cultural category

Attitude	CULTURAL CATEGORY Non-Red White-collar	Inter-mediate	Simple	Other	Semi-Red	Total
Positive	6	19	39	9	18	91
Undecided	3	5	15	3	2	28
Negative	14	23	29	15	2	83
Total	23	47	83	27	22	202

More people with little or no interest in church express a positive attitude to witchcraft beliefs than those with a medium or higher degree of interest (table 33); although here again it is possible that some church people deny it, while in their heart of hearts they still believe in the reality of witchcraft. On the other hand some Christians put forward Biblical grounds for their belief in witchcraft. 'Witches can harm a person; the Bible says they are "killers of the flesh".'[40] It is further interesting to note that a negative attitude was expressed by a larger proportion of persons with a medium interest than of those with a steady or high degree of interest. It may well be that within the 'medium interest' category of church people we have some representing a type which is developing a sceptical outlook generally, both to Christianity (cf. their irregular church attendance) and to traditional beliefs.

There is some difference between the sexes in respect of witchcraft beliefs. Whereas well over a half of the males in our sample expressed a negative attitude, less than a third of the females did.

Twenty-seven persons (about 13 per cent) claimed to have experienced the harmful influence of witchcraft. Some referred to the familiars of Xhosa belief. 'I received incisions on my body which were inflicted by *Hili* or *Tikoloshe* [names for a human-like little rascal of a familiar with features resembling those of a baboon] during the night in my sleep.' This is known as *ukuqatshulwa*. 'I fell one day as a result of tramping on *inyoka* [the snake familiar].' Another claimed: 'When I was in Johannesburg a witch sent *impundulu* [the lightning bird] to me.' 'Bad spirits came as in a dream to separate me from my husband.' Several persons referred to *ukudliswa*, poisoning by harmful medicines in food or drink, and *ukugqwaliswa*, being made unpopular by the mention of one's name in the form of a spell over medicines. 'I get no children; I think I was *ukuthathelwa*', which is a form of bewitching by treating matter from the victim's person with medicine. Other forms mentioned were *ukubekelwa* (to be affected in the sexual organs by a rival male lover using medicines), *ukuphoselwa* (suffering from medicines which are 'thrown at' one), and *umkhondo* (a disease contracted by crossing the tracks of certain familiars).

Some persons mentioned the motives for their bewitchment: jealousy or other forms of tension in inter-personal relations. 'I suffered a nervous break-down as a result of witchcraft. The witch was jealous of my progress in education.' 'I was *ukuphoselwa* by a woman whose child I had fought: I had a persistent headache.'

Various physical and mental ailments and adversities attributed to witch-

[40] The reference is obscure, unless it is to Matt. x. 28 – 'And fear not them which kill the body . . . '.

craft have already been mentioned. Here are some others: 'I had a feeling of invisible insects moving on my face and body and of being quarrelsome and easily offended.' Two had been infested with pig lice. Another ascribed a deformity of his hands to witchcraft. A particular urban slant enters the picture when employment is affected: 'I was made very unpopular by *umgqwaliso* and was out of work for some time.' The belief in witchcraft is also particularly evident in the field of childbirth and early childhood. (See pp. 80 ff.)

Although Western medical services appear to be universally accepted by townspeople, there are many who at the same time still believe in the efficacy of traditional techniques for which there are specialists known as *amagqira*, who, besides treating ailments, also perform divining, and *amaxhwele* (herbalists). Because of his divining activities a 'doctor' (*igqira*) may also be referred to as a diviner (*isanuse*). The doctor's activities are not confined to the purely 'medical' field, but are concerned with all kinds of adversity and their remedies or prevention.

For twenty-six households (nearly a quarter of our sample) information was provided that a traditional doctor or herbalist had been consulted by or for a member of the household during the two years preceding the investigation —in many of these cases it was during the same year. A number of others mentioned less recent cases of consultation. The households reporting recent consultation included all cultural categories, and, surprisingly enough, the intermediate category had the highest proportion. Considering the direct nature of the questioning and the avowed denial of the efficacy of traditional techniques by some people who in fact still rely on them, as well as the possibility of slips of the memory, one may say that the attachment of townspeople to the techniques of the traditional Xhosa practitioners is considerable, even among the more 'westernized' type. A father in white-collar employment, whose East London-born daughter is a student nurse, consulted a diviner and a herbalist during his wife's serious illness. Although this information was not revealed in an interview with a member of the household, it came from a reliable informant closely related to the wife. The wife from an intermediate home consulted a diviner about her stolen clothes. These were subsequently recovered. A woman of 34 who claims to be East London-born, but regards herself as Red and is obviously so, consulted a doctor about eye trouble. An East London-born unmarried mother from a simple non-Red household was undergoing training as *igqira* at the time of the survey, while a mother of another simple family was practising as one. It is claimed that a well-known East London *igqira* counts among his clients some teachers who obtain medicines from him to safeguard their posts.

Here and there among townspeople one comes across some of the characteristics by which the Red category of traditionalists is distinguished from School people in the country and among town migrants. These are mostly of a material nature, and are about the only instances of traditional items of material culture among townspeople. An old woman living with an East London-born daughter of 17, and claiming to have lived in East London since 1911, regarded herself as having always been School, but her former husband was Red. When we visited her, she was wearing a scarf tied round her waist, she was smoking a long Xhosa pipe, and it was obvious that her bare feet did not often see the inside of a shoe. A large tobacco pouch, of the kind Red women sling over their shoulders, was hanging from the bed-post. She danced after the fashion of Red women for a baby she was looking after, and conversed in a boisterous manner which is usually associated with Red people. On the door of the room was a black cross-mark consisting of medicines to give protection against people with 'bad medicines'. Should they enter, 'their medicine will not work'. She claimed that this was prescribed by a doctor she had consulted in Durban about a sore leg. Occasionally one comes across a townswoman wearing a turban folded in one of the fantastic shapes characteristic of Red women, while a few wear beads and bangles. The barefooted man with ear-rings whose wife wears one of these turbans is obviously also a Red or semi-Red townsman.

The extent of adherence to traditional patterns is quite remarkable in the case of male initiation, while the custom of *ukulobola* (making marriage payment) is also widely observed. These subjects are discussed in later chapters.

CULTURAL TYPES

Before summarizing our findings in terms of the different cultural and economic categories we have been discussing so far, we note that it is possible, of course, to distinguish diverse other types cutting across these basic categories. I briefly refer to three such types which appear to be mutually exclusive. We have already mentioned the *zealous church people*, and noticed their distribution among different non-Red categories (p. 43). The other two are the 'socialites' and *tsotsis*.

The term *socialites* is borrowed from the social columns of a local Bantu newspaper. Although they have not been shown up by our survey material as the important type one would expect them to be among urban people, there is no doubt that such a type exists. They appear to be people whose main interest is in regular attendance at get-togethers, in dancing, and perhaps in some of the less common forms of sport. Some of the Combos also come within this type. It is suspected that a significant proportion of them are of the intermediate type, but they are not confined to it. A Bantu university graduate characterized them as social climbers desirous of exhibiting their attainment of 'civilized' manners.

The term *tsotsi* is colloquially used in a loose sense of youths representing widely differing degrees of lawlessness. The 1958 clashes in the location between men and boys[41] started with the men beating up reputed *tsotsis*, but when later they tended to develop into indiscriminate beating of all boys, this action was justified by the allegation that very many other boys have contact with the genuine *tsotsis* and play dice with them. Without doubt there are employed youths and schoolboys who make common cause with the unemployed *tsotsis* in gambling, or even in some of their other illegal activities, so that there is no sharp dividing line between *tsotsi* and non-*tsotsi*. Nevertheless the 'real' *tsotsi* is taken to be the unemployed youth who spends his day loitering around the location, gambling, drinking, and smoking dagga (wild hemp). He is the street gambler who draws his knife on the slightest provocation. His night activities are the waylaying of passers-by, robbing and raping, and the stabbing of people in dark location streets. The more daring undertake outright burglary. Although none of the *tsotsis* interviewed admitted participation in such violence, there were vague references to other activities in which they were

[41] See Mayer, op. cit., pp. 83 ff.

engaged at night, which were their own private concern.[42] They tend to act in groups of three or more members, but it does not appear that there is a close-knit gang organization with distinct leadership patterns among the *tsotsis* of East London.

Tsotsis show preference for certain types of dress, although these are not confined to them. Skull-caps (for which the Afrikaans word *kadotjie* is used), narrow-brimmed 'San Remo' hats, black peaked caps known as *dambuzas*, and convertible 'Cooper' hats are said to be popular, or have been so in the past. Zoot shirts and stove-pipe trousers have long been associated with the *tsotsi*, but nowadays he may also be wearing a pair of striped trousers which used to belong to an elegant White man's morning suit. Recently some have shown a preference for a type of wide-legged trousers said to be worn in Johannesburg by youths who call themselves 'Yanks'.

Besides having their own characteristic forms of gesticulation, *tsotsis* also have a terminology of their own which is particularly evident in in-group relations. Instead of the traditional term *intanga* for an equal, or the modern *itshomi* used by many town young people, they speak of *ntwana*, *khawu*, *bhiza*, *my blaar* (Afrikaans). A senior is called *grootman* or *broer*, and a junior '*lighty*'. Besides Afrikaans and English terms, they are said to be fond of Zulu and Sotho words.[43] This must exhibit the fact that they have been around somewhat, because a real *tsotsi* is one who has seen something of the 'world'. Having been to Johannesburg particularly adds a touch of genuineness. In many ways local *tsotsis* take their cue from the cosmopolitan Rand. It was rumoured that a visit by some Johannesburg *tsotsis* contributed to the increased *tsotsi* activity which preceded the clashes in which they were beaten up.

Some *tsotsis* have no settled place of residence. Here is one who sponges on his nephew (sister's son) and the latter's wife; they have to share their only room with him when he sleeps there. Some nights he sleeps with his sweetheart in the room she occupies as domestic servant in town. He has meals at both these places, as well as with a friend sometimes. 'My nephew and his wife are a bit fed-up with me, particularly his wife. She dislikes continuing to feed a grown-up man who will not work and earn money, and has passed indirect remarks to this effect in my presence.' Not many cases of such unsettled youths were traced. Most of the *tsotsis* interviewed claimed to be living with their parents. It is significant, however, that our sample, both in terms of respondents to the main questionnaire, and in terms of household population, shows a marked deficiency of young men and older boys. I am convinced that many *tsotsis* are unsettled, do not live with their families continuously, and therefore could not be traced in the manner in which our sample survey was conducted.

The *tsotsi* has his female counterpart (*tsotsikazi*), although her presence is still much less obvious than that of the male *tsotsi*. A young man was discussing his sweetheart. He calls himself a Yank and was described by a Bantu research assistant as 'a proper *tsotsi*, but a decent one who dresses like them and speaks their language, goes about with them, but refrains from gambling'. He said of his sweetheart that 'my mother did not like her, for she says the girl is not decent; she is a *tsotsikazi*. It is because she wears very fancy clothes like the

[42] For a discussion of the violence attributed to *tsotsis*, see Mayer, op. cit., pp. 73–5.

[43] For an extensive list of *tsotsi* terms and examples of *tsotsi* language, see Bothma, C. V., *'n Volkekundige Ondersoek na die Aard en Onstaansoorsake van Tsotsi-groepe en hulle Aktiwiteite soos Gevind in die Stedelike Gebied van Pretoria*, unpublished M.A. thesis, University of Pretoria, 1951.

girls appearing in *Drum* and *Zonk*.' He also intimated that 'if I should have other lovers there would be trouble, for she fights a lot, and she is very jealous of me'. An informant described the female *tsotsi* as one who wears large gipsy-type earrings and narrow skirts, who straightens her hair and fights and shouts in the streets.

The majority of *tsotsis* probably come from simple households, and there is evidence suggesting that many of them are the sons of husbandless women,[44] but it is often lamented that even sons of well-educated and responsible people sometimes turn into *tsotsis*.

We now conclude this chapter by summarizing the main characteristics of the basic cultural types that have emerged. This is done in the awareness that the grouping of a population into mutually exclusive categories as we have attempted to do must necessarily suffer from a certain degree of artificiality. Even when applying more exact criteria than we have done, there will always be the borderline cases which do not conform to type. Moreover it is hardly possible to formulate categories for all existing types. Nevertheless the treatment of our material in this chapter in terms of categories has given some indication of the existence of certain types among the urban Bantu of East London. It has also provided us with a basis on which to estimate the numerical significance of some of these.

We have, first of all, the *white-collar* type. The ideal type here is the household with at least one white-collar worker among its members; it has electric lights or a radio and a good suite of furniture. Its members have close connexions with a church of the historic type, and at least one has advanced beyond the Junior Certificate. Its young men take a regular interest in sport as well as other town diversions. With some males hotel drinking is a custom, but females do not drink, or at least do not admit it openly. In all externals, and probably in many of their attitudes also, persons of this type exhibit a considerable degree of 'westernization', but customs such as male initiation and the giving of *lobolo* are commonly observed by them in common with all other types of townspeople. Traditional ancestor and witchcraft beliefs are still held in some cases, and cases of consultation of native doctors are also known to occur among this type.

Approximating to them in 'westernization' is the *intermediate* type, where the bread-winners are unskilled labourers, or occasionally skilled. The ideal type of household here owns a good suite of furniture without any 'luxuries', and has reached the high school education level. Among this type a high interest in church is not as common as among the white-collar type, and although the majority of young men also take an active interest in sport, it is not as general a feature as with the white-collar type. These two types together probably represent about a third of all real townspeople, the intermediate type being the more numerous of the two.

In contrast to these two more westernized types one finds the *semi-Red* type which is historically still close to the Red pagan background. These people do not have impressive furniture, usually have little or no school education, and have only nominal ties with churches, if any. With them open drinking is a general behaviour pattern, but they take little interest in typical town diversions, excepting sport and gambling in the case of young men. Beliefs about the ancestors are also closer to traditional patterns than those of other

[44] Mayer, op. cit., pp. 75, 83.

townspeople. Not more than 10 per cent of townspeople appear to be semi-Red.

That leaves us with the bulk of townspeople whom we have not been able to differentiate further, the *simple non-Red* type. It may be that within this category there exist distinct types which could not be 'unearthed' by our criteria. Personal observation, however, also left us with the impression that for the bulk of townspeople it is difficult to discern distinct patterns of behaviour. These people, whom we shall continue to refer to as a culturally simple type, are those who neither exhibit particular Red characteristics nor strike one as being conspicuously westernized. Their common characteristics are their general poverty and the very simple material culture of their homes, and education that does not advance beyond the standard six level. Apart from this it is difficult to speak of an ideal type, because their ranks include the non-drinking zealous church people as well as hard drinkers, honest-living people as well as the 'urban riff-raff'. There are among them many sports enthusiasts, and also cinema-goers, members of musical groups, and beach-frequenters, but none of these interests predominate. Perhaps these should be regarded as the typical Bantu townspeople of today, a culturally amorphous group relatively poor in dominant patterns of behaviour.

FIGURE 3

Genealogy of participants in sacrifice by members of Maduna clan

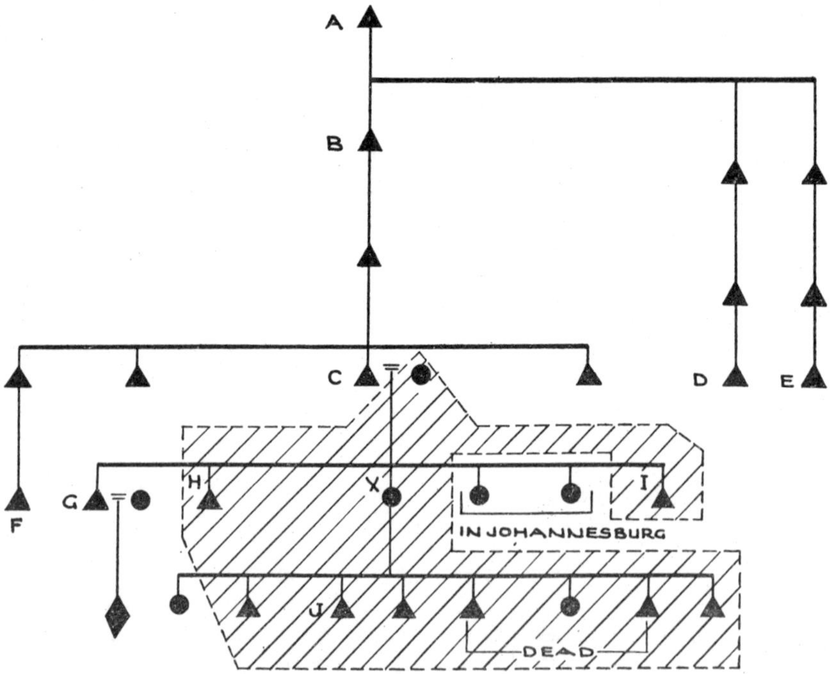

4

Some Townspeople

In this chapter we propose to describe a number of town families and individuals in order to show how the cultural characteristics discussed in the previous chapter are integrated in individual cases. At the same time this case material will provide some background for the discussion of the family in succeeding chapters. We start with a few representatives of the white-collar type.[1]

WHITE-COLLAR TYPE

1. Mr. A is a town-born man in his late twenties who has spent all his life in East London. His wife, a few years younger, was born and educated in a Ciskei reserve, but later came to East London to qualify as a nurse. They were married in church by special licence, with *lobolo* passing in cash after the marriage. According to the date of their marriage and the age of their first child, the baby must have been born within a few months after their marriage. When they were interviewed for the sample survey, they had a baby about six months old. At that stage the husband claimed that he and his wife had not yet resumed sexual relations with each other.[2] When we visited them four or five months later, the young mother had taken up a nursing post and the baby was being cared for by its maternal grandmother in her reserve home.

Mr. A holds a Senior Certificate and is employed by a large department store as a driver earning close to R14 (£7) per week, so that after his wife had started working they should have had a combined monthly income of about R100 (£50). They rent two rooms in a wood-and-iron shack. The building itself is in need of paint and repair, but the interior of their own rooms is freshly painted and neat. The main room contains a new contemporary dining-room suite in a light-coloured wood, and a portable radio. The cooking is done on a single-plate paraffin stove on a table behind the door, where some cooking utensils are also kept. The doorway to the bedroom is screened off by a curtain. All the bedroom furniture is obviously second-hand. Mr. A owns a car which, for a model of some twenty years ago, makes a favourable impression.

He described his daily programme as follows: 'I get up at 6.30 in the morning, wash and dress and have breakfast. All this time the radio is on. I start working at 7.45. During the lunch break I seldom have anything to eat. We play games like cards and draughts, and these keep me so busy that I do not think of eating. If my wife has the day off, I do sometimes go home for lunch. After leaving work at five o'clock I sometimes visit friends, but I do not delay long before coming home. When I get home I have some tea, and perhaps a slice of bread. I read the papers and listen to the radio.' After the evening meal, which they have at 7.30, he goes to bed. On Saturday after-

[1] Names and initials have been changed and certain details slightly amended to mask the identity of the persons described.

[2] Traditional Xhosa custom requires that a suckling mother should abstain from sexual relations. See p. 86.

noons he likes to watch rugby or play golf. Although he is not a full church member, he claims to attend Sunday morning and afternoon services regularly. After the afternoon service he goes visiting.

When questioned whether he and his wife do things together, he said that he helps his wife in cooking, washing-up, laying the table, sweeping and polishing. When the baby was with them, he used to attend to it sometimes. 'We used to go out together, visiting our parents and relatives and going to the movies, but nowadays we do not attend entertainments.'

His breakfast takes the form of milk, bread, butter and syrup, and a cup of milk or tea. Occasionally he has eggs or fried steak. The evening meal might consist of meat, vegetables, rice and samp (crushed mealies). They seldom have a course of sweets. When both are at home, the table is laid and they sit down to the meal together.

2. Mr. X (middle-aged, Junior Certificate) was born in East London, but has spent some of his life in other parts of the country. He and his wife are both employed at the white-collar level, so that between them they have a very good income by location standards. They were married in church, but also observed the customs of *ukulobola* and *ukudlisa amasi*. Both have had previous marriages, but of several living children from the three marriages involved, only one or two are staying with them. They keep a servant but she does not lodge with them.

Mr. X owns a car and always looks well-groomed, mostly wearing flannels with sports jacket and tie. Their house has electric lights, and is furnished as follows:

Reception room: studio couch with matching fireside chairs, an adjustable table, a radiogram, and an old-fashioned flower-stand. It is obvious that all this furniture has been in use for some time, but it is well looked after. On the walls are almost life-size enlargements of Mr. X and his wife and relatives, and a motto 'God bless this house' with an angel. There is further an 'everhot' tea-set, and a number of wooden and porcelain mural and table decorations and souvenirs. A suspended clock has a face in the form of a porcelain plate.

Bedroom 1: a bedroom suite with two single beds, not new, but well-kept.

Bedroom 2: a contemporary single bedroom suite, quite new. (This was said to be Mrs. X's cousin's room.)

Kitchen: a modern kitchen dresser, a wooden table, electric stove and electric kettle.

Mr. X is not a member of any national political organization, but is keenly interested in Bantu national politics and has great respect for ex-chief Albert Luthuli on whom he looks as a genuine leader of the Bantu people. In a conversation in the presence of two politically conscious friends he expressed the opinion that the chiefs and traditional leaders, because of their being in government service, could not genuinely speak for the Bantu people. 'I am not against the chiefs,' he said, 'but the fact is that they are under the government's thumb, and are not free to say what they like.' He does, in fact, have close personal ties with his tribal chief and is highly involved in the politics of his tribe. He has also served on the Locations Advisory Board.

Mr. and Mrs. X are full members of a well-known church and he is also a member of the I.O.T.T. temperance movement. He is a member of rugby and cricket clubs, and on Saturdays plays cricket in summer and watches rugby in winter. Besides going to church, they sometimes attend tea-parties on Sundays. He does a little gardening and sometimes cleans his own car.

3. Mr. B.C. (54) is a non-Xhosa and came to East London from a town outside the Cape Province in the twenties. A brother of his, who had come here some time previously, then already owned a house in the location. Here he married a woman who had been born and brought up in East London. They have three daughters, all born here, of whom the eldest is a nurse in her mid-twenties, but she holds a nursing post elsewhere and was not counted as a member of the family in the survey, so that they were counted as one of the 'upper well-furnished' households of unskilled occupational level. The other two children, both scholars, were with the parents at the time, but were sent to school elsewhere the following year.

The husband is an ordinary labourer who in the course of his work has to carry boxes and clean machines at a wage of R9.60 (96*s.*) per week. His wife earns R5 (50*s.*) per month as an office cleaner. It is an early morning job and she is back at home at about nine in the morning. She keeps herself occupied with household chores and likes listening to the radio, particularly to the Bantu programme. Although she never mentioned it during interviews, it is known that she is a fah-fee sub-runner and goes about a great deal to collect bets from punters. She is a member of the women's *manyano* of her church and claims to attend church regularly. After washing the dishes in the evenings she likes reading the East London *Daily Dispatch*, the Xhosa newspaper *Imvo Zabantsundu* and the women's journal *Femina*. The children like going to the bioscope and concerts, and sometimes one of the parents accompanies them to a concert because of the late hours at which these end.

Mr. C is a simple and quiet type, and in the afternoons after work we would find him attending to his fowls or scratching about in his vegetable garden. He rises early, and after a wash and a cup of coffee, feeds the fowls, and during the planting season waters the young plants. His working hours are from 7 a.m. to 4.30 p.m., with breaks for breakfast and lunch. He does not join any of the groups of men one can always see chatting or playing games beside the street during the lunch-hour. He does have friends and sometimes stands listening to the conversation, but mostly he prefers sitting by himself, somewhere away from the street. In the evenings he likes listening to the radio, making a point of switching on for the news, and reads newspapers and books, generally going to bed at about nine o'clock. He attends church, but not every Sunday, and he rarely goes out.

He does not assist his wife in any of the regular household chores. At most she would ask him to put on water for coffee, which she would then make herself. When attending church, weddings or funerals, they sometimes go together, but often enough each one sets out alone. Excepting a small amount of pocket money, the husband hands all his wages to his wife. She buys food without consulting him, but expenditure on clothes, furniture or the paying of accounts they discuss together. Their furniture was bought on the hire-purchase system.

They live in a four-roomed municipal house with a wooden partition in the entrance room, providing for a separate kitchen. The house has a small cubicle used as bathroom and storeroom. In the entrance room is a new dining-room suite, but the somewhat out-of-date sitting-room suite and bedroom furniture show signs of wear. There is a radiogram with a collection of records, including a number of light Bantu recordings, and a few hymns and recordings of jazz and other light Western music. Special features are two portraits of Mr. and Mrs. C of the large-sized, technically very inferior, type often seen in Bantu homes, and framed newspaper clippings and photographs of the paramount chief of Mr. C's ethnic group.

Mrs. C's description of their meals had much in common with those of Mr. A (case No. 1). She sometimes also cooks *umngqusho*, a traditional dish consisting of cooked samp to which beans are usually added. When her husband is at home, they eat together in the dining-room where she lays a table, but the food is dished into the plates in the kitchen. When the children are at home, the eldest joins them at table, but the two younger ones (14 and 16) mostly eat in the kitchen. She could give no reason for this, apart from saying that the children prefer it that way.

Here the head and his wife are simple people of medium education and in unskilled employment, so that on first contact one feels doubtful as to whether they really belong to the white-collar type. However, the fact that they have an unmarried daughter who is a nurse immediately enhances their prestige, even though she is no more a regular member of the household. This, together with the father's own good income, their material culture and interests (reading, listening to the radio) justifies their classification with the white-collar type.

ELEMENTARY FAMILY OF ZEALOUS CHURCH PEOPLE, INTERMEDIATE TYPE

4. Mrs. Y (38, standard six), was born in East London, and married a Transkei man. She spent several years with his family in the Transkei, from 1940 to 1942 and again from 1943 to 1945. Mr. Y is a messenger (R7 (70*s*.) per week) at the power-station and his wife is 'tea-maker' (R4 (£2) per week) to a wholesale firm in town. They were married by civil rites and the passing of *lobolo*, but the marriage was later consecrated in church after they had joined the Rev. Bhengu's Assemblies of God, of which they are now staunch members. They have a teenage son and daughter in school, and a little boy, all three living with the parents. The eldest son, now in standard seven, has the highest education in the family.

Electricity is laid on to their three-roomed municipal house. Most of their furniture is not quite new, but still in a good condition. Besides a dining-room suite, they also have a studio couch and a small bookshelf, two fairly new and good wooden beds, with a bed-lamp, and an older wardrobe and dressing-table. In the kitchen, where one or two of the children also sleep, there is an iron bed and a home-made cupboard with cooking utensils. They also own a radiogram. On one occasion there were dirty dishes on the kitchen floor, but the reception room is usually very clean and tidy. Besides religious pictures, there are two big enlargements of Mr. and Mrs. Y. In the yard is a small wood-and-iron shack where Mr. Y does some carpentry. There is also a motor-car which appears to have been stationary for some time.

The family attends church every Sunday, and Mrs. Y is secretary of the women's church bazaar committee. Besides relatives, she also visits the patients in a T.B. settlement during her free time. Her husband spends some of his free time reading the Bible. For the baptismal feast of their first child—they did not belong to the 'Assemblies' then—a sheep was slaughtered, 'because of great excitement, the baby being our first-born and a boy, the pride of every mother and father. There was no other motive. With us Xhosa the slaughtering of an animal signifies a deep sense of gratitude or appreciation.' But Mr. Y has not performed any rituals connected with the dead, and adds: 'I do not believe in performing sacrifices to the ancestors; that is meaningless to me.' Mrs. Y stated emphatically that in times of prolonged illness they would try different medical doctors, but would not consider consulting a diviner. However, they attach value to traditional initiation of boys, and intend that their son should be initiated as has been the case with his father. 'I take it to be a good thing, because it is our custom, and our people believe that *ukwaluka* [initiation] has power to change a man's bad character to good. Because of this the *amakrwala* [newly initiated young men] try to show a good character when fresh from initiation. But I believe it is not the mere *ukwaluka* that counts but the upbringing of the boy.'

In terms of occupation, educational level and income this family is still to be regarded as intermediate, but in terms of material culture it compares favourably with some white-collar families, and it may well be that in time the children will go on to a higher educational level and white-collar jobs, and thus draw the family up to the white-collar level.

INTERMEDIATE FEMALE-HEADED FAMILY

5. We are visiting the Maxambeni area on the major survey. The 'street' is a maze of erosion furrows, and we can move about only on foot. We spot our number: the house has a dirty appearance and is badly in need of repairs and paint, but it is flanked by two prim wood-and-iron cottages, the one freshly painted. Across the street is a sombre rust-covered structure which has never been painted. On our making inquiries, Lindile, a girl of 17, comes forward, intimating that her mother is the owner of the place. Yes, they are East London people: she was born here and her mother and brother as well. Quite willing to be interviewed, she leads us along the dirty veranda where we pass some of the tenants, to the family's reception room.

The room of about 9 ft. by 15 ft. has one fair-sized window at the far end of the room close to the door. The other end of the room is on the dark side. There is a curtain to close off the back part of the room which is used as a bedroom, but the curtains are not drawn at the moment. In contrast to the exterior, the room and furniture are clean and tidy, and the walls—wooden partitions and lining—have been painted a bright blue. There are good easy-chairs and a dining-room suite, with a profuse display of crockery and decorations on the sideboard. Besides the wardrobe and clothes hanging from the wall, we notice the old-fashioned iron three-quarter bed with high ends, the spotless white pillow-slips and counterpanes, and an attractive folded travel rug. On the walls are the typical photographs and religious pictures, as well as two maps and a calendar. Lindile says there is one other room in the house which they occupy, in which they have a radio.

In the course of the interview it emerges that Lindile has passed standard five, is an unmarried mother and unemployed. There is no question of her getting married to the father of her baby, which is nearly 2 years old and is now with the young man and his parents. Regarding her religious affiliation she says: 'I was a member of the Assemblies of God, but I got a baby and left the church for good. Now I do not belong to any church.' She can think of no outside activities except visiting her friends.

The household consists of her widowed mother (48), elder brother James (21), Lindile, a sister (14) and brother (9), and a year-old baby of a married sister who left the baby with her mother when she went to join her husband in Cape Town. The mother earns R13 (£6 10*s.*) per month as a cook and in addition collects R13.50 (£6 15*s.*) in rents every month. James has a job cleaning paint-drums at a paint factory which brings in R5 (£2 10*s.*) per week, giving the family a weekly *per capita* income of roughly R1.95 (19*s.* 6*d.*). The mother (standard six) is an attending full member of the Presbyterian Church of Africa and a member of the women's *manyano*. Her only other leisure activity is to visit friends.

Apart from drinking kaffir beer at the shebeens and visiting friends in his free time, James plays rugby for the 'Swallows' and sometimes goes down to the beach. Repair jobs at home also take some of his time. He was baptized and claims allegiance to his mother's church, but has no other official ties and does not attend services. (James and the mother were also interviewed personally after the first visit.)

ELEMENTARY FAMILIES: SIMPLE CULTURE TYPE

6. When interviewed for the basic survey, Simon (42, standard six) and his wife Nomzi were living in a small room with their two children and Nomzi's two brothers aged 18 and 16 respectively. Simon, his wife, and the elder brother were employed, their wages totalling R11.05 (£5 10*s.* 6*d.*) per week. Simon was a labourer at the municipal abattoirs. When we visited them some time later, one of the brothers had gone to work in the mines on the Rand and the other was undergoing initiation in the country. Simon is East London-born, but cannot remember his father—which often means illegitimate birth.

The wife gave us the following account of their marriage. After having passed standard five at her birthplace in the East London district, she came to stay with her mother's sister in town, but after some time in town, she stopped attending school and then assisted her present mother-in-law in her shop. There was as yet no connexion between her and Simon, but her mother's sister and this woman were friends.

Explaining how the marriage originated, Nomzi said: 'My mother-in-law loved me for her son.' She suggested the match to her son and he reacted favourably, so the messengers were sent to her parents. He also proposed to her himself: 'He said he wanted us to be in love', but she did not take him seriously and did not give an answer. His mother also spoke to her mother's sister. Nomzi's own mother now came to town with her husband's elder brother's wife. 'I was then told that I was going to get married. The older woman said: "Today you are going to get married." "To whom?" "To Simon." "I do not want to." "We are not going to hear anything from you." Next I was dressed in marriage dresses which had already been made, and taken by taxi to Simon's home in the company of my mother.' This was on a Sunday, and she had been informed on the Friday before that. Simon's people, both men and women, came to admonish her, and she was told that her name in the husband's home was to be Nomzi. A month later her father came to admonish her: 'You must remain here and serve for us. Never come to us with complaints.'

For the first month she stayed with Simon's parents, but after her father had come to admonish her, she started sleeping in Simon's room, which was not in the parent's house. In the morning she would then go to the parents' home to make coffee and do other work. *Lobolo* was given afterwards. Some time after the admonishing, her father-in-law (apparently Simon's stepfather) slaughtered a goat *ukudlisa amasi*. After the goat had been skinned, she was given sour milk in an enamel dish to take a sip, and a piece of meat to eat—she did not know what it was called. She was told that she was 'being made a woman of this house [*umzi*]'.

The house where we first visited them is in the thick of a densely built-up wood-and-iron area. It does not front on any street, and can be reached only by narrow alleys. On three sides it is almost right against other houses, but on the front side a pathway 8 to 10 feet wide separates it from the opposite building. The house consists of two rows of rooms, of which the front ones open on to the pathway. To reach Simon's family in one of the back rooms, you enter a narrow passage, floorless and open at both ends, from the side of the building, pass a pail of dirty dishwater, and 'climb into' one of the four doors opening on to this passage. Through a small window high above the wall, you see nothing but the metal wall of the next house. In the half-dark of this cluttered cubicle we would find plump Nomzi in her clean, well-fitting dress, looking fresh and friendly, just home from work, or already cooking the evening meal. Simon, more reserved, always in shirt and trousers, would be resting on the bed or chatting to a friend.

An unemployed cripple brother of Nomzi's, who occupies another room in the same house with his family, was often with them. Here are a few extracts from notes on different visits.

Tuesday, 14 April, late afternoon: We found Simon lying on the bed, in conversation with his wife, who was sitting beside him on a chair, and her cripple brother. An insurance agent came in to collect premiums. Later A.M., who lives in another room in the same house, also joined the company.

Wednesday, 20 May, about 4 p.m.: Found only the children at home. Nomzi was not yet back home from work. One of them called their *umalume* (mother's brother) and we had a chat with him. The boy sat in the passage playing with clay: he said he was going to make a pot.

Thursday, 21 May, about 4.15 p.m.: Nomzi was talking outside when we arrived. Simon arrived later. She said there was no particular news, except the abundant rains, and that the roof was leaking badly, but fortunately nobody took ill. A mattress was rolled up against the wall (usually there were two mattresses on the bed). Against the wall was a rolled-up grass mat.

Monday, 1 June (public holiday), 11.30 a.m.: We dropped in for a casual visit. Simon was sitting on a chair chatting to a man we had not seen there before. Both men had their hats on. Nomzi was cooking meat, mealie 'rice', potatoes and cabbage. On the table were one or two dirty dishes, as if somebody had had a meal not long before. The cripple brother's two children were also in the room.

Simon spends most of his free time at home—'I am afraid to walk about'—but sometimes visits his friends. When feeling inclined for a drink, he buys a beaker of kaffir beer and drinks it at home. He claims to be a full member of the 'Ethiopian' Church, but does not attend regularly.

After some months we found them in the house opposite the lane, in a front room which could be reached by wooden steps directly from the path. One afternoon we found Simon giving his 12-year-old son a haircut. The following morning we found the boy with a group of dice players in front of the house, also making a bet occasionally. He was wearing a pair of long black trousers which were too big for him, and a faded khaki shirt, unbuttoned at the neck, revealing some kind of pendant.

We visited them on an afternoon the following week. Simon was not home, as he was doing piece-work somewhere after his regular working hours. Nomzi was there, working at her sewing machine, in the company of several people. Nearest to the door was an old man with light skin-colour and European-like features, obviously a half-breed, but in dress and conversation he was a Xhosa peasant through and through. This was Nomzi's stepfather, who was on a visit to town. There was also a woman with her baby visiting them from Keiskammahoek; she had distant clan relations with Nomzi. A young man whom we did not identify sat near to Nomzi. Perhaps he was one of the two brothers who had been with them before. During our visit a neighbour joined the company; he is of the Tshawe clan like Simon. Another man came in just to ask for something, and a woman looked in at the door but went off again, apparently noticing that the room was now full to capacity, although Nomzi indicated that there was still room.

The room was not as small as the one they had been in. It had a larger window and the walls had recently been painted green. When I remarked that they probably found it pleasanter here, Nomzi agreed, but complained of the bugs that were troubling them. The removing of old wallpaper and paint had not remedied this, and they were now planning to fumigate this room. Meanwhile my assistant was chatting to the old man, exchanging news about people they both knew.

They now had two wooden beds, two home-made tables, two cupboards and four chairs (not matching) in the room. All the furniture was old. An old linoleum square covered the floor. On the walls were some photographs, a large picture of Christ delivering the Sermon on the Mount, two framed insurance certificates, and a calendar.

7. Makhosi (39) is an East London-born illegitimate son of a woman who never married. In school he never proceeded further than Sub A. His mother came to work in town as a young girl from a School home in the country. During the war Makhosi spent several years in the army, and a few years later went to Johannesburg, where he worked for seven years. At the time of the interview he had been back in East London for two or three years. He owns the ten-roomed house in Gomorra shown in figure 2, occupying a small front room with his wife and six-month-old baby. He is not working, but collects R14 (£7) a month in rents, while his wife earns R4 (40*s.*) a month as a domestic servant. Their room, which opens on to the veranda, is not larger than 7 feet by 9 feet. There is a small window about 5 feet above floor level, and on the November afternoon when we interviewed them it was stiflingly hot. On a suspended shelf there are medicine bottles, an alarm clock, shaving-brushes and other toilet requisites, and on another some simple crockery. Space has been found for a single bed, a round table, two chairs and two small cupboards. On one of the cupboards are two pressure stoves and cooking utensils.

Makhosi, who was shabbily dressed when interviewed, spends his time pottering around the house, denies taking any liquor, and can think of no other outside activity than going to church on Sundays. He is a full member of the 'Apostle Church', the name of which he could not specify more accurately.

On the veranda hung a recently painted cross fashioned from tin and wood, on which had been painted an inscription, a few stars and a crescent moon—symbols popular with some Zionist-Pentecostal sects. Apparently it was for the grave of his father, who had passed away a few months previously.

Makhosi admits having had two illegitimate children by different mothers. Both are now girls of about 11 years of age, staying with their mothers in East London. His wife, whose dress suggests that she is a country woman, had three illegitimate children by one man before she got married to Makhosi. These children are with her parents in the country, because 'here is nobody to look after them'. A member of Makhosi's paternal grandmother's clan, whose family is in the country, is staying with them. 'I gave him place as a new-comer.' He has meals with them and sleeps on the veranda, but it seems as if they do not see very much of him. He earns R4 (40*s.*) a week sweeping streets.

FEMALE-HEADED FAMILY OF SIMPLE CULTURE

8. When, on her return from women's *manyano*, Mary found us talking to her 16-year-old daughter, she appeared rather upset, but was soon reassured by our explanation of the purpose for which we were collecting information. There was also a middle-aged man, one of the tenants, and a few smaller children. During the interview, the daughter, her month-old illegitimate child tied to her back, attended to a pot cooking on the stove, and occasionally sold a few fat-cakes to children who came to buy these. Besides the table with cooking arrangements there was another table; also two forms, two beds and a wardrobe. For a room in which cooking was in progress, it was quite tidy, and on subsequent visits it made a clean and orderly impression for this type of family.

Mary, her five children, and the baby occupied only this one room in the house which she owns, the other six rooms being rented. The eldest son, East London-born Ndumiso (24), earned R6 (60*s.*) a week as a messenger, and Mary earned R8 (80*s.*) a month as domestic servant, besides collecting R13 (£6 10*s.*) per month in rents. When we revisited them some time later, the daughter, her baby, and the young children had left for Debe Nek, where they were staying with a brother of Mary's stepfather, so that she and Ndumiso were alone. She was now employed as a factory hand in a pineapple canning factory, taking R5 to R6 (50*s.* to 60*s.*) a week, according to the amount of work done, but she was finding the working hours very long. Ndumiso was giving her R2 (20*s.*) every week as *isiqina* (fixed contribution).

She sent money and clothes to her children in the country. On one of our visits we found her late husband's brother's wife with her. She had arrived in East London that morning to visit her husband, who was working in town. Coming from the same neighbourhood at Debe Nek where Mary's children were, she was able to bring the mother news from them.

Mary was born and brought up in a King William's Town reserve, where she attended school up to standard five. After this she came to East London about 1929, staying with her mother at her employer's in Selborne, and continued her schooling here. But before she could write standard six, she was told that she was 'being courted at home', which meant that a marriage was being negotiated for her at the country home, in this case with a man she did not know, and who was a good deal older than she was. He was in town, but he had a sister at Mary's country home, through whom the contact was established with her family. They were married in church here in town after *lobolo* had been given. Something was slaughtered, but she was not sure whether this was supposed to be for *ukudlisa amasi*. Her youngest child (5) she had by another man after the death of her husband. Before revealing this, she said that since the death of her husband, she had not had dealings with any men, because town men were just *tsotsis*. When the circumstances of the child's birth were mentioned, she said that the child's father was just such a *tsotsi*, and this experience taught her a lesson. She never got any support from him. (Customarily no damages could be claimed for the seduction of a widow.)

Mary regards herself as head of the household, and cites her ownership and responsibility for the house as proof. 'When anything needs repair, I see to it that it is repaired; I order Ndumiso to do it. When there is trouble with the tenants, I attend to the matter and try to settle it.' Asked whether she ever had to call in the help of a senior male person, she said this had been the case when Ndumiso got drunk and would not listen to her, and she called in her husband's elder brother mentioned above. 'But Ndumiso is not a *tsotsi*—he is a good boy. He just stays at home with me. Even when he is drunk, he just comes home.' Ndumiso was usually shabbily dressed, wearing a sports jacket and open-neck shirt. He is a regular kaffir-beer drinker, and sometimes takes brandy as well. Besides drinking, his main interest is in a vocal group to which he belongs. He regards himself as an adherent of the Order of Ethiopia, but apart from having been baptized as a child he has no official ties with the church, and does not attend services. His group sometimes holds rehearsals on Sundays.

The evening meal is the only one they have together. Mostly it consists of the traditional *umngqusho* (cooked stamped mealies and beans), sometimes with some meat. There is no laying of the table. Mary dishes the food into the plates which are placed on the table, and each eats with a spoon. 'We eat in the Xhosa way.'

MULTI-GENERATION FEMALE-HEADED FAMILY OF SEMI-RED PEOPLE

9. Manini is the head of a household made up of three generations of her offspring (see fig. 4). As a family they are a good example of semi-Red

FIGURE 4. *Manini's Family*

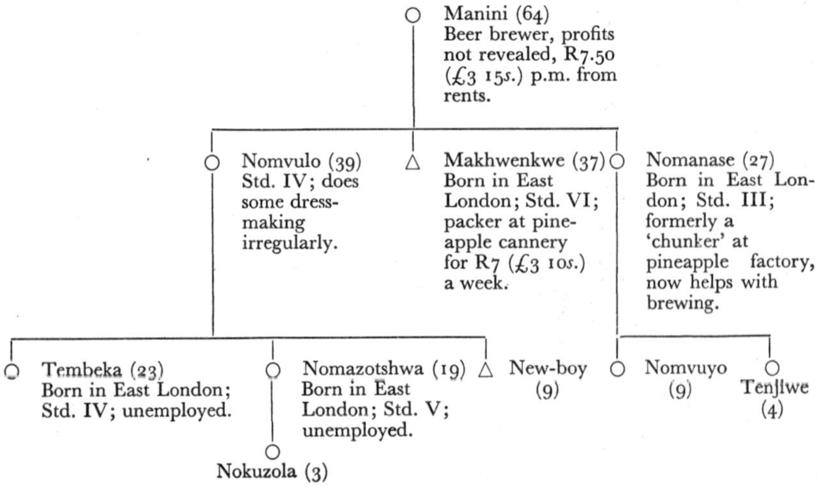

people. Some of them claimed adherence to a well-known church, but this tie appears to be only nominal. Nomanase once said about her children that they 'have not been baptized, for as I have said, we attend no church at our home. If we had been in the country, perhaps we would have been Red people.' Manini and her late husband were Red people when they came to East London in the early twenties.

Manini herself is the only member of the household who has ever been married, and there is no evidence that any of her children were illegitimate. However, Nomvulo calls her *Sisi* (sister) because she was brought up by her grandmother, whom she used to call 'mother'. The grandchildren usually call Manini 'grandmother', but one day she referred to Tembeka as her daughter, and when we queried the point said that she regards her as her daughter, because she is Nomvulo's illegitimate child. Nokuzola also calls her 'grandmother'.

Her reaction to the question of headship was revealing.

Q.: When a mother lives with her children as you do here in town what is the custom: who is taken as head?

Manini: The son, Makhwenkwe, is the head here.

Q.: What shows that he is the head?

M: He has to feed the children. He spent his money on this house. (Further questioning revealed that she had bought the house with her money, but that he had spent money on improving it. Further, another house which she had inherited was sold to help improve this one.)

Q.: Who really rules all the people in this house?

M: I do; all these things are mine; and he [Makhwenkwe] is also mine.

She said that Makhwenkwe gives his whole pay to her, and when he wants to buy something like clothes out of it, he first consults her. The two daughters ask her for everything they want, but the little income that Nomvulo derives from her dressmaking she keeps to herself. In her absence, Manini said, Makhwenkwe would be the one responsible, or Nomvulo, when Makhwenkwe was not there. But this seemed rather a theoretical question to them.

Actually there could be little doubt that she was the head of the family. Makhwenkwe appeared to be somewhat of an outside figure, and we never found him at home. Sometimes it appeared that there might be a little tension between her and Nomvulo over authority. Nomvulo had mentioned her staying with her grandmother while Manini was outside, and we were discussing this when she came back. She scolded Nomvulo for revealing this fact which had not been mentioned at our former interviews. 'There is a Xhosa saying: your tongue is your policeman', implying that talkativeness brings one into trouble. 'These children like to talk. We old people are just things who are not supposed to talk about their affairs now.'

The family live in a back room of their house in Moriva. The house fronts on the street, but to find them one has to follow a narrow alley and passage leading into a yard of about 10 feet square, into which two rooms open. It appears that there are times when they occupy both rooms, but when we visited them they were all in the bigger room of the two, where they slept, cooked, ate and talked. The yard and passage are cluttered with all kinds of junk, but it is dominated by blackened drums used for beer brewing, a barrel which is also used in the process, and numbers of four-gallon tins in which the porridge for brewing is cooked. Their room of about 10 feet by 12 feet is simply furnished with three beds and a collection of small tables and cupboards. On the walls are photographs, including one of a group of young men who usually come there for their drinks, and another of one of the girls with two boy friends. There are the typical calendars and religious pictures, also one of Christ on the cross.

I first visited them personally a few months after they had been interviewed for the basic survey. It was a Monday morning between eleven and twelve. Two little girls were playing in the alley leading from the street, dressing sticks as dolls with bits of left-over material. Inside a door two small boys were eating sweet potatoes from one plate. Somewhere we could hear a penny-whistle. In the small yard we found Nomanase washing. By the time we left, she was bathing Tenjiwe.

Manini was expecting us, sitting on a low form inside the room, wearing a tattered and dirty apron, and soiled black beret on her head. She sat with feet wide apart, emphasizing her corpulence. We discussed her family and her coming to town, Xhosa customs, and sacrifices performed by her long ago, with a minimum of questioning on my part. She belched unceremoniously. Then again she removed her beret, revealing knotted hair which did not appear too clean. At one stage she excused herself, announcing that she was going to pass water.

She has had eleven children, but the three living with her are the only ones alive. Two or three died before she came to town to join her husband here. Thanks to the medicines of an old White doctor, her next child was well and healthy, but at eight months old it was burnt and died. At least one other child was lost through scalding. She connected these accidents with her negligence in making sacrifices for her deceased mother who had asked beer in a dream. She did eventually slaughter a goat to propitiate the spirits.

On another occasion—'Now I am ill; I have had a dream as if my father was saying: "So-and-so [addressing her by her family name], give me meat." "Oh, father! You have two sons. Why is it that you always come to me?" He did not talk, he just looked at me. I saw him holding a dark-coloured he-goat with a white face [*impemvu*], and he handed it to me with the words: "Here you are, child of M——." ' After some delay she bought and slaughtered such a goat, and from that time, for the last ten years, she has been keeping well.

We visited them again a few weeks later, shortly after the annual Mfengu Commemoration,[3] at about ten in the morning. Nomvulo was tidying her bed, and then folded pieces of a traditional costume which she had borrowed for the commemoration, and was now returning to the owner. She was wearing some bead-work which is her own. The first thing Manini mentioned was that her 'children' had been arrested for 'pass'; this proved to refer to her sister's daughter who works in Berea. Some spinach was being cooked for their first meal of the day. Xhosa people use a weed growing in the gardens as spinach (*imifino*), but this was ordinary spinach bought at the market. Manini added some mealie meal, and about five minutes later removed the pot from the stove, stirred it and gave the stirring-stick (*iphini*) to Tenjiwe to lick. She explained that the stick is always given to the child who is most willing to run errands, which is an old custom. The food was now a brownish pulp, tasting both like spinach and raw mealie meal, well salted. She dished all into four plates, but Nomazotshwa dished a portion for herself into a saucer from one

[3] See p. 181.

of the plates. Manini, Nomvulo and Nomanase each had a plate to themselves, but Tenjiwe and Nokuzola shared a plate. The other members of the family were not present. Manini said grace: 'Lord bless this maintenance You give us, through Jesus Christ our Lord. Amen.' Although each had a substantial helping, the food was quickly consumed. There was some handing around of plates in the course of the meal. Besides the food she shared with Nokuzola, Tenjiwe also ate from her mother's plate and was given a lump from Manini's as well. All ate with their hands. They always eat *imifino* and boiled mealies like that, but other foodstuffs are eaten with spoons. There is no particular order of serving, not even when men are present, but a man will not eat from the same plate with a child.

They do not always cook for their morning meal. Often they have only bread and tea, or food left over from the previous night. Other dishes cooked in the middle of the day or in the evening are meat, potatoes, *umngqusho* (cooked samp and beans) and a dish called *umphothulo*, consisting of kaffir-corn or mealies cooked whole, then ground and eaten cold with milk.

Later Nokuzola was playing with a bundle of remnants of material which she tried to tie on her back like a baby. Tenjiwe kicked over the chamber-pot and her mother gave her a quick, hard slap on the buttocks, scolding her severely. She withdrew to a corner without crying while her mother mopped up the mess. Manini blew her nose on her apron, telling us of a tenant of hers who had been killed in an accident while travelling on a bicycle over the week-end. The White driver, who did not stop, was chased by a Bantu taxi-driver who arrived on the scene. He managed to stop him. The police also arrived. The White man pleaded ignorance of his having knocked the man over, but his front light lay near the scene of the accident.

I produced some sweets which were quickly distributed, Manini taking the best kind for herself. Nomanase got nothing because she should not eat sweets during pregnancy, else the baby will be born with a kind of rash known as *ishimnca*. Neither should she eat potatoes, pumpkin and sweet potatoes. Many women eat these foodstuffs though, but Nomanase does avoid sweets. Further a pregnant woman should not expose herself to the cold as Nomanase was now doing, neither should she work hard. She should not have sexual intercourse, said Nomvulo, but Manini disagreed, saying that this depended on the man and the woman themselves.

Manini sent Nomazotshwa out with a sixpence, and she returned soon with half a loaf of bread and a small packet. Tenjiwe was also sent for a penny-worth of snuff. On returning she slipped and fell in the doorway, hurting herself a bit. She went over to Nomvulo for consolation, and Manini made her sit down, gave each leg a good twist, and then she got up quite satisfied. As we left, Nomvulo helped herself to some beer and Nomazotshwa also asked for some but did not get any.

Nomazotshwa was usually the best dressed of the family. On one occasion she was wearing a boldly striped jersey over a skirt, the whole outfit making a neat, clean and well-fitting impression. In addition she displayed a shiny new locket. She appeared cleaner than any of the others, and at one stage massaged her legs with oil. She was often bare-headed, but sometimes wore a white beret. Nomvulo was sometimes quite well dressed by Western standards, but there was usually something careless about her. On one winter's day she was wearing a coat over a two-piece jersey-cloth outfit, all somewhat soiled and worn, with a necklace of Xhosa beadwork. On another occasion she had on what must have been a smart outfit when it was new, consisting of a skirt and a tunic with slits at the sides. It was of black material with a bold yellow design, but it had been 'renovated' by touching up at the neck and cuffs with blue and white. She also had on a necklace of cheap jewellery. Nomanase was often shabbily dressed, perhaps in an old greyish skirt and a tattered black jersey. On one occasion she wore a clean german print dress buttoned up at the neck. Manini also usually wore this type of dress, which is common among the older generation of School women in the country. The two sisters usually wore headcloths. Manini was always barefoot, but the younger women sometimes wore inexpensive flat shoes.

For Christmas the whole family had new dresses. We visited them about ten o'clock on Christmas morning. Nomvulo was busy at the sewing machine, still working on a new dress for Nokuzola. Nomanase came in with Tenjiwe, whom she had been bathing outside. The little girl was naked, except for her clean white socks and very fashionable new shoes. Her mother dressed her in a new cotton frock in which she could stand comparison well with little girls from white-collar homes. Nomanase had on a colourful new dress herself. In the meantime Nokuzola was crying and complaining about wanting to put on a new dress. Nomvulo, still trying to finish the child's dress, ordered her to go and wash, but she loitered around and later threw a tantrum about the new dress. Manini also produced her 'new' (second-hand) dress of a light-blue celanese-like material to show to us.

I quote the report of one more visit to this family on a Friday morning.

We brought Manini a small gift of some coffee, tea and sugar. She was profuse in her thanks, and referred to the topic several times in the course of the visit. 'I shall enjoy this coffee all by myself, sitting on the bed, with those curtains drawn. . . . You see now, it is very good to welcome visitors who come to you: this is the reward . . . God does not come to us Himself, but He works in someone's heart and makes him do the work He wishes to have done. . . . I now have friends among the Whites. Although there is difference in skin colour, love overcomes all things.' Later when they served tea: 'You see now, God has laid this table for me on earth; I wonder whether He will also lay it for me in heaven.'

While we were there a Bantu constable entered, asking: 'What female bugs are you killing here?', which is an indirect way of asking for brandy. Manini answered: 'Oh, it is only starvation this morning. We have nothing at all. Are you all by yourself?' Constable: 'Yes, I am all by myself. I stole away from the others so that I could come here alone to see what I could get from you.' After he had left, Manini commented: 'These are robbers. They will come and ask five shillings from a poor widow. They take advantage of us. We give them these presents so that they should not arrest us. We must do it to close their mouths.'

A little later there was an old man who wanted some beer: 'There is a White man here, what for?' Manini: 'Get away, it's none of your business. Don't be rude here.' 'I'm not rude, I must ask. Give me some beer.' 'You will not get beer if you are rude here. This is our friend. He has got his own business with us just as you have come to us on business.' Then in Afrikaans: 'Come, give the b—— beer.' He was given some beer in the other room in the yard. Manini explained that it was being rented, but the tenant had agreed that beer customers could be served there, since their own room was very full, and there were always children around.

In the course of the morning four young men, obviously *tsotsis*, also came for a drink. They were also served in the other room, and an old gramophone was taken to them to make music. One of them wore a striking blue-and-white striped shirt, bluish-grey trousers and a pair of good, tawny-coloured shoes. The others were not characteristically dressed, but all wore caps and one was definitely slovenly. A woman also came for some beer, and when we left there was a good-natured old deaf-mute who came to Manini's own room for his drink.

We had come with the express intention of asking a few more questions, but Manini was talkative as usual. 'I have this house through God. I never took up employment since I came here, but always just brewed this beer and sold it, saving the money until I managed to buy this house.' She told of her childhood, how she worked hard at her home in the country, milking cows, which is the work of men. This made her strong so that she has always been able to work hard. Then there was the tale of Nomanase's disappointment when she was to have got married. 'But Satan does not want anything that is good. Satan came in: Nomanase got pregnant, so that marriage was spoilt.' Nomvulo discussed her trouble in getting her reference book in order and the possibilities of employment. Manini went on to tell of the 'husband' who had deserted Nomvulo and was now living with another woman not far away. 'You know, this man was very foolish, because he lost a good wife. She was bringing in money. She is a dressmaker. She can make dresses and "two-pieces" and has made wedding dresses.' She was again busy sewing most of the time.

In the meantime Nomazotshwa had a dish of food. Nomanase served tea, for which Manini ordered her to put a white cloth over the table. Grace was said: 'Lord bless this water which You give us. Amen.' Manini held Nomanase's baby, gave it its bottle, and laid it on the bed where it went to sleep. Nokuzola came in licking a sucker and held it up to Nomvulo to taste. The children would not go outside when told to do so, so Manini produced a little thong stuck under her apron belt, and Nomvulo chased them out of the room, giving one a few flicks around the ears. The old woman scolded her and said she should beat her only across the legs.

Before taking our leave we talked about the significance of the picture of Christ on the cross. 'It is to remind us that we need His help', said Nomvulo, without being able to explain any further. Manini said: 'He came to give us advice', and explained his crucifixion in terms of his saying that He was the Son of God, and that there were wicked people who would not accept Him. When this conversation was over, the old deaf-mute was already waiting for his drink, and we took our leave.

TOWN-BORN RED WOMAN

10. Nosanisi (34, no school education, no church connexions) regards herself as a Red person. Her many bangles and particular arrangement of her turban confirm this, while the Bantu fieldworker remarked: 'She uses swear words without consideration as to who is present. Red people are like this.' She was brought up in the country, largely by her mother's brother and his wife, since her parents died while she was still a small child. Both her parents and foster-parents were Red pagans without any schooling. Her parents never

settled in town, but successively lived in two different reserves in the East London district. She claims to have been born in East London during her mother's temporary stay in town. She herself is obviously quite settled in town.

She is living in concubinage with a man by whom she has two children, the eldest aged 6. She has also had four other illegitimate children by two different men. Only one of these children survived, and is living with the aunt by whom Nosanisi was brought up. Her lover has a country kraal where his wife and seven children stay. The wife, to whom he claims to be married by church rites, sometimes comes to visit him in town. For this purpose he has his own room in another part of the location, but otherwise he mostly stays with Nosanisi. When his children come to town, they also visit him in his own room, 'because he does not want them to see his concubine'.

Nosanisi earns R1.50 (15*s.*) a week with washing and ironing. Her lover is a packer for a wholesale firm where he receives R6.50 (65*s.*) a week. They live in a single room simply furnished with loose pieces of furniture, with a few photographs and a calendar on the wall. Nosanisi's only recreation is drinking; although she mostly drinks kaffir beer, she also takes brandy, and particularly *mrara* (cheap wine). She regularly goes to drink in the bushes in the afternoon, but also drinks at the beer brewers' places in the location.

TSOTSIS

11. An unemployed *tsotsi* of 25, who has passed standard six, says that his father and mother died some years ago. Although his father spent many years in town, he always retained a strong interest in the country. He shares a room with an elder brother who often sleeps in his sweetheart's room. There is one bed and a few pieces of old furniture in the room. When interviewed he was barefooted, wearing faded brown stove-pipe trousers and a striped 'skipper'. He described his daily activities as follows: 'In the morning I visit my friends to discuss their movements for the day: "Where do we go for beer? How shall we get money to buy *mrara* [cheap wine]?" T—— answers: "I have only *ingogo* [1*s.*] in my pocket, but if we go to S—— I might get *i-vili* [2*s.* 6*d.*] which he owes me, and which he promised to return yesterday afternoon." The shilling is just enough to pay for *utshevulani* [a gallon-tin full of beer].[4] I go to buy it, because my friend is still in bed and we spend the morning drinking together. S—— might enter the room just after we have had our first round of drinking and he would join us. Then we would move about the location for some more beer until very late in the afternoon. Sometimes I go to look for work in town.

'Late in the afternoon I might leave my friends and go and see my sweetheart and take her to my room if my elder brother is not there.

'I do not play football or take part in any form of sport. I last attended a bioscope over a year ago. I have just lost interest, and my sweetheart has never asked me to attend one.'

There are four young men whom he regards as his particular friends, and they spend most of their time in each other's company. They were all initiated during the same year, three of them sharing the same initiation hut. 'We were small boys together, bathing together in the Ngcabanga stream. When there were functions at the Peacock Hall, we would go to the hall together and peep through the windows to see what was going on inside, because we had no money to pay admission. A man at the door would come and chase us, and we would

[4] These are slang words, but not confined to *tsotsis*.

run away, but come back later. The one who saw the door-keeper would give the alarm. We enjoyed being chased away, and looked on it as a game. We were about 9 or 10 then. We started smoking together, putting some tobacco in a piece of brown paper, rolling it into a cigarette, and smoking the cigarette in turn. We would stay in the shops till the closing hour, playing with girls who would be sent by their mothers to buy something.

'If one of us has dagga we smoke it together in turn. You feel very strong after smoking it, and there is nothing you fear.' Besides drinking, gambling, and playing draughts, they also while away the time in conversation. 'We discuss the scarcity of money and our sweethearts, each praising his own, how faithful she is to him', but when someone approaches, they stop the conversation. They used to go to the beach with their sweethearts, but scarcely do so now.

12. When another young man of *tsotsi* type (25, standard three) was interviewed by the research assistant, he was 'clumsily dressed', wearing an old 'skipper' and soiled trousers secured with pins. His typical day starts with having something to eat in the morning, after which he goes to his friend D, and they go to look for beer. Next they might go to town 'to look for work', but it does not seem as if they are really in earnest about finding employment. 'At about eleven o'clock I feel tired of walking about town without success, and call at my "cherry's" place of employment in Quigney, where I rest in her room. I stay there till about 2.30 to get food from her, and after that I come back to the location to rejoin D, and we resume our rounds for kaffir beer or brandy if we have enough money. But because of the high price of brandy we drink more of the stuff called *mrara*. There is no form of work I do except occasionally repairing a taxi-driver's car when I am requested to do so. The pay is very small, and sometimes it is only a bottle of *mrara*. What I like about these taxi-owners is that one may ask me to take his passengers to a place like Butterworth when he is too busy to drive the car himself. The long journey is a profitable one, because of "tips" along the road—the extra passengers you pick up on the way, and when you get there, there are always people who want to be taken to the locations around Butterworth. That is why I do not mind a bottle of *mrara* as payment for my services.'

Besides D he has two other friends and the four of them are often together. They smoke dagga, gamble and drink together. 'Whoever has money will buy something and we drink equal shares.' He and one of the friends used to go fishing in the Buffalo River, 'but we no longer do it now'. All four were born and brought up in town. They started smoking together as young boys, and would go to the market together on a Saturday morning to earn something as porters to White housewives. 'We did this kind of work in a competitive spirit, to see who could collect the most pay.' They were also initiated together during the same year.

Asked whether he intended marrying his sweetheart, he said that he would very much like to marry her, but suspected barrenness in her. 'We have been sweethearts for some years and we have been having sexual relations all that time, but without any results. This gives me the impression that if we marry, we are not likely to have children, and children are the main thing in married life.' He admitted having 'four or five' other sweethearts besides this one, 'but all others are what we call "side-lines" who are only used when the real one is not available'.

5

Ceremonial Activity Around the Family

The discussion of ritual and ceremonial activity in the present chapter, and of sex relations and marriage in the following two, is intended to lead up to the analysis of the structure of the urban household and domestic family in chapter 8. Since urban Bantu society appears to be in a fluid, transitional stage, in which broad, inclusive structural groupings are still absent or vague, the household is a suitable starting-point for a sociological study. As a group it is easily discernible, it has at least a degree of internal organization, and it is universal (that is, if we also regard the single persons living, cooking and eating by themselves, as household units for this purpose). In the great majority of urban households falling within the bounds of this study, different types of families form the nuclei of the households. The family will therefore be our main concern in dealing with the social structure.

Apart from family prayers, sacrifices, and other forms of traditional ritual, the important family ceremonies or rituals occurring among the urban Bantu take place in connexion with different stages in the life cycle of the individual. A few remarks about the pattern of this cycle in town are therefore necessary before discussing the actual ceremonies.

GROWING UP IN TOWN

The critical period of babyhood discussed in the following section is terminated by weaning, which usually takes place from the age of eighteen months onward, and which—also for many townspeople—marks the advance to a new status. Toddlers are still largely kept off the streets, playing in and around the house under the eye of mother, grandmother or another older member of the household. From 6 or 7 years onward, most children attend school for at least a few years.

Boys, from the age of 6 years, start playing a great deal in the streets, or elsewhere away from home. 'The smallest boys play with girls. At about 8 they start driving wheels in the streets. At about 9 to 11 they build soap-box cars. A lot of fighting takes place at this stage.' There is a tendency to form loose play-groups consisting of boys of approximately equal age, living in the same area. There is some degree of formalization in these groups, in that one who beats all his equals in fighting is promoted to the group regarded as their immediate seniors. There are also fights between boys from different areas. One, for instance, occurred between Gomorra and Moriva boys about a collision of soap-box cars, when Moriva boys came to drive their cars down the slope below Gomorra. Stones are usually the only weapons used at this stage, but among those inclined to *tsotsi* ways, fighting with knives appears, as well as gambling and smoking. Other group activities of young boys are swimming in the stream, playing around in the bushes, marble games, and competing with each other in rolling down slopes inside old motor-car tyres. Some earn money as caddies and market porters.

Girls stay at home more than boys do, play with dolls, and play at touch, hide-and-seek, and skipping. The separation between boys and girls of this age is only partial. A girl of 17, describing what she remembered doing when she was 8 years old, told the following: 'After school I would go to my friend's house to play with dolls which we used to take to school. We would play with boys who would be the fathers of our dolls, and we would be their mothers. We would have dinner from the one plate which was meant for the child of the home where we would be playing. If we had any money left out of what we had been given for refreshments at school, we would buy fat-cakes and sweets and share them with the fathers, just like the mothers in the house.' Other girls go swimming with the boys.

From an early age most girls start taking their share of domestic duties. 'At 8 years there is no definite thing you are doing. Most of my time I spent playing games like hide-and-seek and basketball, helping my mother in whatever she was doing and going where she was going. At 11 years I scrubbed the floors and cooked food for mother and father on Saturdays. I also planted vegetables and flowers in the garden.'

Another girl, who was not attending school, stayed with her sister, who was a domestic servant in town, looking after the sister's baby. 'I usually played with the baby, singing nice songs for it, that it should sleep and not disturb my sister while she was working. When I was off duty, I came home and cleaned my mother's room. I went to the tap to fetch water as many times as I wanted, because my mother was a beer brewer. When I was 12 I took my sister's child home so that I could help my mother in her business. Other unmarried girls with babies asked me to look after their babies as well. I had to wash napkins and feed the babies.' The daughter of a shopowner was one of the few whose parents had their own domestic servant. 'When I was 8, I only went to school after the servant had washed me. After school I played with my dolls on the veranda till I had my bath and supper. I began to do very few things at 12 years, such as cleaning the kitchen only, and doing my washing just when I felt like doing it, because the work had to be done by the servant and my mother.'

A minority of boys also perform domestic duties such as chopping wood, ironing their clothes, sweeping, polishing and washing-up.

Some children start making love from 11 or 12 years onward. At first there may not be any expression of love more serious than kissing, but often it is not long before sexual intercourse comes into the picture. It seems that by the time they are 15 or 16, many girls have already experienced sexual intercourse. Boys are perhaps slightly older than girls when their love-life starts.[1]

Some girls are given a few informal admonitions by their mothers or sisters on the occasion of their first menstruation, and their dresses might be made slightly longer, but others receive no instruction whatsoever. Boys undergo the ceremonies for initiation into manhood from about 18 years onward. These ceremonies definitely still indicate the attainment of a new status implying a responsibility which is in sharp contrast to the irresponsibility taken for granted in a boy. On the other hand, marriage is less important as a step on the ladder of status than it used traditionally to be. As they grow older, unmarried persons seem to be awarded much the same status as married persons of their own age.

There are occasions such as feasts when there is some differentiation between older people and younger adults, including younger married persons. However,

[1]For a further discussion of pre-marital sexual relations, see chapter 6.

this grouping is vague and informal in town, and there is no ceremonial by which a man is promoted to the company of the 'old men'.

CHILDBIRTH AND EARLY CHILDHOOD

Most town-born women regard their condition during pregnancy rather casually. An unmarried girl, or a married woman who knows she has been rendered pregnant by a man other than her husband, may feel concerned, while an early pregnancy after a previous baby, or economic pressure, may also cause anxiety; but the condition as such is not regarded as one fraught with great dangers. All women are agreed that they should avoid hard work or other forms of excessive physical exertion to avoid miscarriage, but some employed expectant mothers carry on working till the end of the seventh month. On the other hand, light activity and exercise are generally recognized as being beneficial to the child. Very often this attitude is connected with the belief that an expectant mother who sits or lies around too much will experience a protracted or belated birth, or the child will be lazy and sluggish and retarded in its development.

Some mothers believe that they are particularly prone to colds during pregnancy, and should therefore avoid going out at night. A woman of medium educational standard and economic level added the following: 'Do not walk about until very late at night, for there is the danger of walking over the "tracks" of the "snake" [*inyoka*, a witch's familiar] from which miscarriage may result. Do not look through the door or peep through the window. This has the result of difficulty at the birth of the child. It will appear to be coming out and suddenly to retreat or move back and disappear. Do not allow anybody to stand by your side when pregnant, for there will be difficulty at birth.'

A few food taboos are observed. The internal organs of an animal should not be eaten, because this will cause the baby to be entangled in the afterbirth or the umbilical cord. Kidneys will cause baldness in the child, pineapples a rash. *Amarewu*, a very light form of beer, will give the child *isishimnca*, a disorder accompanied by a rash and sometimes also by an upset stomach. Sweet foodstuffs will give the baby pimples or *isishimnca*. Some mothers explicity say they do not observe any food taboos, and have not noticed any ill effect upon their children as a result of this. Many women are aware of the value of a balanced diet. An unmarried mother of five children who had passed her second year for the Junior Certificate, said that she ate plenty of fruit during pregnancy, 'and I particularly liked thick milk and vegetables. I would drink plenty of ginger-beer, especially on hot days. These foods are strongly recommended as being very good for the growth of the unborn child which feeds on mother's milk through the umbilical cord. My late mother told me about these different foodstuffs and many other older women in town say the same.' A Xhosa dish particularly relished by pregnant women consists of a kind of wild spinach (*imifino*), boiled and mixed with mealie meal.

Some women wear maternity clothes during the later stages of pregnancy, but most expectant mothers merely adjust their ordinary clothes. Tightly fitting clothes could result in 'difficulty in birth', 'abnormalities' in the child, or fainting on the part of the mother. 'Tight clothes may even cripple a child.' One mother said she 'avoided suspended clothes and many other things like belts, for it is said they would cause the baby in the stomach to be attached to the walls of the womb, and this would cause difficulty in delivery'. A mother aged 45 also mentioned 'things which cross over the shoulders, or braces, suspended vests or petticoats; for they would cause the child to be born entangled in the afterbirth'.

Women of a higher educational and economic level tend to stress what they learnt in their school hygiene, but some of them also observe forms of avoidance connected with different folk-beliefs. On the other hand there are poor mothers with less education who disregard these taboos.

An older town mother held that attitudes relating to antenatal treatment had changed considerably since she had had her first baby twenty-five years ago. 'Then the people were quite country-minded, because our parents still had very strong links with their brothers in the country, as many of them were country-born. The clinics were unknown or very unpopular with the Xhosa community, for they strongly believed in their customs then.' She holds that nowadays taboos are not observed and 'all the pregnant people go to doctors or to the clinic'. It is true that the majority of town mothers make use of the antenatal services offered at the municipal clinic, but they often comment adversely on the harsh and unsympathetic treatment received at the hands of Bantu clinic nurses. It is said that some women taken to be of high status in the location, such as the wives of ministers and teachers, prefer to consult a private doctor, because they are embarrassed, not only by mixing with the 'lower' types, but also by the behaviour of the nurses, which they find humiliating. On the other hand, an unmarried mother with only standard one education, said she did not attend the clinic, because 'the people who go to the clinic have to have very nice underclothes, so that they should not be made fun of by the clinic nurses. They shout and laugh at those with untidy and ragged clothes, and scold them for having too great a liking for sexual intercourse, saying that they should rather stay away from the men and improve their economic position. They forget that the poor girls have the same feelings as they have. Nature is one for every human being.' Women who do not attend the clinic or consult a doctor receive hardly any antenatal treatment. The one quoted above remarked: 'Fortunately I never had worries during pregnancy, otherwise my mother would have shaken [*hlukuhla*] my stomach to make the child settle properly inside.'

Some mothers prepare an elaborate layette for their babies. Most outfits include at least diapers and babies' blankets, nightdresses, and maybe vests, a towel, soap, 'Vaseline', baby powder, a bath or wash-basin, and a pail or bucket. A poor unmarried mother who had passed standard one made 'dresses' and diapers, and 'the child's father gave me money to buy babies' blankets which were of a cheap type, because he does not have much money himself. I used the old baths and buckets and kept a lot of soap in store.'

Women who attend the clinic during pregnancy are usually confined in their own homes, where they are attended to by a clinic nurse, this being the most common procedure among town-born mothers. When complications are expected or arise during labour, they are sent to hospital. Some choose to go to hospital of their own accord. Those who summon neither doctor nor nurse are attended to at their own homes by two or three older women, usually a mother and close relatives or friends. 'I preferred my mother and next-door neighbour for my delivery, because I was not to pay any money. They are more sympathetic than either the doctor or the nurse. They see no wrong conditions as a stranger would and from them I learn more of what is done when one acts as a midwife.' Some do not favour husbands' relatives, because 'they are untrustworthy and always hate daughters-in-law', and are therefore suspected of witchcraft, or may be harsh to the mother.

Although the belief in witchcraft and other traditional beliefs flourishes in the realm of childbirth, town women would not call in a 'native' doctor during labour. An unmarried mother with medium education and income said she went to hospital for the birth of her first child, because 'I was very much afraid and therefore wanted to be nearer doctors in case something of a serious nature happened. I have belief in native doctors and witches, but in cases of childbirth all women in town seem to doubt the knowledge of the native doctor or that of experienced ordinary women in this field. Moreover the native doctor and ordinary women are too boastful: your name will be mentioned at every discussion and all the complications will be divulged' to impress people with their ability. Town women find this humiliating. Women with more than average education stress their confidence in 'knowledge of the Whites' and the need for 'proper training' on the part of persons attending to a woman in labour.

Fear and anxiety during labour are regarded as disgraceful cowardice. A young woman, who was attended to by a nurse 'who is very good and kind to me', said that some nurses could be harsh if patients did not make preparations according to their requirements. Moreover, 'if a mother experiences difficulty in giving birth through fear, they shout and scold at her. They ultimately call for an ambulance, and when the woman goes to the clinic again she becomes a centre of laughter and is made an example of as being a real coward.' Having an ambulance called for one during labour is regarded as a disgrace in itself.

None of the mothers who had been attended to by nurses had experienced any unpleasantness, but time and again one was told of the impatience and harsh treatment some people receive from clinic nurses, 'more especially those they look down upon'. The only adverse comment recorded about hospital treatment was against the separation of mother and child, because of the fear of babies getting 'mixed up'. Moreover, 'babies are left to cry a lot there, and I cannot tolerate hearing my baby crying the whole day'.

When a mother is delivered in her own home, newspapers are often used to avoid blood being spilt. 'Blood of the internal organs should not be smeared on anything.' The mother's bedding is carefully washed after confinement to remove any blood stains, and the blood-stained papers, as well as the afterbirth, are buried in the room if it has a mud floor, or else in the yard. This is done by the woman attending to the mother, usually at night, to avoid being seen by anybody. Often this care is taken because of the belief in the activity of witches or sorcerers, known as *ukuthathela*, in which matter coming from the victim's person is treated by the witch to harm the person. The afterbirth and blood lost at birth are particularly sought by witches in this connexion.

Ten days are regarded as the normal period of confinement, but sometimes it is shorter, as when economic necessity compels the mother to return to work after a few days, or when the attendants are too busy to nurse the mother for the full ten days. One particular woman is usually in attendance on mother and baby throughout the confinement. She is commonly called *umfukamisi* (derived from the causative form of the verb *ukufukama*, to lie in).[2] *Umfukamisi*

[2] Also used of the brooding of a bird. Confinement is *ifuku*, and the place of confinement *efukwini*.

must be a particularly trustworthy woman, again because of the fear of *ukuthathela* and other forms of witchcraft, and the woman's own mother is regarded as the most suitable person. A young married mother of four children who is a qualified teacher had her first baby in hospital, but with her other three children she was confined at home under the care of a nurse. 'In each case my mother was *umfukamisi*. I always wanted my mother to be present for she does everything for me with sympathy and parental love. She is whole-heartedly trusted in every respect. She can never "poison" the food of my baby [*ukudlisa iyeza*, lit. feed medicines, a standard phrase for a particular method of sorcery] through envy or because of being bribed by other people to do so.'

Many women regard the traditionally observed seclusion of the mother and baby during confinement as the ideal, but when housing space is restricted to one or two rooms it is not possible to reserve a room for their exclusive use. Nevertheless it is still common to exclude unfamiliar women and all menfolk, except the confined woman's husband, father and brothers, and in some cases even these males are excluded. The custom is still consciously observed as a precaution against misfortune. Not only could hostile persons wilfully engage in witchcraft or sorcery against mother and child, but the mere association of persons with witchcraft and medicines is also dangerous to babies. A married woman with standard six education remarked that 'a man may have medicines with him, and they may injure the child who is still very tender to the effect of strong medicines. Some people are known as "bad people" [a recognized term for witches], because they always have bad medicines with them which may cause the child to cry of fear.' A semi-Red unmarried mother said that during her confinement 'no men were allowed to come in, because by custom it is believed that the baby is very delicate, and could easily be harmed by smells of medicines carried by certain men. Some have familiars of witchcraft [*izilo zokuthakatha*] which could easily destroy the child before it is resistant to them. Some people have the dangerous shadows [*izithunzi ezinzima*, lit. heavy shadows, sometimes acquired by the use of medicines which make them fearful] which could cause a baby to cry the whole day. Even among women there are such, but not as many as men, who use medicines for many things. If someone should disregard the privacy of the confinement, all the men of the neighbourhood would be informed to take action. He could even be assaulted. He would be regarded as *umthakathi* [a witch or sorcerer].'

An unauthorized person who consciously disregards the privacy of confinement immediately invites suspicion of his being a witch. 'If someone disregarded one's confinement it would be regarded as *umhlola* [an evil omen]. Only a witch would do this sort of thing, and if there are male relatives here, they would have no alternative but to beat up the intruder, thereby averting the coming misfortune.' A young widow who is a teacher, remarked as follows: 'Cases of people intruding *kwa mdlezana* [the place of confinement, lit. at the suckling mother's] are very rare, for Xhosa people have a particular respect for this place. It is one of those places where a Xhosa will not subject himself to unnecessary suspicion, because if anything happens the question will arise: "What did so-and-so want here?" Anyway, as far as I am concerned, I do not mind who comes in, as long as the person has reason to come.'

Some people connect confinement with the dropping of the umbilical cord. They believe it must be carefully disposed of to avoid its falling into the hands of a witch or sorcerer. Should the baby be taken out of the room before it has dropped, it could come off unobserved, where a hostile person might lay hands on it. Rest, the opportunity for the mother to recuperate, and privacy from unmarried persons who should not know all about childbirth, were also mentioned by informants as purposes of confinement. During confinement the mother should concentrate all her attention on the child, and not undertake any work other than the care of the baby. One informant saw in it a parallel to the seclusion of boys and diviners during their respective forms of initiation, of girls during the *intonjane* ceremony observed in the country, and of brides before marriage. 'Some say this is done for *intlahla* [light complexion] which will make people admire one.'

On the termination of confinement at home the room is usually thoroughly cleaned and the floor is scrubbed, polished, or, in the case of a mud floor, smeared with fresh dung. The smearing is 'for the sake of cleanliness and to hide the spot where the afterbirth and other things like the umbilical cord are buried, so that witches and their familiars will not be able to trace the place where these have been buried'. 'When I go out of confinement, I scrub the floor of the room, wash my body and my baby's body, and make sure that I do not leave on the floor anything dirty which will betray me as a careless person. People usually like a suckling woman to be very tidy, and their odours, if unclean, tend to nauseate people.'

At the end of, or during, confinement neighbours, friends and relatives bring gifts for the mother and child. Often these are in the form of cash which is termed 'soap' for the baby or mother, and many people actually give soap, but the gifts often take the form of articles commonly included in a baby's layette. Others donate groceries like candles, tea, sugar or meal. These gifts are mostly regarded as an expression of congratulation and gratitude for the birth of the child and the mother's safe delivery. 'Many people send gifts in money from as far abroad as Johannesburg and Cape Town. This is very common for a first-born baby, when not only the grandparents and the parents are excited, but other well-wishers also. The gifts are to praise [*ukuncoma*] the parents of the child. These gifts are as good as Christmas presents: if there was a reason for the Wise Men from the East to bring presents to Jesus, this bears the same significance. These gifts are an expression of appreciation for the precious gift. A baby is a great pride of any good-hearted person.' Some people refer to these gifts as *ukubona umntwana* (seeing the child). 'The face of the child is not uncovered till the person pays something. This is only done for relatives or very close friends.' Occasionally the mother of a new-born baby receives a dress from her own mother. 'My mother bought me a printed dress, saying that it was the customary dress for suckling mothers coming out of confinement.' A father of an illegitimate child may also donate something soon after the baby's birth.

Where ordinary women act as midwives and assistants to *umfukamisi*, they receive no payment, but after the termination of confinement some mothers prepare a simple treat for them, known as *izibembe*. 'This is always baked bread, cakes, sweets, tea and cool drinks.' They may be joined by other friends and neighbours. Some people believe that if a woman has not been attended to during confinement by her own mother or grandmother, but by a friend who offered to help her, it is essential that this *umfukamisi* should receive a special gift, usually in the form of cash, which is known as *intlambazandla* (washing of hands). 'As this woman has been handling you, and sometimes helping in washing your dirty linen, the general belief among us is that her contact with you or any of your articles of clothing renders it an obligation that her hands be washed, failing which her contact with you or your clothes has the power to create ill-feeling between the two of you. This ill-feeling is unavoidable and neither of you can say it is caused by this or that. You will quarrel over something very insignificant, and the only cure will be to give *intlambazandla*.'

The traditional custom of slaughtering a sacrificial goat (*ukubingelela*) after the termination of confinement is not often observed. In some cases it has become merged with the custom of some church people to hold a baptismal dinner. Most children receive baptism at an early age, but some unmarried mothers have several unbaptized children because their church discipline does not allow children to be baptized while the mothers continue to have loose liaisons. Other churches baptize such children, even when the mother belongs to a different church. Some form of celebration usually takes place after the christening of the child. It may be an informal party for which there are no special invitations, where tea and cakes are served, informal congratulations are expressed, and, perhaps, one or two prayers are said. With others it takes the form of a baptismal dinner which may vary considerably in its details. It may be little more than a specially prepared meal, consisting of meat bought from the butcher, dried and fresh cooked vegetables, cool drinks and sweets, without any speeches, or it may be an elaborate affair, marked by the slaughtering of an animal, brewing of beer and speeches.

A couple who, on the birth of their daughters, had held dinners without inviting people or slaughtering anything, specially slaughtered an animal and prepared an elaborate feast after the mother had given birth to a son. 'My husband was very excited because he was very keen to have a boy. He invited all his friends to the dinner. He brewed beer and had some liquor [Western]. There was meat, cakes, and soft drinks for the non-drinkers. There were church people also. The drinkers drank outside in a place representing the *inkundla* [the open meeting place in a country homestead] and cattle-kraal. Many gifts were given to the baby. Money went up to two pounds, with many other gifts like toys and drapery. My husband opened the proceedings by saying that he thanked God and the ancestors in responding to his request for a baby boy. He liked a boy, because the name of Tyamzashe [the father's lineage] will not come to an end if males are born. The people should not wonder why he mixed God and the ancestors, for God was the greatest of all ancestors. They sent the request to God when one referred it to them. An old man who is a neighbour said that the ancestors of the Amangwevu clan [the father's clan] proved that they liked me for making me give birth to a boy and satisfying my husband. The Amangwevu people were pleased with me, and would never allow my husband to ill-treat me, for I have retained the name of the Amangwevu. I had done all required of me. I should not forget the love of God on my part. He hoped that my husband would praise God, for He had given him everything he desired.' There were more speeches in a similar vein. Among those present were a brother and maternal cousin of the father, and 'the old men of the neighbourhood'. (Mother East London-born, standard six education; a full member of an independent Bantu church. Father country-born, regarded as church adherent, but does not attend church.)

Even in the case of an illegitimate child, the baptismal dinner may be the occasion for stressing kinship ties, in this case the patrilineal ties of the maternal grandfather whom an illegitimate child often regards as its father. An unmarried mother of the Limakwe clan (passed standard seven and member on trial in church) described the baptismal dinner held for her child. Nothing was slaughtered, but beer was brewed. A member of the clan spoke in the following trend: 'Well done, you of the clan of Limakwe! Although we are in town, the place of the White man, we must not deviate from our customs. Whatever may be said, the child for whom we have gathered here is an additional member of the clan of Limakwe. I am sure the mother's father fully realizes this, which is evidenced by the fact that beer has been brewed in spite of their being church people.'

Eighteen months is the most common age at which town mothers wean their babies. Occasionally a baby is weaned before it is a year old. The tendency is therefore toward a shorter suckling period than the traditional two years or more, but a young widow who holds a teacher's qualification claimed that she weaned her child at the age of 3. The traditional rule that a mother should abstain from sexual relations until her baby is weaned is still observed by some. Others abstain for some months, but do not wait till the weaning stage to resume relations. An unmarried mother said that when she is suckling, 'I meet my boy friend [for sexual relations] only once in two weeks. I am only afraid of pregnancy when I have a baby. To have two babies who are both small and need nursing would be a great nuisance.' It is also felt that having two babies in quick succession would result in the neglect of the elder one, and some people simply regard it as a disgrace. Besides wanting to avoid pregnancy, many women also have the belief that intercourse has an injurious effect on the baby. During intercourse, or even when she becomes sexually excited, the mother's blood becomes heated—so the belief runs—and this 'spoils' her milk. The 'bad' milk may upset the child's stomach, and in any case has a weakening effect on it, and causes it to lose weight. A mother who weaned her baby at eighteen months said that sexual relations could be resumed at ten months, 'when the child is strong enough to resist the bad milk', but even then 'we have to limit ourselves: our usual practice is only once a week'. Some think it important to have sexual relations only with the father of the child while still suckling, because he will have more consideration for mother and child and endeavour to avoid pregnancy. There are mothers who no longer believe that intercourse during the lactation period has a detrimental effect. An unmarried mother who maintained that she does not abstain from intercourse held that 'many women sleep with men while suckling, but their children are very healthy and look nice. Sexual intercourse is only prohibited to prevent pregnancy.'

Babies are usually weaned by applying a bitter substance to the mother's nipples. Two species of aloe are commonly used, but some mothers use cascara. In addition the child may be given sweets or food for which it has shown a particular liking. Most babies receive bottle-feeding in addition to breast-feeding from an early stage. Complete artificial feeding is uncommon. The custom of shaving the baby's hair when it has been weaned is still very commonly observed. To some people it is merely a custom without any known significance. Others recognize it as a sign that the child has passed from one stage to another. It is no longer an infant (*usana*), but is now a child (*umntwana*). The shaved hair is commonly burnt or buried, in some cases in the belief that witches could use it to make the child insane if it should fall into their hands. To others the burning also is just another custom. A woman who is a teacher also burnt the child's hair, but explicitly denied that it was a precaution against witchcraft. 'I burnt it to destroy it, because I do not like hair being scattered about.' The wife of a school principal who has passed her Junior Certificate, said the hair of her child was burnt after being cut, to avoid witchcraft, but added: 'Although my husband and I do not take these beliefs very seriously we must take care of what has not happened', implying that it may yet happen if the precautions are neglected.

For the common ailments in children like diarrhoea, excessive windiness (*umoya*), sore eyes (*imvuma*), teething, and different forms of chest complaints, mothers commonly consult the municipal clinic and occasionally a doctor. Patent medicines are also used in some cases. Commonly known traditional cures such as dropping mother's milk into a child's sore eyes are also applied by some. For teething one mother ties *itantyisa* (a shell necklace) round the neck. Referring to sore eyes, another woman says: 'My husband usually gets a Xhosa medicine for this.' One mother consults a white female herbalist who has good medicine for flatulence.

A substantial proportion of town mothers believe that certain ailments lie outside the scope of medical doctors, and although they readily make use of Western medical treatment in other cases, they resort to traditional Bantu doctors in these. This is particularly the case when witchcraft or sorcery is suspected. After mentioning the use of eye lotions bought from the chemist for sore eyes, milk of magnesia or a doctor for stomach disorders, baby powders for teething, a standard six unmarried mother said: 'I would go to Xhosa doctors when I notice that the child is bewitched, for example, by stomach medicine [of sorcery] which could not be identified by medical doctors. Witches and their familiars do exist in town. There would not be such beliefs if there were not such things.' An unmarried mother with Junior Certificate, whose own mother is a schoolteacher, mentioned the ordinary diseases for which the clinic is consulted, and added that excessive crying may be caused by the baby's 'seeing bad things which are invisible to the grown-up people: it sees *inyoka yabafazi* [the snake-familiar kept by female witches] and *u-Hili* or *Tikoloshe* [different names for a very common familiar]. A baby also senses a bad person who is in possession of *istofile* [a small tin in which medicines are kept]. Such ailments [caused by seeing things] are best treated by a herbalist who burns something on the fireplace and the smoke from this has the power to drive away the familiars.' Some mothers also believe that a baby's refusing to take the breast may be caused by *Tikoloshe* or the snake-familiar feeding on the mother's breast when she is asleep. 'In this case the services of a diviner are employed to say where the familiars come from. They could come from elsewhere and might have come across the mother accidentally during their wanderings, or they may be the property of the mother given to her by her own mother. The diviner will give medicines to chase away these dirty things.' A baby may also become upset by 'being walked over' (*ukuhanjwa*) by a snake-familiar. The snake may be driven away by smearing the baby's body with a pulp made by grinding the bulb known as *isibumba-mpunzi* (a kind of wild garlic). It has an offensive smell which is believed to be repulsive to familiars also.

Where the belief in witchcraft persists, babies are regarded as particularly susceptible to attacks of witches. A town-born wife of a teacher who passed her Junior Certificate said that a baby should have its own towel, basin and bath, because if it uses the same implements as other people 'there is the danger of the baby contracting misfortune [*amashwa*] from adults.[3] The life of a baby is one of innocence [*ubumsulwa*] but that of an adult is defiled [*bunezinto ezimdaka*, lit., it has dirty things[4]]. This is our belief, and I firmly believe in it.' The same mother holds that 'you must never attend a funeral or any social gathering with your baby on your back. A baby has no resistance and easily contracts diseases. When there is a gathering of all sorts of women, who knows the good ones and who the bad ones? The smell of a medicine which some bad women keep in *istofile* is sufficient to choke your baby to death or cause a disease known among Xhosa as *isifo sabantwana* [the disease of the children], a form of fits.' For this she would consult a Coloured woman in the location who is regarded as a specialist in the treatment of this malady, whereas other common ailments in children 'are treated at the clinic as far as I am concerned'.

The intensive interviews with town mothers on childbirth and infants' diseases substantiated the impressions from the general survey as discussed in chapter 3. There is no evidence of resistance to the medical services introduced by Whites as such, and medical doctors, clinics and chemists are readily patronized. There are some who combine this acceptance of Western techniques with the denial of any belief in the existence of witchcraft or the ability of native doctors. Among the mothers interviewed on childbirth, those who expressed disbelief had all proceeded as far as standard seven or further in school, but some well-educated women make no secret of their belief in witchcraft and sorcery. Others 'do not take it seriously' but nevertheless observe certain customs, so as not to take chances. With others it lies dormant but not dead. 'Everybody of Bantu descent believes this, though some think they are too civilized to believe in witchcraft, but when even such people take ill, they believe in it.' However, many women openly combine the acceptance of Western medical techniques with a strong belief in witchcraft and the efficacy of traditional methods of treatment in this respect. Even a semi-Red town mother took this inclusive attitude that 'I would go to the clinic, [medical] doctor, and diviner and use any medicine that I believe would help my child'.

BOYS' INITIATION

Boys' initiation is the traditional institution most tenaciously adhered to by the urban Xhosa-speaking people. It is still almost universally observed, even by youths born and brought up in town. Some of them go to relatives in the country to be initiated with boys of that neighbourhood, but many are initiated in town, where most of the traditional ceremonial is still observed.[5] During June–July 1959, thirteen seclusion huts were traced in the bushes on the outskirts of the location and it may well be that there were a few more which escaped our notice. Ten huts visited had an average of 4.3 youths per hut so that it may safely be said that at least fifty boys were initiated in town during that winter.[6] Their ages ranged from 19 to 23. About two-thirds of them were

[3] Traditional Xhosa belief also has it that if one washes in the water of a fortunate or influential person, one may 'contract' some of his characteristics.

[4] This is often a reference to witchcraft.

[5] About thirty years ago initiation ceremonies did not take place in town (Hunter, op. cit., p. 477).

[6] Permission has to be obtained from the municipal commonage ranger for the erection of these huts. No records are kept of the permits issued, but the ranger regarded the number of applications received during the 1959 winter as normal.

East London-born youths. Occasionally a scholar is initiated during the longer Christmas holidays to avoid interrupting his attendance at school.

A number of boys and young men of varying educational level, including scholars as well as employed and unemployed youths, were questioned about their reasons for having been or wanting to be initiated. The following remarks by a scholar in his final year for the Senior Certificate, who had been initiated three years earlier, reflects most of the reasons mentioned in these interviews. 'I went to be initiated because it is a national tradition [*isiko lesizwe*]. It is good because it gives one a recognized status as a member of society. It allows one the privileges of marriage and independence from the rule of one's parents. Among the Xhosa, where initiation is regarded as a necessity, an old uncircumcised man is never dignified until he is initiated. In fact, he becomes an object of laughter [if not circumcised], and they usually say an uncircumcised person becomes half-witted in the long run. It is because he is made a scarecrow and laughed at. The idea of a new world makes one become responsible. Other black nations do not circumcise at all, and they are disregarded by the Xhosa, taken to be unreliable and incomplete persons. When a person comes from initiation he comes back prepared to abandon careless life and intends to live a new life as a responsible member of society. I do not know whether there could be any other belief or practice which would make a person change his manner of living as quickly as this one. If one had been an undesirable member of society previously, after circumcision one becomes a trusted, dignified and respected man.'

In town, then, as in the country, initiation is still commonly regarded as an honourable traditional custom indispensable for making the transition from the irresponsible stage of boyhood to the status and responsibility of manhood. The traditional view that an uncircumcised boy is an 'unclean being' (*inqambi*), a 'dog', or a 'half-witted person' (*umntu onengqondo engaphelele*) still prevails, and therefore 'no good can be expected of him' and 'he is not disgraced by doing shameful things'. Yet, although an uncircumcised man or youth is often looked down upon by the circumcised, the cleavage is not as sharp among townspeople as it is among the rural Xhosa, so that newly initiated young men often continue their friendships with uninitiated youths much the same as before they were initiated.

The privileges attached to the new status follow traditional patterns in some respects. Although it would be possible for an uncircumcised man to get married, most people still recognize initiation as an essential prerequisite to marriage, and if an uncircumcised man got married, a stigma would be attached to the couple in the eyes of most people. Further, initiation is still commonly regarded as opening the way to the attainment of recognition and respect in location society. 'If he does not go [to initiation] at all, he will never be regarded as a fully grown-up man; he is not allowed to marry; he is despised. The people will not listen to his word, so he cannot enjoy a fully developed life.' 'Initiation is a ladder to humanity [*ubuntu*] and respect.' Recognition as a man implies the right to voice an opinion at public meetings and informal gatherings. 'One is promoted to the full status of being a resident [*ummi*] who may have a say in location affairs.' 'It allows one's word in every social matter to be listened to.' The independence from parental control mentioned above represents a new interpretation of the privileges of the initiated. Another informant said: 'It is the road and gate to independence [*ukuzimela*, lit., standing for oneself] in all spheres of life.' It is significant that both these informants were scholars in their final Senior Certificate year.

That the new status implies responsibility was referred to in one way or another by every informant. Most men regard the ceremonies as having a definite effect on initiates to bring about the change from irresponsibility to the responsible behaviour associated with manhood. 'Initiation is very good, for it makes people change their childhood behaviour and they become very responsible.' It is described as 'a school to mould [*ukwakha*, lit., build] the unclean people to attain understanding'. This change does not seem to be regarded as being effected by some magical influence of circumcision as such, and some informants even revealed an appreciation of the psychological nature of its effect. 'The operation itself does not change a person's character, but the meaning implied in initiation reminds one that one should be a well-balanced citizen [*ummi ozinzileyo*].' Some regard the admonitions given to boys during initiation as the vital influence making for change of character. 'The operation by itself does nothing to mould one's character, but it is a sign that one has been admonished.' 'It is not the actual circumcision which makes one a changed man, but the admonitions made to one.'

It is recognized, however, that in many cases the ceremonies fail to effect any permanent change, particularly among town youths of the *tsotsi* type. It is among them, then, that one also finds the sceptics who doubt the effectiveness of the ceremonies. Their comments also reveal insight into the psychological factors involved. A typical *tsotsi* who had been initiated himself remarked: 'Initiation makes one a changed person. If before initiation you were reckless and irresponsible, you try to do good, *because you are expected to do it.* It is the belief that initiation has the power to make you a better man, that helps *amakrwala* [the newly initiated] to behave well, even if their good behaviour will not last long. I say this because in town young men resort to the things they used to do when they were boys. Some will go to the extent of associating with uncircumcised boys in spite of the admonitions received when they came out of initiation. From what I have seen, initiation in town does not make any difference, because hardly three months after initiation these young *amakrwala* get drunk openly, and start waylaying womenfolk at night with the intention of robbing or raping' (23 years old, standard three, unemployed). Another one who still intended being initiated, said: 'Personally I do not think initiation has any effect on anyone. It has no power to change you. You remain what you were when you were a boy. Take *amakrwala* in town: they join the company of unitiated boys and walk about the location together, behaving in the same manner [as the uncircumcised]. They also get drunk, and at night you hear of a woman who has been raped by *tsotsis*. Among these *tsotsis* there were *amakrwala*. Initiation helps only those who were good boys and who were determined to live a good life' (19 years old, standard three, unemployed).

What is regarded as responsible behaviour is reflected by the admonitions given to the initiates on different occasions in the course of the ceremonies, but particularly when they finally come out of seclusion. It should be appreciated that there is a strong element of rural-minded persons among those present on these occasions. Not only are town-born boys initiated together with migrant youths from the country but even the contacts of town boys who attend—fathers, relatives, neighbours—often include migrants whose homes are still in the country, both School people and Reds. At least some of these men also address the boys, so that the sentiments inculcated on these occasions often have a strong flavour of the traditional values still recognized by country people.

The following summary of three speeches held at a coming out ceremony in town was related a few days later by a man who acted as 'father' to one of the boys, his sister's illegitimate town-born son.

A. 'You have today entered into manhood. A circumcised man is a man of various responsibilities which cannot be evaded, but must be faced and overcome. The burning of your seclusion hut and your things represent the casting away of all your old bad habits of boyhood.

'A man must not sleep or spend the night away from home unless there is good reason to do it; he must always be at home to see what things have gone wrong, what needs his attention. If you keep these admonitions you cannot go wrong in life. You were fortunate in having M—— as your *inchibi* [surgeon] for he is a man from whose hands good things have come. He has a wife and children who are very well cared for by him. He is in employment, and not a loafer, and I hear he has a home in the country as well. Follow in his footsteps.'

B. 'Now that you are men, much is expected of you. A knife is only used for eating meat, and for nothing else. A young man does not argue with a man who is old enough to be his father. Do not embrace a girl in full view of the public. Have respect for old age.

'In a man's life there are three very important stages when elderly men come together to talk to him. You are today going through the first stage; the second stage will be when you get married, and the third stage is when the ancestors have called you to them; that is death. On that occasion we will not speak to you, but speak about your deeds.'

C. (a man speaking on behalf of the master of the initiation ceremonies [*usosuthu*]). 'During your period of seclusion no mischievous deeds on your part were reported to me. This, my sons, gives me hope, because evidently you kept the words these men said to you when you were circumcised. [There is some admonition immediately after circumcision.] I therefore have reason to believe that the words which have been said now have fallen into your ears and have been locked into your hearts. It is not the actual cutting of your foreskin that matters, but these admonitions.'

The responsibilities of manhood mentioned here are, then, the proper care of one's home and family, diligence, not indulging in violence (stabbing with knives), and respect for age. Young men discussing their own initiation mentioned similar admonitions, as well as injunctions to aid one's parents, to try to improve one's living conditions, and to participate in local meetings. We have also observed the implication that circumcised men are expected not to partake in excessive drinking, robbery and rape.

The normal procedure in town is for a boy to express the wish to be initiated. The parents then make the necessary preparations. A son of an unmarried mother may be assisted by his mother's brother or another patrilineal kinsman of the mother. It often happens, however, that a boy joins a group of boys being initiated, without the consent or knowledge of his parents. All the preparations he need make are to obtain the consent of the men responsible for the ceremonies of the group and to buy the special blankets needed during the seclusion period. This usually happens when the parents are not in a financial position to meet the necessary expenses, and put off the initiation after the boy has indicated his desire to attend. This procedure on the part of the boy is referred to as 'stealing oneself' (*ukuziba*). In the way the ceremonies are performed in town, there is no occasion when the physical father's presence is essential. In the ceremony observed by the author, the father of one of the boys who was, in fact, the 'owner' of the lodge (*usosuthu*) or master of ceremonies, was absent at work during all the important stages of the ceremonies, and a patrilineal kinsman acted as his substitute.

The ceremonies of a group of four youths, two of them born and brought up in East London, were followed step by step, the author personally observing the most important stages, excepting the 'coming out', and it was remarkable how closely they resembled the ceremonies as performed in the country according to the fairly recent observations in the Keiskammahoek reserve.[7] There are the same major officiants, the master of the initiation ceremonies or 'owner' of the seclusion hut (*usosuthu*), being one of the boys' fathers, the surgeon (*inchibi*), and the guardian (*ikhankatha*). There were, however, several men who attended to the boys during their seclusion and were referred to as *amakhankatha*. The different stages in the ceremonies are also the same.

June and July are the common months for performing the ceremonies, and those observed commenced during the first week-end of June. The ceremonies started with the customary shaving of the boys' hair, undressing, and covering of the body with a blanket only, while the thong which is later used to tie the penis in position after circumcision is already tied round the waist. The custom that the youth does not wear the discarded clothes again after initiation is also observed in town, though it is said that some who have expensive clothes do wear them again later. The *ukungcamisa* slaughtering takes place, at which the boys each eat the portion known as *intsonyama* which figures so commonly in Xhosa ritual. This is performed for each boy separately at his own home. A small enclosure of branches is usually specially built in the yard to represent the cattle-kraal where the ritual takes place. Occasionally it takes place in one of the kraals in the location. Some boys are also given an *ubulunga* necklace which serves as a protective charm.

There were three Fingo boys, and one Xhosa, and the customary tribal differentiations were observed, the Fingo boys having *ukungcamisa* on the Friday afternoon, with the customary dancing and singing known as *umguyo* at their homes during the night, and their circumcision following early the next morning shortly before sunrise. For the Xhosa youth there was no *umguyo*, the *ukungcamisa* taking place on Saturday morning and circumcision at two in the afternoon. While a group of men accompanied each boy to the place of circumcision in the bushes just outside the location, young men playfully fenced with sticks but were warned not to start fighting in earnest. A stream was crossed where each boy had to take a dip. Near the seclusion hut the boy was made to sit down, the surgeon unobtrusively emerged from behind a bush, hiding his knife behind his back, and in the flash of a moment completed the operation, after which the boy had to say 'I am a man'. The surgeon bandaged the wound, the boy's face was smeared with mud and he was told to walk to the seclusion hut in a stooping posture. In the hut the boys were briefly admonished, both in the morning and in the afternoon, mostly about their behaviour during seclusion, but with references here and there to their attainment of manhood and its responsibilities. The hut, which had been completed

[7] Wilson, Monica (and others), *Social Structure, Keiskammahoek Rural Survey*, vol. III, 1952, pp. 199–220.

the previous day, consisted of a framework of saplings, covered with a layer of reeds and another of grass, with an outer layer of sacking. (Most of the other huts visited were also covered with sacking or old canvas.)

The customary *izichwe* (or *izigqutsu*) leaves were used to bandage the wounds, and later on an outer cover of mealie husks was used, but immediately after the operation on the Fingo boys, a whitish powder was applied to the wound, it was bandaged with a piece of brown paper torn from a paper bag, and tied up with a thread of cotton. The guardians sometimes attended to the wounds, but the surgeon also kept on attending to the boys personally. At some stages he seemed to be in control of the activities and when two guardians arrived late for the *ukojiswa* ceremony he punished them by inflicting a few strokes on the hand with a switch.

During the seclusion the boys—now called *abakwetha*—observed the customary taboos on certain foods, such as meat, beans, bread, potatoes, fruit, and salt, as well as clear water and tea. They drank water made muddy by the addition of earth from molehills and during the first week they ate only boiled whole mealies. On the Saturday following circumcision the slaughtering known as *ukojiswa* (roasting) was performed, and they again ate the *intsonyama* which had been roasting on branches of *umthathi* (sneezewood), after which they were free to eat meat and some of the other foodstuffs which were taboo during the initial period. They observed the smearing of their bodies with white clay, the taboo on the use of certain words and the use of *abakwetha* substitutes, and certain customary responses to questions or the calls of men approaching the hut. The usual troop of younger boys were always hanging around the hut but were ordered away when the wounds were treated. On the day after *ukojiswa* they were visited by girl-friends who had not yet had children, who gave them new names. They further mentioned the following rules which they had to observe or which applied to them: to sit down when smoking; not to walk about singing; not to whistle or shout loudly; not to eat fowls, wild birds or honey from a beehive; not to walk about unsmeared (with clay); to hide when they see women; not to quarrel in the hut; that the fire in the hut must be kept burning the whole night; that the ashes should not be thrown outside, but buried inside the hut; that a woman who has had a child may not come near the hut; and that boys may not watch while their wounds are being treated.

After the wounds had healed enough to allow them to start moving about, they spent their time collecting firewood and the leaves used for treating the wounds, hunting birds with catapults, visiting other *abakwetha* and playing a traditional game known as *iceya.* One or two were sometimes found reading cheap English novels. They did not receive any instruction during seclusion. Later on they walked about without their blankets in the neighbourhood of the hut, wearing only a piece of old blanketing as an apron covering the private parts.

Some of the boys intended returning to their previous jobs at the beginning of August, so that the ceremonies were concluded on the last Saturday in July, the seclusion having lasted seven weeks. At the coming-out ceremony, the boys had to wash in the stream, were anointed with fat and were given new blankets and a black stick. Their seclusion hut was burnt and they were taken to *usosuthu's* home where they were given the admonitions quoted earlier, and received small gifts. They spent the night together there, and were escorted to their own homes the next day, where there was feasting and more admonition.

There does seem to be a certain degree of laxity in the observance of all the ceremonial detail in town. At the Xhosa boy's circumcision, the man acting as his father, and another male relative, both members of the Xhosa royal clan, came up in the rear of the party escorting the boy to circumcision. The operation was performed before they had arrived on the scene and without the boy's having been made to wash in the stream, and this was adversely commented upon. The boy's guardian also regarded the fact that *usosuthu*'s deputy undertook the anointing of the boys with fat on his own accord, instead of someone being specially elected beforehand, as a deviation from the 'proper' custom. He also mentioned the fact that the official guardian of the boys (*ikhankatha*) should be responsible for burning the seclusion hut, and that he should carefully collect whatever the boys had been using to be burnt as well. But in this case 'nobody seemed to take particular care about these articles and nobody seemed to care who burnt the hut'. The bandaging of the wound with brown paper in some cases was, of course, also not in keeping with custom. A trusted informant also mentioned the burning of the foreskin in the fire by at least one of the boys, and the use of greenish mealie husks for bandaging instead of dry ones, as irregularities. The foreskin should be disposed of by hiding or burying in a secret place, or dropping it into an ant-hill. The boys were also not very careful about keeping the body white, often smearing only chest and arms instead of the whole body. It is said that the duration of seclusion is shorter in town than in the country, but it is known that even in the country some of the boys are secluded for less than two months.

It is not known how many boys go to medical practitioners to be circumcised, but it does not seem to be common. Many men do not regard such a person as a real man, and they say that in order to be accepted into manhood he would still have to go into seclusion at some another stage.

GETTING MARRIED

The majority of townspeople who have settled down to a 'married' life, claim to have been married in church. The rest have either been married by civil rites, or the wife was either 'taken' by the *ukuthwala* custom, which often implies the consent of her parents, or they are living together by mutual agreement without any form of regularization. Marriages such as the one described in case No. 6 in chapter 4, in which there are no church or civil rites, but the bride is publicly handed over to the bridegroom's people after payment of *ukulobola*, or at least some agreement about it, are not common in town. In many cases *ukudlisa amasi* is performed in addition to other rites.

Although it is common for a young man to propose personally to the girl he intends marrying, this is usually followed by a formal request to the girl's parents by representatives (*oonomazakuzaku*) of the bridegroom or his parents. Some negotiation follows, amongst others about *ukulobola*, in which the girl's parents sometimes also act through representatives.

Prior to the wedding-day the bride remains in seclusion (*ukuhota*) for some time. Sometimes this seclusion starts with the first publication of the banns, but in other cases it is only observed for a few days. Some people say this seclusion improves the looks of the bride, but it is also referred to as 'an old Xhosa custom'.[8] A feast is also made, to which relatives and friends bring their wedding-gifts (*amabhaso*), which nowadays often take the form of cash. A report

[8] Seclusion of the bride for two or three weeks did form part of traditional Xhosa marriage festivities: Wilson, *Social Structure*, p. 83.

of such a party for a sophisticated couple, in the local Bantu press, referred to it as a 'wedding presentation party'. A close acquaintance of the couple remarked that the main purpose of the party in this case was probably to raise funds in view of the heavy expenses the bridegroom would have to incur, amongst others to hire cars to take guests to the wedding which was to take place in the Transkei.

In the evenings young people may gather at the bride's home for singing and refreshments. These gatherings may last till about midnight or later, and in some cases some of those attending may sleep there for the rest of the night. Referring to these gatherings, one town-born informant said: 'The real *imibholoro*, such as I had, are not common in town weddings, but it is not unusual to notice some kind of singing going on at night at a place where there is going to be a wedding. In my case my late husband came from Gcalekaland, the place of *imibholoro*, and my mother was also born and brought up in the country' (widow of 38, married in 1936).

On the wedding-day bride and bridegroom proceed to church separately, each accompanied by a number of male and female companions (*abakhapi*). If the bride has not yet had a baby, she wears a long white dress with a veil, and the marriage takes place in church where she 'is publicly given away by the father, or brother, or any male relative'. '*Inkazana* [a girl who has had a child][9] wears an ordinary dress and is married in the minister's office in church privately.' On arriving at the bride's home after the ceremony in church, the bridal party parades around or in front of the house. This is called *ukunyathela inkundla* (to tramp on *inkundla*), *inkundla* being the open space between the huts and cattle-kraal of a Xhosa homestead. 'We did this in front of the house as there is no *inkundla* here. The people had formed a circle in front of my mother's house and were chanting wedding songs.'

The rest of the day is spent in feasting. First there is usually a dinner to which the guests sit down at one table in relays, the most important guests taking precedence. Where there is a large crowd, some may be served outside. Later in the day there may be a tea-party, for which bride and bridegroom change their clothes (*ukutshintsha*), while the bride may even change for a second time for the gathering where the couple are admonished. The colour of these dresses for 'changing' are according to the bride's personal choice. In the evening the bride is sometimes taken to the bridegroom's home to be handed to the groom's people. There again light refreshments may be served before her companions return. Here now are accounts given by town-born persons of their own weddings.

A town-born woman, after completing two years of a teacher's training course, was married in 1936 to a Transkei man who had been in the employ of the Native Affairs Department in East London for some years before that. Before marriage she was attending college elsewhere, but he had noticed her during vacations. 'Without first consulting me he sent three men as *oonomazakuzaku* to negotiate with my mother about marriage. Through her *unomazakuzaku* my mother agreed to the marriage proposal. My mother had a high opinion of the bridegroom on account of his service of long standing in the Native Affairs Department, and two of the *oonomazakuzaku* were men of high standing. The one was a senior court interpreter and the other a clerk in the

[9] Among Red people *inkazana* is a mature woman who bears children but remains 'outside marriage': Mayer, op. cit., p. 235.

Native Affairs Department. The Xhosa judge the social position of the bridegroom by his *oonomazakuzaku*, who will not agree to act for him without first making sure that he is a man of substance. When mother told me about these negotiations, I first objected on the ground that I had not completed my education, but she replied: "My child, it looks as if this thing is someone," implying that he had the necessary qualities. I was not adamant in my objection, as mothers have the final say where daughters are concerned.'

After publication of the banns, the wedding-dress and 'change' dresses were procured, and besides provisions for the feast, the mother bought her some kitchen pots, three-legged Xhosa pots, dishes, enamel and porcelain plates, knives and forks, a tea-set, a large suitcase and a bedroom suite. There was *umbholoro* at night attended by girls of her age, and older ones, as well as young men. Refreshments were served every night, and those who did not sleep there left at about 1 a.m. There was a gathering for *amabhaso* for young people at which she was presented, amongst other things, with a tea-set by members of the staff of the school she had attended in East London. Her mother's particular popularity was the reason for this unusual gesture. There was a separate *amabhaso* feast for the older people. Besides cash, she received gifts like mirrors, tea-pots, vases, and a wash-basin and water-jug. For each feast a sheep was slaughtered and other food prepared. The bride also observed the custom of seclusion, 'avoiding publicity as much as possible'.

On the wedding-day they drove to church by car, accompanied by a procession on horse-back (*umkhwelo*), a custom well known in the country, but not in town. Singing by a school choir in church was also regarded as rather unusual, also indicating the bride's and her mother's popularity. At home they performed the march *ukunyathela inkundla* before sitting down to dinner. An ox and six sheep had been slaughtered, and there were samp, beans, rice, potatoes, and cabbage. Besides tea, minerals and kaffir beer, a case of brandy had also been provided. 'The women who did the cooking were experienced cooks who had done cooking as servants in White homes.

'Among those present were men and women of high standing. Some were elderly men whose sons and daughters were either schoolteachers, court interpreters, or nurses, and they themselves were retired teachers or church stewards. Most of the local ministers were present, as well as teachers, besides less important people and even the simplest location people. All the ministers and principals of schools were served at the first session at table.' Besides the table in the bride's mother's house, some people were served in a house across the street, and others had their food outside in dishes. In front of the house women and girls sang Xhosa wedding songs. After dinner bridegroom and bride, each with their *abakhapi*, went to separate rooms to rest and change. For 'changing' the bride put on a green dress. Afternoon tea followed, and at about 5 p.m. the bride again changed into a yellow dress for the admonition speeches, which lasted till about 6.30.

The bridal party now went to the bridegroom's house in the Thulandivile area, some by car and others on foot. They were welcomed by women singing: 'Come with her! Come with her!', some of them waving their arms. 'This was the handing over of *umtshakazi* [young wife] to the groom's people.' Bread and tea were served, also beer for those who drank, and 'small groups of men met in one room, probably to drink brandy'. At about 9 p.m. the bride's party returned home, 'leaving me as *umtshakazi* in Thulandivile'.

On this fairly elaborate pattern there are numerous variations. This wedding, of course, took place more than twenty years ago, and although we should allow for possible inaccuracies on account of lapses of memory, it may be accepted as a good indication of what an older townswoman regards an imposing town wedding to have been like in her day. It may be that the present trend is toward simpler weddings, but it was not possible to collect enough descriptions of weddings to establish with certainty the existence of such a trend. In a recent wedding of a 'white-collar' couple described below, the negotiations were quite elaborate, but the actual wedding ceremonial was simpler. The bride was an East London-born nurse, the bridegroom a teacher who grew up in another town, and they were married in 1959.

The couple were sweethearts for a time, and the bridegroom proposed marriage to the girl. He then sent two *oonomazakuzaku* to the bride's father, the bride seeing to it that her father knew of this beforehand. The father had invited two of his relatives to be present. After stating their errand, the *oonomazakuzaku* made him a gift of a bottle of brandy, a customary gift to establish good relations, known as *uswazi*. Acceptance of this gift was regarded as a sign that the proposal was acceptable. There had been no particular preparations for the visitors, but during the discussions they had bread and tea, and then returned the same day.

Three weeks later they came again to hand over part of the *lobolo*, which was being given in cash, and to receive permission for the publication of the banns. A sheep was slaughtered to honour them and beer was brewed. The two relatives of the bride's father were again present to take part in the discussions, and there were neighbours and some other people who had come to share in the eating and drinking. The women sang till about midnight, when most of the guests left. On Sunday the 'bridegrooms' went to church in the company of the bride and three of her girl friends. (An informant explained that the *oonomazakuzaku* must receive public recognition, and in this respect taking them to church on this occasion is a recognized formality with School Xhosa.) After church there was a dinner to which the bride's father had invited some of his clansmen. The *oonomazakuzaku*, relatives and some neighbours sat down for the first session. The *oonomazakuzaku* left in the afternoon. On the following Saturday bridegroom and bride and their respective fathers visited the minister to ask for the publication of the banns.

There were no parties for gifts, no singing at night, and the bride did not observe seclusion. She was at work till the day before the wedding, and resumed her duties as soon as it was over. Besides her wedding and 'change' dresses, she had to provide two dresses for each of the two student-nurses who were to act as her *abakhapi*. 'It is the custom that the bride should buy the dresses for her *abakhapi*.' A wedding-cake was also ordered from a confectioner in town. The bridegroom did not acquire any special clothes, as he had enough clothes 'in very good condition'. The bride maintained that 'it was a simple wedding, and the bridegroom's aim was to avoid as much expense as possible. After a big wedding the bridegroom is usually up to the neck in debt. This is very foolish when one cannot afford a big wedding.' Nevertheless, when describing the wedding-feast itself, the bride referred to it as 'a big *umtshato*'.

The church was about half full for the wedding service which took place in the afternoon. Besides some nurses and teachers and a handful of some of the respectable residents of the location, there were quite a number of the general public who had seen the cars at the church and came to watch. When the party came out of church there was spontaneous singing by the women who had gathered in this way. As the cars approached the bride's home, there were the customary exclamations of welcome by womenfolk: 'Hi-hi-hi-hi! Ha-la-la! Ha-la-la! It is it! It is it! It is a wedding!' They immediately sat down to dinner without marching (*ukunyathela inkundla*). The meal included meat—two sheep had been slaughtered—*umngqusho* (samp), rice, vegetables and sweets. The first session was made up of the bride and bridegroom, their *abakhapi* and their parents, and a sister of the bridegroom with her husband. Relatives of the bride's father 'were also squeezed in'. The bride did not notice any particular order followed for the other sessions, but 'men who were not particularly smartly dressed' sat around in the yard where food and beer were served to them. Besides the groom's *abakhapi* and relatives mentioned above, his *uduli* (bridal party) also included a few of his close friends who were Thembu, as he was.

After dinner the two bridal groups changed clothes, the groom and his *abakhapi* going to a house next door where the whole *uduli* was accommodated. After changing there was a tea-party, and then followed the speeches of admonition. The feasting was over by about 6 p.m., when the bride accompanied the groom and his party to his home where the day ended on a modern note with a 'cocktail party' (champagne, cool drinks, tea and cakes). Besides members of the bridegroom's party, there were schoolteachers and nurses and other friends of the bridegroom, all of the better-educated type of Bantu.

In the following case (marriage in 1951) much simpler people were involved. The bride had only standard four—she now sells vegetables—and the bridegroom was a 'minister' of a small Zionist sect of which the bride was also a member. Nearly always ministers of this type are unskilled labourers with a low educational standard for whom the ministry is only a part-time occupation. The woman had been recommended to her present husband by Rev. X, another minister of the same church. 'He was very much older than I was, and was not my personal choice. I was forced to marry him by my widowed mother and her brother, very much against my will.' As the future bridegroom 'had no male relatives near by', Rev. X acted for him as *unomazakuzaku*, and the girl's mother was represented by her brother. About a month before the wedding the mother bought material for wedding-dresses which were made by a White dressmaker. She had a blue dress for admonition, and a dark brown costume for afternoon tea. 'After the second publication of the banns the girls and young men who attend my church gathered at home every night to sing. This gathering is known as *umbholoro*.' Tea was served during the night, and because the people were in employment, the gathering dispersed after about eleven o'clock every night.

The gathering for *amabhaso* was held at home two weeks before the wedding. 'My mother issued notices in writing to all our church people, friends throughout the location, and neighbours. She notified them of the date of the wedding, and invited them to the *amabhaso* ceremony as well. A large number of people turned up. Mother slaughtered a sheep for the occasion, and there were *umngqusho*, potatoes, rice, cabbage and soft drinks. The donations amounted to £10 [R20] in cash, besides tea-sets, vases, pots, plates, forks and knives. The gathering took the form of a religious meeting. Hymns were sung, and prayers and short speeches were made.' The bride also observed seclusion for four days prior to the marriage.

'We went to church by car. It was myself, my mother's brother, his wife, and my three *abakhapi*, and we found the bridegroom and his *abakhapi* and all the other people already assembled in church. My mother's brother gave me away in the presence of the congregation. After the service we drove home—I and my husband and all the *abakhapi* in one car.' At her mother's house they first performed *ukunyathela inkundla* before going into the house. 'There was a wedding-cake in the centre of the table, and the table was neatly laid for a meal. My husband and I took our seats at the head of the table, and our *abakhapi* were seated alongside each of us. Church dignitaries such as Rev. X and his wife, and Rev. Y and his wife, and others were served during the first session. Other sessions followed.' The meat for the occasion had been bought from the butcher. The same kind of foodstuffs and drink were served as at the *amabhaso* ceremony.

After dinner the bride and bridegroom changed into different clothes before returning for the speeches of admonition. Here are some extracts of what the informant remembered of these speeches. 'You are now a married woman. You have now been married into the family of B——. Do not disgrace us in that family. Let us not hear any bad things about you. In fact, I would be very much surprised if such could happen in your case, because in all these years you have been living with us, nobody could point a finger at you. . . . Go then, my sister's daughter, and create friendship with the family of ——.' Rev. X also spoke: 'I thank God for sparing my life that I should also witness the wedding of these two. I will not say anything to you, Rev. —— [bridegroom]. Nobody can address you better than yourself. You have spoken eloquently at many a wedding, and today the speeches you have directed at other people must be referred to yourself. Bride, I rightly claim you to be my daughter. You have been a promising member of my church, and I hope you will continue to be good, not only to your husband, but to all people. May God bless this marriage.'

In this case the bride was not taken to the bridegroom's home on the evening of the wedding. In fact, she refused to go and stay with him in his room, and only joined him after two months, during which time her mother spoke to her, 'trying to convince me that married life was a call to all womenfolk. Most women were married to men they never fancied, but later in life they learnt to love their husbands.'

The ceremonial accompanying a marriage by civil rites is usually less elaborate, and for second marriages most of the ceremonial is also usually dispensed with. An interesting case is quoted below of an East London-born teacher who was quietly married to a nurse while he was teaching elsewhere. The bridegroom's father was a very highly educated professional man whose name is still held in high esteem in the location. On the couple's first visit to East London, a full eighteen months after they were married, an imposing wedding-feast was held. 'There was a love-affair between us for some months and I proposed marriage. The matter was between the two of us; there were no preliminary marriage negotiations. After we had come to an agreement on marriage, we decided on a convenient day to appear before the native commissioner for the marriage to be solemnized. On that Saturday morning we dressed ourselves neatly and proceeded to the native commissioner's office.

Instead of the usual *abakhapi* we only had witnesses. These were clerks we found at the office. After the marriage we returned home quietly, and on the afternoon of the same day my wife returned to the hospital for duty. The only people who knew I was married were those present at the native commissioner's office.

'When I came home with my bride for the first time, for her to be seen by my relatives, my widowed mother advised me when we were together in one of the rooms that it was necessary, since I was the son of a great man, that the community here and abroad should know that I was now married. She suggested there should be a marriage feast at the community centre where there was plenty of room for all the people who would attend.' A few days later he called a meeting of 'relatives and friends' which was attended by his two sister's sons, two close friends of the family, 'a prominent resident' of the location and the vice-principal of the local high school—all of them males. 'This family meeting was unanimous that blood should be shed', that is, something should be slaughtered. 'Invitation cards were sent out to many people: teachers, nurses, prominent residents and ministers. There were also those who came on their own without invitation cards.'

At the feast one of the family friends who had attended the meeting acted as master of ceremonies. He spoke with appreciation of the bridegroom's 'decision to postpone the marriage feast, for it shows how much he values his home. Home refers to you in this case. He felt his wedding would have been incomplete without you playing your part in it.' A number of tables had been joined to form one long table in the hall, so that 'there was room for all those who had been invited. Many young men and women were seated along the sides of the hall, waiting for their turn to be served at table.' The bridegroom regarded the food served as a 'square meal'. There was meat, for which a sheep had been slaughtered, potatoes, rice, cabbage, samp, beans, sweets, and cool drinks. Kaffir beer was also brewed 'not at home, but elsewhere near by, because of church rules'. A band provided music.

After the meal the guests were invited to deliver speeches. No particular persons had been asked to do so. The man described as a prominent resident of the location spoke in the following vein: 'M——, now that you are a married man, you have to be quite different from what you were before marriage. In married life your will is not your own, and your life belongs not to yourself, but to your family. Your movements today will be controlled by your wife who is your lifelong partner, and it behoves the two of you equally to see that you do nothing that will cause the walls of your marriage to crack and tumble down.' One of the bridegroom's sister's sons also spoke: 'The life of a man is divided into three stages, namely childhood, manhood, and married life. The fourth stage is death, when the living have to speak openly about the good qualities of the dead man. We look to you, M——, to follow in your late father's principles. He did not live unto himself, but unto the public. That is why he achieved greatness. I must further mention this important fact that any man's success depends entirely on the co-operation of his wife. We therefore cherish the hope that your wife will be your fountain from which cool waters will flow.'

After the speeches the tables were removed for dancing for which the band provided the music.

It seems to be regarded 'proper' that a marriage should be well publicized, and the elaborate marriage ceremonial serves this purpose well. A quiet marriage tends to raise suspicion. A teacher proposed marriage to an East London-born girl, 'but it was to be a quiet and hasty sort of wedding because of enemies'. On this the father of the bride commented to a fieldworker: 'I cannot be sure of the reason for this privacy, but I think the bridegroom had committed himself to several other girls he had promised to marry.' That this kind of trouble is not imaginary is proved by a press report of an objection that was raised against an East London marriage while the rites were in progress in church. The minister upheld the objection and the marriage was not solemnized. This must have been rather a catastrophe, because we learnt from other sources that it was to be a very elaborate wedding. Rumour has it that the objection was raised by a nurse who claimed that the bridegroom had promised to marry her, and further that the couple were eventually married somewhere in the Transkei.

When the bride is pregnant it is also usually a quiet wedding in which elaborate ceremonial is dispensed with, but in such cases also a marriage feast may follow later. 'There were none of the marriage negotiations which usually precede a marriage, because of my pregnant condition. My husband proposed marriage when I reported my pregnancy to him. We had been sweethearts. No preparations were made, except arranging with the minister of the —— Church, and we approached him together. The marriage was in a rushed kind of manner, to avoid publicity.' The idea behind this was to get married before the girl's pregnant condition should become noticeable. Observance of all the customary negotiations and marriage ceremonial would have caused too much delay. They did not officially seek the girl's father's permission, but she did discuss the matter with her mother. 'We quietly went to church between six and seven in the evening and thereafter returned to my husband's room in my father's house. There was no dinner, tea-party or particular clothes. The proper marriage feast is still pending. It definitely will be performed in the country where my husband's parents and relatives are' (woman of 24, standard six, married in 1957).

Besides these special cases (second marriages, civil rites, pregnant brides, promises of marriage to other persons) there are also many other instances of marriages taking place with little or no ceremonial. In the case described below the bridegroom is represented as somewhat of a rogue who schemed, not only to obtain a wife, but probably also to avoid the expense of elaborate ceremonies.

The couple were not sweethearts before marriage. The man approached the girl's widowed mother directly and negotiated with her. He claimed to have applied for a house in the new township Eziphunzana, and to have been told that he could not get a house until he was married. Having looked around a bit, he found her daughter to be a suitable wife and now asked her in marriage. 'The matter was very urgent. There would be none of the usual negotiations and he would *lobola* after the marriage had been consummated. It was therefore my mother who influenced me to marry this man and she would not listen to my excuse that I had a lover at Fort Hare who had promised to marry me. There were no preparations by the bridegroom, whose people were not here. It was my mother who on the day of my wedding prepared a dinner on a small scale and invited a few of her friends and some of my girl friends. She bought meat from the butchery and vegetables from the market. There were cool drinks and cakes. My husband's friends organized a reception in Eziphunzana in our honour on the following Sunday where cool drinks, cakes and tea were served.' The wife held that the husband had merely desired her for sexual satisfaction, but he could see that his chances for this were remote, 'because of my strong connexions with my former sweetheart who was a Fort Hare student, and he realized he was no match for my lover. He therefore decided a marriage proposal would be the best line of approach.' They stayed with her mother in her house, but were separated after three months of married life. 'He abandoned the idea of getting a house in Eziphunzana on the excuse that the rent was very high. His promises of *ukulobola* never materialized. His failures sort of drove him away from my home.' The mother kept on reminding him of his promises and eventually he just disappeared. (Standard six, waitress in a tea-room in town, married in church, 1959.)

DEATH

When news of a death spreads, neighbours and other friends proceed to the bereaved family as soon as possible 'to show their practical sympathy and to strengthen them in their grief'. Throughout the following days till after the funeral there are always other people about the house. Visitors make donations of money as they come, and these are entered on a list. Young women of the neighbourhood take charge of domestic work, particularly the task of providing visitors with refreshments. Female members of the household just sit quietly huddled up in a corner during all the preparations for the funeral. In time relatives from other places also arrive. Regulations forbid keeping a corpse in the house, and it is removed to the funeral parlour on the day of the death. Pictures are removed from the walls when a death has taken place and are only replaced long after a funeral.

During the night a watch service (*inkonzo yomlindo*) is held, which is often attended by a large crowd. Hymns are sung and prayers are said. No particular person is appointed or requested to lead, but usually one woman is tacitly accepted as leader 'because of seniority and experience of night watches and other devotions'. The women tend to take a more active part in singing and praying than the men. At a night watch in a four-roomed municipal house where there was a large attendance, all the women were in one room and the men in another. Candles are often burned in the room where the night watch takes place, even if better lighting is available. Tea and bread are served in the course of the night. All tea and coffee consumed from the time of death till after the funeral is taken without milk.

The body is returned to the house a few hours before the funeral where the coffin is opened to allow the face of the deceased person to be seen. After the main funeral service everybody present files past the coffin to look at the deceased before it is finally closed. A funeral of an adult church member usually consists of a short service at the home of the deceased, a service in church, devotions at the grave, and then a gathering at the home where those who took part in the funeral wash their hands in a dish of water specially provided for the purpose, refreshments are served, and speeches of thanks are made. Some form of free transport is always provided for as many persons as possible.

No particular persons are singled out for certain duties such as carrying the coffin, or filling-up the grave, but a number of neighbours are usually with the family during the first few days after bereavement and they spontaneously play a prominent part. Commenting on a funeral attended, an informant said that in the case of a funeral for which a large attendance is expected, there may be some organizing and assigning of duties to certain persons, as in the case described below.

The 14-year-old stepdaughter of a prominent East London-born business man had died unexpectedly. There were the usual visits of neighbours and friends and the night watch. I quote further from the research assistant's notes of his observations.

A day before the funeral a meeting of neighbours was held. It was open to any man, even to those who came from far away. No particular man was appointed to lead the meeting. Anyone could get up and say: 'Gentlemen, lend me your ears, I wish to draw your attention to the fact that this is the best time to arrange the programme for tomorrow to avoid the last-minute rush.' All men responded more or less as one: 'Quite so, son of——', mentioning his clan name. Two men who were close neighbours were appointed to see to the smooth running of the programme, and to see that the buses were first occupied by elderly people who were not able to travel long distances on foot. There would be six buses and about seventeen private cars, all at the disposal of the people free of charge. Further the time at which different parts of the programme would start and the speakers at different places were discussed tentatively. As most men would be away at work, it was decided that those men who would not be in town should make a special effort to be present when the coffin arrived, so that they could help carry it into the house. No particular men were appointed for this.

The hearse arrived at 11 a.m. on the following day and the coffin was taken into the house where it was placed on forms in the main room. The White driver of the hearse opened the coffin a bit, exposing the corpse from the neck upwards. A hymn was sung, while the mother sobbed bitterly. As it continued verse by verse, most of the women were overcome by emotion. The service at the house started at 1 p.m. and was conducted by a church elder. A speech was also made by a prominent business man and former school principal in the Transkei, who had close connexions with the deceased child's father (now divorced from her mother). He spoke of traditional burial customs which indicated that even the ancestors of the Xhosa had a belief in life hereafter. With the arrival of the Whites, Christianity was introduced, by which 'our original idea of death has been improved, for we now know that the death of Jesus Christ on the cross sanctified death'.

In church the minister, who was new to East London, called upon the elder to speak about the deceased. He spoke of death being an axe which chops down a tree irrespective of age, and of the girl's promising future. 'We all mourn the death of——, but we have the consolation that her life had not been spoilt like yours and mine. It was perfect in its purity.' The girl's class teacher spoke of her outstanding record at school, and of other good qualities. After this the people filed past the coffin to have a last look at the deceased. Because of the large crowd, this took about half an hour. Two of the church officials screwed on the lid, and others, with some churchmen, carried the coffin to the hearse. The procession to the graveyard was headed by about two hundred school-children. Besides the buses and cars there were large numbers of people on foot. At the grave there was a short service with speeches. One of the schoolteachers read out the telegrams from friends and relatives as far afield as Durban and the Transvaal. No particular men were appointed to lower the coffin into the grave. 'Anybody near enough is good.' After the burial formula, a hymn was sung during which all the women filed past to throw handfuls of earth into the grave, first the mother and relatives. After the women, elderly men followed, and then the grave was refilled. All who could returned to the home, where there was the washing of hands, followed by tea or coffee, still served without milk, and a speech by a male neighbour on behalf of the family.

The many speeches by persons connected with the deceased or his family are a feature of funerals.[10] On the death of a country-born shopowner who had built up an impressive business during a stay of many years in town, a memorial service was held at his place in town before the corpse was taken to the country for burial. After the service the author was asked to address the gathering and the research assistant was requested to thank him. On the arrival of the corpse, the crowd, which had dispersed, reassembled, and the assistant, being a very well-known figure in the location, was asked to make a speech on behalf of the community. These requests came spontaneously, without having been planned beforehand. A number of friends of the deceased now also came forward to make spontaneous speeches, and at the end a man suggested that some Methodist preachers who were present should say a prayer. Incidentally the deceased was not a church member, but a Baptist minister was asked to lead the service. Being unable to do so, he requested the Presbyterian minister to take his place. A Seventh-day Adventist evangelist was prominent among the audience, and seemed to make some of the suggestions about procedure.

These speeches always dwell on the 'good works' of the deceased. Much is made of his concern for his family and love and kindness to fellow-men. A few extracts illustrate this.

'C—— was a man of deeds, in spite of his little education. He had suffered a great deal in order to provide all his children with the highest education.' Speaker referred to the youngest son who was doing his first year B.Sc. at Fort Hare, and the fact that the deceased had kept on working in spite of severe asthma. 'It is not every father who is prepared to suffer for the future of his children. He was great in heart, because in his heart there was not only room for the members of his own family, but for everybody.' Speaking of the death of a shopowner whose family life was known to be somewhat irregular, the minister found it possible, nevertheless, to commend him for having provided well 'for the women and the children'. Other speakers spoke of his loving all people equally, 'and he helped as much as he could where help was really needed'. 'He did justice without discrimination. He was very kind to everybody, and I assure you of the clan of —— [the deceased's clan name], the death of X will be more felt by the poorer ones in this neighbourhood, those who did not always have cash to pay for goods bought from his shop.' The speaker concluded his speech by calling out the name of the deceased and repeating the word for a human being (*umntu*) three times while pointing at the coffin. On occasion the weaknesses of a dead man were discussed with unexpected frankness, but reasons were given for condoning them. An old man, who had once been a preacher in a well-established church, had lost interest in church, and according to current rumour, taken to women and drink. The minister therefore found it necessary to explain why he was being given a full church funeral. I quote from the field report. 'One may ask: was Y a church person

[10] In fact speeches figure prominently on most ritual and ceremonial occasions of School Xhosa, both in urban and in rural communities, often taking the form of admonition (*ukuyala*).

up to his death? If not, why should his funeral be conducted in church? My answer to this is: Y was an outstanding church member for many years, during which time he worked conscientiously for God. It is true that after the death of his first wife about three years ago he stayed away from church, but he did not sever his connexions altogether, for his children and his present wife continued to attend. This means that his thoughts were still with the church, but that he had been overcome by the desires of the flesh. We feel certain that if God had spared his life, he would have come back to church to occupy his former position.' The minister also related how he had summoned the deceased to his office on several occasions to talk to him about his lapses. 'I could see that he was a different Y, in that he had a different smell.' (An informant interpreted this as referring to the smell of liquor.) Yet the preacher commended him for admitting his fault on such occasions.

Funerals often draw large crowds, and are occasions for engendering a community spirit. Thanking the guests after a funeral, a speaker said: 'I have lived with you since 1914, and for one thing I must give you credit. That is that on such occasions you have always shown unity. It is the time when we realize we must sink down our personal differences and petty quarrels and come together as one body. This is admirable about you, tribes of Rarabe.[11] I do not feel like thanking you as the previous speaker has done, for according to our custom a man is never thanked for fulfilling his obligation. The living bury the dead.'

Besides the mourning observance of removing pictures from the walls, some women wear black for mourning, and men wear black armbands or buttons in coat lapels. For a shorter or longer time after the funeral, the women of the household confine themselves to the precincts of the house as far as possible. A year or more after the funeral a feast is held to bring the members 'out of the forest', indicating the termination of mourning. Sometimes this feast is consciously connected with the traditional rite of *ukubuyisa* ('bringing back' the deceased), but people also refer to it as the unveiling of the tombstone.

CONCLUSIONS

Most of the ritual and ceremonial described in this chapter is associated with transitions between different phases in the life-cycle of the individual, which indicate changing relationships. The seclusion of mother and child and the mother's concentration of all her attention on it during the first days of the baby's life is typical of the first phase in which it is 'totally confined within the matricentral cell'.[12] After taking its place in the larger domain of the whole domestic group or household, it is in most cases also introduced into the 'visible church' through baptism, and simultaneously through a party or dinner into the circle of kinsfolk, friends and neighbours. This may also be the occasion for stressing its relation to patrilineal kinship groupings and ancestors. The second phase of Fortes's paradigm of the life-cycle in which the child first belongs to the patricentral nuclear family unit before it moves into the

[11] The origin of the two major divisions among the Xhosa proper is traced to the chiefs Gcaleka and Rarabe. Practically all the Rarabe tribes eventually settled in the Ciskei, while generally speaking the Gcaleka remained in the Transkei. (See Hammond-Tooke, W.D., *Tribes of the Willowvale District*, Dept. of Native Affairs, Ethnological Publications No. 36, 1957, p. 34.)

[12] Fortes, Meyer, 'Introduction' to Goody, Jack (Ed.), *The Developmental Cycle in Domestic Groups*, Cambridge Papers in Social Anthropology, No. 1, Cambridge University Press, 1958, p. 9.

domain of the whole domestic group (say an extended or compound family) is characteristic of traditional Xhosa household structure, but in town it is usually either non-existent, as in the case of children born to unmarried mothers or women who have lost their husbands, or it coincides with the third phase, as when the domestic group consists of a nuclear family.

Weaning and the associated cutting of the hair of a child is also connected with change in status from 'infant' to 'child', but is probably less closely associated with changes in relationships than used to be the case traditionally. In the urban household there is more diversity in respect of the age of weaning, and it generally takes place earlier, through bottle feeding, which may very soon supplement mother's milk, and may be administered by any member of the household. The baby is also less completely dependent on its mother during the suckling period. The 'psychic' weaning therefore starts earlier and proceeds more gradually, and the definite physical weaning may not lead to immediate changes in relationships. In time, however, the child becomes less confined to the domain of the domestic group and starts building up its own contacts with other persons in the same house[13] and in the neighbourhood.

Male initiation confers certain rights of 'independence' and imposes responsibilities in the eyes of the urban Bantu community, but these rights and duties have no recognition within the legal system of the modern state, and there are no legal sanctions to guard the rights or enforce the duties and responsibilities in question. In the eyes of the location community, however, it confers certain meagre citizenship rights, such as voicing one's opinion in a public gathering. It confers the right to get married, but scorn is the only sanction by which this right can be withheld from the uncircumcised. It imposes the duty of responsible behaviour generally, and the responsibility for an individual's own actions in the eyes of the location public. In town initiation is therefore only in a very slender sense related to the youth's future status in the politico-jural domain. In traditional Xhosa society, however, initiation in a much fuller sense indicated a youth's admission to the politico-jural domain, and in present-day rural Xhosa communities where more of the traditional Xhosa political system still functions at the local level—often unofficially—it also has greater significance in relation to the politico-jural domain than in town. It is significant that as a complex of behaviour patterns the initiation ceremony persists in town, relatively unchanged, and with great tenacity, whereas it has lost much of the significance it had in relation to the structure of tribal society. This is a theme to which we shall return in chapter 10.

'Initiation ceremonies, in the strict sense,' writes Professor Fortes, 'are often regarded as the prelude to marriage, if they do not actually end in marriage. In general, what finally terminates jural infancy is the emergence of the family nucleus for the new domestic group that is destined to replace that of the parents.'[14] The significance attached in the location to some form of marriage feast to publicize the marriage, in contrast to the privacy in which the religious and civil rites can be, and often are, performed, seems to imply the consciousness that a new status and new relationships within the wider community are involved. Church and civil rites may meet the requirements of church rules and state laws, but when they are conducted without the publicity that accompanies a wedding-feast, they are ineffective in ratifying the couple's

[13] The relation between house and domestic group or household is discussed in chapter 8.
[14] Fortes, op. cit., p. 10.

new status in, and relationships with, the wider community. Where a high degree of anonymity prevails within an urban population, this ratification in the eyes of the wider community might be unimportant, but we shall indicate in chapter 9 that the East London Bantu population is not of this kind.

This chapter has further illustrated the varying influence of traditional and Western behaviour patterns respectively in moulding modern urban behaviour patterns. In the case of marriage ceremonial one could say that in broad outline the pattern is largely determined by Xhosa tradition—protracted negotiations through intermediaries with special reference to *lobolo*, singing at night, seclusion of the bride, and feasts at both homes, where attendance is not restricted to invited guests—but the details are largely determined by Western behaviour patterns. The cocktail party is, as far as the Bantu are concerned, a specifically urban phenomenon. In the case of male initiation ceremonies again, we have a whole complex of behaviour patterns determined by Xhosa tradition, in over-all pattern as well as in smaller details. In mortuary rites the influence of Western patterns prevail, but in certain details, such as the washing of hands and the ritual for the termination of mourning, the influence of Bantu tradition is obvious. The background of some details such as removing pictures, night watch services or wakes, and taking beverages without milk is uncertain.[15]

[15] Creoles in Freetown turn pictures and mirrors to the wall and also have a wake the night before the funeral (Banton, *West African City*, p. 210). 'Black' tea and coffee could be related to Western-orientated customs of wearing black for mourning, but blackness also has symbolic connotations in traditional Xhosa culture which may well be associated with death.

6

Pre-marital Relations

A common characteristic of many African urban populations is the diversity of forms of sexual union found among them,[1] and East London is no exception to this. First of all there are the *pre-marital love-affairs* mostly between young people, in which the partners do not live together as spouses, but sexual relations are a regular feature of their relationship. Then there are the cases of men and women '*staying together*' as husband and wife (*masihlalisane* or *ukushweshwa*), without their relationship having been regularized in any way. This relationship figures more prominently among migrants, particularly the Red category, than among the long-established town population. The great bulk of real townspeople living as husband and wife claim to be married by *Christian* or *civil* rites, or by the custom of *ukulobola* (giving marriage payment), or by a combination of two or all three of these. This also applies to widowed, divorced and separated persons. In addition there is the prevalence of *extra-marital love-affairs* of married persons, as well as of those who once were married, but are now without spouses.

MARITAL STATUS OF A SAMPLE OF TOWNSPEOPLE

Before discussing the marital status of our sample of permanent town-dwelling Bantu, attention must be drawn to the irregular nature of the sex-age structure of the sample. Reader's sample, on which our own was based, suggested that there were more females than males among the East London-born adult Bantu, but in our own sample the ratio of 60 males per 100 females is unusually low. Reader related the irregularity in the shape of the population pyramid of East London-born persons, as reflected by his own sample, to the fact that many East London-born young men are away working elsewhere, and my own impression confirms this. However, it would appear that, in addition to this, our own sample has been affected by the inadequate representation of certain categories of single males. If a population pyramid were to be constructed for the present sample, irregular formations for the older age groups might well be accounted for by the small size of the sample. But the extraordinary preponderance of females in the 15–19 age group (15 males to 35 females) calls for explanation. I suggest that besides youths away working elsewhere, this sample also missed the unsettled type of *tsotsi* youths who are not attached to any particular household. The fact that in the total population of our sample households there were hardly any unmarried sons of heads between the ages of 15 and 29, whereas there were quite a number of daughters of this age category, further supports this explanation. It may also be that in the age groups between 35 and 54 some disparity is caused by husbands who

[1] Cf. amongst others Clement, Pierre, 'Social Patterns of Urban Life' (Stanleyville), in *Social Implications of Industrialization and Urbanization in Africa South of the Sahara*, Unesco, (1956), pp. 394 ff.; Southall, A. W., and Gutkind, P. C. W. *Townsmen in the Making*, East Africa Institute of Social Research, Kampala (1957), pp. 153 ff.; Levin, Ruth, *Marriage in Langa Native Location*, Communications from the School of African Studies, University of Cape Town (1947), pp. 40 ff.

die or desert, or who are deserted by wives who take their children with them. Some of these husbands may have left East London, but others may be of the type having no fixed domestic arrangements, or they may be living singly, in which case they are more easily missed than persons living in a larger household.

TABLE 13

Marital status by sex and age

Age	MARITAL STATUS						
	Single unmarried	Staying together	Married	Tempor. separated	Divorced or separ.	Widowed	Total
			MALES				
15–19	15	—	—	—	—	—	15
20–24	14	2	2	1	—	—	19
25–29	8	—	2	1	1	—	12
30–34	2	—	6	1	—	—	9
35–44	1	—	7	—	—	—	8
45–54	1	—	3	1	—	1	6
55–64	1	—	1	1	—	1	4
65 plus	—	—	3	—	—	—	3
Total	42	2	24	5	1	2	76
			FEMALES				
15–19	34	1	—	—	—	—	35
20–24	18	2	3	1	—	—	24
25–29	13	—	4	2	—	—	19
30–34	3	1	4	—	—	1	9
35–44	4	1	7	—	1	6	19
45–54	1	—	6	—	2	3	12
55–64	—	—	—	—	—	4	4
65 plus	1	—	—	—	1	2	4
Total	74	5	24	3	4	16	126

The marital status of persons in our sample is analysed in table 13. We note the preponderance of females over males among unmarried persons, which is a concomitant of the disparity in numbers between young males and females discussed above. Another point of interest is the small number of separated and divorced persons and widowers, whereas there are quite a number of widows. There is reason for suspicion that some of the women who claimed to be widows, particularly the younger ones among them, were in fact separated women, since some people do feel a certain degree of shame over broken marriages, and women commonly feel somewhat humiliated about having been deserted by husbands. Location talk also leaves the impression that broken marriages are more common than our figures suggest. On the other hand, as we have suggested, it is possible that divorced and separated men are not adequately represented in our sample.

The age grouping shows that although both males and females get married from 20 years of age onward, the majority of both sexes remain unmarried up to their thirtieth year. Thereafter only a minority remain unmarried. This suggests a relatively late age for marriage, which is in keeping with a tendency toward a later marriage age among the Bantu of South Africa generally.[2]

In our sample 83 per cent of the males and 77 per cent of the females over 30

[2] Holleman, F. J., 'Die Bantoehuwelik op die Kruispad', *Journal of Racial Affairs*, 11, 2 (1960), pp. 82–117.

years of age claimed to be or to have been married. Therefore, although some people do remain unmarried, the great majority ultimately get married. It is important, however, to analyse the position of those persons over 30 who were unmarried and not staying with a spouse at the time of the survey. Of the five males in this category, two, aged 30 and 32 respectively, were members of households of which their widowed mothers were the heads. Both denied having fathered any children; but it seems quite probable that they may still get married. The other three were over 40. One was living by himself; another was with his brother and family; and the third lived with his father and family, the mother and other members of the family looking after the father's homestead in the country. Other details are set out below.

	AGE	ILLEGITIMATE CHILDREN			
		By mother No.	Number	Ages	Remarks
X	43	(1)	3	7–14	Mother alive in East London, children with her.
Y	45	(1)	2	14 & 19	Do.
		(2)	1	18	Do.
Z	55	(1)	1	28	Mother dead, son in King William's Town.
		(2)	4	12–20	Mothers alive in East London, children with them.
		(3)	6	7–17	

The point to note is that these three 'bachelors' had been far from sexually inactive, each having fathered his first child during his twenties, Z claiming to be the father of as many as eleven illegitimate children. Significant also is the tendency to claim more than one child by the same mother, suggesting relationships which lasted for several years. Further, relationships with different women overlapped chronologically in the case of Y and Z, which indicates that they had affairs with different women simultaneously, unless it happened that they returned to a former lover after an interlude with another. It is possible that the men could at some stage have stayed with women, but the questionnaire was not framed to bring this out. It emerged that at the time of the survey X had a visiting relationship with a lover, but it was not made clear whether she was the same one by whom he had had the three children.

Of nine 'spinsters' over 30, only one aged 46 denied ever having had a child. She owned a house and had a few male relatives staying with her as members of her household. Of the rest, four were heads of households, and the other four were members of households of which their widowed mothers were the heads. Further details are summarized below.

	AGE	ILLEGITIMATE CHILDREN			
		By father No.	Number	Ages	Remarks
A	31	(1)	1	14	Fathers alive; children with A
		(2)	2	5 & 7	
		(3)	1	$1\frac{3}{4}$	
B	31	(1)	3	$\frac{1}{4}$–8	Father alive, two children with B, one with B's mother's mother.
C	34	(1)	3	3–14	Father alive; children with C.
D	35	(1)	1	17	Father alive; child with D's father's brother.
		(2)	1	10	Father alive; child with D.
E	37	(1)	4	11–19	Father alive; one child dead; others with E.
		(2)	2	—	Father alive; children dead.
F	39	(1)	4	3–12	Fathers' whereabouts unknown; five children in the country with F's mother's sister; baby with F.
		(2)	2	$\frac{1}{12}$ & 2	
G	39	(1)	3	9–23	Father alive, children with G.
H	68	(1)	2	—	Father's whereabouts unknown; children dead.

All these women had been sexually active from an early age, and each had two or more children, the great majority of whom were living with the mothers. Some of these women could be considered still young enough to get married, but other factors than age made marriage improbable. A, for example, was well established as the head of a household made up of her children, her unemployed younger brother, and two younger unmarried sisters and their children. In all cases the possibilities of getting married would usually depend on the chances of their children being cared for by relatives, because it is unusual for a man to take responsibility for his bride's illegitimate children by other men. Even women living with their widowed mothers are themselves largely responsible for providing for the needs of their children, and few of these mothers would be able to provide for their daughters' illegitimate children, should the daughters get married. In view of the numbers and ages of their children, the chances that even the younger women might get married seem remote.

Females, like males, also show the tendency to have more than one child by the same partner, although quite a few of the women have had successive sets of children by different fathers. Some of these women may have been involved in 'staying together' relationships for some time. This is known to have been true of at least one. Another had a man living with her in the room some months after the survey.

Summarizing, we may say that although a minority of persons do remain unmarried, the genuine bachelor or spinster who remains sexually inactive for life appears to be highly exceptional. Many of the sexual relationships of unmarried persons last for several years, but they do not seem to last for life. The material also establishes the presence of a category of unmarried mothers who rear children without ever getting married, often as part of their own mothers' domestic families.

THE PRE-MARITAL STAGE[3]

Sexual activity commonly starts at an early age, long before marriage. Traditionally this was also the case, but there was strict enforcement of the rule that a girl must not be rendered pregnant. Only external sexual intercourse (*intra crures*) was permitted to unmarried young people. Amongst town Bantu it still remains an ideal with most people that a girl should not conceive before marriage, but among the majority of young people full sexual intercourse is accepted as a normal feature of the relations between sweethearts.

Very little is done in the line of sex instruction, and among the girls interviewed the majority had not been consciously prepared beforehand for menstruation. One, who was typical of quite a number, said that she was surprised and felt unhappy when she experienced her first menstruation, 'thinking that there was something wrong with me internally, or that I was cut by something. . . . I told my mother what I had. She told me I was a big girl now and I must never have intercourse with boys. I was surprised, because that was the first time I had heard my mother saying those funny words to me.' A friend had, in fact, told her of her own experience of menstruation, but she had not paid much attention.

It is commonly believed that milk or sour milk (*amasi*) or anything associated with milk should be avoided during menstruation, since it causes an excessive

[3] Most of the information in this section is drawn from interviews with nine youths (25 years old and younger), nine girls (25 and younger) and two married women (25 and 35 respectively).

flow. Unmarried girls should avoid intercourse during menstruation, since it is believed that a woman very easily conceives at that stage. Some also have the belief that playing with boys causes an excessive flow. Strict privacy should be observed in connexion with the menstrual flow and garments in contact with it, especially towards males. Some women give hygienic reasons for this, and compare the behaviour of White women in this respect. Others relate it to the belief that it may be used by witches to make the woman barren, and that it has a weakening effect on the man who sees it.

One related how her mother instructed her on the occasion of her first menstruation, when she was only 11, 'She told me that these are the signs that I am a girl, not a double-sexed person', and in very plain language the mother went on to describe what she should not allow a man to do with her, as this would make her pregnant. Other mothers only give a vague warning not to play or laugh with boys, because they are 'dangerous', 'mischievous', 'cruel', or 'rough'. A few girls claimed that they did not realize the significance of their condition when they became pregnant. One of these added: 'My mother used to tell me that babies are bought at the market when you are grown-up. But what puzzled me is that I never saw babies on beds at the market.' (First pregnancy at 15.) More open discussion of sex matters takes place with older sisters and other girls. They warn the younger girls against pregnancy, but may on the other hand encourage and guide them in their love-affairs. The following is typical: 'My sister told me I must have a boy as a sweetheart, but I must never sleep with him, because I will get pregnant. I must be friendly with the boys, because they are always rude if they notice that you do not want to pay attention to them if they pet you.'

Sex instruction was not discussed in detail with boys, but it is our impression that in the home they get even less of this than girls. Admonitions during initiation may include warnings against making girls pregnant, and immodesty (e.g. not to embrace a girl in view of older people), but there is no evidence of any instruction in sexual technique as part of the initiation ceremonies in town. This the boys also learn from the older ones. A matric scholar said that he first had sexual intercourse when he was 18. When he was younger, 'I did not know how it was done. I heard what is done from other friends who were more experienced. Sometimes I listened to the young men talking by themselves about sex matters.'

Children start having 'sweethearts', 'boy-friends' or 'girl-friends', 'cherries' (girls), or *iintokazi* (lit., female things) from 10 or 11 years onward. Of those interviewed, the majority were 15 or younger when they had their first love-affair. Sometimes these early sweethearts are not much more than playmates. 'I started to be in love when I was 13, but I will not say that was love, because it was the time when we used to play with those small boys who only pick the girls they want, but do not propose love. I started the true love when I was 15.' This was when she first experienced sexual intercourse. (Girl of 19, passed J.C., prospective student nurse.) Others have more serious affairs when still very young. 'I was 11 when I started to be in love with a schoolboy. I kissed him, and bought him sweets and hankies.' (Married woman of 25, standard eight.) Kissing, going to a concert or bioscope together, and the giving of sweets or other small gifts, are common. The exchange of photographs of each other, writing love-letters, and walking together from school, were also mentioned.

Some informants suggested reasons why love-making starts so young. Several referred to conditions which make for lack of discipline and control in the homes. 'They are always free, without their mothers' care, as the whole family is sometimes busy working.' 'Most of the children have no fathers. The mother has to leave her children and go to work, and the person looking after the child will do everything in front of it.' A girl said she started having a sweetheart when she was 12, 'because my mother and father were living in separation that year, and I was left with my father who let me go wherever I wanted to, without caring what time I came back, whereas my mother had been very strict'. Another mentioned the children's having very little to keep them busy in the room which is the family's home, 'and they play all sorts of funny games such as hide-and-seek'. Others referred to the lack of privacy which causes their being aware of their parents' sexual relations from an early age. Moreover, 'they see what is going on in the streets and what is done by their sisters'. The unsupervised and uncontrolled playing together of boys and girls offers ample opportunity of putting into practice what they have seen the older people do. Some nevertheless avoid being involved in early love-affairs. A girl of 19 whose mother was a teacher said she started to be in love only when she was 17 because before this she had wanted to pass her Junior Certificate. Now that she had a sweetheart, she also had sexual relations with him, but has not been rendered pregnant yet.

When discussing the reasons for their falling in love with a particular girl, most young men mentioned physical beauty, particularly bodily features. Characteristically, one said he first fell in love with his 'cherry' when he saw her at the beach in her bathing costume. Some referred to smartness, particularly in dressing habits, or their liveliness or ability to make pleasant conversation. Another, again, admired the girl for being 'soft-spoken and respectable'. Several referred to the girl's good character. A young man who had passed only standard four had obviously a high opinion of his girl-friend. 'I loved her because she looks beautiful and lovable to me. She has a good character, because she does not keep other boy-friends and she does not fight in the street. She is very clean and neat, and works hard in her home. She is a good singer and likes to sing for me and others when we are relaxing.' Others held that their girls were not a 'cheap line' or a 'street girl'. A well-dressed *tsotsi* had a girl whom his mother disliked because she regarded her as a *tsotsikazi*, but he liked her, 'because she is very lively and beautiful, and dresses nicely. She does not keep on asking for money to buy clothes, but is always employed.'

Girls do not want lovers who are drunkards, who are 'cruel', or who use force to make them submit. Better-educated girls like boys who are well-educated or civilized.[4] 'The thing which made me love him was that he was very smart and he was a qualified teacher.' (Girl with Junior Certificate.) A boy-friend must have good manners and show respect for the girl's parents and for people in general. Cleanliness, not being younger than the girl, and being employed, were also mentioned as requirements for a lover. One girl felt that a boy 'should know how to romance if necessary, and he must know how to express himself, to be able to say how much he loves you'.

Traditional rules of clan exogamy are still observed, in respect of love-affairs also. Many maintain that they inquire about the clan name before embarking on a love-affair. A girl with Junior Certificate said: 'You cannot be in love with

[4] The word *ukuphucuka*, to become smooth or polished, is used. *Impucuko* is used in Xhosa for 'civilization'.

a boy to whom you are related, although they do not tell us. If you eventually happen to find out that he is related to you, you have to leave him because that is incest [*umbulo*]. Relations are prohibited with your brother, your uncle and your cousin. I do take care of this rule and before meeting him I first have to ask him his clan name [*isiduko*], because if you happen to have a baby when you get married, the baby will not suck unless you confess that you once had intercourse with your brother or cousin. That is taboo [*inyala*].' Others said a child born of an incestuous union would be a cripple. Another girl with Junior Certificate who said she regarded any male of her own or her mother's clan as her brother or cousin, held that 'they usually say' that a brother or cousin of a girl will be incapable of having intercourse with her, because he will not become sexually excited.

Some young people are careless about clan exogamy in relation to love-affairs, but even the careless ones would avoid a relationship with a partner who has the same surname.[5] 'It is not common for us in town to ask the clan name. As long as the surnames are different, we go on loving the boy. If eventually I find out that we have the same clan name, I shall never reject him, because he is not my brother.' 'The clan name is of minor importance because we have no time to ask the clan name. Only the surnames are important. You cannot reject a boy who is in love with you for the sake of the clan name if your surnames are different.'

It is obvious that there are innumerable possibilities of contact between young people of different sexes. Mothers often warn their daughters not to play or go about with boys, and some consciously try to prevent this, but usually there are numerous 'loopholes' for such girls to accept and meet boy-friends. They find excuses for delaying after school or when they have been sent on an errand, inform the boys of the times their parents are not at home, or sneak away at night when their parents are asleep. The persons interviewed had got to know their sweethearts as school-mates, or playmates out of school; they met at friends' homes, or saw them at functions, at the beach or passing in the street. If nobody is available to introduce a young man to an unknown girl, he simply introduces himself.

A proposal of love may be made very soon after the first introduction, or the boy may first pay attention to the girl for some time by visiting her when possible, making gifts, taking her to a cinema or for walks, accompanying her from school or when meeting her in the street, and by often passing her home in order to see her. Some girls cherish the ideal of a boy-friend who owns a car, but not many young men possess the means to fulfil it for them. Girls also go out of their way to attract a boy's attention or to encourage a prospective lover. A girl may make a special detour to meet the boy, try to put on an attractive appearance and make pleasant conversation, or give him gifts, and is anxious to keep appointments.

Proposals are made verbally and personally, but sometimes also by letter or through a third party. It is regarded as a matter of course that a proposal may have to be repeated several times before it is accepted. But if the girl is eager to have the boy, she 'must not be fussy', as he may lose interest. Sometimes the girl confirms acceptance of the proposal by a special kiss known as *isivumo* (from *ukuvuma*, to agree). 'He fell in love with me first. I used to regard him

[5] In the case of School people some surnames are shared by lineages or lineage segments of several generations' depth.

just as a friend, because he was the only boy who used to take me to the bioscope and give me bus fares when I was short of money. All the time I did not know that he was aiming at anything, till one day he told me that he had been loving me for a long time, but did not want to say it, because I would be surprised, since we had been friends all the time.' (Girl of 19, J.C., from well-furnished home.) 'I met her at her home and she used to accompany me outside where I proposed love to her. I used to pretend to go about school matters, so that her parents were never suspicious. I wrote proposal letters till she loved me.' (Male of 25, 'matric' scholar.)

Boys or young men sometimes use force in order to make a girl accept their proposal. 'He always waited for me when I went to Annie who stayed near his room. She used to go to his room, and he would send her to the dairy to buy milk, and I would wait for her. He would keep on proposing love to me while she was out. One day he locked me in the room and told me to accept him. I first refused, but he broke my finger, so that I accepted his proposal, hoping that he would let me go. . . . He said the day I wanted to reject him, he would beat me. . . . I have no other sweetheart because I am always afraid that he may see me with another one, and he will beat me to death.' This girl (22, standard three) was 14 and the man 28 when their affair started, and she already has two children by him, but they are not married.

Intensive petting—referred to as *ukuncokolisa* (to excite sexually), *uku-phatha-phatha* (the intensive form of the verb *ukuphatha*, to touch or feel), or by the English word 'romance', used both as noun and verb—and with it sexual intercourse, are often part of a love-affair from an early age. Cases of pregnancy are known to occur from 12 years of age onward. Among the male informants 14 was the youngest age at which one of them first experienced sexual intercourse. From 16 years onwards most young people have love-affairs in which intercourse is a common element. Of the eighteen unmarried informants, only one denied having a sweetheart, but she was an unmarried mother who was still being visited by the father of her two children. With one young man who admitted having a sweetheart, conditions of interviewing were not favourable to discuss his relations with her. All the others spontaneously mentioned sexual intercourse as a regular feature of their relationship, and most of them stated explicitly that they practised full intercourse, not merely the traditionally sanctioned external intercourse.

Couples mostly meet in the young man's room, if he has one to himself, very seldom at the girl's home. If the latter happens it is usually secretly. Sleeping together at the boy's home may take place with his parents' cognizance. A youth of 22 mentioned his girl-friend spending a night with him, and added: 'My mother knows her, and she usually sees her when she has visited me, and she says I must not spoil her; I must marry her in church.' Another man of 30 broke away from his parents and their six younger children to take a room of his own, because he had nowhere to meet his girl-friend. He had quarrelled with his father who once found him sleeping with a girl on the veranda at home and then chased them away. Occasionally a boy who has no room of his own takes his sweetheart to a friend's room. Domestic servants 'sleeping in' are often visited by their lovers in their rooms on the employers' premises. The bushes in and around the location are a common meeting place for lovers who have no room to go to, particularly younger ones.

The amount of common activity between lovers, apart from love-making, varies considerably. Some young lovers often go about together: they attend places of amusement if they have the money, wander about the streets, play games, or just enjoy each other's company. Conversation may be in the nature of love-talk, or just casual, with some joking and teasing. 'She is not shy to cause monotony when we sit together. When we are in each other's company during the day, we kiss, talk about school matters and about bioscope pictures.' (Matric scholar.) 'When we are together my sweetheart usually tells me how he behaved when he was a schoolboy and he passes jokes.' (Girl of 20, J.C.) 'I pay her visits and take her to my home. Sometimes I take her to the beach, to concerts or the bioscope. When we are together we kiss, play cards, drink, sing songs, and we play and tease each other.' (Male of 24, standard five.) 'When we are together we sit close to each other, holding hands, chatting, laughing, and looking at each other with eyes full of love. If one is worried, you console him, kiss and romance him, so that he can be happy. If you are with your boy-friend, you feel in your seventh heaven. You cannot explain it, but you feel it.' (Girl of 20, student-midwife.) Some *tsotsi*-type young men hardly meet their girls otherwise than for love-making.

Girls make their boy-friends gifts in the form of handkerchiefs, sweets, cigarettes, and money. Some unemployed young men sponge on working girl-friends for their smoking-requirements and an occasional meal. Working young men sometimes make gifts of clothes to their girl-friends. Several girls stressed the requirement of obedience to their boy-friends when discussing their relationship. This particularly pertains to warnings against dealings with other men. Some girls use love-medicine to keep their lovers faithful. A young female teacher held that if her boy-friend's love should wane, 'I shall go to the herbalist and buy *isivamna* ["listen-to-me" medicine] so that he can think about me wherever he goes'.

Many young men and some girls also keep two or more lovers simultaneously, but then they usually distinguish between major and minor lovers. One is the 'known lover', sometimes also referred to as *makhonya*.[6] The others are 'subs', 'side-lines', or 'private' lovers. The English words are commonly used, but the Xhosa term *osecaleni* (one on the side) is also heard. Keeping 'side-lines' seems to be more common among the *tsotsi*-type of young men. One of these maintained he had two or three, 'but they have their lovers, and I am only a thief in each case. When an opportunity presents itself, I will go to any of these women. They drink and smoke cigarettes, and when I want one of them in my room, I wink an eye and whisper that I have something nice in my room, and she will follow me.' On the other hand a scholar now doing his Senior Certificate, who sometimes attends church and church choir practice on Sundays, said that besides the known lover, who was a scholar like himself, he had two others who 'work in town, and they are very helpful in supplying me with money. They are free and easier to be visited.' With his schoolgirl lover he gets a chance of spending a night about once a month, when she pretends to her parents to be attending a concert, but any of the others he can visit once a week. A young female teacher, again, kept an extra lover because she wanted to avoid the humiliation she had once before experienced, of being deserted by a lover in favour of another girl. 'If this man is full of nonsense, I can leave him

[6] *Ukukhonya* is used of the bellowing of a beast, the crowing of a cock, the cooing of a dove, etc. An informant explained that using the term *makhonya* of a lover indicates that she is the one who has the say.

for a night and spend the night with another, happy and in peace.' A *tsotsi*, again, said he had only one lover, but occasionally he slept with other girls he liked, 'just for a change'. A well-educated girl said she had previously had more than one lover, to be able to boast about it to her friends.

Occasionally one finds a youth or a girl maintaining that affection for the lover prevents him or her from taking on a second one, but the more common reason for avoiding multiple relationships is that these cause a lot of trouble. In case of pregnancy a girl with several lovers may find that the father of her child can easily deny paternity on the ground that she had these other lovers, or a young man may find he is accused of making a girl pregnant, while another is actually responsible. For this reason a young man found it better to stick to one faithful lover, because if you have more than one, 'you cannot easily check on them'. Multiple relationships also give rise to fighting between competing parties, even when they are females. Some girls, again, are afraid their boy-friends will ill-treat them if they should discover their having private lovers. For unmarried mothers it also involves the possibility of being made pregnant again sooner.

Occasionally young lovers think in terms of marriage when embarking on a love-affair. A girl with a Junior Certificate, training for a white-collar occupation, accepted her boy-friend's proposal of love because he also said he was going to marry her. 'I was interested because this was what I wanted, and not to get a baby without marriage. So I accepted his love.' However, she had had three lovers simultaneously before this. 'I left them because I did not love them with all my heart; I was just pretending, although they did not have any aims.' She maintains that she merely accepted them for sexual gratification 'and to tell other girls that I am a play-girl with three boy-friends'. Her new lover did eventually make her pregnant, but he told her he knew what he was doing: 'he wanted a child from me and not from anybody else, and he was responsible for that'. She is still anxious to marry him, and claims to have gone to the extent of stealing money from her parents to buy groceries for her prospective parents-in-law, 'so that he can realize that I will be a good wife for him and please his parents also'.

At the other extreme is a girl who intended keeping her lover until she had passed standard six, 'because I knew quite well that when I went to the institution, as I intended doing, I would not have boys of low classes to be in love with me. I would rather choose the teachers, because a person with very little education will not help me to increase my knowledge.' Her plans for higher education had to be postponed, however, since her lover rendered her pregnant and she had a baby soon after passing her standard six examination. At the time of the interview she still intended doing her Junior Certificate, but in any case still did not consider getting married to him, because the fact that he made her pregnant 'shows that he has no manners; he did a thing of which he was not sure'. A girl whose boy-friend had used force to make her accept his proposal did not want to get married to him, while another in the same position said he had promised to marry her and she was willing to have him as a husband.

The majority of informants seemed to consider the possibility of marriage favourably when it was suggested to them, without the prospect playing any significant role in their relationship. 'I should like to marry him if he is prepared' reflects the typical attitude of many girls, while the following non-committal answer is representative of many young males: 'I should like to marry her, but

I am not yet thinking of getting married, and if I should consider it while I am still in love with her, I shall marry her.' One male informant said he was not yet considering marriage because of unemployment, another because he was not yet initiated, another because he was still at school (doing his Senior Certificate): 'But I will marry her if we complete our education still in love.' A *tsotsi*-type said he would like to marry his sweetheart, but he suspected she was barren because they had been sweethearts and having sexual relations for some years 'without any result' (see p. 77). Another typical *tsotsi* who also adopted a wait-and-see attitude added that 'in fact I do not think our people think of marrying when they make love to each other. To propose marriage to a girl depends on the choice of the parents at times. This happens here in town. If I choose a girl for marriage, I may not choose the most beautiful one, because she will be tempted to commit adultery.'

These pre-marital love-affairs, then, although they may last for several years, and may even result in the birth of more than one child to the female partner, are essentially temporary liaisons, entered into only with a view to sexual gratification and companionship for the present and immediate future. The desire to be in step with one's friends and equals acts as a further urge toward such affairs. It follows that the majority break up without leading to a marriage. This is usually the result of loss of interest on the part of one of the partners, often as a result of another love-affair, or disagreeableness. Some admit that they never really loved a former lover. A love-affair seldom lasts after one partner has left East London.

PRE-MARITAL PREGNANCY

The majority of town Bantu girls have at least one baby before they get married. Over 60 per cent of the unmarried females in our sample (15 years and over) were mothers (table 14) and for the age groups between 20 and 35, the years during which most girls get married, the percentage was 74. Even of the girls in the 15–19 age group, nearly half were already mothers. It is obvious that pre-marital pregnancy, and that from an early age, is extremely common. There is further a tendency for unmarried mothers to continue having more children as they grow older. Nearly half of the unmarried mothers in the sample had more than one child, and two had as many as six children each.

TABLE 14

Unmarried females: pregnancy by age

	EXPERIENCED PREGNANCY		
Age	Yes	No	Total
15–19	16	18	34
20–24	12	6	18
25–29	10	3	13
30–34	3	—	3
35–44	4	—	4
45 plus	1	1	2
Total	46	28	74

(Table 34, appendix I.) The average for different age groups steadily increases from 1·1 for the unmarried mothers of the 15–19 group, to 3·8 for the age group of 35 and over. Of the twenty-one who had more than one child, thirteen claimed that they were by the same father, seven said there were two fathers, and one said there were three.

On the whole, the earlier pre-marital pregnancies are the outcome of the young people's love-affairs described in the previous section, not of mere chance meetings. Although one may find girls who have children by married men, this is not the rule.[7] These young unmarried lovers are usually anxious to avoid pregnancy. Mostly they resort to practising *coitus interruptus*, but some use contraceptives. A small number restrict themselves to external intercourse in the traditional way.

Although pre-marital pregnancy has become very common, most girls are nevertheless upset when they discover that they are pregnant. Some have intense feelings of guilt and shame, and may even consider suicide. Others are only worried because their parents are upset, or because they have to face a period of loneliness, staying at home, deprived of entertainment and the company of friends. Some also grieve over an educational career that has been cut short.

The following reminiscences of a girl from a well-furnished home, undergoing training for a 'white-collar' occupation, is an example of the more intensive type of reaction. 'I felt so unhappy and lonely that I kept on crying, but did not want anybody to see it, because I would not tell her my secret feelings [*umvandedwa*, lit. the feel-it-alone]. I thought I should drink poison and die, because I was completing my Junior Certificate. I thought of my parents, who sent me to school so that I could help them in future. I did not take poison, because I was afraid of death, since pregnancy is sin, and I thought I would not see heaven. I thought of one who could procure abortion, but I remembered a song which I used to hear: "These children whom you aborted await you up there in heaven",[8] so I decided to leave all those bad thoughts. . . . I did not tell anybody except my boy-friend, because I was afraid they would tell the teachers at school, so that I would be out of school, while I intended still to write my examinations. Fortunately I could still write and pass my Junior Certificate already pregnant.' A girl of a lower educational level (standard three) seems to have been less upset. She had stopped menstruating, 'but I did not realize that that was how a person got pregnant. I would have kept on going to school if my mother had not told me not to go. When I asked why I should not go, she shouted at me whether I could not see that I was pregnant. Now I began to feel it. . . . No boy-friend to be seen now. I was just a lonely thing that was kept indoors. My father did not want to speak to me for a long time because of the bad thing I had done.' Attempts to procure payment of damages failed, because the girl had been in love with two boys at the same time. 'I felt very unhappy, because the whole of my family was cross with me because nothing was going to be obtained from pregnancy except the baby, which would have to be provided with everything by them.'

Parents' reactions also vary from feeling deeply distressed, to just being fed-up, as in the case just quoted. Some do not seem to worry very much as long as the girl's lover offers some redress. 'My mother and father did not swear at me, but they only became sick, because they did not know that a child of 13 years could become pregnant.' However, when she became pregnant a second time 'my parents now swore at me, and sometimes my mother did not give me supper, saying that we had done it purposely now'. 'I did not go back to school [after having the baby]. My mother said I had had enough education. She did

[7] Married men often have love-affairs with older unmarried mothers (see p. 131).

[8] '*Aba 'bantwana nibaqhomfayo banilindele kweli phezulu.*' (A Xhosa wedding-song.)

not send me to school for boys but to learn, and that she would not even care for that baby.' (Both these girls became factory-workers.) Another girl, whose own mother is also unmarried, said her mother's attention was drawn to her condition by other women. 'She said she did not know I could get pregnant at that age [14]. . . . My mother said I should not be worried, because they were not cross with me, since I did not think of doing anything that would procure abortion and they had obtained something from my pregnancy, which is not common in these days.' (The girl's lover had made two payments amounting to R48.00 (£24).) When a girl's pregnancy does cause tension between her and her parents, it is usually temporary.

The parents usually make some attempt to find out who is responsible for their daughter's pregnancy and try to obtain a sum of money as damages or as *lobolo* for marriage. The amount claimed varies, and parents seem to regard themselves fortunate if they get anything at all. Some lovers undertake to make a regular maintenance contribution, and sometimes the matter is taken to the Bantu Affairs Commissioner to compel the young man to pay maintenance.

The following cases illustrate the confusion in regard to the steps that are taken about pre-marital pregnancy. The girl who was 13 when she became pregnant for the first time, said that her family 'went for the *lobolo* business. They were promised to be paid fifty pounds in instalments of five pounds per month.' She went to stay with her lover after becoming pregnant for the second time, but returned to her parents when she took ill after the birth of the second child. 'When my boy-friend came to fetch me, they told him that he had to pay twenty pounds for the first baby, which he had not paid, and another twenty pounds for the second baby. He did not seem to take any notice, until he was taken to "Native Affairs", where he promised to pay £2 10*s*. per month.' Another girl (standard three, pregnant at 15) said that when her parents went to the boy's home, the boy was not even called, and the mother insisted that 'her son of 16, my boy-friend, would never make a girl pregnant. My mother then told me to go with them, but I refused, because I knew that my boy-friend would not admit responsibility, because he knew that I was in love with another boy. My people never went again; they left the matter there till today.' In the case of the girl who had passed her Junior Certificate the family went to ask for *intlawulo yesisu* (damages, lit., payment for the womb). He promised to marry her, and he was expected to pay R200 (£100): '£25 was for the books they had bought for my schooling, £50 for my pregnancy, and £25 to make sure that he was willing to marry me. The money was to be collected the next time they visited him. When they went, they only got £25, and he told them that they would be receiving it in instalments, because he had to buy everything that was needed for the baby, so they should come after the baby had been born.' The boy-friend of a girl with standard three, who was 14 when first pregnant, sent his brother with R34 (£17) as damages and the request to have the girl as his wife, but her family demanded R100 (£50) for *lobolo*. Only a further R14 (£7) was sent. 'I had the second baby from that man, but he never married me, because he never finished paying the £50. My brother went to look for him, but they could never find him, and they decided to leave him as he was. On the second baby there were no questions, and he did not give my parents anything', but he does contribute regularly towards maintenance. Another girl with standard six maintained that her parents demanded R150 (£75) 'damages'.

ATTITUDES TO PRE-MARITAL SEX RELATIONS

The widespread practice of full sexual intercourse and the common occurrence of pregnancy among unmarried young people reflects a behaviour pattern conflicting both with traditional Xhosa ethical notions and the Christian norm of complete chastity before marriage introduced by the missionaries. On the whole, complete chastity before marriage is still upheld as moral norm by the majority of Whites in South Africa, and Bantu, even those in towns, have not been exposed to the propagation of free love to any significant extent. It is important, therefore, to know in what terms the urban Bantu frame their judgement on pre-marital sex relations.

In an attempt to test this, the following four questions were put to the persons in our general sample:[9]

What do you think of a young man (*umfana*)—

(1) who renders a girl pregnant?

(2) who has never rendered a girl pregnant, but has full sexual intercourse with one?

(3) who does *ukumetsha* without full sexual intercourse? [By this is understood intercourse *intra crures*.]

(4) who is in love with a girl, but never has sexual intercourse with her or any other girl?

The great majority of answers could be easily classified as expressing a positive or negative attitude to the behaviour mentioned in each case. Positive attitudes were usually expressed in terms such as 'right', 'good', or 'better', and negative attitudes in terms like 'bad', 'wrong', 'not right', 'disgraceful', 'foolish', 'do not like it', 'spoils her future', or 'leaves her in the lurch'. The results of this classification of answers, given in table 15, show that hardly anybody explicitly sanctioned pre-marital pregnancy, and a small number sanctioned full sexual intercourse. A small number expressed opinions which left their attitude undecided on these matters, for instance, in the case of question 1, by giving answers like 'He must be made to marry her', and 'Bad, but good if damages paid or marriage follows'. Undecided answers to question 2 were those merely expressing the opinion that such a boy is abnormal or needs a doctor's attention, showing that what struck the respondents in these cases was not the occurrence of pre-marital intercourse, but that pregnancy did not occur when intercourse had taken place.

TABLE 15

Attitudes to pre-marital sex relations

Attitude to young man who—	Positive	Undecided	Negative	Total*
(1) renders girl pregnant	2	6	167	175
(2) has not rendered pregnant, but practises full intercourse	8	3	164	175
(3) practises only external intercourse	134	5	36	175
(4) is in love, but abstains from intercourse	60	16	99	175

* The answers from 27 persons in the sample who were interviewed by one particular assistant were so uniformly patterned, in contrast to the diversity of answers returned by other assistants, that a strong suspicion of bias could not be avoided. They were therefore rejected.

[9] These questions, which were embodied in questionnaire A (see appendix II), were discussed beforehand with Bantu field assistants who were unanimous in their opinion that matters such as these are often openly discussed, and the questions would not be regarded as improper.

External intercourse, the traditionally sanctioned pattern of sexual behaviour for young people, was positively valued by the great majority of persons in the sample, but one of these remarked on the divergence between ideal and actual behaviour, saying: 'It is right, but not common today.' Others went further, expressing a negative attitude with answers like the following: 'In olden days it was right, not now'; 'It is out of fashion today—no girl likes this'; 'He does not follow' (*akalandeli*)—the latter also indicating that such behaviour is old-fashioned. Several commented on the fact of this being traditional behaviour, and in two cases where no further opinion was expressed the remark was classified as an undecided attitude.

Corresponding with this attitude to external intercourse, the majority expressed a negative attitude in respect of the lover who practises no sexual intercourse whatsoever, indicating that, on the whole, the Christian ideal of pre-marital chastity is rejected in favour of the traditional permission of external intercourse for unmarried persons. It is revealing that many of the answers regarded such behaviour as indicating physical abnormality—these being classified as negative. Another expressed doubt that such behaviour exists. Two answers to the effect that 'It is right, but I doubt his health', indicate an undecided attitude. A few just described such a boy as *bhulu* or *isishumane*, terms indicating shyness in love-making, but not physical abnormality. If no more explicit attitude was expressed, such answers were also classified as undecided.

The full significance of the answers can only be judged when the patterning of the whole series of four answers is analysed. The following are the patterns observed.

A. The dominant pattern is that which clearly follows *traditional values*: a negative attitude to pre-marital pregnancy and full intercourse, as well as to complete chastity, but positive to external intercourse. *Forty-five per cent* of the sample followed this pattern.

B. Acceptance of the *Christian ideal*—positive valuation of complete chastity, negative of all three other cases—was expressed by *thirteen per cent.*

C. Where the attitude to pre-marital pregnancy and full intercourse was not explicitly negative, one could deduce a *tendency to sanction or at least condone the present common sexual behaviour* of unmarried persons which runs counter to both traditional and Christian values. *Eleven per cent* (19 persons) gave answers along these lines. (Explicitly positive attitudes to pre-marital pregnancy or full sexual intercourse or both was expressed by ten persons, undecided attitudes by nine.)

D. A considerable number disapproved of examples 1 and 2, but expressed conflicting attitudes in approving of both the traditional (3) and the Christian (4), or, by giving an undecided answer, avoiding making the choice. *Such conflicting or uncertain attitudes* were expressed by forty-nine persons constituting *twenty-eight per cent* of the sample, as follows:

Approved of both 3 and 4	31
Approved of 3 but undecided about 4	11
Approved of 4 but undecided about 3	2
Other undecided	5

An interesting example of an undecided attitude is that of a girl who disapproved of all forms of intercourse, but said about the chaste lover: 'This is good to church people, but I think he is sick.' A semi-Red woman who approved of the traditional practice for unmarried persons, expressed an ambivalent attitude to the chaste lover: 'It may be that he is not well, or he has no real love, or he is fooling, or he does not want to spoil my daughter.'

E. Six persons expressed negative attitudes to all four cases. This also apparently involves conflicting attitudes by disapproving of external intercourse as well as complete chastity. However, three of these were members of the Assemblies of God, and it was explained that with their negative reaction to question 4, they did not disapprove of the absence of sexual relations, but they had in mind love-affairs as such. They held that their church did not approve of young people being in love at all.[10]

Although actual behaviour suggests that the traditional ideal of restriction to external intercourse is outmoded and the Christian ideal of complete chastity is regarded as untenable, there are not many people who openly advocate the complete sexual freedom which is practised. There is, therefore, divergence between actual behaviour and the norms to which lip-service is offered.[11] Further, the attitudes expressed are obviously patterned much more according to traditional moral values than Christian sex teaching, but there is a distinct tendency to avoid an explicit choice between the two. This divergence between behaviour and norm and the perpetuation of conflicting values may either point to an inner conflict which is building up, or to the absence of strong convictions in matters of sex.[12]

Occasionally, however, one finds an attempt to compromise, or to adjust the values to the existing reality. One respondent regarded external intercourse as 'better' but none as 'best'. A young wife who is a member of the Assemblies of God, and has a high degree of interest in her church, approved of the traditional ideal and regarded the completely chaste lover as being unhealthy sexually. But she commented that 'though biblically fornication and similar things are unholy before marriage, one may do it with someone he intends marrying'. Her older husband, a member of the same church, compromised, but did not really resolve the conflict. Of the traditional practice he said: 'This is wrong before marriage for earnest Christians, but I accept it as necessary', and of chastity: 'In church we are told that is right, but I think it is a sign of weak health.'

Our sample does not suggest that attitudes to sex relations vary much with the degree of interest in the church (table 35). It is notable, however, that only two of the persons with little or no interest in church expressed attitudes conforming to the Christian ideal. Marked variations cannot be claimed either between persons of different educational levels (table 36), or between different cultural categories (table 37). Therefore the conclusions arrived at seem to apply relatively evenly to all types of urban Bantu, with the exception, perhaps, that among people with few or no church ties, the Christian ideal of sexual morality receives the least support. Altogether it is clear that Christian sex teaching has only a restricted impact on the attitude and practice of East London's urban Bantu, at least as far as pre-marital relations are concerned.

[10] This extreme attitude is somewhat understandable against the background of the fact that to most urban Bantu young people being in love implies having sexual relations.

[11] Material collected under different conditions suggested that the norm has, in fact, changed —the new norm being full intercourse, with care to avoid pregnancy—but when a moral judgement had to be quickly formulated by the respondent, as in answers to our questionnaire, there is the tendency still to fall back on the traditional norm. (Cf. Mayer, *Townsmen or Tribesmen*, pp. 254–5.)

[12] See further, pp. 163–164.

7

Marriage and Children

Although this chapter does not deal with household structure as such, some of the material discussed here is relevant to the question of the structure and growth of the domestic group. It is therefore appropriate to preface our discussion of marriage and children with a few remarks to indicate the points around which our discussion of the household will be focused. Our major aim is to indicate what the urban Xhosa household is like, and what changes are taking place in its structure and in the values connected with it, as part of the processes of 'westernization' and urbanization. The stress has been on getting to know the urban household, systematizing facts, and distinguishing a type or types.

Recent studies in social anthropology have emphasized the importance of the 'developmental dimension' in the study of domestic groups.[1] It has to be recognized that the domestic group, even where rapid social change is not involved, is always involved in a cyclical process and that it takes on a different structure during different phases in this cycle of development. When identifying different 'types' of household structure observed in a certain population at a given time, we should take care, therefore, to ascertain whether we are, in fact, dealing with different types or merely with different phases in the developmental cycle of the same structural type. In the present case the concept of the developmental cycle needs to be applied with caution, however, since urban Bantu society is a 'new' phenomenon, and in East London most urban families have hardly completed their first full cycle, so to speak. It may be difficult to tell whether the changes in the structure of individual households represent changes of a cyclical order or the emergence of new structural forms as part of the process to which Fortes refers as 'the amorphous subject-matter usually labelled "culture change" or "social change" '.[2]

Another aspect of the study of the household which has been emphasized is that of the varying roles and statuses of father and mother in societies which are neither patrilineal nor matrilineal. Various studies have drawn attention to household patterns among New World Negroes and elsewhere, as in, for example, British labour class families, which exhibit what has been termed matrifocal tendencies.[3] The position of the urban Bantu in the wider social structure has certain characteristics in common with that of the communities or classes for which matrifocal families have been recorded—characteristics which have been connected with the matrifocal trend. On the other hand there is the tradition, from which the urban Bantu are not yet far 'removed'—neither in time nor in space—of a social structure and values in which patrilineal ties were strongly emphasized. In view of these considerations the positions of mother

[1] e.g., Goody, Jack (ed.) *The Developmental Cycle in Domestic Groups*, Cambridge Papers in Social Anthropology, No. 1, Cambridge University Press, 1958, and Smith, Raymond T., *The Negro Family in British Guiana*, Routledge and Kegan Paul, 1956.

[2] Introduction to Goody, op. cit., p. 1.

[3] Cf., e.g., Smith, op. cit.; and Young, M., and Willmot, P., *Family and Kinship in East London*.

and father in the urban Bantu family require particular attention. Our material leaves no doubt that there is a strong matrifocal trend in households, but where the father is present his role is still conditioned by traditional ideas about male authority and the importance of descent through males.

Their positions are also significant from another angle. In a study of British families, Bott has paid particular attention to conjugal roles and distinguished between 'segregated' and 'non-segregated' conjugal role-relationships, according to the degree in which husband and wife shared in common activities and social networks.[4] She suggested, amongst others, that the degree of segregation of conjugal roles is related to the nature of the social network. Traditionally the roles of Xhosa husband and wife were highly segregated, while the social network was particularly close-knit. This also renders the question of the roles of father and mother in the Xhosa urban situation particularly interesting.

However, let us first consider the question of marriage. When Bantu couples live together as husband and wife, their relationship may be based either on a legally recognized marriage contracted by civil or religious (church) rites, or on a 'customary union, which enjoys only "indirect and partial" legal recognition as an inferior matrimonial union'[5]; or they may be living in concubinage without legal sanction. In our sample the great majority of couples who regarded themselves as legally married claimed to have been through church or civil rites. The rest claimed that *lobolo* had been given in respect of the marriage, which, although not the only grounds on which a relationship could be regarded as a customary union, is sufficient reason to classify it as such. Before discussing the different forms of marriage, we may first consider some of the preliminaries to marriage.

THE CHOICE OF A PARTNER: INDIVIDUAL CHOICE AND ROMANTIC LOVE

A general feature of the changes which marriage is today undergoing among many African peoples, particularly in urban areas, is the tendency toward marriage based on individual choice of the partners concerned, in contrast with the selection of partners for young people by their parents and other kinsmen, which used to prevail in many African societies. In East London this trend is also obvious, but there is considerable variation on this point. We have noted the extremely individualistic approach in the case of the teacher who fell in love with the nurse while both were following their respective professions away from their homes. The two of them by themselves decided to get married and the marriage was solemnized by civil rites with a minimum of publicity.[6] At the other extreme is the case of a young husband (standard five, married 1957) whose parents took the initiative. 'An old man in our church, called grandfather M——, recommended the girl to my mother. I did not know the girl before, except by sight. I was told by them and my father to go and propose marriage to her and I successfully did so.' A prospective bridegroom himself sometimes also turns to other people for suggestions about a suitable bride.[7] Quite often marriages are arranged for daughters without their having accepted the marriage proposal. This does not necessarily happen without their cognizance, but it does sometimes take place against their wish. Examples of this have been noted in chapter 5.

[4] Bott, E., *Family and Social Network*, Tavistock Publications, London, 1957.

[5] Holleman, op. cit.; cf. Simons, H. J., 'The Law and its Administration', in Hellman, Ellen (ed.), *Handbook on Race Relations in South Africa*, Oxford University Press, Cape Town, 1949.

[6] See p. 99–100. [7] See p. 98.

However, it is common for a young man to propose marriage to the girl of his choice, and for the girl to accept or reject him according to her own wish. After the two have come to an agreement, the young man generally refers the matter to his parents, not only for their consent, but also in order that they should formally make the request to the girl's parents through chosen messengers. Although a number of relatives and friends are usually drawn into these negotiations, which are sometimes still quite elaborate, they do not have much influence to oppose the choice of the young people themselves. Parents do at times express disapproval of their children's choice, but if the couple persist in their intention, the parents can hardly force the issue. Unless one of the couple is a minor—and mostly this is not so—there is nothing to prevent them from getting married by church or civil rites. Parents may even be forced into co-operation if the girl is made pregnant by her would-be bridegroom. In relationships in which the question of marriage has never yet been discussed, the girl's pregnancy may also precipitate the marriage, although this seems to happen only in a minority of cases of pregnancy nowadays.

Marriage by individual choice does not necessarily imply romantic love as a preliminary to marriage. Often enough a relationship of romantic love does lead to marriage, but we have noticed that a pre-marital love-affair tends to be something apart from marriage, existing in its own right. Moreover, a person acceptable as a lover is not always acceptable as a marriage partner. Outstanding physical beauty or handsomeness may be desirable in a lover, but not in a marriage partner, because it easily leads to infidelity. Barrenness in a girl does not lead to her rejection as a lover, but throws grave doubts on her suitability as a wife. The girl's family background may also count in the choice of a wife, and cause a man to marry a girl other than his lover. A married clerk related the following about his paramour: 'It was during 1954 when we first met, and I loved her very much. Her beauty was the main attraction, and she was very smart. This was before I got married. I met my wife in the middle of 1955 and we were married towards the end of that year. My wife was not as beautiful and as smart as my lover, but when it came to the choice of a good wife, she outshone my lover. The parents of the woman count a great deal when considering marriage, and my wife came from a respectable family of townspeople.'

CUSTOMARY UNIONS

Of the 34 males in our sample who had been married, 8 had been married by traditional custom only. For females the figure was 4 out of 52 (table 16). In several cases the partners to customary unions were quite young. Customary unions therefore appear still to be of some significance among East London's urban Bantu. In a number of cases, however, particular conditions existed to which attention must be drawn. In three cases it ultimately emerged that neither of the two marriage partners in each had actually been born in East London. In another, the East London-born partner came from a 'double-rooted' family which, although long and firmly established in town, still kept a homestead in the country. The wife of the man in question was still living in that country homestead, while the children appeared to alternate between the two homes. Of the rest, three cases were in the same family: three East London-born brothers, all relatively young, were living with their wives as members of the same household, of which their widowed mother claimed to be the head. It

TABLE 16
Forms of marriage

Group	Form of marriage	MALES Marital status: Living together	Married	Temporarily separated	Divorced or separated	Widowed	Total	FEMALES Marital status: Living together	Married	Temporarily separated	Divorced or separated	Widowed	Total
	Living together (No form of marriage)	2	—	—	—	—	2	5	—	—	—	—	5
Christian Rites	Christian rites only	—	—	—	—	—	—	—	1	—	—	—	1
Christian Rites	Christian rites and *lobolo* (and *ukudlisa amasi*)	—	15	2	—	1	18	—	21	—	3	13	37
Christian Rites / Civil Rites	Christian rites and civil rites and *lobolo*	—	1	—	—	—	1	—	—	—	—	—	—
Civil Rites	Civil rites only	—	—	—	—	—	—	—	—	1	—	—	1
Civil Rites	Civil rites and *lobolo* (and *ukudlisa amasi*)	—	3	—	—	1	4	—	1	1	1	1	4
Civil Rites	Civil rites and *lobolo* and *ukuthwala*	—	—	—	1	—	1	—	—	—	—	—	—
Customary Union Only	*Lobolo* and *ukuthwala* and *ukudlisa amasi*	—	1	2	—	—	3	—	—	—	—	2	2
Customary Union Only	*Lobolo* and *ukudlisa amasi*	—	1	—	—	—	1	—	1	—	—	—	1
Customary Union Only	*Lobolo* and *ukuthwala*	—	3	1	—	—	4	—	—	—	—	—	—
Customary Union Only	*Lobolo* only	—	—	—	—	—	—	—	—	1	—	—	1
	Total in sample	2	24	5	1	2	34	5	24	3	4	16	52
	Total Christian rites	—	16	2	—	1	19	—	22	—	3	13	38
	Total Civil rites	—	4	—	1	1	6	—	1	2	1	1	5
	Total *lobolo*	—	24	5	1	2	32	—	23	2	4	16	45
	Total *ukudlisa amasi*	—	16	3	—	1	20	—	14	—	2	16	32
	Total *ukuthwala*	—	4	3	1	—	8	—	1	—	—	2	3

may well be, therefore, that customary unions are not as common as would appear from our sample.

Traditionally there was a customary form of ceremonial, accompanied by feasting, by which the bride was officially handed over to the bridegroom and his people. In the reserves such wedding feasts are still common, although in modified form, but in town they are hardly known, although an instance of such formal handing over of a bride in connexion with the customary union was noted in chapter 5. An alternative form of marriage was by the custom known as *ukuthwala*, a form of elopement or abduction which has become more common in the reserves in recent times.[8] Often this takes place with the connivance of the girl's father and after he has formally been asked for his daughter's hand. It may also happen that the parties agree to the girl being taken by *ukuthwala* after *lobolo*-payment has already been made. Most of the customary unions in our sample were said to have been *ukuthwala* marriages, but informants hold that in town the term usually implies nothing more than that the couple start living together, with or without the consent of the parents.

Another aspect of traditional marriage ceremonial is the slaughtering of a goat for the rite of letting the bride drink milk (*ukudlisa amasi*). Before performance of the rite, which often takes place some time after the marriage, the bride may not drink the milk of her husband's clan. The ceremony is regarded as establishing a ritual bond between the bride and her husband's ancestors. Some people nowadays regard performance of the rite as the form of legalization alternative to Christian or civil marriage rites, but it was not performed for all customary unions in our sample. On the other hand, many of the couples married by Christian rites maintained that *ukudlisa amasi* was also performed for them.

LEGAL MARRIAGE AND 'LOBOLO'

The most common form of marriage is by Christian rites. In our sample this type constituted a majority of all marriages. The proportion of marriages by civil rites is still small.[9] In spite of this large-scale acceptance of legal marriage, it is significant to note that it is mostly accompanied by *lobolo*,[10] and often also by the rite of *ukudlisa amasi*. Urban *lobolo* has received considerable attention in recent times,[11] so that we did not attempt an intensive investigation on this point, but we shall indicate what evidence there is of the existence in East London of some of the phenomena mentioned in other studies.

Throughout southern Africa cash is now often being substituted for the cattle or other stock traditionally given in settlement of *lobolo*, and with it a commercial element is being introduced into marriage.[12] This is particularly prevalent in

[8] Wilson, Monica, and others, *Social Structure*, Keiskammahoek Rural Survey, volume III, p. 84.

[9] Some allowance could be made for customary unions being returned as legal marriages in a survey, and for persons living in concubinage claiming to be married, but I do not think this happened very often.

[10] According to unpublished figures collected by Dr. D. H. Reader in 1955 the proportion of East London-born persons legally married without payment of *lobolo* is larger than in my sample, but in those figures they also constitute quite a minority.

[11] e.g. Brandel, M., 'Urban Lobolo Attitudes', *African Studies*, 17, 1 (1958), pp. 34–50; Mathewson, J. E., 'Impact of Urbanization on Lobolo', *Journal of Racial Affairs*, 10, 3 (1959), pp. 72–6; and Holleman, F. J., op. cit.

[12] Mair, L. P., 'African Marriage and Social Change', in Phillips, Arthur, *Survey of African Marriage and Family Life*, London: Oxford University Press, for International African Institute (1953), pp. 26, 37, 67, etc.

urban areas, and in marriages of townspeople in East London, the usual procedure is for *lobolo* to be settled in cash. Nevertheless, cases in which part or the whole of the *lobolo* payment was in the form of cattle are not uncommon. Thus, for the marriage of a couple married in 1956 *lobolo* consisted of two head of cattle and R160 (£80) (representing eight head of cattle). Both were town-born young people, and their educational qualifications were Junior Certificate and standard six respectively. It is perhaps significant that the man's family owned cattle and that he slaughtered goats to perform the *ukubingelela* rite for the birth of his daughter and a rite of mourning (*izila*) for his late father. Even when in the form of cash, the amount of *lobolo* payment is still commonly expressed in terms of cattle, R20 (£10) being regarded as the equivalent of one beast. In the majority of cases the amount is from six to ten head of cattle.[13] Only occasionally does it exceed ten beasts.

The bridegroom usually has to provide *lobolo* out of his own resources, and there is also the tendency for the recipient, not uncommonly the girl's widowed mother, to use the money in her own interests. One mother used *lobolo*-money to build additional rooms to her house. An informant also commented on the tendency for *lobolo* to be spent in connexion with the wedding or the bride's trousseau. 'People will tell you here that after the wedding there is hardly a penny left over of the *lobolo*: it has all been spent on buying things for the bride.' On the other hand, a woman of 36, whose town-dwelling mother received ten head of cattle, a mare, and R20(£10), said that her mother sold some of the cattle and bought sheep from the proceeds, and 'we still have the progeny of the original cattle and sheep'.

The weight of opinion values *lobolo* positively, even in the urban setting. 'It is a must', as one informant put it. Some feel that it should be maintained because of its being traditional custom, and even when no additional reasons are mentioned, there seems to be more behind this attachment than mere sentimentality. *Lobolo* is commonly regarded as a compensation to the parent or guardian for the cost of the bride's upbringing, particularly that of her school education. A teacher, married to a nurse, who also held this view, explained that his wife had been brought up by her mother's brother after the death of her own parents. Her guardian 'did more to her than he did to his own children in the way of education. From the information I received from my wife in our conversations before marriage, I felt he deserved compensation for his kindness.'

The wife's status is regarded as depending on the giving of *lobolo*, and to be married without it is a disgrace. 'If no *lobolo* has been paid, you are a cheap wife', said one married woman. A husband again held that he would not have been willing to get married without *lobolo* because 'I do not want to have a wife for nothing'. On the other hand, it may be regarded as proof of the man's worth as a future husband. 'Some people say that payment of *lobolo* is a test to see if the bridegroom is a man of substance. If he cannot afford to pay *lobolo* there is no guarantee that he can maintain a family. I share this view. If a man has money or cattle when he decides to get married, that proves beyond doubt that he is thrifty, which is the principal thing today and tomorrow.' The stress is therefore on the status of the marriage, and on the guarantee of future economic security, rather than on legalization of the union.

The adherence to *lobolo* in conjunction with legal marriage has been interpreted as an attempt to bolster the institution of marriage, which, particularly

[13] Reader, D. H., unpublished figures.

among urban Bantu, is in an uncertain and insecure condition.[14] Other phenomena pointing in the same direction are the observance of *ukudlisa amasi* alongside Christian rites, and other elaborate ceremonials surrounding the marriage. We have noted the importance attached to the wedding feast, even though it may be postponed, to such an extent that months after the solemnization of marriage a mother insists on the celebration (chapter 5). We suggested that the display and publicity to which the feast gives occasion, ratify the new status and relationships of the couple in the eyes of the public. Thus the feast gives status to the marriage, and attracts the interest of the community, and this may compensate to some extent for the loss of the interest of whole kin groups on either side, which used to be a potent stabilizing factor in marriage, particularly through co-operation and common responsibility in connexion with *lobolo*. The status which the marriage is afforded in the eyes of the community through *lobolo* and the wedding feast may contribute to increase the couple's feeling of responsibility in respect of their marriage. The element of publicity in connexion with the wedding feast may also stimulate this by counteracting the tendency toward a purely individualistic approach. Instead of the marriage resting on the frail foundation of the mutual agreement of two individuals recorded in the 'secrecy' of a commissioner's or a minister's office, its foundation is bolstered by making it the concern of a wider community. The community aspect is stressed by the fact that not only personal friends, but also community leaders, and usually anybody else who wishes to attend, may be found taking part in these feasts. The adherence to *lobolo* may also tie up with emotional factors which are discussed at a later stage.[15]

EXTRA-MARITAL RELATIONS

Extra-marital relations of married persons constitute another type of sexual union which may be discussed in connexion with marriage. Although it is difficult to assess the extent to which such relationships occur, the available evidence indicates that they must be very common. Intensive interviews on extra-marital relations were conducted with fourteen married men and twelve married women, all town-born, selected at random to represent varying educational levels, although medium or more highly educated persons predominated. Nine of the males and seven of the females admitted having extra-marital affairs at the time of the interviews. Although one cannot claim that these proportions are representative of the urban Bantu, it indicates at least that the numbers of married persons involved in such love-affairs must be considerable. All the male informants, as well as the females who admitted having lovers, were of the opinion that among married persons those who do not have lovers are in the minority: they are 'a few', 'very few', 'one in ten', 'three in a thousand', or married persons with lovers 'are even more than the unmarried persons [who have lovers]'. Four of the females who denied having lovers, however, thought there were many married women like themselves in this respect.

The occurrence of extra-marital relations does not seem to be associated only with certain types or levels in the community, such as the less-educated people with simple material culture or those who lack close church ties. Informants who admitted such relationships included full church members taking an active

[14] Holleman, op. cit.
[15] See pp. 196–7.

part in church activities. Several had a Junior Certificate or teacher's qualification and came from well-furnished homes. However, they may be less common among staunch church members than among those not interested in the church. A number of informants, including some who admitted love-affairs, expressed the opinion that staunch Christians, 'those who fear God and the people', '*manyano* women', or men 'who come from Christian homes' are the kind of married persons who do not have extra-marital love-affairs. 'I would describe them as Christians who fear to do anything wrong because of God and because of the people. At the same time they realize that although the desire to do these things is there, there is no gain but a bundle of troubles. Because church people and ordinary people in the location speak highly of these men, that admiration gives them more strength to resist the temptation, and once you practise self-control, the desire becomes less and less' (a lay-preacher who has no lover). On the other hand some thought that the people who disapprove of love-affairs do so merely to pretend innocence, while they are the very ones who have them. In this connexion one informant referred to 'staunch members of the church, particularly the members of the young men's *manyano*'.

Often such a liaison is between two persons who are both partners to legal marriages, but many married women prefer unattached males as lovers, and men prefer unmarried mothers or widows, to avoid trouble with legally married spouses. 'I shall never be in love with a married man, because I will always be afraid of his wife, that she will come and shout at me, so that it will be known that I am committing adultery.' The unmarried mothers whom married men take as their lovers are usually not the young girl mothers, but mature women who are called *amankazana*. Traditionally this word was used of married women who had returned to their fathers' homes and continued bearing children there, or of mature unmarried women who became unmarried mothers.[16]

Love-affairs are often associated with an unsatisfactory state of married life. One woman referred to quarrels with her husband and not being at peace with him. Several women claimed to have accepted lovers because their husbands were having affairs with other women. This is not only to repay them in their own coin, but also because husbands readily neglect their families when they keep lovers, which gives some wives all the more reason to accept lovers who in their turn will assist them. 'My husband had too many girl-friends and did not want to sleep in my room. He did not give me any money and did not provide me with clothes. . . . My lover gave me money so that I could buy all I wanted.' A woman whose husband had been away for three years said: 'I have got a lover, since I noticed that my husband did not want to come back from Johannesburg, as he started to be a poor correspondent.'

A love-affair may also be associated with a spouse's loss of interest in the other marriage partner as a result of age. A woman of 56 told of her lover buying her sweets 'whereas my husband now thinks of his grandchildren when he has sweets'. Further she complained that there was no 'romance' between them and that he very seldom had intercourse with her. 'Love is not plentiful now.' Loss of sexual interest is also associated with husband and wife becoming too accustomed to each other, or with the drudgery of married life. A married woman justified her love-affair by saying that it gave her the opportunity of having 'a nice time, because when you are married, there is no love, but you

[16] Cf. Mayer, op. cit., p. 235.

have to look after the children, keep your husband clean to be seen by the other girls, and keep the room clean and tidy'.

It is significant that several informants mentioned men or women who were being satisfied by their legal spouses, in sexual matters as well as in domestic relations generally, as the ones who do not keep lovers. A man of 40, who had been married some nine years, claimed that he had abandoned his former lovers after a few months of married life 'because of entire satisfaction' with his wife. He still felt that way about her, because 'she is faithful to me; she loves me and I love her. She is very sympathetic with me; she takes my word when I say I have no money today. In all I do she is at my side to encourage me.'

Some husbands cite the traditional custom that a suckling mother should abstain from sexual intercourse as reason for their taking a lover. An unemployed teacher one day casually remarked to the author that 'we Africans all do it: we keep *amankazana*, and when the wife is "wet" [i.e. suckling a child] it is the opportunity to visit one's *inkazana*. I think the ministers are the only ones who probably do not do it.'

Some people have no scruples about their extra-marital affairs. 'I think it is right to have a lover, because you get all you want, which your husband is not giving you.' The woman whose husband had been away for three years felt that having a lover was right, 'because these men leave us without any reason, and you cannot do without a man when you have been married, although you say "I am stealing" '. Or another: 'It is quite right, because I do it, and nobody has seen me yet.' A husband of 47 thought it was good, right, and necessary to have a lover, citing as reasons the loss of sexual interest in one's wife, and the custom relating to a suckling mother. On the other hand, many of the informants who admitted having lovers nevertheless thought it was wrong. A husband who spoke in terms of its being 'foolish' and 'unwise', more than its being morally wrong, maintained that most men would agree with him, but 'it is only when these things are discussed that some people realize how foolish they are. But strange enough, we all continue doing it.' However, he did feel that it was excusable for a husband to have children by a lover in the event of his wife's barrenness. A widow admitted that the last child born during her husband's lifetime, when he was already an invalid, was born of an adulterous union, but added by way of excuse: 'What could I do? My husband was laid up, and I was active and well.'

Some informants admitted marital fidelity to be the ideal, but felt it was difficult to attain. A woman with strong church ties maintained that an extra-marital affair was wrong 'but I do it . . . because Satan is strong'. A male informant qualified his disapproval—which rested on considerations of personal safety rather than on moral convictions—by adding: 'but it is difficult to have nothing to do with other women.' Another maintained that 'with us love for other women is always there, and it is difficult to exercise self-control. If you love a woman you have sleepless nights until you win her.' It is significant that among the categories mentioned as not being involved in extra-marital affairs disabled persons and shy and timid men known as *izishumane* figure prominently. By implication it appears that many people regard extra-marital relations as 'normal' behaviour for normal persons. Thus a man expressed the opinion that 'it is not good to have a lover who is not your wife, but at the same time it is difficult to resist the demands of nature'.

The main objection against extra-marital love-affairs, raised by those who had lovers, as well as those who did not, is its adverse effect on family relations. It leads to disharmony between husband and wife, and the wife whose husband has a lover is neglected, both sexually and otherwise. One husband went the full length of admitting that this was selfish. Again, if the wife has a lover, she 'will pay little attention' to her husband, or the husband 'will not give you your rights as a wife, as he usually does, although he does not tell you why, because he wants to see with his own eyes, and beat you'. Time and again love-affairs were cited as leading to the separation of husband and wife.

Although a man has no legal responsibilities toward a lover, unless he has a child by her, he usually gives her a certain amount of economic aid, and this usually happens at the expense of his own wife and children. 'People argue that no man can satisfy two women, particularly in sexual matters and maintenance of the family. . . . I have practical experience of this: [sexual] weakness at home, no money for Saturday's groceries.' Moreover, the fatherless children born out of extra-marital affairs are regarded as prospective delinquents.

Another objection concerns personal safety, as these liaisons easily give rise to violence. 'Your life is not safe, because you do not know what other lovers this woman has.' 'It is a risk to have a lover who is not your wife. I have seen married men who have been attacked and stabbed to death in a lover's room, and men have been poisoned by their lovers for marrying other women.' Another informant thought in terms of a man's lover 'swearing and challenging his legal wife to a fight'. An unfaithful wife, again, may fear violence on the part of her husband.

Informants disapproving of love-affairs also referred to religious convictions. Most of these denied having lovers themselves. It is regarded as 'a sin', 'against God's law' or the Ten Commandments, and 'God does not allow it'. It means breaking the vows of a church marriage that one would 'keep to this man for better or for worse'. A husband who admitted a love-affair, nevertheless disapproved of it: 'We are Christians and not Red Xhosa who take this to be a game for men.' A wife who did not have a lover felt that 'heathens will never want to go to church, because they will say that church people [*amagqobhoka*] commit adultery, yet they say they are believers'. Some degree of social control is ascribed to the church in this respect. One reason given for disapproval of love-affairs is that 'you cannot get your rights [the sacraments] from the church if it is found that you have a lover who is not your husband'. Two wives who had lovers stressed the fact that church people should not know of this. A husband claimed that 'I have no lover, and even before marriage I was not mad after women. My church kept a close check on me, in that I became a server when I was a small boy, wearing the red cassock and white surplice', serving on Sundays and attending church choir practice daily. Faithfulness in marriage also raises one's prestige with fellow-members of the church. 'I am a preacher in my church, where all members seem to have confidence in me. I would not therefore like to disappoint them [by having a lover].'

Some wives without lovers also expressed concern for their parents' feelings or for public opinion. 'By carrying on with lovers you are making your parents down-hearted because your husband can take you to them and tell them that you need to be trained anew, because you have not yet had enough of girlhood.' Or if you have a paramour 'the people around will call you *ihule* [harlot]', or you will be 'the talk of the street, even among children'.

One informant believed that infidelity could lead to childlessness. 'In my own way of thinking it is very mean for a married man to have private lovers. You are only draining yourself, with the result that when you now want children from your wife, you are very weak. The doctor will tell you your blood is too weak to produce children. Many girls get pregnant before marriage and they commit abortion to evade unmarried motherhood, but when these women get married they cannot have children when they really want them.'

In spite of the fact that so many married persons have lovers, they tend to be very secretive about their affairs. Wives particularly mentioned all sorts of measures to be taken, so that the husband should not find out and separation follow. They are also particularly wary of the husband's relatives, as they are sure to inform the husband of anything suspicious. There should be no correspondence, and no messages through intermediaries, or otherwise only through one trusted person. The lover must never be allowed in her room, and meetings must only be by appointment. Should the children see the mother in the lover's company she calls him *buti* (brother), so that they should regard him as an uncle. Husbands also tend to avoid publicity, but they appear less afraid that detection may lead to their marriage breaking up. It is rather avoided because 'a man must have consideration for his wife'; or 'she will never trust you again' if she should find out.

Married women are particularly anxious not to become pregnant by their lovers, but married men are less concerned, particularly when their lovers are unmarried mothers or widows. Some men hold that their lovers dislike precautionary measures, while it is even maintained that pregnancy is welcomed by some. 'There is nothing to be careful of in the case of an unmarried mother. If you love one another you are equally eager to have a child. I have nothing to do with young girls or wives of other men, where I would have to exercise great care.' Those who do try to avoid pregnancy either use contraceptives of Western origin, or practise *coitus interruptus*.

In view of the need for secrecy there is little other common activity between partners in illicit unions than love-making as such. The man who takes out his paramour by car is an exceptional case. Sometimes love-gifts, known as *amahogi*, are given. Men give their lovers small amounts of money to attend concerts or bioscopes, 'to buy soap and sweets', or to meet casual needs. There are also cases where the money given constitutes a considerable contribution to the woman's maintenance, as in the case of a neglected wife whose paramour is an unmarried man: 'he gives me money for everything I want.' Male lovers may receive articles of clothing, tobacco, money for a drink, or be treated to an occasional meal, but some do not receive any gifts from their lovers.

Most of these affairs are steady relationships, often lasting for a number of years, but some are of a fleeting nature, like those with so-called 'five-minute lovers'. 'To this type of woman there is no love proposal. You visit the woman in her room when you are certain she will be all by herself and when you are with her, you behave suggestively. These five-minute lovers are solely for sexual satisfaction. Should pregnancy follow, you stand a good chance of denying responsibility. This type of woman is even reluctant to take action against you.' Partners in less serious affairs are also referred to as *imixhuzulo*.[17] 'Since getting married in 1946 I have not had a standing lover known as *isigxina*,[18] but have had the type known here in town as *imixhuzulo*. These are

[17] From *ukuxhuzula*, denoting a jerking action. The term *umxhuzulo* is said to imply drawing the person's attention stealthily, as by light jerks at a jacket or dress.

[18] *Isigxina* denotes that which is one's own, also an intimate friend.

not lovers in the full sense, but are visited merely for sexual satisfaction. Such a woman cannot claim me to be her lover nor can I claim her to be mine.' Relationships with five-minute lovers or *imixhuzulo* are not associated with direct payment for sexual favours. One informant did remark about the presence of women who are willing to offer sexual privileges for direct payment, but our evidence indicates that prostitution proper does not figure prominently in the sex life of the location.

'LIVING TOGETHER'

Living together in concubinage is a common relationship in town and a partner to such a union is referred to as *masihlalisane* (let us stay together) or *ishweshwe* (a concubine). Many male migrants enter relationships of this kind in town,[19] but it is less common among town-bred men. Only five couples in our sample came into this category, and only two of the male partners concerned claimed to have been born in East London. The partner of one town-born woman (34) was in fact a migrant labourer (45) whose legal wife was living in the country kraal with their seven children. The woman in town was unmarried and had had four children by two other men, and two by him. Another case involved an East London-born woman (38) whose partner (37, not East London-born) claimed to be unmarried. Other cases of migrants living with older East London-born women were also encountered outside the survey sample.

Although relatively lasting relationships are common among young townspeople, these do not commonly lead to the establishment of common domestic arrangements outside marriage. Under particular circumstances this does however occasionally occur. In the three remaining cases of concubinage, all the persons concerned were under 25 years of age, excepting one male partner who was 33. A girl of 19 who had had three illegitimate children, of whom two were by the young man living with her, had been with him for three months in a room they were renting. When her own mother was asked whether she and her husband had given their consent to the couple's living together, she avoided giving a direct answer and explained that being staunch church members they could not continue keeping the daughter in their home as an unmarried mother. The girl was nevertheless on good terms with her parents. Just the opposite occurred in a case where a couple were living with the young man's father, because the latter, having been deserted by his wife, had no one to keep house for him. Sometimes it also happens that a girl goes to stay with her lover if relations with her parents become strained, say, when she becomes pregnant for a second time.

It seems probable that some of these young couples may ultimately get married, while others may become separated again. Living-together relationships which start as early as these do not usually last for life without being regularized ultimately.

TEMPORARY SEPARATION

A number of persons in our sample claimed to be married, but were temporarily not living with their spouses. In a few cases this arrangement was forced on them by the shortage of accommodation, since they could not find

[19] See Mayer, op. cit., pp. 256 ff.

accommodation together. At the time of the survey towards the end of 1958, X was staying with his mother's brother and the latter's wife and child and two other male relatives, all in one room. When in the location, his wife stayed with relatives of hers, but she had a room where she was working in town as domestic servant, and X sometimes slept with her there, 'but secretly, because of the police'. They were married in 1957, and he said they had this arrangement because they could not find a room where they could stay together. Another young woman was sharing a room and eating with her unmarried sister and the latter's child. Her husband was sharing accommodation with other men, so that she could not stay with him. She performed certain domestic chores for her husband and his room mates, with whom he shared his meals. When they wanted to sleep together, the husband had to find a room with friends somewhere else for the occasion.

In other cases the temporary separation was a symptom of a rift between husband and wife, which might, or might not, have led to permanent separation. Shirley (married by Christian rites, with *lobolo* and *ukudlisa amasi*), had left her husband and two small children shortly before their home was visited for the survey. The reason given by her husband himself was that he had had an illegitimate child by another woman. He expected that she would return, but about two months later she had not yet done so. Mary and Ernest (married by *ukuthwala*—carrying away—and *lobolo* only) and their baby were living with Ernest's widowed mother and his two elder brothers and their families. A few weeks before the survey there had been a 'misunderstanding' between the two, after which she left alone, presumably going to Johannesburg. It was still too soon to know whether the separation would become permanent. Nomathemba (married by civil rites and *lobolo*) and her husband and child had been living in their own room in her parents' house, cooking their own food. When interviewed, she and the child were living with her parents in a single household unit, and she intimated that her husband was in Johannesburg 'for a little while', but she appeared reluctant to discuss their relationship. The fieldworker, in fact, knew that the husband had been away for 'several years'.

The separation may also indicate their keeping up country ties. A Red man of 63, who claimed to be East London-born, was staying all by himself in a room of the house he owned, while his wife stayed in their homestead in the reserve. When he was interviewed about his family history some months later, it emerged that he was not actually born in East London, but it is evident that he is of the double-rooted type with long-standing interests in town and spending more time in town than in the country, while his wife, staying in their homestead in the reserve, maintains their land rights there.

THE POST-MARITAL PERIOD

In view of the small numbers in our sample there is not much that can be deduced from our statistics in table 16 about the termination of marriage. It is significant to note, however, that there were nearly as many women who were widowed, divorced, or separated (twenty) as there were married women (twenty-four). This suggests an unusually large proportion of women in the post-marital stage. We have already mentioned our suspicion that a considerable proportion of these are women whose marriages have broken up—more than the figures suggest. There is continual talk of broken marriages in the location, and women who were being unfaithful to their husbands repeatedly mentioned the breaking-up of their marriages as the one thing they feared if their husbands should discover their infidelity.

Divorced or separated men should also be more numerous than would appear from our sample. (Only a minority of persons living in separation from their spouses are legally divorced.) It is not strange that widows should outnumber widowers, since husbands are usually a few years older than their wives, and Bantu females have a longer life expectancy than males.

A variety of domestic arrangements is possible after the termination of marriage. Some divorced or widowed spouses of course do remarry, but often they enter into relationships with lovers whom they visit or who visit them. Occasionally they live in concubinage with new spouses. In our sample half of the females who had remained single after termination of their marriages had had post-marital illegitimate children. Some had returned to their parents' homes after losing their husbands, but the majority, both males and females, had carried on independently and were the heads of households, usually made up of their children, and often also grandchildren.

CHILDREN

The most notable feature about family growth among urban Bantu is the large proportion of children born of illicit unions. More than 40 per cent of the children (alive and dead) of the females in our sample were returned as born of extra-marital unions (table 17). The majority were the children of females who had never been married. For the women who had been married, only eleven children were returned as born premaritally, compared with 181 born

TABLE 17

Distribution of children

Whereabouts of children	Children of unmarried mothers	Children of existing 'living together' unions	Children of women married, widowed, divorced, separated				Total
			By most recent marriage	By previous marriage	Pre-marital by husband	Other extra-marital	
With:							
father and mother	—	4	56	—	5	—	65
father*	1	—	—	—	—	—	1
mother*	65	—	58	—	—	16	139
mother and step-father	—	—	—	6	—	—	6
father's parents	—	—	2	—	—	1	3
mother's parents	—	—	—	—	—	2	2
other relatives	12	—	2	—	—	1	15
Elsewhere:							
at school	—	—	4	—	—	—	4
working/training	—	—	5	—	2	—	7
married/independent adult	—	—	10	—	1	—	11
diverse	—	—	1	—	—	—	1
Total alive	78	4	138	6	8	20	254
Total dead	12	—	37	—	—	5	54
Total births	90	4	175	6	8	25	308

*These include many cases in which the child and its parent form part of the household of which its grandparent is the head.

of marriage. A comparison in this respect between married and unmarried females must not be made without reserve, since it is much easier for a married woman to conceal illegitimacy of birth in a child than for an unmarried mother. Nevertheless it is probably true that the proportion of premarital births has been increasing, and that a smaller proportion of married women, who on the whole belong to older age groups, had premarital children than the unmarried girls of today.

The fact that only one woman admitted the birth of an adulterine child during the lifetime of her husband must be treated with the same reserve. In view of the prevalence of extra-marital relations and the absence or inadequacy of contraceptive measures in many cases, one suspects that more married women have adulterine children than this solitary one suggests. We have seen that among women who have lost their husbands post-marital pregnancies are common. Of 127 children returned as born of illicit unions, 21 were post-marital. Altogether it seems probable that our sample figures for extra-marital births are on the conservative side.

Although often deplored, illegitimate birth has become a regular and accepted feature of the social structure, and illegitimate children are usually integrated into the domestic families to which their mothers belong. In rare cases an illegitimate child is taken by the father and his family. If the mother is a daughter in a two-generation family, her illegitimate child is often treated as her sibling and as a child of its physical grandparents. As the difference in age between the three succeeding generations increases, and as more illegitimate children are born in the family, they tend to become socially differentiated as a third generation, but still taking the surname and clan-name of their maternal grandfather. In such cases mother and grandparents are jointly responsible for the child's care and upbringing, the mother usually taking an increasing share of the responsibility as she grows older. Post-marital children also sometimes grow up in their grandparents' households, as when a woman returns to her parents after termination of her marriage. In all the cases mentioned, the mother's family of origin may already be without a male head through death or separation, so that the child grows up without even a substitute father, under the authority of mother and maternal grandmother.

Where a widow or separated woman continues to run an independent household she rears her post-marital children along with the children of her marriage. Some unmarried mothers also rear their children in their own households, usually being left in control after the death of their parents. There are also unmarried mothers who came to town many years ago in their youth, whose parents never lived in town, who have also reared their children in their own households.[20]

When considering both legitimate and illegitimate children, we find that the great majority of children are living with both parents or with the mother, that is, speaking in terms of physical descent (table 17). But those who are with their mothers only, and not in the care of their fathers, constitute more than two-thirds of this number. This means that of the children of the females in our sample, only a minority could have belonged to domestic units consisting of elementary or nuclear families. Contrary to what might have appeared to be the trend in earlier stages of urbanization,[21] the elementary family is not the

[20] Figures in table 17, however, refer only to the children of women who claim to be born in town.

[21] Hunter, op. cit., p. 459.

predominant form of domestic family among that part of the population which has been established in town longest. Our figures also point to the overriding importance of the mother in the family structure. Even though some of the children enumerated as being with their mothers were also under the authority of grandfathers, all of them had their immediate genealogical ties with the domestic families to which they belonged through their mothers. These conclusions about the elementary family and the position of the mother in the family structure are substantiated by our analysis of the composition of households in the following chapter.

It is further significant that not many dependent children live away from their mothers. Of those who do, a few are with grandparents and the rest are with other relatives. In these cases there are usually particular reasons for this arrangement, such as the need or desire of the relatives concerned for the child's aid or company, or the inability of an unattached mother to care for the child alone, often on account of having to work. We should further note that, excepting one who was with the father, the children of unmarried mothers who were not with the mothers were all with other relatives, not with grandparents. This is a concomitant of the fact that, if it is at all possible, unmarried mothers tend to live with their parents. If this is not possible, it is usually neither possible to leave the children in the grandparents' care.[22] An unattached unmarried mother may then find it difficult to care for her children, and may need the assistance of a relative. Mary (22), the unmarried mother of two children, was not staying with her widowed mother because the latter was staying with her own brother, and, as Mary put it: 'I do not like the place.' Her son (6) is therefore staying with a sister in the country 'since my mother has no house of her own'. Mary is working, and a maternal cousin is helping her to look after her three-month-old baby, the three of them making up a single household. Of two girls sharing a room, one was an unmarried mother of 22, whose mother had died long ago, and whose two children were being cared for by her mother's sister in Queenstown as she intended entering training as a nurse.

A question that remains to be answered is what happens to the children of unmarried mothers when the mothers get married. The numbers of such children enumerated in our survey were very small, but it is my impression that if the children's physical father married the mother they will be taken by the couple when they establish their own household. If it is another man, they remain in the household of which they are members when the mother gets married, although cases are known where such children have also become integrated into the newly established household.

The pattern of family development emerging from the foregoing is that of a female contributing to the growth of her family of origin before she gets married, causing its expansion into a three-generation family if it is not one already. On marriage she and her husband either start developing an altogether new family, or some or all of the children of the woman are transferred to the new domestic unit, and the couple continue developing the family which the woman initially started developing within her own family of origin. This might cause the latter to revert to a two-generation span. For some time the domestic

[22] It should be remembered that hardly any of the living grandparents (i.e. parents of the unmarried mothers) were living in the country, nearly all of them being in town as first generation townspeople.

unit is a complete elementary family.[23] The husband ultimately drops out, often before the wife is past the child-bearing age, but the family may continue its independent existence, now centring upon the mother. It may also continue to grow, perhaps by the addition of the mother's post-marital children, but also by her daughter's pre-marital children, thus attaining a span of three generations. (The three-generation span may of course also be reached while the husband is still in the family.) Alternatively, after the husband has dropped out the woman may return to her own family of origin, causing it to expand, not only in membership, but also in its span of generations.

We have also observed that there are unmarried mothers who never get married, but nevertheless families develop around them which never pass through a stage of being a complete elementary family.

[23] This may not be quite clear from the present chapter, but in the next chapter we shall see that this is the position.

8

Household and Family Structure

In the location situation where a large proportion of the population lives in tenement-type houses, and where what are obviously separate households often occupy only part of a house, or even a single room, it would clearly make no sense to regard the inhabitants of a single house as constituting the household unit. The most appropriate criterion seems to be the sharing of common eating and cooking arrangements. The group thus identified is also one which can be easily distinguished in the vernacular, as the Xhosa have a standing expression referring to them as 'those who eat from one pot' (*abatyela 'mbizeni 'nye*). Usually there was no problem in applying this criterion. Occasionally a case was encountered where a daughter with children sometimes cooked in her own room, or a member of the household sometimes ate at home and sometimes elsewhere, but it was always possible to make a distinction between what was regular and what was a deviation from regular practice.

This group of people almost invariably lives under the same roof. It does happen that a daughter of the household head, who belongs to the household in terms of eating arrangements, has a separate room in the house for herself and her children; but, even apart from eating, their life is so closely tied up with that of the extended family of which they form part that it seems only reasonable to regard them as part of the same household. On the other hand there are cases of married sons and their families, living in the same house as their parents, where the son and his family have a separate room or rooms, while his wife does her own cooking for the family. In this case again, the son's family is regarded as a separate household, although it may happen that the children often eat also with the grandparents, much as the case used to be in the traditional Xhosa *umzi*. Cases such as the latter, however, are not very common.

For collecting information on household composition, questions were planned in such a way as to include all persons who could possibly be regarded as belonging to the household, such as those sharing accommodation with the household but eating elsewhere, for instance at their place of employment, as well as members absent at the time of investigation. Many such names were listed, including those of persons who had been absent for several years. Further information about such doubtful cases concerning date of departure, expected return, visits home, and their participation in the household economy, was collected, and on this evidence only a small number were counted as members of the household. In the sample households' total population of 631 there were only seventeen such persons.[1] Of these, six could be called 'partially present'.

[1] Questions on the household formed part of the major questionnaire applied to our sample of 202 presumably East London-born persons of 15 years and older. They belonged to 109 different households, which constitute our household sample. Our total household population is therefore a more inclusive group than the sample of professedly East London-born adults with which we have been dealing in chapters 3, 6 and 7. (For further details on method and sampling, see Appendix II.)

They were persons who would normally be 'eating from the same pot' with the household, but were accommodated at their place of employment and visited the household at least once a week. Usually they also contributed to the household income. The others, classified as members of the household temporarily away, were mostly children attending school elsewhere, whose board was being paid from the household's resources, and who came home on holiday at least once a year, and members in gaol, or in hospitals and sanatoriums, who were expected to return to the household when discharged. Persons away visiting or working, and expected to be absent for more than six months, as well as children in the care of relatives, for whose boarding expenses no contribution was made, were not regarded as members, even if contributions were made in respect of clothes, school-books and pocket-money. In the present study, therefore, the household is virtually a group sharing meals and living together in the same house, although it seldom has the whole house to itself.

KINSHIP COMPOSITION OF THE HOUSEHOLD

Although the urban household generally extends beyond the elementary family, it is essentially a group of kin. Of the 631 persons in the sample households, only 9 were not returned as kinsmen or affines of the household head.

The key figures in the household are the head and the head's spouse. In nearly half the number of households in our sample these were a male head and his wife (or occasionally his concubine). However, in one case of a couple just living together, and one in which they claimed to be married, the informants maintained that the female was the head, so that in these cases the key male figure should be described as the female head's spouse. A large number of households had 'husbandless' women as heads, so that in these cases there were no key male figures. A few male heads were men without wives. We shall refer to the male and female key figures respectively as the 'fathers' and 'mothers' of the households. This designation is of course not quite accurate, since one does find households where the key figures are not father or mother of any members of the household. But for convenience' sake we use the terms 'father' and 'mother' for the concepts 'male head or female head's spouse' and 'female head or male head's spouse' respectively.

The accompanying figure 5 indicates the different types of kinship and affinal relationships between members of the households and the 'fathers' or 'mothers' respectively, as well as the frequency with which each relationship occurred in the sample households. We note first of all that mothers outnumber fathers considerably, so that we may expect to find a large number of households without fathers, with mothers as heads.

Descendants of father or mother or both[2] account for the largest single category of kin. This is not unusual, but the considerable number of grandchildren, and even a number of great-grandchildren, is significant. This suggests the existence of domestic families with a span of more than two generations. Further, the great majority of grandchildren are the children of daughters, while the great-grandchildren are all daughters' daughters' children. This, together with the fact that there are only a few wives of sons, indicates that households become extended in the matriline, rather than the traditional patriline. The only

[2] In material on household composition we did not draw a distinction between the children of a head and spouse by each other and those each one had by other partners (e.g. by previous spouses or lovers).

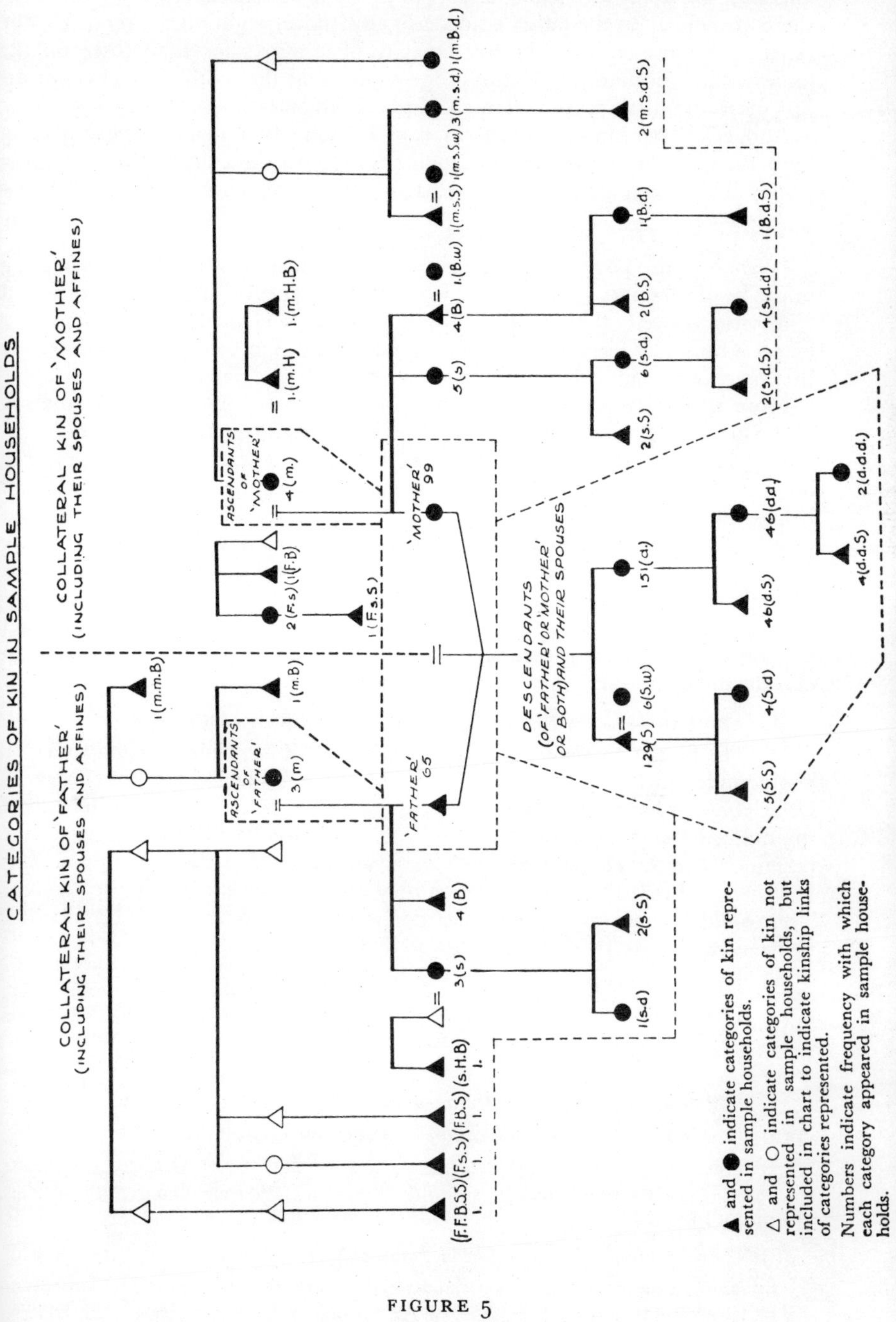

▲ and ● indicate categories of kin represented in sample households.

△ and ○ indicate categories of kin not represented in sample households, but included in chart to indicate kinship links of categories represented.

Numbers indicate frequency with which each category appeared in sample households.

FIGURE 5

ascendants are a few mothers of fathers or mothers of households. Of *collateral kin* there are fifteen on the father's side as against thirty-eight on the mother's, the latter also representing a larger diversity of relationships than those on the father's side. Siblings and siblings' descendants on the mother's side count for just more than half of all collateral kin on both sides.

Altogether the kinship composition of households indicates a very distinct slant towards the mother's and daughter's side, to the extent of accentuating purely matrilineal ties, much more than patrilineal relationships.

TYPES OF HOUSEHOLD STRUCTURE

In spite of the presence of a considerable number of kinsfolk not belonging to the head's families,[3] it is obvious from the frequency with which the different relationships occur that an actual family, whether elementary, compound or extended, usually forms the basis of the household. Households could therefore best be classified in terms of the structure of the 'basic' family.

From the analysis of kinship composition it has become clear that the sex of the head, and the generation span, constitute significant criteria for differentiating various types of family structure. By the application of these criteria the households in our sample could be grouped into a number of types as indicated below. In the case of two-generation male-headed families it seems important to make a further distinction between families that have mothers and those without mothers. By multi-generation families are meant families with a span of three or more generations, that is, where all three or four generations are represented in the family. Where one generation was skipped, the generation beyond the gap was not regarded as part of the 'basic' family for purposes of classification. We have then the following:

(1) The *male-headed multi-generation* family: eighteen households.

(2) The family consisting of *father, mother and children*, whether elementary or compound: thirty-five households. In this type of household the father is invariably the head, although in the case of one such household the informant maintained that the mother was the head. They were said to be married, but certain circumstances gave rise to a strong suspicion that they were just living together, and that the house in which they were living belonged to the woman. This would explain why she was regarded as head. For purposes of classification this exception may be disregarded.

(3) The family of *father and children*: five households.

(4) The family consisting of a *man and his 'wife'*, without any children, although in two cases grandchildren were living with the couples: four households.

(5) The *female-headed multi-generation* family: twenty-one households.

(6) The family of *mother and children*: seventeen households.

(7) The family consisting of a *female without husband or children*, to whom *other persons* are attached: five households. (Two of these included grandchildren of the head.)

(8) There were four *single-person households*, three males and one female.

[3] By 'family' is meant here ascendant and descendant kin of the mother or father. This means that for purposes of this typology only ascendant and descendant kin of the 'father' and 'mother' are considered members of the head's family. This does not allow for the identification of joint families made up of siblings and their children, but these are not common, and allowance for their separate identification would have complicated our typology unnecessarily.

The numerically important types, therefore, are the male-headed and female-headed multi-generation families, the father-mother-children type, and the mother-and-children type. As will appear from table 18 the rest are small households, and in terms of members even less significant numerically than has already appeared from the numbers of households in each type. They are therefore usually not treated as separate types in our subsequent discussions.

TABLE 18

Type of household structure by numbers of members and average size

Type of household	Number of households		NUMBER OF HOUSEHOLD MEMBERS: Members of head's family	Other relatives	Others	Total	Average size
Multi-generation, male head:							
without add. members	12	18	146	11	2	159	8·8
with add. members	6						
Father-mother-children:							
without add. members	23	35	159	13	4	176	5·0
with add. members	12						
Multi-generation, female head:							
without add. members	18	21	157	6	1	164	7·8
with add. members	3						
Mother-children:							
without add. members	8	17	69	18	2	89	5·2
with add. members	9						
Other		18	33	10	–	43	2·4
Total		109	564	58	9	631	5·8

Table 18 shows that no single type we have formulated can be said to predominate numerically, but the two types of multi-generation households together represent more than half the total population of the sample. Fewer than one-third of the households (in terms of population of the sample the proportion is about the same) are based on the elementary or compound family of father, mother and children. The proportion consisting of only this unit, without any attached members, is less than a quarter. It cannot be said, therefore, that the elementary family, usually associated with Western patterns of living, is at present the predominant form of household unit among the urban Bantu. On the other hand, it appears from our analysis of kinship composition of the household that, although so many households consist of multi-generation families, they usually do not grow into three or four generations along the traditionally important patriline.

The multi-generation households are distinctly the larger ones, while the father-mother-children and mother-children households are medium sized. The remainder are small. Detailed figures on the distribution of household size confirm this trend indicated by average size. All types of households contain members not belonging to the head's family, but female-headed multi-generation households seldom extend beyond it.

With regard to the kinship relations of members to head, there do not seem to be specific trends correlated with the different types of households, apart from such obvious facts as that mothers, grandchildren, and great-grandchildren are exclusively found in multi-generation households, with the exception of a few grandchildren in the non-classified ('other') households. It does seem worth mentioning, however, that the small number of great-grandchildren all belong to female-headed households. Another obvious fact is that where a woman is the head one hardly ever finds relatives of her 'husband' (present, late or separated) as members of the household, whereas it is not so unusual for male heads to have relatives of their 'wives' as members of the household.

HEADS AND THEIR SPOUSES

A remarkable feature of the urban Bantu household is the large proportion of female household heads. In our sample more than two-fifths (forty-six households) had female heads. With two exceptions, already mentioned, they were females without husbands, i.e. widowed, divorced or separated women, or unmarried mothers.

In the two-generation household where there is a father, as well as in the household of a married couple without children, the father (husband) is invariably the head, but when a couple are living together in an unmarried state, there appears to be a tendency for the woman to be regarded as head, particularly if she owns the house, or is the more permanent tenant of the premises which the household occupies. There are, however, also cases of couples living together where the male is regarded as head.

In the household of a woman with her unmarried children the mother is the head. Even when additional members are attached to such a family or to a woman without her own children, the woman is still regarded as head, because these attached members are mostly children, while the few adults are mostly single persons who have found accommodation with the woman who is the original occupant of the premises. Where 'husbandless' sisters and their children stay together in one household, the eldest sister, or the one who owns the property, may be regarded as head. The sample also included a household of a widowed woman with her younger brother and his wife, where the sister was regarded as head, and the brother and his wife as temporarily accommodated with her while trying to obtain their own accommodation.

In the multi-generation household where there is a male belonging to the eldest generation, he is invariably the head. When there is only a female of the eldest generation, the position varies. When the household consists of such a female and her husbandless daughters and their children, the grandmother is generally the 'mother' and head of the household. But there are such households in which the female of the eldest generation is employed outside the home and is only 'partially present', her daughter (second generation) then being regarded as head and mother of the household. It even occurs that a female of the second generation is regarded as mother-head, in spite of the permanent presence of her own mother, although no such household occurred in the sample.[4] This seems to be the case where the daughter is responsible for the main household income, particularly when she provides this through some form of trade which enables her at the same time to remain in the home and run the household. The ages of mother and daughter probably also play a role in deciding which of the two is regarded as head. There may even be a certain degree of tension or uncertainty over authority in such situations.

In multi-generation households with only a female in the eldest generation,

[4] For an example of such a household, see pp. 51, 53 (fig. 2), household of X.

but with a married male in the second generation, this male is generally regarded as head. The household then actually centres upon the elementary family of man-woman-children to which the man's mother or mother-in-law is attached. It does, however, happen that the older female is regarded as head, in spite of the presence of a married son. In the only instance which occurred in the sample, a widow of 63 had her three married sons, the eldest 30 years old, living with her together with their families. Her age and some degree of economic dependence of the sons—the mother owns the house—seem to be the deciding factors.[5]

TABLE 19

Type of household structure by marital status of heads

Type of household	MARITAL STATUS OF HEAD: Married	Living together	Widowed	Div./sep.	Unmar. mother	Other unmar.	Other*	Total
Multi-generation, male head	16	—	2	—	—	—	—	18
Father-mother-children:								
Male head	30	2	—	—	—	—	2	34
Female head	1	—	—	—	—	—	—	1
Multi-generation (female head)	—	—	14	3	4	—	—	21
Mother-children (female head)	—	—	11	1	5	—	—	17
Other: Male head	2	1	1	2	—	1	4	11
Female head	—	1	3	—	2	1	—	7
Total	49	4	31	6	11	2	6	109
Total male heads	48	3	3	2	—	1	6	63
Total female heads	1	1	28	4	11	1	—	46

*The 'Other' consists of one whose marital status was unknown, one married man whose wife had recently left him, and who expected that she would return again, and four married men whose wives and some or all children were living in a country home. It has subsequently emerged that some of the latter households did not include East London-born adults.

According to the details about marital status of heads summarized in table 19, male heads—almost without exception—and the great majority of females, were married or had been married. For the same reasons as those mentioned in connexion with the marriage sample, more females may have been unmarried mothers or separated women than the figures indicate. In spite of the possibility of such a bias, nearly a quarter of the female heads were returned as unmarried mothers. This establishes without doubt the existence of a distinct type of family which is mother-controlled, not because the father has disappeared from the family, but because it lacks a father altogether. Let us analyse the composition of these families with unmarried heads more closely.

(*a*) Of the four multi-generation households in this category, two had unmarried grandmothers as heads, who were 45 and 57 years old respectively. Both had unmarried daughters and the latter's children living with them, so that three-generation families had developed without a marriage ever taking place. In the other two the heads were of the second generation, their own mothers being employed and only partially present. One of these two grandmothers was a widow, the other was living with a man who sometimes slept at her place of employment, and sometimes with the rest of the family in the location. In this kind of household the unmarried mother-head is usually largely dependent economically on the grandmother, and it might be more appropriate

[5] For the authority structure of the family, see also pp. 155 ff.

to regard the older woman and her daughter as joint heads, the former providing, planning and advising, and the latter holding more of an 'executive' authority.

(*b*) Of the five unmarried mothers who were heads of mother-and-children households, one was 22, while the other four were between 30 and 40 years old. One had a married sister living with her, who had had trouble in finding accommodation together with her husband. Another had an unmarried brother and her two sisters, both unmarried mothers, with their children, living with her, the eldest of the three sisters being regarded as head. The third had only her baby with her, her other five children being cared for by relatives in the country. Another had her cousin, a girl of 14, living with her to look after her baby. One had, besides her own children, an adopted daughter (also an unmarried mother) and her baby, making the household in effect a three-generation household.[6]

(*c*) The remaining two households consisted, in one case, of two girls of 21 and 23 respectively, both unmarried mothers, staying together with none of their children with them, and in the other of a woman of 68 who had only a sister's daughter staying with her.

Summarizing, we see that of the eleven households discussed, two consisted of unmarried mothers and their children, with the mother's mothers (on whom they were heavily dependent) partially present; three were actually or virtually three-generation families, with two generations of unmarried mothers; one consisted only of mother and baby as a remnant of the family, the rest of the children being under the care of relatives; two had other females staying with them, one with the express purpose of providing assistance with the care of the baby, while the remaining two did not have any of their children with them. This suggests that, as one can easily understand, it is difficult for the family consisting of an unmarried mother and her children to exist completely independent of outside help in the care of the children, but that by the time the family has attained the three-generation stage, such independence becomes possible and does occur.

In the previous chapter the existence of certain patterns of family development was suggested, which, if valid, could mean that some of the structural types we have formulated represent different stages in a developmental cycle, rather than distinct family types. We have to ascertain, then, whether the different types tend to differ in respect of their relative 'age'. Although the head's age cannot serve as an absolute indication of a family's age—because of different factors making for variability, for instance the generation to which the head of a multi-generation family belongs, and remarriage to a young spouse—it does have tentative significance. With this view in mind the ages of heads are analysed in table 20.

This shows that the male heads in the sample who were younger than 40 usually had father-mother-children families. The only male head of a multi-generation family who was younger than 40 was a young man whose mother was living with him and his wife and children. Among older male heads there were some with father-mother-children families, but those with multi-generation families predominated. As regards male-headed families, therefore, father-

[6] A slight inconsistency in classification must be admitted here: a household consisting of a married couple with only an adopted child was classified as 'father-mother-child' so that the household mentioned above should strictly have been classified a multi-generation household.

mother-children families predominate at younger levels and the multi-generation families at older levels, suggesting that generally speaking the latter are at a later stage of development.[7]

TABLE 20

A. Male heads: household type by age

TYPE OF HOUSEHOLD

Age of head	Multi-generation I	Father-mother-children II	Other III	Total
20–29	1	4	1	6
30–39	—	11	2	13
40–49	5	11	4	20
50–59	5	4	2	11
60–69	3	2	2	7
70 plus	4	2	—	6
Total	18	34	11	63

B. Female heads: marital status by age

MARITAL STATUS

Age of head	Unmarried mother I	Widowed/ divorced/ separated II	Other III	Tota
20–29	4	—	—	4
30–39	4	1	2	7
40–49	1	11	1	13
50–59	1	9	—	10
60–69	1	8	—	9
70 plus	—	3	—	3
Total	11	32	3	46

Female heads under 40 were predominantly unmarried mothers, while most of those older than 40 were women who had been married.[8] When a further analysis is made for females in terms of family type, we note that heads between 40 and 60 represent both mother-children and multi-generation families, but over 60 the heads of multi-generation families predominate. Our analysis of families with unmarried mother-heads has already indicated the existence of a distinct type of fatherless family which has a tendency to develop a three-generation span. The most apparent inference from the analysis of head's ages would then be that apart from the completely fatherless type of family, the father-mother-children family, which is usually an elementary family, does tend to be the common initial stage of family growth—the pre-marital stage apart—and that multi-generation and woman-children families develop out of elementary families. The elementary family is then the basic type, but it shows a strong tendency on the one hand to lose the father at a relatively early stage and on the other hand to develop a multi-generation span.[9]

[7] If column III is eliminated from table 20A, and age groups are lumped (20–39, 40–59, and 60 plus) the resulting table is significant at a 1 per cent level.

[8] If column III is eliminated from table 20B, and age groups are lumped (20–39 and 40 plus) the resulting table is significant at a 1 per cent level.

[9] Another way of assessing the relative ages of families is to compare the ages of the 'mothers'. (Cf. table 39.)

MEMBERS OF THE HOUSEHOLD: SEX, AGE AND MARITAL STATUS

A feature of the composition of the households in our sample is the marked numerical predominance of females over males (table 38, col. XI). The masculinity rate of the total population of sample households is 81. Closer analysis reveals that this discrepancy does not exist in the under 15 age group, so that the predominance of females is even more notable when the adults of 15 and over are considered by themselves. For this group the masculinity rate is 68.

As regards heads and their spouses we know already that there are a large number of husbandless female heads, while male heads without spouses are few. Further there is a very distinct excess of daughters over 15 over sons of the same age. In the category of 'other members' the discrepancy is more than accounted for by the presence of seven mothers or mothers-in-law, and six sons' wives, whereas there are none representing the corresponding male categories. We are confronted, therefore, with the 'disappearance' of husbands, both in the heads' and heads' parents' generations, as well as of adult sons.

The age distribution of children in different types of households (table 38, cols. III and IV) is particularly interesting. Except in the father-mother-children households, sons and daughters are present in virtually equal proportions in the under 15 age group in the main household types. (The larger proportion of young female children in the ratio of about 130 : 100 in father-mother-children households, is difficult to explain.) In the 15-and-older groups daughters predominate in multi-generation families, and this is much more in evidence in the male-headed families than in the female-headed ones. This may mean that as households grow 'older' (having attained a three-generation span) adult sons tend to disappear to a greater extent, or sooner than daughters, but that this tendency is not as strong in the female-headed multi-generation household as in the male-headed one. In this connexion it seems important that both sons and daughters are relatively older in the mother-children household than in the father-mother-children household (in that a smaller proportion are under 15). This also suggests that the mother-children household is on the whole older than the father-mother-children one, but it does not yet show the tendency to lose its sons earlier than its daughters. The over-all impression is then that sons stay on longer in female-headed households than in male-headed ones.

If sons do not disappear from different types of households equally soon, it is obvious that their age distribution cannot be an indication of the developmental level of different types. In the case of daughters this is different, and their age distribution points to the same developmental order we have already suggested. The proportion of daughters in the under 15 group is largest in father-mother-children households, while it diminishes from one type to the next in the order mother-children household, male-headed multi-generation household, and female-headed multi-generation household (table 40). The female-headed multi-generation households, moreover, are the only ones with a number of daughters of 30 years and older. This also supports our earlier impression that on the whole multi-generation households are older than two-generation households, and female-headed ones again older than those with male heads.

In the category of grandchildren, which is largely confined to children under 15, the numbers of males and females are almost equal.

The most important fact emerging from the figures on the marital status of household members (table 41) is that unmarried mothers figure prominently in all female categories of members. Of all the females 15 years and older, 28 per cent were returned as unmarried mothers.[10] The father-mother-children household is the only type in which they do not appear, but in this type there are very few adult females other than heads' spouses, who obviously cannot be unmarried mothers.

Another significant fact is that there are very few households where married children of the head and their spouses are members of the household. Of the four married sons in multi-generation households, three were in the same female-headed household, and one in a male-headed one. All of these also had children with them. In one of the 'other' households a son, and the woman with whom he was living together, belonged to the household, but they had no children. Two male-headed multi-generation households each had a married daughter, but both were living with their parents in temporary separation from their husbands. In only three households, therefore, were there sons with their spouses.

We may say, then, that apart from the male heads, the majority of adult males in the households are single men, of whom it is difficult to assess the proportion who have already fathered children. Adult daughters are largely confined to multi-generation households. Just more than half of them are unmarried mothers, a small number are widowed, divorced or separated, and the rest, accounting for only 37 per cent, are said to be single. Female-headed multi-generation households have a larger proportion of daughters who are unmarried mothers than the male-headed ones. It is also significant that of ten granddaughters of 15 years and over, six are unmarried mothers, and all of them belong to female-headed households. Very few of the 'other' females are unmarried and single, while the majority are other 'husbandless women'.

We have observed that many households include persons not belonging to the head's family. Diverse reasons were given for their belonging to the household. Of those related to the head, about a quarter were children under 15 of whom more than half had lost their parents or were neglected. Nearly all the others were the children of other adult members in the household, while one girl was said to be living with the head to aid in household duties. The reasons for the presence of adult relatives were mostly framed in terms of their being related: that these were their closest relatives, that they had no other relatives to stay with, or no other home, while three sisters (unmarried mothers) and a brother said that they had been staying together as one family with their mother, and continued to do so after her death. A few siblings and a mother's mother's brother were staying with the respective heads because they were said to be sickly, mentally ill or blind, and had no other care. A number of related persons did not refer to their relationship, but merely said that they could not find other accommodation. Two were aiding in household or business, while one young girl from the country who had come to her relatives in town in order to see an eye specialist had simply stayed on with them and was giving casual aid in the care of the baby. Two young unmarried mothers had merely decided to stay together (without their children) on their own, giving no specific reason for their choice.

[10] This refers to all adult females in the *total household population* of our sample. From tables 11 and 12 it will be seen that of the professedly *East London-born* females 37 per cent were unmarried mothers.

Of the nine non-related persons, three were adopted children, one the child of an adopted child, two were boarders, and one a servant. One man was described as a member of the head's father's mother's clan who was a newcomer in town and for this reason had found accommodation with the household. A woman, again, was said to belong to the household because she was a friend, having been a neighbour of the family in the country.

Most of these attached persons seem to belong to the household on a relatively permanent basis, regarding it as their home. Not many are typical migrants from the country, but there are some who would branch off on their own if they could obtain more suitable permanent accommodation.

CHARACTERISTICS OF DIFFERENT TYPES

We may now co-ordinate the main characteristics of the major types of households that have emerged in the course of this chapter.

Father-mother-children households: The overwhelming majority in this category consist of married couples with their children, in some cases also with other relatives or non-related persons, of whom there are about 0.5 per household. In terms of the ages of head and spouse and of children, these are relatively young households with a fairly equal proportion of sons and daughters, few of whom are over 15. Almost all the other members are over 15, the majority being males, most of them unmarried. There are no groups of other members constituting sub-families of parent(s) and children. Their structure is therefore relatively simple. On the average they are distinctly smaller than multi-generation households.

Mother-children households: These consist of widows, separated wives and unmarried mothers, with their children and sometimes other persons. A few families are on the borderline between two and three generations, in that they include unmarried daughters who have lost babies or are expecting their first. One includes an adopted unmarried daughter with her child. Nearly 40 per cent of the children are 15 and older, while the numbers of sons and daughters are about equal. Measured by the ages of the female head and her daughters, these households are on the whole older than the man-woman-children households, but younger than the multi-generation households. Actually these families represent two distinct types, namely (*a*) families with unmarried mother heads, which are conspicuously younger, and (*b*) families of 'post-marital' mothers, which tend to be older. Other persons are present at an average of just over one per household. In only two cases such persons constitute sub-families. More than half of the other members are children under 15. Nearly all of them are related to the female head as siblings, siblings' descendants, or mothers' siblings' descendants. They do not differ much in size from man-woman-children households.

Multi-generation male-headed households: These show a considerable degree of variety in structure. (*a*) Most of them consist of a married couple with husbandless daughters and their children, the majority of these daughters being unmarried mothers. (*b*) Occasionally there is a married son of the head, with his wife and child(ren), or a deceased son's widow and her children. In both (*a*) and (*b*) there may, of course, also be other children of the head who are still single. (*c*) Sometimes the household consists of the head, his wife and children, and the head's mother or mother-in-law. (*d*) Another variation occurs where there is a couple with their unmarried children, and grandchildren whose parents do not belong to the household. In such cases occurring in the sample the parents were alive, but the children were given in the care of the grandparents, as often happened in the traditional Xhosa family. Modern labour conditions, including migrant labour, may also necessitate this, while illegitimacy, and neglect by or the death of parents may also be the reason. Combinations of the four variations described also occur, while it also happens, though seldom, that the head is a man without a wife.

In the sample households, other persons than those mentioned above were present as members at an average of 0·7 per household, the great majority being adults. In a few cases they formed sub-families of husband and wife or parent and child, further adding to the complicated character already imparted by the multi-generation aspect of the household. In terms of the ages of head, spouse and daughters, these households are distinctly older than the two-generation types, but they still have a considerable number of children under 15. There are few adult sons, but there are many adult daughters, a majority of whom are unmarried mothers.

In spite of their being male-headed, their structure reveals a female-orientated tendency in that nearly all grandchildren in such households are linked to the heads through their mothers, and adult daughters are much more numerous than adult sons. In some cases the attached relatives consist of only the wife's kin, while it also happens that almost the whole household consists of a man's second wife's children by her first marriage, and her daughter's children.

Some of these households may be regarded as being in a transitional stage, or in the phase of 'replacement'.[11] They have been assigned their relative age, not from the first and second generations, but from the second and third, since headship has already passed to the male of the second generation, but they still retain a multi-generation span through the presence of a parent of the head or his wife. They are in the process of becoming households based on elementary families. It may be that this factor is partly responsible for giving the male-headed multi-generation households a somewhat younger appearance than the female-headed ones. Although there are female-headed ones in which headship has passed to a female of the second generation, it seems as if a grandmother-head does not relinquish her position as head to a husbandless daughter as readily and as early as she does to a married son.

Multi-generation female-headed households: The family consisting of a woman with unmarried children and the children of unmarried daughters is very distinctly the main representative of this type, but the same kinds of variations as found in the male-headed counterpart (where one respectively has the head's widowed daughter, mother, married son and his family, or grandchildren without their parents) also occur. However, only here do we in some cases find unmarried granddaughters with their children. These households are also large, but include few other persons. Most of the heads claim to be widows.

Measured by the ages of head and daughters, they are older than any of the other major types. Although adult daughters numerically predominate over sons, this tendency is not as strong as in the male-headed household. This, together with the greater tendency to develop a four-generation span, suggests the possibility that the female-headed type has a stronger cohesion than the male-headed one.

It seems that in the four or five 'types' of household structure we have been

[11] Cf. Fortes, 'Introduction' to Goody (Ed.), *The Developmental Cycle in Domestic Groups*, p. 5.

discussing, we have, in fact, only two basic types, namely that of the household consisting of or based on an elementary family during its earlier phase of growth—this being the major type—and a minor type based on the group consisting of an unmarried mother and her children. Both have the tendency to develop a multi-generation span, while the major type often loses the male head at an early stage. One should remember, however, that the emergence of an urban Bantu family is a recent phenomenon, and urban society is still very much in a state of flux. It may well be that from now onward a tendency may be revealed for certain households continually to maintain a multi-generation span, growing into four generations before the eldest generation departs from the scene. Such multi-generation households would then have to be distinguished as a type on its own.

We have been speaking of trends and developmental patterns, drawing conclusions of a diachronic nature from material which is strictly speaking of a synchronic nature, in deducing developmental trends from differences in age of certain significant household personnel. Actual case histories bear out our deductions, however, that multi-generation households have developed out of two-generation ones. (Cf. cases 5, 7, 9 in chapter 4.) We also have the evidence of Hunter's study indicating that a generation ago the household structure of the settled town population was that of the elementary family.[12] Out of these the multi-generation families must have developed.

STRUCTURAL TYPE AND CULTURE

It still remains to be seen how households of differing structural 'types' compare in terms of their economic and cultural characteristics. In table 21 they are compared in terms of economic and cultural categories, and the only inference to be drawn from this is that 'white-collar' households are, almost exclusively, male-headed.[13] As regards the semi-Red cultural category it will be remembered that it is a category applying to individuals, not to households; but we may note that semi-Red individuals came from hou eholds of varying structural types, the female-headed ones being well represented. Our impression is that matrifocal tendencies are not confined to certain cultural types, but they do appear to be somewhat restrained among the small minority of families of the 'white-collar' type.[14]

TABLE 21

Household structure by cultural (economic) category

Type of household structure	CULTURAL CATEGORY White-collar	Inter-mediate	Simple	Other	Total
Multi-generation: male head	3	3	11	1	18
Father-mother-children	7	10	14	4	35
Multi-generation: female head	—	4	14	3	21
Mother-children	1	3	9	4	17
Other: male head	2	2	6	1	11
female head	—	—	6	1	7
Total	13	22	60	14	109

[12] Hunter, *Reaction to Conquest*, p. 459.

[13] One could perhaps claim a general tendency for male-headed households to a 'higher' cultural and economic level than female-headed ones (table 42B).

[14] In an investigation of Bantu white-collar families in East London which formed part of the economic section of the Border Regional Survey, it was found that in only eight of fifty-five 'true families' there was no male head. (Houghton, D. H. (Ed.), *Economic Development in a Plural Society*, O.U.P., 1960, p. 265.)

When we consider the question of housing type, we note that a larger proportion of multi-generation male-headed households in our sample were living in municipal houses than any of the other structural 'types' (table 22). If the sample is representative here of a general trend, this trend is difficult to explain. A possible explanation may be that the spaciousness of municipal housing lends itself better to the development of the larger multi-generation households than the cramped wood-and-iron surroundings, but that there are factors making it more difficult for female-headed households to procure municipal houses. One might have thought that administrative regulations could have some bearing on the problem, but according to the municipal Manager of Native Affairs there are no regulations which have the effect of making it more difficult for a female head than for a male head to obtain a municipal house, even though she be an unmarried mother. However, the absence of an older male bread-winner might place many female-headed households at a lower income level, where the rent charged for a municipal house is felt to be outside their reach. In some way or other house-ownership may also be involved. Of the twenty-one female-headed multi-generation households, twelve owned the houses in which they lived (all of course in the wood-and-iron areas) while only five of the eighteen male-headed ones owned houses.[15] One could argue that in the case of female-headed multi-generation households house ownership is a stronger force keeping them in wood-and-iron areas than it is in the case of the male-headed ones, though it is not clear why more female heads are owners.

TABLE 22

Household structure by housing type

Type of household structure	HOUSING TYPE		Total
	Wood-and-iron	Municipal	
Multi-generation: male head	9	9	18
Father-mother-children	27	8	35
Multi-generation: female head	17	4	21
Mother-children	14	3	17
Other: male head	10	1	11
female head	6	1	7
Total	83	26	109

FATHER AND MOTHER

Marwick's recent prediction that 'with a few more generations of urban living' we may expect the emergence among urban Bantu of the type of matrifocal family common among Negroes in diverse parts of the New World[16] already seems to be materializing in East London. Following Raymond T. Smith's use of the term 'matrifocal',[17] we could apply it to many households among the East London urban Bantu. If 'matrifocal' is taken to indicate a system of domestic relations in which the father has a 'marginal' position, then

[15] This contrast between male-headed and female-headed households is not confined to the multi-generation ones. Of the total of 63 male-headed households, only 13 (21 per cent) owned their houses, while 25 out of 46 female-headed ones (54 per cent) owned their houses.

[16] Marwick, M. G., 'The Modern Family in Social Anthropological Perspective' (Inaugural Lecture), Witwatersrand University Press, Johannesburg (reprinted from *African Studies*, 17, 3), 1958, p. 17.

[17] Smith, *The Negro Family in British Guiana.*

the type of fatherless 'family', developing and sometimes even attaining a three-generation span without marriage, may be said to be matrifocal in the extreme. A case could, in fact, perhaps be made for applying the term 'matrilineal' to these domestic groups. However, the classical use of the term implies a persisting system in which marriage is legalized and the father-role exists—albeit that 'matrilineal fatherhood' is then 'primarily a domestic relationship with only a minimal function in the politico-jural domain'.[18] This does not apply to these completely fatherless households. Moreover, although sufficiently numerous to be regarded as representing an emergent type, they are of too recent origin to be called part of a persisting system.

More numerous are the households with mother-heads, which did have legal fathers at an earlier stage of their development, but lost them relatively early and continued without them. The trend for households, even those with male heads, to become extended in the matriline, also indicates a trend toward matrifocality in household structure. Although a multi-generation household may have a male head who is not merely marginal, there is no father linking the 'matricentral cell' of unmarried daughter and her children to the domestic domain as a whole,[19] and this may continue throughout the period of the rearing of her children. The general tendency for more kin on the mother's side to be included in the household than kin on the father's side is another feature making the urban Bantu family comparable to the matrifocal Negro families.

We may now briefly examine the respective roles of father and mother, firstly that of the mother-head, and secondly those of father and mother in male-headed families. The authority of the mother-heads is sometimes subject to a certain amount of restriction. In some cases there is a degree of conflict, or at least uncertainty, over authority between a mother and an adult son in the household. This is the position in case no. 9 described in chapter 4, where the mother-head of the multi-generation household at first tried to create the impression that her unmarried adult son was the head. There was no evidence of real conflict between the two, the son being very much a marginal figure and the mother obviously the *de facto* head, but it seemed that in the light of traditional patrilineal values it was felt proper to suggest that he was the head. When eventually she did put forward her claim to being the head, she based it on her ownership of house and household property and on her being in charge of household economy.

A widow (44) who was a house-owner, with children and a grandchild (illegitimate), said her son (25) could never be the head of the household, because he was *isiza-na-nina* (lit. 'a come with mother', i.e. mother's premarital child). 'He knows my late husband was not his physical father. He refuses to go by his clan-name and claims rather to be —— [his mother's clan]. Moreover, he has no respect for me. For instance in his room in the house in which I am living, he stays with a young woman (under *ukushweshwa*) very much against my will.' Once the son became violent about the mother's sleeping in the house with her lover, attempting to throw the lover out by force, and the police had to intervene. Eventually the son asked to have his own room and be independent of the mother. In this case the mother seemed to imply that the son might have had a claim to headship but was disqualified on the ground of his not being linked with the patrilineal kin of the late father

[18] Fortes, op. cit., p. 12.
[19] Cf. Fortes, op. cit., p. 8.

of the household. Paradoxically values relating to a patrilineal system have here contributed to a matrifocal set-up. But the son's lack of respect for his mother was also a reason why he could not be head.

A widow living with an adult son (26) and daughter (22), both unmarried, owns the house in which they live and which she inherited from her husband. Some of the rooms are let. Her son gives her two rand (20*s.*) out of his weekly income, keeping the larger portion for himself. She buys all food and her own and her daughter's clothes. Asked why she regarded herself as head, she explained that the site was registered in her name, and since inheriting the house, she had added two rooms costing 'well over a hundred pounds', while her son helped with only 'a few pounds occasionally'. 'If you want to know why I rule and not my son, this is my answer: If the house were registered in my son's name, and he seduced a girl, there would be the danger of the property being attached for damages. . . . Moreover, I do not like to give my son the impression that I am under him. He must know he is under me and that there is nothing he can do without my consent. But I do consult him about everything I do.'

One could say that authority tends to be balanced between mother and adult son. Both have a certain claim, and who will, in fact, be head, depends on the interplay of diverse factors. House-ownership or original tenancy, contribution to household income, the son's participation in household activities, whether or not he desires to exercise his authority, respective ages of mother and son, and legitimacy of birth (where the mother has been legally married) are some of the factors affecting the issue. Where a son living in the same household with his mother is married, he is more readily cited as head, but we have seen that even in such a case the mother may be regarded as head.

In the absence of a potential male head, authority tends to pass from mother to mature daughter only when a daughter is well established as a mother herself. This may involve a period of uncertainty and even a degree of conflict before the daughter becomes head. In the following case the 'divorced' daughter seems to be well established as head. She is a qualified teacher in her forties, her mother was a teacher as well as a nurse, and her daughter (20) and son (16) are both far advanced in their educational careers. 'All domestic matters are settled by me in consultation with my mother', she says. 'I am the head. I pay rent and food. Mother refers to me if someone comes on small business.' Another woman, separated from her husband, 40 years of age, is living with her mother and has two working sons (aged 22 and 20 respectively) and two younger daughters with her. The younger woman regards herself as head, in spite of the fact that her mother is the registered tenant of the municipal house which they occupy, and she came to live with her after being separated from her husband. She stated the grounds for regarding herself as head as follows: 'If anybody comes for a loan of money, mother will refer the person to me. For any other matter mother will say: "We cannot discuss about this until B—— comes." I am responsible for running the house. My contribution is much larger than that of my sons, and though they might fail to give me theirs, I cannot fail. I am the head, because my mother is well advanced in age, and her only income is the old-age grant amounting to £3 7*s.* 6*d.* per quarter.'

Some grandmothers retain authority much longer, as in the case of Manini (chapter 4, case no. 9). Since her son is so much of a marginal figure, one might have expected that authority would by now have passed to her eldest daughter who is already a grandmother. The main reason why this has not happened seems to be that her daughters are economically dependent on her to a high degree. The fact that the grandmother owns the property may also throw some doubt on her daughter's claim to headship. In the family in connexion with which the ritual described in chapter 3 took place, the unmarried daughter gave the impression of being in complete control, and of the home being hers. However, when her brother stressed the importance of the mother's presence, she admitted that the house legally belonged to the mother and that she herself was an unmarried mother. Although factors of respective ages and house-ownership play their role, the daughter's taking over responsibility for household economy is probably the most important factor, deciding the replacing of mother by daughter as head. Sometimes, of course, this only takes place at the mother's death.

Another indication of the restricted nature of female headship is that there are occasions when a 'substitute father' is needed by female-headed households, as for controlling an errant son, negotiating about a daughter's seduction, negotiations for children's marriages, sons' initiation, and traditional ritual. It should be remembered, however, that male heads usually also summon one or two kinsmen or friends on such occasions, and some widows, in fact, said that they summoned the same men as their husbands had done during their lifetimes. Nevertheless, female heads are more dependent on these male advisers than male heads. In the case of widows the males who are summoned are usually patrilineal kinsmen of the late husband. Mary called in her husband's elder brother when her son (24) got drunk (chapter 4, case no. 8). A widow, who has an unmarried son (20) living with her, first consults her son and then a clansman of the late husband on important matters. When the son took ill, she consulted the clansman about the advisability of seeing a diviner, and he accompanied her to one. The widow whose son tried to evict her lover first called in two of her husband's *imilowo* (patrilineal kinsmen) to intervene, before the police were summoned. When her daughter got pregnant, 'these two men were called again and they ordered a messenger to interview the young man who was responsible'. A woman recently widowed said that she would call her late husband's younger brother 'to act as head' if there was anything of importance to be discussed.

In the case of separated or divorced women, relations with the husband's kinsmen might be strained and they might summon one of their own kinsmen instead. This would also be the case with an unmarried mother. We noted the case of the youth who is sponsored for initiation by his unmarried mother's brother (p. 91). There is also the instance of the unmarried mother whose brother was summoned about the children's misbehaviour and started negotiations about performing a sacrifice (p. 53). A separated mother also summoned her brother for her two sons' initiation. On the other hand, a woman who claims to be a widow summoned her elder sister's two adult sons when her daughter was seduced, explaining that these were the only male relatives she had.

In spite of certain disabilities or limitations, then, the households without fathers seem to manage fairly well without them, and urban Bantu households are therefore comparable to those of British Guiana Negroes, in that the husband-father is 'dispendable'. However, whereas in the latter, the father, when present, fulfils a 'marginal' role and is not the *de facto* head, although he may be the *de jure* head, this cannot be said of the East London Bantu households which do have husband-fathers. Here the father is not marginal, and often spends much of his leisure time at home, and is seldom away for long periods. There is seldom any doubt about his being the head, not only in name, but also in practice. Except in some white-collar households in which the mother earns more than the father, he is the main bread-winner. Both tenants and landlords would leave the payment or collecting of rent largely in their wives' hands, but when trouble arises the husband usually steps in. Many wives refer all important matters to their husbands, and during fieldwork we often had the experience, when calling on a family, of being told by a woman that she did not wish to give information without her husband's approval. It must be noted, therefore, that in spite of the matrifocal trend evident in family structure, the father—if there is one—still wields the major authority in the household. There are cases where the wife in practice wields the greater authority, in spite of her husband's presence, as when the husband is a loafer and she has to shoulder economic responsibilities alone, or when her education or income is considerably higher than that of her husband—but this cannot be regarded as representing a general trend.

Generally speaking, relations between husband and wife are no doubt closer in the urban household than they used to be in the traditional Xhosa *umzi*, where avoidance customs and ritual emphasized the position of the wife as an outsider in her husband's homestead, particularly during the earlier years of married life.[20] Where marriage takes place in town a young couple usually choose each other in the first place, rather than being selected for each other by their parents, and in married life they tend to be less involved with their parents and in-laws and more aware of their exclusive responsibility for an own household[21] from an early stage.

Quarrels and disputes are affairs between husband and wife in which the wife tends to act with less submissiveness than tradition requires. The grandfather in a patrilineally extended family mentioned below (p. 161) contrasted his own son and daughter-in-law's behaviour with traditional custom: 'When they get cross with each other, instead of the wife reporting the matter to her mother-in-law, she just tries to solve the problem by exchanging words with her husband. This cannot be helped in these days. Traditional customs are quickly disappearing. Women shout at their husbands and they even return blows when beaten by them. Husbands in these days assault their wives in the presence of their elders and even of parents.'

Economic roles are also less clearly distinguished in the urban household. At all economic levels it is common for the husband to hand over the greater part of his earnings to his wife, and for her to finance the running of the household from this with relatively little interference from the husband. However the working wife with an income of her own is not only found in the poorer households, but very often also in those of white-collar level, and in the latter it is not unusual for a wife who is, say, a nurse, to have a higher income than her husband.

Consultation between husband and wife on matters of household economy, children's education, and the performance of ritual are common. There are instances of husbands sharing domestic chores with their wives, though it must

[20] For 'role separateness' between Red Xhosa couples, see Mayer, op. cit., pp. 98–9.
[21] Cf. Hunter, Monica, *Reaction to Conquest*, pp. 460–1.

be said that on the whole, even if the husband does perform certain tasks at home, it is understood that duties are fairly clearly divided and that his participation in household chores is regarded as voluntary assistance in what are primarily the wife's duties. Some husbands and wives of the white-collar level go visiting and attend entertainments or church services in each other's company, but in households of simple culture this is very unusual, if not non-existent. Our case material suggests that there is some tendency with white-collar couples to what Bott[22] has termed a 'joint conjugal role-relationship', but conjugal relations of the majority of couples are more segregated, though not as highly segregated as in traditional Xhosa marriage.

A town-born man who is in white-collar employment and whose wife is a nurse, viewed traditional conjugal roles as highly segregated. 'The man was a boss', he said, 'and a very big one too. The wife had to be very far from the husband. She just had to be busy with her own work inside the house. She had to respect her husband as *utata ka bantwana* [father of the children]. The only time they would meet, was when something was to be discussed. It was a way of maintaining dignity, so that women should not be despised [*ukudelwa*].' He and his wife are quite different, in that 'we share almost everything; we are always together. She has to be very near. As my partner she has exactly the same rights in everything: in love, in everything we are equal.' This may read like a rather self-conscious attempt to emphasize the acceptance of 'Western' values as contrasted to traditional ones, but in our conversation it did not strike me as having been made merely to impress. Moreover, what he had said about his own and his wife's activities before making this statement also points to a relatively non-segregated relationship. He hands his earnings to his wife because 'we [men] can be extravagant'. They consult each other whenever there is something extraordinary to be spent. When he needs clothes, he tells her about it, and she gives him the money. 'All men do not take this attitude, some regarding that "a woman is a woman". I was trying to nurse [the idea] that there should be some understanding between her and me.' When she comes off duty after him, he fetches her at the hospital by car. She cooks the dinner and they sit down to their meal at table together with the wife's brother (18), who is staying with them. (At this stage they had no children.) He sometimes helps his wife to wash the dishes—'when we are both tired'—and also to clean the house—'when the boy [her brother] is ill'—but he added laughingly though with emphasis: 'only when I feel like that; it is no work of mine here in the house.' The three of them attend church together about twice a month. They have family prayers every night, when the wife chooses a hymn and he says a prayer. Besides visiting and film shows, the two of them also attend 'social gatherings' such as wedding receptions and graduation parties together. He has, however, also a great diversity of sporting and other interests, which his wife does not share.

In the first case described in chapter 4, we also have an instance of a white-collar couple of whom the husband claims to help his wife a great deal in household chores and who used to go out together. In case no. 2, there is also evidence of their attending church and tea parties together.

Couples with conjugal role-relationships of this kind are only a small minority, however, wife and husband usually having much less joint activity. Case 3 in chapter 4 illustrates this for a household which we classified as white-collar,

[22] *Family and Social Network*, p. 55.

although neither the husband nor the wife were in white-collar employment themselves. A factory 'head boy' (54) with standard seven does not accompany his wife to church on Sundays, but goes to watch sport or to visit his friends. His wife maintains he has never assisted her in her household chores, except in moving heavy furniture when she is doing a thorough spring-cleaning. In the great majority of cases in town, it seems that conjugal relations are of an intermediate nature, falling between the highly segregated pattern of traditional custom and the joint pattern found with some white-collar couples. In the following chapter we shall examine the relation of changes in conjugal roles to other structural changes.

We have seen then, that in spite of the unmistakable matrifocal trend in urban Bantu households, there is this difference from the British Guiana families, that where there is a father in an urban Bantu household it cannot be said that his role is marginal or that he is merely the head *de jure*, but not *de facto*. The reason for this seems to be that in spite of structural conditions working towards a matrifocal family structure, traditional values relating to patriarchy and patrilineal kinship ties are still strongly in evidence, even among urban Bantu. This is not difficult to understand, since, otherwise than the Negroes of the New World, they are close, both in space and in time, to a society patterned on patrilineal kinship. It is only one or two generations ago since their ancestors migrated to town from the rural areas where this type of society existed. Moreover, in spite of changes, patrilineal kinship still figures prominently in present-day Xhosa rural society, and there is continual and intensive interaction between the Xhosa of East London and those of the reserves. Consequently the tradition of male authority and patrilineal descent still has considerable force, even in town, and is valued in spite of the deterioration of the father-role in structural terms.

This valuation was aptly illustrated in the case of an aged father whose town-born son (47) was living in a neighbouring house with his family, while they formed a single domestic group, sharing meals, household chores and the care of their cattle. The son used to inform his father of 'anything important' he intended doing at his house. The grandfather took pride in this pattern of the patrilineally extended family. 'D—— is still supporting me and looking after me. Our close co-operation gives me respect from all the people. My equals praise me that I can bring up and train a child properly.' Thus the patriarchal patterns still found in town by way of exception are still generally valued. In other words, traditional values are retained although they have lost much of their structural significance. This means that the culture has not yet changed to the extent that the structure has.

But let us return to the similarity between urban Bantu and British Guiana Negro households in terms of their matrifocal structure. Smith argues that the matrifocal character of the British Guiana household 'can be regarded as the obverse of the marginal nature of the husband-father role', and that this is related to the economic system and the system of social stratification in the total society, in that 'men, in their role of husband-father are placed in a position where neither their social status nor their access to and command of economic resources are of major importance in the household group *at certain stages of its development*'.[23] Broadly speaking this hypothesis would hold for the urban Bantu family too. For their income households depend mainly on labour,

[23] Smith, op. cit., p. 221.

trading, and rentals, and none of these are controlled exclusively by the husband-father. Mothers freely take up employment, venture into large- or small-scale trading and can own properties through inheritance and purchase. Even an unmarried mother can manage to rear her own family without a husband-father, and even without her own mother, although it might be difficult at times, and, as we have seen, she would need the help of other relatives while her children are young.

The Bantu urban father also does not fulfil a critical function as link with the status system. We shall indicate later that traditional status differentiations have lost much of their significance in town, while in terms of emerging class differentiations the bulk of the urban Bantu belong to a lower stratum, holding an inferior position to the bulk of Whites on the other side of the racial division, and also to the small minority of the white-collar type who are set apart as an upper stratum among the urban Bantu. With class-differentiations unimportant, the father has no critical function to fulfil in relating the household group to the status system. On the other hand, in as far as class differentiations are growing in significance, the high educational standard and 'respectable' occupation of children may contribute more to the greater prestige of the domestic group than the father's income or occupation. The indication that the matrifocal tendency is less in evidence in white-collar households in our sample suggests, however, that as class distinctions increase in importance the husband-father role in the system of domestic relations may increase in importance.

I would, in fact, go further than economics and the status system, and suggest that the matrifocal tendency is related to the insignificance of the father-role over the whole series of important external relations of the household. To illustrate this we may compare a few aspects of urban Bantu society with the traditional social organization of the Xhosa. Traditionally status differentiations were closely related to the political structure and to ritual procedure, these different fields all being largely patterned by kinship relations. Distinctions between royalty and commoners were based on clan membership, and seniority in terms of patrilineal descent was recognized on ritual and ceremonial occasions between members of the same clan or lineage. Patrilineal descent was also the most important factor deciding access to the hierarchy of leadership roles in the political system. In ritual the emphasis was on clan and lineage ties and patrilineal ancestors. A child was linked to the structurally important kinship groups through its legal father, and its position in the kinship structure largely decided its status generally, and in particular its position in the political and ritual fields. This was combined with a distinct patriarchal organization of the domestic group, and with the concept that wives and children were minors at law who had to be represented by their husbands and fathers. This was a case, therefore, in which, in Professor Fortes's terms, the 'conjugal relationship and patrifiliation' were effective in establishing a child's jural and ritual status, and the husband-father was 'the critical link between the matricentral cell' of the mother and her children and the domestic group—which commonly extended beyond the elementary family—and through the domestic group 'with the environment and with the structure of the total society'.[24] To this we may add that the matricentral cell was highly dependent on the husband-father for access to the economic resources of land and cattle. In other words, mother and children had all their important links with the domestic domain as

[24] Fortes, op. cit., pp. 8–9.

a whole and with the external field of the total social system through the husband-father.

Under modern conditions the situation has changed even in the rural areas. For instance, to some church people the 'ritual status' a child acquires through baptism, quite independently of its position in the patrilineal kinship system, is of greater significance than his ritual status in terms of ancestor cult and patrilineal descent. Chieftainship and traditional patterns of political organization orientated to patrilineal kinship, though still in evidence, have lost much of their significance to Western-orientated government institutions. Nevertheless, rural Xhosa society is still largely organized on principles of kinship, and patrilineal kinship groups remain of vital importance, so that the father may be regarded as normally still fulfilling a critical function in relating the matricentral cell to the total society, particularly within the Red sector.

In town the father-role loses almost all the significance it had in relation to the external field in the traditional structure. We shall see[25] that although kinship ties are still recognized, they have hardly any significance in urban society for political roles and for status generally, while the significance of kinship in its ritual context is greatly diminished. Generally speaking patrilineal kinship groups have lost their significance as important categories of interaction in day-to-day relations, and with this the husband-father role has lost the significance it traditionally had as link between the matricentral cell and the total society. As we have noted above, the father is also 'dispendable' as a link with the economic system in town and in most cases so far has no critical function to fulfil in relating his wife and children to an emergent urban status system. With very little effective participation in urban local government, as well as in tribal or national government,[26] the politico-jural domain is an undeveloped field and the urban husband-father has neither in terms of modern institutions any significant role to fulfil in relation to this field. I argue, then, that the matrifocal trend is related to this general insignificance of the husband-father role in relating mother and children to the total social system.[27]

The question of attitudes to sex relations, however, also seems to have a bearing on the matrifocal trend. Both traditional and modern Bantu attitudes tend to view sexual gratification as something not necessarily associated with the conjugal bond. Traditionally a large degree of sexual gratification could be sought before marriage (*ukumetsha*, external intercourse), not necessarily with a prospective marriage partner. Married men, mature unmarried women, and women who had lost their husbands were also allowed opportunities of sexual gratification outside marriage. The serious transgressions were the impregnation of a nubile girl and adultery which involved a married woman. What were guarded were not the exclusive rights of present or future spouses to sexual favours but the *rights to the 'procreative powers'*[28] of nubile girls and married women—the rights, that is, on the part of the kinship groups into which the

[25] Chapters 9 and 10.

[26] See chapter 9, and Mayer, op. cit., pp. 51–4.

[27] Brandell writes that the loss of men's 'tribal functions', humiliations resulting from the colour-bar, their restricted earning capacities, increasing independence of women and women's growing status as persons in their own right 'have given the men a sense of their own futility and uselessness'. (Op. cit., p. 47.)

[28] These form part of what are termed 'genetrical rights' as distinguished from 'uxorial rights' which include the rights to 'sexual services'. (Cf. for example, Mitchell, J. C., 'Social Change and the Stability of African Marriage in Northern Rhodesia', in Southall (Ed.), *Social Change in Modern Africa*.)

women were married and the girls were eventually to be married. To put it differently: the bearing of children was guarded by marriage, but not sexual enjoyment. Further, the children a woman bore in marriage belonged not only to her husband, but to his whole patrilineal kinship group. *Lobolo* essentially established the right of the husband's kin group to his wife's children. For a married woman to commit adultery was a serious breach of fidelity, not only toward her husband, but also toward his lineage and clan. Moreover, it gravely annoyed his patrilineal ancestors.[29]

I argue, then, that a woman's procreative powers were 'fenced in' by marriage to guard the rights of the patrilineal kinship group, and that the increase in extra-marital pregnancies is related to the weakening of kinship ties. The more kinship groups lose their solidarity and corporate structure as in towns, the less is the concern over procreative powers of women, and the less is the pressure on nubile girls to avoid pregnancy.[30] This fits in with the impression that in the reserves premarital pregnancy is more common among School people than among Red people, and that kinship ties are less affected among the latter than among the former.[31] It further fits the urban situation where extra-marital pregnancy has become a 'normal' phenomenon and lineages and clans have virtually no structural significance.

In an analytical sense, then, sex relations were always potentially something apart from the conjugal bond among the Xhosa, and they remain to be regarded as such by the majority of townspeople. But in addition the bearing of children has now also become divorced from marriage. In the light of this development the domestic group needs the male only as genitor but not as a permanent husband-father, and in terms of social structure the conjugal bond becomes 'dispendable'.[32]

This is, of course, only the one side of the picture. On the other hand Christian concepts of chastity and marital fidelity have been introduced, and there are those of the urban Xhosa who genuinely and earnestly seek to order their sex and family life accordingly. We have seen, however, that the impact of Christian teaching on attitudes and norms pertaining to sex still appears to be very restricted.

In arguing as I have done, I do not subscribe to the relativistic belief that with the given structural situation the present moral situation was inevitable. I do not believe that the only valid moral norms are those deriving from the prerequisites for the continued existence of society, in other words that moral norms merely reflect a particular structural situation. No doubt, what people regard as moral norms are often nothing more than the dictates of a particular structural situation, but this does not mean that absolute norms which transcend the structure of the particular society are non-existent. This is, of course, a matter of belief, but it inevitably enters into our interpretation of a situation

[29] For a more detailed exposition of a similar argument up to this point in respect of Zulu marriage and kinship, see Gluckman, M., 'Kinship and Marriage among the Lozi of Northern Rhodesia and the Zulu of Natal' in Radcliffe-Brown, A. R., and Forde, D. (Ed.), *African Systems of Kinship and Marriage*, O.U.P., 1950. In broad outline Xhosa marriage and kinship structure is similar to that of the Zulu. The absence of age-sets among the Zulu, which Gluckman mentions, does not affect the argument up to this point.

[30] Cf. Mitchell's point that in the urban situation genetrical rights in a woman — which include rights over procreative powers—fade in favour of uxorial rights. (Op. cit., p. 325.)

[31] Mayer, op. cit., pp. 37–9.

[32] The argument is related to that proposed by Gluckman (op. cit.) and developed by Mitchell (op. cit.), which relates a high degree of marital stability to a kinship organization based on corporate patrilineages, genetrical rights being acquired by groups in the latter type of system,

as the one we have discussed. What I wish to point out then, is that I do not view the fatherless urban Bantu family as a phenomenon which is the inevitable result of the prevailing structural situation, nor that it is a satisfactory domestic arrangement because it is reasonably adapted to the wider social system in which it exists. To my view true moral norms transcend any particular social structure and have an absolute validity. These norms may be accepted in spite of structural conditions which militate against them, and their acceptance may eventually change the whole structure of a particular society.

I believe, therefore, that the church has a definite task in relation to the prevailing moral situation among the Bantu. It has something to say to those who wield political influence, about the way in which social structure militates against moral norms, but it also has something to say to the urban Bantu themselves. Towards them its task is not only to proclaim those absolute moral norms relating to sex and the family, but more important still, to proclaim a gospel of salvation from the powers, including the forces exerted by a particular structural situation, which militate against conforming to these norms. Perhaps the reason why Christian teaching seems to have had so little impact on the sex life of the Bantu is that too much stress has been laid on norms, and too little on salvation and redemption.[33]

[33] Cf. what I have written elsewhere about the moralistic and legalistic trend in Tswana churches. (Pauw, B. A., *Religion in a Tswana Chiefdom*, O.U.P., London, 1960, pp. 218–19).

9

The Social Universe of Bantu Townspeople

It is a well-known fact that Bantu society has now for some time been becoming less rigidly structured in terms of kinship and kinship groupings, and that the 'thawing' of this kinship structure is most pronounced in towns. Usually it is indicated that as kinship groupings dissolve, social relations of the Bantu become increasingly individualistic in character, and that urban living produces a growing spirit of individualism. This does not apply to East London without qualification. It is true, of course, that settling in town generally tends to attenuate ties with the structurally significant traditional kinship groups, and that the townsman need feel himself under no great compulsion in terms of behaviour prescribed by kinship relations. He is relatively free to make his own individual choice from varying behaviour patterns according to personal inclination.[1] The social relations of East London Bantu are indeed much more individualistic in character than those of their rural ancestors, but theirs is not the individualism of loneliness and anonymity sometimes associated with urban societies.[2]

It has not been possible to study intensively the wider social network (outside the domestic family) of urban Bantu in East London, so that our treatment of the subject is admittedly somewhat impressionistic. Nevertheless there is considerable evidence for what I would regard as the main impression, namely that in spite of the development of individualism, social relations are not characterized by an extreme degree of isolation of the individual. Not only is the individual generally involved in a number of dyadic relations of an intimate and personal nature, but often also in one or more relatively small, intimate groups.

FAMILY AND KIN

Within the domestic family there is often a considerable amount of joint activity. This has been illustrated by several of the families described in chapter 4. Most families have at least one meal per day together, and the females—and sometimes also the males—share domestic duties, often working in each other's company. The pleasant conversation of several members of a family over a cup of tea on the return of the working members after the day's work was often observed during fieldwork in the location. Male adults, however, particularly unmarried ones, tend to share less of this family life. Group activity within the family is further more obvious in the large, multi-generation families than in the smaller ones, while the adult members of a multi-generation beer-brewing family may spend most of the day in each other's company.

Frequently there is considerable contact with relatives who are not members

[1] Cf. Mayer, op. cit., pp. 13–17.

[2] Cf., for example, Ogburn and Nimkoff, *A Handbook of Sociology* (revised ed. 1953), pp. 349, 351, 447.

of the domestic family. In the wood-and-iron areas it is not uncommon for families to have relatives living in the same house or in the one next door or just across the street. Nineteen households in our sample (109) had kinsmen as neighbours. In five cases the relationships were reminiscent of traditional patterns: father and son, two brothers, or two more distant patrilineal kinsmen. But in six cases the relationships reflected the modern matrifocal trend: mother and daughter, two sisters, or sister's daughter and mother's sister. Other cases consisted of sons who were neighbours to their husbandless mothers, two unmarried brothers living close to their sister, and pairs of cross-cousins or cross-cousins once removed. Only two of these cases occurred in municipal housing areas.

Relations with kin certainly figure more prominently among the urban Bantu than they do among urban Whites in South Africa. Within the domestic household we find evidence of this in the numerous multi-generation households, and in the frequency with which collateral kinsmen are members of households. We have noted the fact that these people are usually said to have no other shelter and have found a haven with their relatives. Generally the kinship connexion is fairly close, but our chart of the kinship composition of households (fig. 5) shows that in some cases even a distant kinsman may be accepted into the domestic family. These facts already indicate that kinship obligations are honoured to a considerable degree.

Many townspeople have close kin besides their own parents, siblings or children living in the location, or at least somewhere in East London. In time of need they would commonly turn to those most closely related, but when these are not at hand they would also seek assistance from parents' siblings or first cousins. Informants often cited actual cases of having received or given such help. This mostly takes the form of material assistance, generally a loan of money and sometimes a gift or performing a service. A certain amount of contact is kept up with kinsfolk in the country and in other towns through correspondence, visits, and sometimes through gifts. However, the contacts observed in this manner seldom extend beyond kinsmen of the third degree. Moreover the contacts are often confined to certain kin within these limits. In other words, there is selection, albeit that this selection is often conditioned by circumstances other than mere likes or dislikes.

Frequently a very particular bond is felt with one particular kinsman. A married man (31, std. six) said of his cousin (F.B.S.) who is a teacher: 'Of all my relatives he is next to my soul [*usondele emphefumlweni wam*]. We are of the same age and he is very generous to me.' He also used the expression '*siyaphefumlelana*' (lit., we breathe on each other). The cousin has given him money 'up to £3' during informant's visits to him in Port Elizabeth and on occasion he sent him a new sports coat. 'I have bought shirts for him and a smart pair of trousers.' A female liquor trader (36, std. six) singled out her cousin (F.s.d.) among her relatives. 'She comes number one. When I was ill she offered to come and look after me when none of my other relatives seemed to care. They did not even come to see how I was progressing.' A well-educated young man keeps up a regular correspondence with a cousin (m.B.S.). 'He stayed with us in East London as a small boy and I have spent holidays at his home.'

Attitudes to the observance of contacts with kinsfolk vary from enthusiasm to dislike. As an example of an enthusiastic attitude we may take a young father who mentioned the following in connexion with his contacts with kinsmen:

A, father-in-law, and B, wife's sister: saw them several times a week and had on occasion received material assistance from each of them;

C, a clansman believed to be descended from the same patrilineal great-grandfather as informant;

D, another clansman, and

E, a 'sister' of his father, who was, however, not an actual sibling, 'but they were of the same clan, had close contacts, and regarded each other as brother and sister': from D and E he had received financial assistance some years previously.

C, D, and E were also in East London and were seen occasionally. He also mentioned a cousin of his wife's father (her F.m.s.S.) with whom he and his wife had spent a week-end in the King William's Town district when a revival meeting of their church was held in the area. He felt that these contacts were too few, and wished to have more. 'In the event of an early death the relatives are there to look after your young children, and the more relatives there are, the better, because they cannot be all equally poor or equally heartless. One of them must be sympathetic to your children and would make a special effort to see them through in life.'

Another young man (28, std. six) mentioned five male relatives who were all in East London and all of whom he had seen fairly recently, 'but we do not help one another. They are much older than I am, but have never helped me or my mother and therefore I am not prepared to help them.' He had a personal non-kinsman friend from whom he sought assistance when in need and was unenthusiastic about keeping up ties with kinsmen. 'They have failed to indicate in a practical manner that they are my kinsmen. For instance, when I was circumcised in 1955, *umguyo* [the feast preceding initiation] was largely attended by my "teeth friends" [intimate friends] who were no kinsmen but merely friends. None of my kinsmen made any contribution towards my circumcision ceremony.'

Others are not as sceptical as this informant, appreciating the contacts they do have, but they are wary of contacts with too many relatives, because 'some become a nuisance and become beggars because they are too lazy to work'. Complaints of this kind are common. Moreover, it is felt that one cannot meet the justified expectations of kinsmen with whom one has contacts if these are too many. Another young father who had contacts with several of his kin, felt that these were 'just enough'. If one has too many, one receives too many invitations and one cannot accept all. 'One sometimes attends a marriage or any other ceremony of one relative and forgets or neglects that of another, and this gives rise to ill-feeling.'

The traditional grouping into patrilineal clans is recognized in various ways by the urban Xhosa. We have seen that clan exogamy is still universally observed in respect of actual marriage, and to a large extent also in extra-marital sex relations. Breach of the rule of exogamy is commonly regarded as incest (*umbulo*) and uncleanness, sometimes still combined with the belief that it will result in the birth of deformed children. The taboo on a bride's drinking the milk of her husband's clanspeople seems to be of little significance in town. The ritual slaughtering of a goat in connexion with marriage, referred to as *ukudlisa amasi* (to cause to drink sour milk), though still performed, appears to have lost much of its significance as a clan ritual. The clan name is in common use as a form of greeting or addressing mature men. Many people harbour some sense of obligation towards fellow clansmen. A young man who had passed his Senior Certificate, and was planning to proceed to Fort Hare for a degree course, mentioned a young married man whose home he regularly visited over the week-end, and commented: 'They are people of my clan. Our grandfathers were brothers. When we have family matters like weddings or sacrifices, he always attends.' He regarded the following as his duties towards members of his clan:

- to help them financially and otherwise when they are in need;
- to visit them and make them feel that there is one of their relatives who keeps an eye on whatever happens to them;
- to attend when they make a sacrifice, when someone has died or is seriously ill;
- to intervene and console when they have domestic troubles; and
- to extend protection in the event of troubles and quarrels of any kind;
- to be 'the feet and hands of those who are old and disabled'.

Not all townspeople would feel that their clan obligations are as wide as this, but the recognition of a certain degree of obligation is common.

Our material is insufficient to indicate whether recognition of kinship obligations are affected by the matrifocal trend in the domestic family, but persons whose ties with their mother's kin are much closer than with those of their fathers' are not uncommon. Several married men said they went to their wives' parents for assistance in time of need, without mentioning their own parents or patrilineal kinsmen. However, patrilineal kinship comes to the fore in the recognition of clan ties, and particularly on ceremonial occasions such as sacrifices, baptismal feasts or *ukubingelela*, and initiation.

Kinship ties are valued, then, but in practice most urban Xhosa have effective ties with only a restricted number of kinsfolk. The selection of these 'effective kin' is not based on principles inherent in the traditional kinship system, but depends on their availability, on the way they have reacted to ego's needs, or merely on personal likes. Occasionally a number of members of a clan or lineage gather for ritual or ceremonial purposes, but in contrast to rural Xhosa society, where kinship ramifies throughout the whole social structure, it constitutes only one among many categories of relationships figuring in the total social network of a townsman. Clan and lineage are not highly significant categories in the urban structure compared to neighbours and friends, churches, associations, and relationships at work.

Our East London material substantiates Southall's major generalizations about kinship in modern African towns. He points out that kinship does not break down, but 'the scope of kinship rights and duties has narrowed and become more uncertain and the body of kin included in them become reduced', so that 'the individual is left to cast about and pin obligations of kinship on to whom he can. . . . Most of the rituals of kinship cannot be performed for this reason, or only in a truncated form.'[3] In East London the latter remark is vividly illustrated by Mayer's interesting material on substitute rituals in town.[4] The Red migrant particularly regards the rural home as the more appropriate place for a sacrifice, especially because of the close connexion of

[3] Southall, *Social Change in Modern Africa*, pp. 31, 32, 34.
[4] Mayer, *Townsmen or Tribesmen*, pp. 151 ff.

the ancestral spirits with the cattle-kraal, but also because the real centre of his social network, including kinship ties, lies in the country. The School migrant and his town-born descendant[5] tend to build up a completely new town-centred network into which they draw whichever kin they can and wish to.[6] Hence, should townspeople wish to perform a ritual, as occasionally happens, they may find it easier than Red migrants to muster a number of kinsmen.[7] However, the group that gathers is a less compact and less closely knit group than that which would meet for a ritual in the country.

This contrast between Red migrants and townspeople proper agrees with Southall's conclusion that 'the urban situations most inimical to the development of local kin groups are probably those associated with the maintenance of strong rural ties'.[8] In East London, however, the situation is determined, not so much by 'extrinsic factors' such as wages, influx control and housing conditions, which apply to Red and School migrants alike, but rather by the contrasting values with which Red and School migrants come to town.[9]

NEIGHBOURS AND FRIENDS

The extremely crowded conditions in which the majority of location inhabitants live make for daily close contacts with large numbers of people. Generally people living in the same house or in adjacent ones are not merely in close contact, but are also friendly towards each other. People who are always attempting to withdraw from their neighbours are not common. In the crowded wood-and-iron areas it is of course extremely difficult to attain even a minimum of privacy from neighbours, but even in the municipal houses, where privacy could easily be established, neighbours freely come and go in each other's houses in a very informal way. Few of our own visits to location homes passed without a neighbour being present during part of the visit. When making room-to-room visits in a certain area a group of children recruited from different families in the same house would often follow us about from one room to the next. Although friends are not predominantly drawn from among neighbours, many people have their closest friend living in the same house or yard, or in the immediate neighbourhood.

Of the people in the location who are active and well, there are probably few who do not have friends. Often a person is able to single out someone whom he regards as his closest friend, and most people have several friends with whom they have frequent contacts.[10] Close friends are usually seen at least once a week and often almost every day. Generally these friendships are not family affairs, and every member of the family tends to have his own little circle of friends. A youth might count his sister's sweetheart among his friends, or he might be on friendly terms with a female friend of his sister, confiding his love problems to her, or asking her to convey messages to his own sweetheart. A particular friend of one member is often also on friendly terms with the whole family, while neighbours may be friendly to each other as families. But the kind of family friendship in which one family, for instance, visits another in a group, is uncommon.

[5] Most townspeople are descended from School immigrants. (See chapter 1.)

[6] See pp. 187 ff.

[7] Southall remarks about the 'more permanent' elements of urban populations: 'Here there are families, there is a network of kinship [although 'reliance on kinship is less'] and also considerable continuity with tribal life.' (Op. cit., p. 43.)

[8] Southall, op. cit., p. 36.

[9] See Mayer, op. cit., chapter 18.

[10] About friendships among School migrants, cf. Mayer, pp. 217–19.

Among children and teenagers there is a distinct tendency to form small groups of friends. We have already mentioned the small play-groups of children which sometimes become fighting groups (p. 78). Teenagers, among whom a close friend is known as *itshomi* (from English, 'chum'), also perform many of their activities in groups of three or four friends. According as the interests of its members vary, such a group may join for conversation, games, loitering about the streets, drinking or dancing, going to the beach or for fighting. A semi-illiterate girl of 16 spoke of 'my group' with whom she goes drinking in the bushes, while on Sundays they gather in a room for dancing. They go to do their washing together at the taps where 'we talk about the gifts we have received from our boy-friends and plan to collect money so that we should have enough *isigomfane* (a potent brew) for the week-end. We talk about a girl who had a quarrel with my *itshomi* and that we should go and fight her, all of us.' Incidentally fighting is not uncommon among girls and is not restricted to semi-illiterates such as this one. Often these fights are about lovers.

Among boys and youths it seems that this clustering together is sometimes associated with a form of age-classification in which uncircumcised boys distinguish between equals (*intanga*), seniors and juniors. This is vaguely reminiscent of pre-initiation age divisions in the reserves, where, however, they are much more explicit and organized.[11] A town-born young man who was well-acquainted with the word, said of *intanga* in town: 'They grow up together, share the same views and are inclined to follow each other's example. If one fights and defeats a senior, they will all try individually to defeat that equal of theirs, so that their senior should be regarded as their equal, instead of their equal being promoted to the seniors. Of course, if he is a violent fellow he is left alone to join the seniors, and for his brutality is accepted by the seniors as their equal.' Often, however, youths do not consciously associate their friendship groups with age divisions. Moreover, when one member of such a group is initiated before the others, this does not disrupt their friendship, and after his return to normal life, they share common activities as before. These groups of older boys lack all form of formal organization or conscious leadership patterns.

A married person generally also has two or three close friends who are also friends of each other, but there is usually not quite as much joint activity between these mutual friends as in the case of younger people. Some men, however, usually play cards or draughts, gamble or drink with such a group of friends. We may also mention here the lunch-hour groups formed at places of employment. Bantu employees seldom take more than a sandwich and a cup of tea at lunch-time, usually on the premises where they are employed or outside where they gather in small groups, spending the rest of the lunch-break playing cards or draughts, or in conversation.

When a family is confronted with a serious problem, such as a daughter having been rendered pregnant, or when a marriage proposal has to be considered, male friends are usually called in for an informal meeting to discuss the matter, in much the same way as such matters used to be discussed by kinsmen in the past. Often the advisers who are summoned are in fact still kinsmen.

CHURCHES, ASSOCIATIONS AND GATHERINGS

In chapter 3 we noted a considerable degree of participation in churches and religious associations, and in the case of men, also in sport, while some other

[11] Wilson, Monica, and others, *Social Structure, Keiskammahoek Rural Survey*, vol. III, pp. 159 ff.

associations and groups are also important. There we dealt with these in terms of the interests and activities of the individual, here we look at them as groups.

The most important religious associations are the so-called church *manyanos* (*umanyano*, an association) which differentiate along lines of sex and age. In nearly every church *Umanyano Lwamanina* (the Women's Association) figures prominently, often more prominently than its male counterpart. Some churches also have girls' and men's associations. Some of the latter are designated young men's association (*Umanyano Lwamadodana*), but even then older men often form a considerable proportion of the membership. The main activities of these associations are meetings held for the purpose of religious exhortation, but they also play an important role in the organization of fund-raising functions, which often provide an opportunity for social intercourse and recreation. Most churches have Sunday Schools, but few persons of 15 years and older belong to these. More belong to church or Sunday School choirs. An important association working in close affiliation with the churches is the Independent Order of True Templars (I.O.T.T.), a Bantu temperance movement of which there are several branches in the location. Officially it is an interdenominational body, but in practice different local branches tend to be associated with the denomination on whose premises they meet.

Although some of the churches have large congregations, there is nevertheless often an intimacy of relationships which prevents the individual from being lost in the crowd. The *manyanos* play an important role in providing smaller groups within the church, within which all members are personally known to each other. Some people build up intimate friendships with fellow church members and small groups of friends may act jointly in church activities. Commenting on the three persons outside his own household with whom he had the closest connexions, a young father belonging to the 'Assemblies of God' mentioned the names of three men. 'We met each other in church and we are about the same age. I am a Sunday School teacher and S takes the collection on Sundays. We are always together in church on Sundays and sometimes also during the week.' (The 'Assemblies' have several gatherings on weekdays also.) In spite of its large membership, the local Assembly is known for its particularly close in-group relations.[12] The Methodist class system again assigns each full member and member on trial to a small 'cell' which regularly meets for instruction and mutual exhortation.

Clubs exist for all the types of sport mentioned in chapter 3,[13] and particularly in connexion with rugby a considerable organization has been built up, which, however, experiences phases of strife and fission. Among townsmen the 'Swallows' club is the most popular. Not only is it regarded by many people as the East London home club *par excellence*, but it is also regarded as particularly connected with the Ndlambe tribe.[14] 'In my younger days', said a town-born Ndlambe of 52, 'I was an active member of the Swallows club, and I did my best, because Swallows was and still is the club of Ndlambe.' A number of rugby clubs are thus associated with particular tribal groups and areas, for example the Bush Bucks with Gcaleka from the Transkei, the Tembu R.F.C. with the Tembu from Glen Grey and Cala areas, the Black Lions with the

[12] See Mayer, *Townsmen or Tribesmen*, pp. 200–3, and Dubb, *The Role of the Church in an Urban African Society*.

[13] See p. 45.

[14] This is because East London is in the area at one time coming under the jurisdiction of Ndlambe chiefs.

Gqunukwebe of Middledrift, the Winter Roses with Xhosa from Stutterheim, and the Spring Roses with Xhosa from Peelton and King William's Town. Membership of each club, however, is not confined to the group with which it is associated.

This tribal and regional slant is not an important feature of the organization of other forms of sport, and it is true, as Mayer has indicated, that the majority of sport clubs are formed on some other principle.[15] However, in view of the much larger numbers involved in rugby clubs than in any other form of sport, its significance must not be underestimated. There are also clubs catering for particular groups of employees, such as a soccer club sponsored by police authorities for Bantu members of the South African Police, and the Vusomzi Rugby Club, which is said to cater specially for railway workers. In tennis clubs distinctions of occupation and social status seem to play a role, while the 'Stone Breakers' Rugby Club is said to attract the more educated players, particularly civil servants.[16] A cricket club goes by the name of *Abonwabisi* (Entertainers), and a rugby club is called *Vusomzi* (awaken or rebuild the home), but most sport clubs have English names, some rather fanciful: there are the 'Breakers' ('Stone Breakers'), 'Boiling Waters' and 'Busy Bees' (rugby), 'Highlanders' and 'Silver Stars' (tennis), 'Bosco Body-building Club' and 'Gunpowder Soccer Club'. A few merely use the designation 'Bantu' or 'non-European' with the name of the kind of sport they represent.

Masazane, a women's association of particular interest, is a kind of burial society, but its activities extend beyond mere assistance in connexion with funeral expenses.[17] It has no written constitution but nevertheless appears to be well organized. Membership is confined to the two major locations in East London. Whenever a death takes place in a member's family, specially appointed 'messengers' go about to inform the other members, and they are expected to visit the bereaved member and contribute to the collection which is always held when a death has occurred, and to which neighbours, friends and relatives contribute. The bereaved member's name is now placed on a waiting-list for the performance of a ceremony referred to as being 'washed'. It may take a whole year before a member's turn comes, but when she is about to be washed, a messenger is sent to inform her beforehand. 'She will have to make tea and buy bread, and we will enjoy the time together.' Speeches are made 'to explain things to her in order that her heart should subside'. On this occasion a collection, to which each member must contribute ten cents (1*s*.), is handed to her. Every Monday such a 'washing' ceremony takes place. Further, the organization is specially adapted to dealing with disputes among members.

Masazane was founded in 1944 by a widow who had come to East London in 1925. She was moved to start this organization when noticing the hard plight of bereaved women who had nobody to help them in town, but she feels that she was inspired by God to this undertaking. 'God said: "Let me collect these people, that they may love each other." What God likes in a person is love. How can you claim to be a friend of a person if there is not love in your heart?

[15] Mayer, op. cit., p. 221.

[16] Ibid.

[17] This association reveals features which recur in voluntary associations among diverse populations in modern Africa, for instance those concerned with diverging activities such as aid in time of bereavement, entertainment and settlement of disputes, and the use of titles connected with offices of authority introduced by the Whites. (Cf. for example Banton, *West African City*, chapters IX and X.)

I cannot claim to have brought these people together; it is God, it is not my power.' About the name *Masazane* (let us know each other), she said: 'We must all get to know each other, so that we may be one.'

The location is divided into three areas for purposes of organization. The senior office bearer in each area is called *umkangathi* (one who presses down),[18] but the founder, who is *umkangathi* in her area, fills the role of a general president for the whole association. In each area there is also a 'prosecutor' (*umtshutshisi*), a secretary and a number of messengers. There is also one 'judge' and one 'magistrate' (*u-mantyi*). Disputes are first investigated by the founder-president. If necessary she calls a meeting which takes the form of a court session at which the prosecutor leads the evidence by questioning. The verdict is passed by the magistrate or judge. The only form of punishment is that the guilty woman has to apologize before the judge. Besides informing members of deaths, the messengers also collect the contributions for the weekly 'washing' functions.

The office bearers have been appointed by the founder, but it is said that the names of new office bearers are laid before the members for their approval. Offices are held indefinitely. Membership is open to women of all denominations. There is no uniform or special induction ceremony. There are no subscriptions or permanent funds, but every member must contribute her ten cents (1*s.*) every week for the member who is being 'washed'. The only penalty for non-payment is that one's name remains at the bottom of the waiting-list of persons 'entitled' to being 'washed'.

What has been said about face-to-face relations in churches and religious associations applies to *Masazane* as well. Although it has a large membership, it is also characterized by the personal interest of members in each other, and it has at least a nucleus of members between whom close personal contacts exist. Membership of a sports team, dancing club, choir or combo also makes for contact with a small, regularly co-operating group within which relations are of a personal nature.

It is my impression that on the whole the interests of voluntary associations are internally directed, concerned with the interests of the group and its members. Characteristically the most important non-denominational women's association is altogether a mutual aid association which also aims at 'knowing each other' (*Masazane*). The type of association directing its main energies toward philanthropic activity is still relatively unimportant. A recently formed Y.W.C.A., however, seems to concentrate on work of this kind. It is maintained that its membership is drawn from the ranks of the more educated women, whereas we have seen that in *Masazane*, for instance, the lower educational and cultural levels are well represented. During 1959 several public meetings were held in the location to form an organization for combating juvenile delinquency but this seems to have petered out. Some church associations would, of course, contribute to funds for undertakings in the interests of the whole church, such as Sunday School work or theological training, but generally this accounts for only a small amount of the association's activities.

The reason for this internally directed nature of associational activity is probably to be found mainly in the economic set-up. The great majority of urban Bantu just do not have the money and time to work for other people's

[18] The verb *ukukangatha* means to press down, thereby making something smooth. It is also used of an influential speaker who rounds off a discussion, but it is not common as a translation for terms like 'president' or 'chairman'.

interests. Where they do find time for associational activities, such funds as are collected are generally needed for the running of the association or of the church with which it is connected. Coupled with these facts of bare economy one should mention the fact that class differentiations are still much less obvious than in Western societies where participation in associations often tends to be associated with particular social strata, and may be the means by which a person climbs the social ladder.[19]

Judging by the columns of a local Bantu newspaper combos and similar entertainment groups are often troubled by internal disputes. Amongst others the columnist mentioned one of these groups dissolving for the third time. He referred to lack of co-operation and 'gross irresponsibility' as reasons for these crises. 'But the paramount one is that everybody wants to be a leader.'[20] A different kind of dispute took place around one of these groups described as the 'local beauty queen promoters'. Following some altercations between the elected queen and the promoters, another girl was elected in her place. The 'dethroned' queen claimed that she was rejected because she was not an East Londoner, because 'they say she lacks education', and because the promoters were 'in the habit of wanting their friends and relatives as queens'.[21]

In connexion with ballroom dancing dissensions have arisen from the differing educational accomplishments of interested persons. From observation it would appear that dancing is most significant among the higher educated and more particularly the 'white-collar' type of people, but it appears that some of the 'professionals' are men of lower education and this divergence in education appears to cause some friction in dancing circles. The following excerpt appeared in connexion with a dispute of a local dancing teacher, a certain Mr. M——, described as a Border champion, with the local dancing association: 'Mr. M—— complains that all the members who have little or no education at all are subjected to ridicule and are put in subservient positions by members who happen to be well educated in the Association. But, says Mr. M——, it so happens that the vast majority of local dance teachers are uneducated. But is that a good enough reason why qualified teachers should be treated with utter contempt by people who only a few months ago knew nothing about dancing, and who, after taking but a few dancing lessons from these very teachers feel that they know better than the teachers who taught them how to dance?'[22]

Such conflicts, tensions and splits are a common feature of urban Bantu associational activity at the present stage. We have drawn attention to phases of strife and tension in the local rugby union. Political organizations of the Bantu have also thus far revealed fissiparous tendencies which Reader has illustrated in respect of East London.[23] The location further has its full share of small 'separatist' churches, although the larger, well-established churches are perhaps the most stable organizations in the community. All this seems to reflect the transitional stage of Bantu urban society. Authority based on ascribed status is of little significance in the urban structure, whereas the Bantu have not fully adapted themselves to leadership patterns based on mutual consent. Now that leadership in terms of ascribed status has lost its predominating position

[19] Warner, W. Lloyd, and Lunt, Paul S., *The Social Life of a Modern Community*, Yankee City Series, vol. I, New Haven, 1941, chapter XVI.
[20] *Indaba Zasemonti* (East London News), Saturday, 21 November 1959.
[21] Op. cit., Saturday, 10 October 1959.
[22] Op. cit., Saturday, 30 May 1959.
[23] Reader, *The Black Man's Portion*, pp. 25–6.

'everybody wants to be a leader'. The lack of tradition in respect of the aims and interests of clubs and associations generally, as well as of individual organizations, might also be expected to contribute to instability at the present juncture. Some of the churches and their associations, however, have existed long enough to allow the developing of some tradition in this respect. The more rigid and formal nature of proceedings required to control the activities of voluntary associations also requires adaptation among people with a tradition of government in terms of ascribed status and whose legal and political proceedings were of an informal nature.

While we have stressed the prevalence of intimate personal contacts, it does not mean that 'crowds' are insignificant in the social universe of the urban Bantu. In town the individual daily moves in crowds on the street, in the bus, at film shows, and concerts, at public dances and 'get togethers'. Some religious meetings also take on the nature of crowds and there have been times in the past when large crowds were mustered for political meetings. It is my contention, however, that the average individual Bantu townsman in East London is involved in sufficient intimate contacts with individuals and small groups to prevent his getting 'lost' in the urban crowd. To mention one more illustration—it is revealing to note how many people greet each other as acquaintances in the busiest location streets even at the time of peak activity after 5 p.m.

MAJOR SOCIAL DIFFERENTIATIONS IN THE LOCATION

Generally the traditional distinction between nobles and commoners is of little significance in the life of townspeople. Real townspeople may join in expressions of honour and respect offered to chiefs during their visits to town and on ceremonial occasions one is aware of a certain degree of deference paid to close kinsmen of Xhosa chiefs if any are present. It may well be, however that this is largely fostered by migrants taking part in the ceremony while the real townspeople merely follow suit. For instance, at the initiation of a fatherless town youth whose ceremony was arranged by a male relative of his mother the man being a member of the Xhosa royal clan of the Tshawe, local and visiting kinsmen of the Gcaleka chief tended to form a group apart, and when one of them made a speech, a member of the audience kept on interjecting '*Mhlekazi*!' (Your honour!) as is the custom during speeches by persons of high rank. The person taking the initiative here was obviously a rustic migrant Further, the boy concerned was regarded as a Tshawe and the pre-eminence of the clan was stressed in some of the speeches made. On the other hand many Tshawe live in the simplicity of urban poverty where there is nothing to dis tinguish them from their neighbours.

Mayer[24] has distinguished three major categories in the locations, namel (*a*) townspeople proper, with whom the more sophisticated 'School' migrant easily identify themselves, (*b*) 'School rustics', and (*c*) migrants who belong to the 'Red' section of the rural population. He affirms that all School migrant share the townsman's idea that comparative status is measured 'in terms of education, occupation and living standards—the more civilized the better' and that 'in this kind of ranking the Red migrants must clearly find a place at the bottom, uneducated and uncivilized as they are'.[25] The Reds, however do not apply a common ranking system to the whole Bantu community, bu

[24] Op. cit., chapters 4 and 13.
[25] Ibid., pp. 76, 77.

nterpret their social relations in terms of two parallel systems of ranking, one pplying to their own, and the other to the non-Red part of the community. On the School side of the Red-School contrast some attitudes reflect 'what one s tempted to call a class-conscious preoccupation with manners and minor onventions', but Mayer points out that in some respects the attitudes of School migrants tend to be more aligned with those of Red migrants than with hose of townspeople proper.

If this representation is combined with the analysis of cultural types presented n chapter 3, the whole of location society falls into the following categories:

A. 'White-collar' type;
B. 'intermediate' type;
C. non-Reds of simple material culture;
D. semi-Reds;
E. 'School rustics' (migrants); and
F. 'Red' migrants.

While categories A to D have been formulated strictly with reference to persons who were born in East London, or may be regarded as completely settled in own, many migrants and more recent immigrants may be identified with one f these categories. In fact, in influence, and perhaps also in numbers, more ecent immigrants seem to predominate in the white-collar category. The few octors and attorneys, and most of the ministers and teachers and most pros- erous business men have come to East London from elsewhere, and many of hem were born and brought up in the country. The same applies to some of the nen who have exercised political leadership in the past and some of the present nembers of the Locations Advisory Board.

Reds are sometimes singled out to represent the opposite pole from the ighly educated people,[26] but they do not appear to constitute a *separate* lower ratum by themselves. In fact, I do not think that any of the distinctions etween the categories C, D, E and F represent emergent class distinctions. In a ossibly emerging class structure all these still belong to a single lower stratum f society. One might be tempted to regard the white-collar category as an pper stratum, B as a 'middle' class and the rest of the population as a lower ass, but the relation between cultural distinctions and class structure is not s simple as this.

When approaching the question of class merely from an objective point of iew, the white-collar type clearly does represent an upper level in terms of lucation, income, occupation and material culture.[27] Type B again represents n intermediate position in terms of education and material culture, but in rms of occupation and income there is a considerable degree of overlapping etween this type and types C and D.[28]

If we approach the concept of 'class' in subjective terms as relating to a odel or different models operated by the members of society, we find different ctors making for differential status. As an indication of the criteria by which

[26] Cf. Mayer, op. cit., p. 77.

[27] For a discussion of standards of living of white-collar households in East London, see ughton, D. H. (Ed.), *Economic Development in a Plural Society*, pp. 264–74.

[28] I do not mention the migrant types here, because the reference is to the quantitative aterial in chapter 3, which was collected from a sample of townspeople. However, what is said re of categories C and D may well apply also to E and F.

status or prestige may be accorded, I quote from an interview with a shop-owner, who, although not town-born, has associated himself closely with town life and is a member of the Advisory Board. He had spoken of finding 'all types of people' living together in the same location street. When asked of what types he was thinking, he mentioned 'nurses and teachers, ordinary people with medium education [only J.C. or standard six], some who can only read and not write, and some who cannot even read'. About the concept *udidi* (kind, status, rank)[29] he commented: 'It is difficult to distinguish which of two people has higher *udidi* than the other. A has money, owns a car, runs a business, but has only standard six education. B is a graduate but does not have all that A has. A has a better life than B: no financial difficulties, he gets what he wants, he can afford meat every day. Educated people know a lot, and therefore want a lot. Taking myself, I must have a black suit for funerals as well as an ordinary suit, two or three pairs of trousers, several shirts, and many other things, whereas a Red-blanketed man needs very little.'

I had previously come across references to 'high people' (*abantu abaphakamileyo*) and 'low people' (*abantu abaphantsi*) and questioned the informant about these expressions. To him 'people who can afford everything they want' were high, whereas those who cannot afford it were low. Questioned about the expression 'great names' (*amagama amakhulu*) of the location, which one sometimes hears, he answered: '*Igama elikhulu* does not depend on financial position, but goes with the way a man behaves. If he is a man who knows how to maintain discipline, who assists every person who is in difficulty, who works hard—such a person comes to be regarded as belonging to *amagama amakhulu*.' The reference is always to *izenzo zakhe* (his works).

Educational achievement seems to be the most important single criterion by which town Bantu grade each other. This was the first distinction our informant made when he was asked to indicate different types, which to him obviously constituted a descending order. But as his comments on *udidi* and 'high people' show, wealth also counts for something.

In a discussion of the matter with three well-known location men of white-collar level, they came to the conclusion that 'high' could refer to well-educated people, 'but some people also take wealthy persons to be high, though one might find that when one starts talking to such a person, he cannot discuss a matter intelligently, which shows that he is not well educated'. One of them concluded that in his opinion 'high' people are those 'like teachers, the well-civilized class, those who behave in a dignified manner, irrespective of whether they have money or not'.

A semi-Red woman contrasted 'high' and 'low' in terms of wealth. The people like themselves who continually had to borrow essential commodities like sugar, for instance, were low, whereas the high people were the ones like prosperous business men, people who always had sufficient for their needs. On second thoughts, however, she added that they were the people with 'good homes' where there was an orderly family life. 'The next thing you hear about them is that visiting rugby players have been staying with them.'

One is, then, held in esteem also for 'dignified' and 'civilized' behaviour, 'decency', helpfulness and a 'good home', which is generally distinguished by disciplined children who are respectful to adults, but this makes for prestige generally, rather than for particular class status. However, when a teacher

[29] Cf. Mayer, op. cit., pp. 76–7.

becomes a drunkard or starts 'carrying on' with women openly, he usually loses status and may not be given the public recognition that is granted to other members of his profession on certain occasions. (See below.)

Without doubt the highest status is generally accorded to persons like doctors, teachers, trained ministers and nurses, as well as prosperous business men who are also well educated. On certain social occasions they are clearly set apart as a class, for instance by being ushered to front seats at a concert or beauty-queen contest, or by being called to the first sitting at a wedding-feast. Menfolk of this level nevertheless tend to mix easily with 'lower' people, but there is some indication of a growing tendency among women of this level to keep somewhat aloof by not mixing on the personal level and by forming a more exclusive type of association.

This setting-apart of the white-collar type, which is on the whole also the best-educated and most wealthy section of the community, is the only indication I see of the emergence of a class structure among urban Bantu. To apply the term 'middle class' to them, as is already commonly done, seems somewhat confusing. They do not, as yet, occupy an intermediate position in any way in the structural sense of a class. In view of the strict segregation of the total South African society on racial lines, the Bantu class structure must be viewed apart from that of the Whites, existing partly beside and partly below the latter, so that the Bantu white-collar section does not share a common middle-class position with a White middle class. Within the Bantu community, however, they represent an upper stratum at present. Admittedly, what is now the upper stratum may still become differentiated into different strata with increasing economic and industrial advancement of the Bantu, but it cannot be merely assumed that the future upper and middle classes will be distinguished on precisely the same lines as those of Western societies. 'Middle class' could perhaps be used merely as a cultural concept, to indicate that sector of Bantu society which approximates Western middle-class patterns of living, but then it should be applied with the necessary reserve, as in the case of the term 'westernization'. But even then the term causes confusion when it comes to discussing the class structure.

I do not think one could indicate a further stratification besides this setting-apart of the white-collar type, although some persons may operate a kind of 'three-valued' model of the class structure.[30] An illiterate semi-Red town-born informant who had always lived in town, except for some years during childhood, and who was incidentally also an admirer of the African National Congress, distinguished between highly educated persons, those with less education, and the uneducated ones. 'The highly educated people are very humble and are most friendly with all kinds of people. Those with less education are very dangerous, because if they get a chance to cheat the poor uneducated person, they will readily do so. They boast about their little education and they harbour tribal prejudice as one finds between Xhosa and Fingo. The uneducated are never happy with the less educated people. We, the uneducated people, like the highly educated, are friendly and peaceable. It is our aim always to make anyone feel at home in our midst.' This comment came quite spontaneously when the informant discussed the educational ideals he would hold for his children, and was given by way of explanation to a statement that 'your child must either receive the highest education or remain uneducated'.

[30] Cf. Bott, *Family and Social Network*, p. 75.

The remarks are suggestive of a three-valued model of the class structure, with antagonism between 'adjacent' classes and a friendly attitude between alternating ones.

TOWNSMAN, TRIBE AND NATION

The attitude of the majority of townspeople towards the contrast between tribalism and an inclusive Bantu nationalism is one of compromise: the ideal of the different tribal groups moving closer together finds considerable support, but a significant degree of tribal consciousness and pride is retained. A middle-aged man holding a teacher's qualification gave his tribal connexions as a member of the Ntakwenda clan of the Ngqika section of the Xhosa. Answering various questions about the value of such connexions, he said: 'Oh yes, it certainly is good to remember that one belongs to a particular tribe. A tribe is made up of different families [*izintshapo*] which come together and form one big family and the chief is the head or father of the tribe. To my way of thinking this is very important because it resembles a single family, but on a large scale. Moreover, you are not an isolated individual, you are one of many. I feel very proud that I am a Xhosa and a Ngqika.' As to the desirability of the disappearance of tribal distinctions, he commented: 'It would be a good thing if all tribes became one, or came under one nation [*ubuzwe*]. This would end tribal prejudice by which Xhosa claims to be better than Mfengu.' A younger man (24, std. six, unemployed) felt that remembering one's tribal identity was important, 'because these tribes were set up by our forefathers. I feel we must not deviate from our ancestors' footsteps.' Nevertheless he favoured closer unity of the different tribes. 'We are told that all Bantu tribes are descended from one common ancestor. It would therefore be a good thing if we could look upon one another as brothers and sisters of one very large family.'

There are, however, minorities respectively representing either pole of the contrast. A messenger-clerk (20, std. nine) commented on his tribal and clan origins: 'All this is meaningless to me. Clans and tribal connexions divide us into sections hostile to one another.' He strongly favoured greater unity and the disappearing of tribal oppositions, but added that 'these tribal differences are deep-rooted among all of us'. A bus conductor (26, std. six) who is a Mfengu by descent, but calls himself a Ndlambe because of being born and brought up in East London, which used to be the area of the Ndlambe tribe, also regarded this aspect of his identity as unimportant 'because the result of these tribal connexions is tribal prejudice. Tribes become jealous of one another, or hostile, for no reason. If I had the power, I would make all my people remember we are Africans and nothing else. I would fix a day once a year when all black people would come together as one unit and not as different tribes.' On the other hand a girl (22, std. six) whose late father was a teacher of Mfengu descent, but also regarded himself as Gcaleka because his rural home was in Gcaleka territory, was not enthusiastic about the disappearance of tribal distinctions. 'No change is needed. We are right as we are. The Bantu should go by their tribal connexions. What is the use of wishing that the Bantu tribes should come under one name when that is impossible. Even if it could be tried, it would never work harmoniously because the tribal spirit is there. We have this Mfengu-Xhosa opposition even in Church.' (She might have been thinking of church members voting along these lines in the election of office-bearers.) A young skilled factory-worker holding a Senior Certificate also expressed scepticism about the practicability of an actual merging of tribes, although he regarded it as a 'noble idea' in principle, feeling that it would be a good thing 'that we should come together and regard ourselves as one large family'. The trouble he foresaw was that in the event of such a fusion each tribe would claim superiority over all others and each would continue along the path of its traditional custom.

Tribal ties are valued for offering a sense of 'belonging', and tribal identity as a symbol of having an historical tradition. 'A tribe is something that was formed by our first ancestors. It is something that reminds us of our origin.' Lack of such a tradition is deplored, and Bantu in East London often point to the Coloureds, with some feeling of superiority, as people who lack such a tradition. 'We Xhosa say the Coloureds [*Amalawu*] are no nation because they have no chiefs of their own.' 'We are not *Amalawu* who do not care for these things.' 'I know I am not like *Ilawu*: I belong to a distinct group of people who have their own chief.'

The tribal consciousness of townspeople is not restricted to mere sentiment, but is on occasion concretely and jointly expressed. The two major tribal groups of Xhosa and Mfengu (Fingo) each observe an annual 'national' celebration. That of the Mfengu takes place on 14 May every year, commemorating the day in 1835 when the Mfengu pledged their allegiance to the colonial government. Annually numbers of Mfengu gather at an historic tree in the Peddie district, where the pledge is said to have been made. In the location the day is marked by festivity. Sometimes a meeting is held where speeches are made. During the afternoon groups of people, mostly women, wearing the traditional costume of the Mfengu, walk about singing, stopping to drink and dance where there is beer. It is customary to tuck a stalk of grass or a green twig in some part of the costume, or even in ordinary clothes. To most townspeople the significance of this seems to be obscure, but an informant suggested that it is a symbol commemorating the fact that the Mfengu 'were wearing grass' when they came into this part of the country, fleeing in destitution from the Zulu. Some young town girls also dress up in men's clothes, wearing coats inside out and trousers unevenly rolled up, as at Christmas-time. Red migrants predominate in this type of feasting, but there are non-Reds who normally wear Western-type clothes, but keep special traditional costumes which they wear on these occasions, while others borrow costumes. People value the celebrations 'because it makes us think of the ways of long ago'; 'it gives us an opportunity for wearing our costumes' (two young girls), and 'it is a day to remember the ancestors'. Some townspeople proper also take part in the celebration or at least regard it as an event which sustains their tribal consciousness.

Round about Easter there is usually some celebration commemorating the prophet Ntsikana, one of the earliest Xhosa converts to Christianity who 'made so great an impression on the members of his own Xhosa tribe that he has become a figure of legendary proportions, credited with seeing visions and uttering prophecies that were fulfilled long years after'.[31] Some of his visions are associated with an ox to which he is said to have been particularly attached. A hymn which is believed to have originated with him has been included in the Xhosa hymnals of various denominations. The Xhosa have come to regard

[31] Shepherd, Robert H. W., *Lovedale South Africa*, Lovedale Press, 1940, p. 20. Some Xhosa place him long before the advent of Christian missionaries.

the annual Ntsikana commemoration as a Xhosa national festival. In East London, as in a number of other towns, a special committee is responsible for organizing the celebrations, which usually take the form of a religious service.

Many townspeople attach significance to these celebrations and even townswomen wear traditional coloured costumes and beadwork for the occasion. 'In towns the occasions which revive our Ngqika-consciousness [*ubungqika*] are very rare. For instance, the commemoration of the prophet Ntsikana comes once a year when all Ngqika come together to remember Ntsikana. This is predominantly observed by the Xhosa, although other tribes are welcome as well.' (Town-born male ex-teacher of 52.) 'Ntsikana's commemoration is the only occasion which reminds me that I am *umxhosakazi* [a female Xhosa]. Then I wear my Xhosa dress with beadwork ornaments and we Xhosa chant Ntsikana's hymn. When we sing this hymn we have a clear picture of Ntsikana the prophet, with our ancestors watching in surprise at his unusual behaviour.' (Town-born female of 30, std. six.) 'Our chiefs, Velile Sandile and Ngwenyati Makinane [two Xhosa chiefs from the Ciskei reserves] are always present at the Ntsikana commemoration [in town], and if they do not attend they send their apologies through representatives who attend. There is nothing I do to show that I am Ndlambe, except attending the Ntsikana commemoration.' (Town-born male, 36, std. six, packer for tea merchants.)

We have already noted how tribal consciousness is expressed in the association of certain rugby clubs with different tribal groups (p. 172). Some town-born people donate to tribal funds instituted in the reserves for the building of schools or for expenses in connexion with special tribal gatherings. Some people also regard the observance of initiation and sacrifices as expressions of tribal consciousness. 'It is on the occasion of the Ntsikana commemoration that I like to remember what I am, and when I visit other places, people greet me: "*Molo Mngqika*!" I have already been initiated and my father slaughters goats as *idini* [sacrifices] in remembrance of the ancestors. All these things show beyond any doubt that I am Ngqika, not partly but wholly.' (Unemployed married male of 24, std. six.) 'I have relatives in the country who have sometimes performed sacrifices and they have not omitted to invite all Ngwevu [his clan], even those who are in town, and it is on such occasions that one's clan consciousness and all that it represents is stimulated and revived. These activities and the fact that we have come together as Ngwevu go together with Ngqika-consciousness [*ubungqika*] because they are a continuation of the performances of our forefathers. There is no material gain or privilege, but it gives a feeling of satisfaction.' A Ndlambe (52) who was born and brought up in East London except for two years spent at St. Luke's not far from town, during childhood, and a few months at the time of his initiation there, attached great significance to the fact that he had been initiated in the country as an indication of his being a genuine Ndlambe. He repeatedly said: 'My foreskin was eaten by the ants of Ndlambe's land.'

Chief Velile Sandile of the Ngqika has a number of councillors in East London who act jointly as a council (*isigqeba*) in town. When fieldwork was drawing to a close, there was some confusion over the composition of this council because of a dispute involving an 'old' and a 'new' council. One or two of the men involved were town-born, while others had been permanently settled in East London for many years. According to one councillor this *isigqeba* is nowadays regarded as a council of the Rarabe, representing both the Ndlambe and Ngqika sections of the Xhosa. A major function of the *isigqeba* in town is to make arrangements for visits of all chiefs to East London—even visits of other than Rarabe chiefs—which is regarded as territory of the Rarabe, more particularly the Ndlambe. The council sometimes convenes meetings to discuss 'matters of the Great Place' (the chief's headquarters).

Many townspeople know of the existence of the council and what the names of some of the members are, but generally they do not exhibit any great interest in its activities. However, a middle-aged townsman, who has been quoted above, commented on the value of these meetings: 'Men from the reserves as far afield as Kentani attend these meetings in town. Our coming together with country people to discuss matters of common interest is important in itself. For instance, there has been the matter of shifting the chief's Great Place, and there were negotiations with the government which were conducted by men from the country and town-dwellers. That is good.' The informant himself had never attended any of these meetings, however, because they were held in the evenings 'and I am just lazy to attend any gathering at night'.

The established town Bantu do not differ much from the total Bantu population of East London in terms of tribal composition, consisting almost exclusively of Xhosa and Mfengu. Our main sample was made up of 126 Xhosa, 66 Mfengu, 4 Tembu and 6 Southern Sotho.[32] I did not come across any indication of tension between the different sections of the Xhosa proper, but the longstanding hostility between Xhosa and Mfengu[33] has not quite disappeared, not even among townspeople. There is not much open tension, casual contacts between members of the two groups are friendly and easy, and many close friendships reach across the tribal distinction, but Xhosa townspeople often still regard the Mfengu with suspicion. 'A Mfengu will do anything to be praised by a White man. The leakage of private information always takes place through the Mfengu. We take decisions together at our meetings, and we warn the people not to talk about this until we reach a certain stage, but to our surprise the White man knows of all that was said at that meeting first thing the next morning. Who told him? It is the Mfengu, good-boy of the White man.'[34] (Youth of 24, Senior Certificate.) 'In employment or anywhere where there is a White man, the Mfengu will do anything to create a good impression, even at the expense of a Xhosa.' (Ex-teacher.) It is maintained that in the election of committees some people tend to be partial to members of their own tribe when Mfengu and Xhosa are involved.

As regards attitudes to other tribes and ethnic groups, there is awareness of linguistic and cultural differences where these exist, and sometimes a degree of disdain. The Bhaca, for instance, are regarded as 'backward', and the people who do the work which the Xhosa will not do, but this is because the Bhaca in East London are virtually confined to a corps of illiterate migrants who have come to regard certain forms of employment such as street-sweeping, refuse-removal and work in connexion with sewers and night soil as their particular

[32] In 1955 the tribal composition of the East London location population was as follows: Xhosa, 56 per cent; Mfengu, 34 per cent; other Bantu, 4 per cent; Coloured, 6 per cent. (Reader, op. cit., p. 49.)

[33] It has been alleged, but also denied, that the Mfengu were subjected to a form of slavery by the Xhosa. (Soga, J. Henderson, *The South-Eastern Bantu*. Johannesburg, Witwatersrand University Press, 1930, pp. 179 ff.)

[34] *I-good-boyi-yomlungu*—a commonly used expression, said to have originated with Clements Kadalie during the heyday of the I.C.U. For the Xhosa view of the Mfengu as traitors, see Mayer, op. cit., pp. 31–2.

domain, and these are by no means representative of the Bhaca people. Of the Zulu the urban Xhosa-Mfengu do not have a very high opinion either. 'They are foolishly scared of the Whites and do not become adapted to the town way of life easily as the Xhosa do.' Other expressions used of Zulu were 'big babies', 'childlike showiness', 'position seekers', and they were also denounced for acting as informers. No doubt these opinions are often based on contacts with small numbers of Zulu who are not representative of their people either, as the following comment suggests: 'The Zulu are very primitive with their big holes in their ear-lobes. Most of the Zulu in East London are prison wardens—a job of which they seem to be very proud.'

It would be dangerous to generalize about the attitude of the urban Bantu to national politics. There is obviously a great deal of spontaneous resentment of government policy and the way it is enforced, but two impressions come to mind, which, if correct, complicate the picture. The one is that opinions on politics are often dominated by the cliches of press and political leaders, both White and Bantu. The other is that the Bantu are subject to a certain degree of pressure from within their own ranks, the extent and nature of which it is difficult to define. An informant confided, for instance, that many people were pleased with the clean-up of the *tsotsi* element by the police early during the 1960 emergency, 'but of course they would not say it openly'. The scope of the present investigation did not allow for the careful and detailed study which this particular topic requires, but since it can hardly be disregarded in a general study of the urban Bantu some elementary facts and a few examples of the political ideas expressed are offered.

In his study of the migrants, Mayer briefly indicated recent trends in the field of politics among the Bantu in East London: how the once active and widely representative Vigilance Association, working in loose connexion with the Location Advisory Board and concerning itself mainly with local interests, was superseded by the African National Congress and its Youth League, and how, since the 1952 riots, interest in these organizations greatly dwindled.[35] The results of our own investigation also support the conclusion that interest in political activity is at a low ebb at the moment. Ten per cent of the males and only two females in our sample claimed membership of the A.N.C. or the I.C.U.,[36] members of the former being in the majority. The small numbers in our sample do not suggest any particular trend in terms of cultural category, education or age.

There has been some activity of the more radical Pan-African Congress and the All-African Convention, but these do not seem to have gained substantial support as yet. The anti-pass campaign initiated by the Pan-African Congress did not have a marked effect in East London and the stay-at-home orders issued in connexion with the campaign and also after the Sharpeville disturbances were not widely observed by Bantu in East London. Although the atmosphere in the location grew tense after Sharpeville, no open clashes occurred. A few weeks earlier the Pan-African Congress leader, Mr. Robert Sobukwe, was prevented by the authorities from conducting a meeting in the location and was summarily ordered out of the area.

Examples of a radical and largely negative opinion abound in the columns

[35] Op. cit., pp. 52–4.

[36] The Industrial and Commercial Workers' Union which was particularly active in the Union and also in East London during the late twenties.

of a local weekly paper which was published[37] in Xhosa and English under the name *Indaba Zasemonti* (*East London News*). A leader commenting on the break-away of the 'Progressives' from the United Party criticized almost every shade of political opinion existing among White South Africans. Reference was made to the 'illiberal liberals of the Ballinger type', while the Progressives were said to be attempting to 'reconcile the irreconcilable', there being 'no middle of the road in political matters as things are today'. It went on to say that the Progressives were 'trying to strike a happy mean between the so-called liberalisticism of the South African Liberals and the steely hand of domination' of the government of the day, 'but especially the silver-gloved version of domination that is espoused by the United Party'.[38] On another occasion the South African Institute of Race Relations was accused of 'selling-out', and it was hinted that ex-chief Albert Luthuli's 'followers' could no longer be happy about his association with the Institute.[39]

These were more in the nature of interludes in the sustained criticism of the government and its apartheid measures, but some of the most vehement criticism was reserved for those Bantu who had decided to co-operate with the authorities in connexion with Bantu Authorities, Bantu Education, or segregated nursing organizations. It was stated, for instance, that 'the pronouncement by the quisling chiefs at the opening ceremony of the reconstituted Bunga in the Transkei . . . will go down in the history of the non-European oppressed people . . . as an act of betrayal by a handful of selected sycophants of tyranny whose duty it is to worship on the altar of domination or lose their blood stipends. . . . The voice of shameful capitulation came, fittingly, from none other than the notorious —, "the blue-eyed boy of the government". Genuflecting at the feet of the great gods of domination he read out the prayer that the policemen-chiefs had carefully prepared for the consumption of the gods of Apartheid.'[40]

I am not aware of *Indaba*'s openly criticizing the African National Congress, but some A.N.C. supporters felt that it was boosting supporters of one of the more recent and more radical organizations. The paper did not seem to be extremely popular in the location. This may be due in part to the radical nature of its political views, but the personal tone of some of its social columns was also criticized.

Although the African political organizations existing prior to the 1960 emergency no doubt enjoy a large degree of sympathy among the urban Bantu, criticism of these and of their leaders was not absent from some of the research interviews with East London-born Bantu. One informant felt that 'the Bantu are not yet mature to lead their own people to a happy future. Such leadership needs people who know what to do and how to do it.' He also commented on the tendency among the Bantu to quarrel about positions in organizations. 'This would happen if any of the African organizations would be called upon to lead the people.' Another said: 'We definitely need the lead of the White

[37] Publication stopped in the course of 1960.

[38] 21 November 1959.

[39] 23 January 1960.

[40] 30 May 1959. A leader attacking the same chief gave rise to prosecution of the owners and editor, which resulted in the owners being found guilty of criminal libel under the Cape Act of 1882. The editor, was, however, acquitted, since the court found that it had not been proved that he had been editing the paper at the time of the article's publication. (*Daily Dispatch*, East London, Saturday, 30 July 1960.)

people, but they must be White people who sincerely want to do justice to all alike. I think the United Party would lead the Bantu to such a happy future. The government of the Afrikaner is oppressive, and there is too much colour bar in it. In the eyes of the Afrikaner the black man is no better than a baboon.' The same informant criticized the A.N.C. for 'bringing about misery in the 1952 riots when innocent people were shot by the police. When trouble comes, the illiterates always suffer, while the leaders escape in time.' (Male of 25, std. seven.) 'It would be a tragedy to choose any of our political groups to take over leadership, because of inefficiency. We definitely still need White leadership.' (Male of 49, std. six.)

Some particularly favour 'the English people' for political leadership. 'During their reign there were no such things as Bantu Education and Bantu Authorities. All people received the same education and our boys and girls trained at Wits [Witwatersrand University] with Whites, Indians and Coloured.' (Male of 39, std. six.) Another suggested that the problems of the Bantu could be solved by South Africa becoming a British Protectorate, and that 'the right persons who would lead our people to a happy future are the Queen of England and her Councillors'. (Male of 49, std. six.)

A middle-aged business man holding a Junior Certificate argued for the reintroduction of direct parliamentary representation of the Bantu, not by Whites, but by Bantu parliamentarians representing their people by tribal groups—'Xhosa for the Xhosa, Zulu for the Zulu, and Sotho for the Sotho'.

Apart from an occasional careful hint that there is something to be said for certain aspects of government policy by people who usually still had strong country ties, opposition to the National Party Government is general. Usually the Afrikaner is associated with the government as the enemy of the Bantu, the Government being regarded as '*u-rulumente wamabhulu*' (the government of the Afrikaners).

My over-all impression of the relation of the East London Bantu townspeople to tribe and nation is that there is an obvious consciousness of an inclusive Bantu nationalism, either in aggressive opposition to the Whites, or envisaging varying degrees of co-operation or integration with the White population of the country, more especially with the English-speaking section. At the same time, however, they generally remain conscious of tribal distinctions and are keen to retain tribal identity, but the more explicitly anti-White their attitude, the more cynical they seem to be of preserving tribal identities.

As elsewhere in Africa, tribal feeling has not disappeared, but has become modified.[41] However, East London differs from towns like Freetown and those on the Rhodesian Copperbelt where 'tribal systems' are seen as persisting in adapted form as 'sub-systems' or 'secondary systems' within the larger total urban system, so that Africans of tribal origin sometimes act and group themselves in terms of tribe and sometimes in terms of more inclusive urban categories according to the situation involved.[42] Although there is tribal consciousness in East London, it is only occasionally that people act in terms of their being Mfengu or Xhosa (or one of the subsections of the Xhosa proper), and although certain 'tribal' customs persist, the tribe cannot be regarded an important

[41] Cf. for example Banton, *West African City*, p. 183, and Gluckman, M., 'Anthropological Problems Arising from the African Industrial Revolution', in Southall, op. cit., pp. 70 ff.

[42] Cf. Mitchell, J. C., *Tribalism and the Plural Society*, O.U.P., 1960; Epstein, A. L., *Politics in an Urban African Community*, Manchester University Press, 1958, p. 234, and Banton, op. cit., pp. 162, 178.

category of interaction. This is probably because of the high degree of linguistic and cultural continuity between Xhosa and Mfengu who make up the overwhelming majority of the population, and the overruling importance of the Red–School dichotomy.[43]

THE SOCIAL NETWORK

In summarizing the 'extra-household' relations of townspeople we use the concept of social network as it is being applied by some social anthropologists, and as Mayer has also done, in the sense of 'the total of ego's interpersonal relations with other individuals'.[44] Networks may vary in their degree of 'looseness'. At the one extreme there is the very close-knit network of the 'integrated' or 'clearly structured' type of community in which ascribed relations predominate, such as that of the rural Xhosa. By contrast the network of, say, a British middle-class family is very loose-knit, relationships being formed according to free choice and not through structural ascription. By comparison with the latter again, the network of a member of the British working-class may be close-knit though not as close-knit as that of a member of a rigidly structured small-scale society. Using these concepts, Mayer has indicated that the Red migrant coming to East London tends to retain his rural close-knit, structured network, 'stretching' it, as it were, to cover as far as possible, all his social needs in town, and avoiding new relations as far as possible. The School migrant, on the other hand, tends to avail himself freely of the opportunities in town for forming new relationships, building up a completely new, very loose-knit network.[45]

By contrast with the structured network of the rural Xhosa, in which ascribed relationships are pre-eminent, the networks of proper townspeople tend to be loose-knit. Relationships with kinsfolk are still important, but there is a relatively free choice as to with which of them to keep in touch. There is a wide range of different forms and places of recreation and of religion from which to choose, entailing so many different groupings of people, none of which is identical with any of the others, or with the group in which ego is involved at his place of employment. From these, or some of these, diverse groups the townsman builds up his network with a much larger degree of choice than his rural counterpart. However, there seems to be some variation in the degree of 'looseness' of the networks of different types of townspeople. Although I cannot produce quantitative evidence, the material collected suggests that the networks of townspeople of the white-collar level tend to be more loose-knit than those of townspeople of simpler culture. Cases no. 1 and no. 2 described in chapter 4 illustrate the relatively loose-knit type of network of the white-collar level. Mr. A (case no. 1) regularly plays cards and draughts during the lunch-break with his work-mates and visits friends after work. He plays golf, watches rugby, attends church services and used to go visiting and to the cinema with his wife. He is therefore involved in a diversity of leisure activities each of which involve relationships with sets of people which probably do not overlap very much. Mr. X's network (case no. 2) is more obviously loose-knit. Though not a member of a political organization, he has close friends active in these, but also maintains close connexions with his tribal chief's 'Great Place' in the

[43] See Mayer, op. cit., pp. 40–1.
[44] Op cit., p. 9.
[45] Op. cit., pp. 124, 284–9.

country. He is a member of the Locations Advisory Board and of a school committee. He and his wife are regular church-goers and he belongs to two different sports clubs. Here and there the sets of persons involved may overlap, but they are certainly not identical in any two cases.

An attempt was made to investigate the networks of a small number of persons in greater detail, and one of these is presented below. Ego (P), whose wife is a nurse, is in white-collar employment. (Their conjugal role-relationship is discussed in chapter 8, pp. 160 ff.) He is a full member of a church with a large membership—attends about twice per month—as well as a member of the I.O.T.T., and of a rugby and cricket club respectively. He is enthusiastic about film shows and goes 'whenever there is a nice piece. I do not care much for concerts, though I go at times if my wife likes to go to one.' They also like to attend wedding and graduation receptions and P often goes to the community centre. The following is a summary of details about the more important persons in his network.

Person No.	Sex	Kinship relation	Residing in E.L.: YES/NO	Frequency of contact	Nature of contact
1	M	Nil	YES	Once per week	Met for first time at *Vigilance Assoc.* where he interested P as a speaker. P was once the member of a *band* of which no. 1 was the 'manager'. Now *employed at same place* where they often converse about location affairs. (He is not highly educated but 'brainy'.)
2	M	Brother	YES	Every week	*Visits* P at his home.
3	M	Nil	YES	Often	Met for first time at *social centre* where no. 3 is 'manager' of a *boxing club* and P sometimes goes to watch the boxing. Also seen at *rugby club* meetings where no. 3 is an official. (He is sociable and belongs to many bodies.)
4	M	Nil	YES	Often	Were contemporaries at school, though not attending same school. Met at *school competitions*, rugby matches and athletic contests. Still often carry on conversation when *met in the street* in town (i.e. White business area).
5	M	Nil	YES	Often	Met for the first time at *church*. They still meet at church and no. 5 sometimes *visits* P at his home. Conversation turns around church matters. (P likes him for being a good preacher.)
6	M	Nil	YES	2–3 times per month	P knows no. 6 through *rugby* and receives *visits* from him.
7	M	Nil	YES	2–3 times per month	Employed in *same firm* where they see each other. Also *visits* P at his home.
8	M	Nil	YES	2–3 times per month	P knows no. 8 through *rugby* and *church* and receives *visits* from him.
9	M	Nil	YES	2–3 times per month	P knows no. 9 through *cricket* and *church* and receives *visits* from him.
10	M	Nil	YES	2–3 times per month	P knows no. 10 through *rugby* and receives *visits* from him.

Person No.	Sex	Kinship relation	Residing in E.L.: YES/NO	Frequency of contact	Nature of contact
11	M	Nil	YES	Occasionally	Met for first time at *dancing club* where no. 11 was a teacher. Now they meet at *receptions*.
12	F	Nil	YES	Occasionally	A sister at the hospital where P's *wife* is *employed* as a nurse and whom the two of them occasionally *visit*.
13	F	Nil	YES	Occasionally	P and wife sometimes *visit* her.
14	F	Mother's cross-cousin	YES	Occasionally	Mutual *visiting* between P (and wife) and no. 14 and her son (no. 15) and daughters. P and no. 15 also see each other at *rugby*.
15	M	Son of No. 14	YES	Occasionally	
16	M	FBdH (H. of No. 17)	YES	Occasionally	Mutual *visiting* between P (and wife) and no. 16 and wife.
17	F	Fbd. (w. of No. 16)	YES	Occasionally	
18	M	wF	NO	1–2 times per year	P and wife *visited* by nos. 18 and 19. (No mention of return visits, but P feels obligation to *assist* them financially when necessary, and has done so during past year.)
19	F	wm	NO	1–2 times per year	
20	M	Nil	NO	1–2 times per year	P got to know no. 20 through his coming to visit P's Fsd who used to stay with P, about once or twice a month. He still *visits* P about once every six months. No. 20 is a very good story-teller, 'and when he is here we lock the door and start telling stories'.
21	M	wB	NO	Seldom	No. 21 has *visited* P and wife on occasion, but no mention of return visit.
22	F	Mother	NO	Seldom	No. 22 has *visited* P and wife. No mention of a return visit, but P feels obligation to *assist* her *financially* when necessary, and has done so during the past year.

After this list had been compiled, P said that there were still more he could mention, and added: 'We add up friendship through friends we visit. Wherever I am I like to learn and I like talking.' Quite unassumingly he remarked: 'I am a very popular person and know very many people. Whenever there are two or three or more people together, I like to be there and see what is going on.'

It will be easier to comment on this network by comparing it with that of Q, an urban male of simple culture. He is 28 years old, has been married for about a year and claims a standard six education, though a close companion maintains it is much less. He is not a member of any association or church but occasionally goes to see a 'Tarzan' film and attends boxing tournaments two or three times a year at the community centre. He is not interested in concerts or meetings of any kind. Together with his mother, wife and child he occupies a one-roomed municipal house in Ezikawunsileni.

Person No.	Sex	Kinship relation	Residing in E.L.: YES/NO	Frequency of contact	Nature of contact
1	M	Nil	YES	Every week	Homes in *same neighbourhood* (Ezikawunsileni) and *grew up together*. *Initiated together* in same initiation hut. Mutual *visiting* and 'discuss our problems together'. (Also married, with one child.) Q and no. 1 have *assisted* each other *financially*.
2	M	Nil	YES	Every week	*Grew up together*. No. 2's *home near by* in Thulandivile. Were *initiated* during *same year*. Mutual *visiting*.
3	M	Nil	YES	Every week	'Went about *together' as boys* and attended bioscopes and concerts. Mutual *visiting*. His home in Mekeni (also *not very far* from Q.)
4	M	Same clan	YES	1–2 times a month	They are much older than Q and are the only kinsmen with whom he has contact. He does not visit them regularly, and *contacts are casual*. Re mutual assistance, Q remarks: 'They have never helped me and I am therefore not prepared to help them'. No. 4 is domiciled in same neighbourhood as Q.[46]
5	M	Same clan as mother	YES	1–2 times a month	
6	M	Same clan as mother	YES	1–2 times a month	
7	M	m s S	YES	1–2 times a month	
8	M	m s S	YES	1–2 times a month	
9	M	Nil	NO	Hardly ever	A friend, now teaching in Umtata, whom he hardly ever sees now.
10	M	Nil	NO	Hardly ever	A friend whose home is in E.L. but who is now in Johannesburg. No contact during last two years.
11	M	Nil	NO	Hardly ever	A friend whose home is in E.L. but who is also now in Johannesburg. No contact during last two years.

Besides the three friends outside East London with whom he has virtually lost contact, Q could not mention any others outside town with whom he had contact through visits or correspondence.

P's network is much more loose-knit than that of Q, in that he has regular contacts with a much larger number of people, and his contacts with them are through a great variety of institutions and interests between which there is little connexion. They range from dancing club to church and from Vigilance Association to a diversity of sports clubs. Moreover, he consciously aims at forming new relationships. Q's network, on the other hand, is strongly centred in his three close friends whom he has known since childhood and who all live within a short distance from his home. (P's friends are scattered over the whole location.) His three friends who have left East London seem virtually to have moved out of his network, and the few kinsmen with whom he has contacts are the ones he happens to see, because they are in East London, but he is not very enthusiastic about his relationship with them and he only mentioned them

[46] Q's relationships with these five kinsmen are quoted on p. 168.

when specifically questioned about his contact with kinsmen. His range of interests is restricted, and when he goes to boxing or the cinema he goes as a spectator so that this does not necessarily result in enduring relationships as would be the case if he were to join a club or association.

What we got to know of Q indicates that he would fall into our category of semi-Reds, and this may be significant. The proximity of his Red background may have held him back from launching out into the diversity of activities offered by urban life. However, among the networks collected the pattern reflected by that of Q was common for males and females: close contacts with a small number of friends, mostly known to each other, more tenuous ties with certain kinsmen, and, perhaps, involvement in one or two voluntary associations. Most people, however, do still have contacts with people in the country.

Some of the cases of simple culture described in chapter 4 seem to have close-knit networks. Ndumiso, the young man in case no. 8 seems to have a close-knit nucleus in his network, consisting of the co-members of his vocal group—in which all would know each other since these groups seldom have more than eight members—and perhaps some friends with whom he drinks—if the latter do not coincide with the former. Makhosi (case no. 7), in spite of his army career, cited no other extra-household activities than those in connexion with one of the small sects characterized by face-to-face relationships. The two *tsotsis* (cases nos. 11 and 12) with their sets of friends who have known each other since childhood also illustrate the point. A further example of a close-knit network is given in appendix III.

In compiling networks, one cannot expect to get an exhaustive picture of all ego's social relationships—he would usually mention only those which 'matter' to him. Thus, in the case of Q, there was no mention of his contacts at his place of employment until he was questioned about White people with whom he had regular contacts. He then mentioned two White men working in the firm where he is a messenger. The true pattern of his network, and apparently of many other townspeople of simple culture, appears to be one of a close-knit core set within a wider network which is more loose-knit, involving casual ties which, though implying regular contacts, are to him unimportant. Casual contacts at work, in the street, and with next-door neighbours who are not close friends would come within this category. Relationships with members of other racial groups also usually belong to the loose-knit part of the network. This means that although it is more close-knit than that of the white-collar urban Bantu which is relatively evenly loose-knit over the total field of social relationships it differs from the rural network which, in view of its being more of a structure, is more evenly close-knit over the whole field.

The recent nature of the process of urbanization and the high degree of mobility within the location, which makes for a high population turnover in any particular area, even as far as town-born persons are concerned, largely still prevent the formation of the type of close-knit network found, say, among the British working class. Even the more close-knit networks of urban Bantu are continually changing as persons move out and others come in.

There remains still the question whether there is any connexion between the degree of looseness of the network and the degree of segregation in conjugal roles, and whether these are related to class status. In her study of British families Bott found that a close-knit network tended to go with a high degree of segregation between the roles of husband and wife, whereas a loose-knit network tended to go with a joint conjugal role-relationship. She suggested that a close-knit network makes for uniformity of norms and constant informal pressure among the members of the network to conform to the norms, keep in touch with and help one another. If both spouses come to marriage with such close-knit networks 'rigid segregation of conjugal roles will be possible because each spouse can get help from people outside'. On the other hand, when the network is loose-knit, norms are more varied and 'social control and mutual assistance will be more fragmented and less consistent'. Couples with such loose-knit networks are more dependent on each other for emotional satisfaction and assistance in household tasks.[47] Network may also be related to class distinctions in that 'families with close-knit networks are likely to be working class'.[48]

Our own material also suggests the possibility of some connexion between network, conjugal role-relationship and social class. Not only did we find the most loose-knit type of network and the least segregated conjugal role-relationships in households of the white-collar level, but they actually occurred together in the same households. The three cases quoted as examples of joint conjugal roles (p. 160) are the identical ones used above to illustrate loose-knit networks (cases nos. 1 and 2 in chapter 4, and P). Among people of simple culture belonging to the lower social stratum, joint conjugal role-relationships do not occur and there is a tendency to have more close-knit networks.

Although the material is not sufficient to prove the hypothesis, I do think that there is some connexion between class, network and conjugal role-relationships in urban Bantu society also, but the connexion is of a different nature than in the British families studied by Bott. As yet the connexion between these three factors is less direct, resulting from their each being connected with a fourth factor, namely education. We have shown that (*a*) as regards '*class*', education seems to be the most important single factor by which urban Bantu grade each other, and that the white-collar category is also the best-educated. Although education may not be closely connected with occupation at lower levels, access to the best-paying occupations can only be had through a higher educational qualification. Prosperous business men will only be classed with the upper stratum if they are also well educated. (*b*) As regards *network*, a higher education makes for a wider range of interests and an open mind to innovation, which are important conditions for a loose-knit network. (*c*) As regards *conjugal roles*, the development of joint conjugal role-relationships has required a conscious move away from traditional patterns implying segregated roles, and a conscious striving toward Western middle-class patterns of 'companionship'. The better-educated Bantu are the ones who tend to follow Western patterns most consciously, and the type of Western family pattern they have come to know best from educationists, missionaries and magazines is not the working-class pattern of segregated roles, but the pattern of companionship between, and 'equality' of, the spouses in marriage.[49]

The tendency toward segregated conjugal role-relationships—in 'lower' families generally, and even in many of the 'upper' stratum—seems to be caused more by traditional patriarchal values than by conditions resulting from a high degree of connectedness in the network. In fact, we have pointed

[47] Op. cit., p. 60.
[48] Op. cit., p. 112.
[49] Cf. ibid.

out that the networks of urban Bantu, even at the lower levels, are probably less connected than the close-knit networks of British working-class families. Bott indicates that in as far as there is a connexion between a low class status and a close-knit network it is the result of the fact that only in the working-class one is likely to find 'a combination of factors all operating together to produce a high degree of connectedness'.[50] Some of these factors do not exist in the situation we are dealing with. There is no 'concentration of people of the same or similar occupations in the same local area'. All Bantu live together in the location, but there is still very little territorial grouping according to occupations. A teacher may have an office messenger, a labourer on the railways and a domestic servant as his closest neighbours. The factor of 'jobs and homes in the same local area' does not apply either. Homes are in the location, jobs are 'in town'. A third factor required for a really high degree of connectedness is a 'low population turnover and continuity of relationships'. The urban Bantu still often change their homes and their jobs, which means that they develop contacts with new neighbours and new work-mates. Thus the network is still prevented from becoming as close-knit as it can be among the working class in Europe and Britain, and it cannot be regarded as significantly contributing to the 'segregatedness' of conjugal roles at the present stage.

The absence of a direct connexion between network and the degree of segregation in conjugal roles may also be viewed from the angle of change. In the change from traditional to present-day urban structure the two aspects did not change at the same tempo. The change in network is more directly related to 'structural' urbanization.[51] The close-knit rural (and traditional) network 'exploded', as it were, with the move to town, particularly in the case of the School migrant who settled in town where he started building up a new network which was inevitably disconnected.[52] With continued residence in town the network now seems to become more close-knit among the bulk of the town-born population of the lower stratum. The change was therefore not one of simple progression, but involved first a relatively sudden change from extremely close-knit to very loose-knit and then gradually moved in the opposite direction towards being more close-knit. The change in relationship between husband and wife has been in the nature of a more simple progression from highly segregated roles towards a somewhat lesser degree of segregation. It seems probable that the 'explosion' of the traditional loose-knit network has contributed towards de-segregating conjugal roles to the extent that this has taken place, but the patriarchal tradition has strongly deterred the process in the lower social stratum generally, and to a large extent also in the upper stratum. In the upper stratum the network remains more open and the de-segregation of conjugal roles has in some cases progressed further—a process in which more advanced education seems to have played a significant part.

[50] Ibid.

[51] See Mayer, op. cit., pp. 5–7, for a discussion of urbanization as a structural process as distinguished from a cultural process.

[52] Cf. Mayer, op. cit., pp. 282–9; and Bott, op. cit., p. 106.

10

Conclusions

THE TRIANGLE OF FORCES

Our main findings may be summarized in terms of the 'triangle of forces'—Western culture, traditional Xhosa culture, and urbanization—referred to at the outset.[1] In terms of the contrast between 'Western' and 'traditional' we may say that the culture of the urban Xhosa of East London is predominantly orientated to Western cultural patterns. In the economic and technological field patterns are almost completely Western. For their means of livelihood the urban Xhosa rely almost exclusively on Western forms of occupation such as wage labour in industry and commerce or domestic service, white-collar employment, trading, or returns from investment of capital in property. In respect of material culture one may point to housing, furniture, clothing and transport, all of which follow Western patterns, although houses and furniture are often of a very simple nature. Formal education in schools on Western patterns is 'normal' and a large proportion of town Bantu have a real connexion with a Christian denomination, while many of the rest claim allegiance to one. Western medicine is generally accepted. Diverse forms of Western sport, concerts, the cinema, ballroom dancing and jiving, and vocal groups represent large-scale westernization in the recreational field. Visiting and drinking are more or less 'neutral' in this respect. Fah-fee is of oriental origin but reflects the cosmopolitan nature of the Western urban pattern.

In respect of marriage and values connected with the family it is more difficult to decide whether Western patterns predominate. Love-making is obviously influenced by present-day Western ideas, but patterns of pre-marital relations as such can hardly be classified as either Western or traditional, although lip-service is paid to traditional sex norms. Where marriage does take place it is usually legalized by church or civil rites, but this is often accompanied by the customary negotiations through intermediaries on behalf of the parents, and giving of *lobolo*. In *amabhaso* parties and wedding receptions there is a merging of tradition and patterns of Western origin. Conjugal relations are closer than they used to be, but the traditional patriarchal patterns are still valued and continue to influence relations between husband and wife. In some white-collar families, however, Western 'middle-class' values are consciously fostered.

In the political field there is a desire to participate in a system based on Western democratic patterns in concert with non-Xhosa peoples, but the traditional chiefs are still respected by many, and people attach a positive value to clan and tribal identity.

There are, however, significant instances of the persistence of behaviour patterns orientated to traditional Xhosa culture. We have already referred to *lobolo*, which is almost universal where marriage does take place. Male initiation is also very widely adhered to and is probably the 'purest' example of a tradi-

[1] See 'Introduction'.

tional institution persisting in town. Witchcraft beliefs and other traditional beliefs relating to the causation of illness and other forms of misfortune are common, and continue to influence the behaviour of many townspeople. Beliefs relating to the ancestor cult are still held by many people, and are occasionally given concrete expression in ritual.

The general orientation towards Western culture is not the result merely of urban living, because the process of westernization started long ago during the time of the present townspeople's rural ancestors. Most of the parents who moved to town, and even the majority of grandparents, already belonged to the category of School people, the acceptors of church and Western education and of 'civilization' generally. Even in the rural areas, School people are orientated to Western patterns in much of their material culture, religion, education, norms of cleanliness and in their relative readiness to accept innovations on Western lines where possible.[2] Migrant labour in urban areas has of course contributed its share towards the westernization of the rural School Xhosa, but it is largely the result of 'agents' and institutions acting directly within the rural environment, such as missions, schools, government agencies and white traders. The School migrant coming to town has found there the opportunities for greater fulfilment of those Western-orientated ideals fostered by his School background in the country.[3] Urban living has therefore merely contributed to a process of westernization which started within the rural environment, and it is difficult to distinguish cultural characteristics of the urban Bantu which are the result specifically of being born and brought up in town.

In the case of the small proportion of townspeople whose parents were Red, the degree of westernization they have attained is more closely related to urbanization. They themselves often connect their departure from Red behaviour patterns with urban living. However, they are often less westernized than the children of School immigrants, some of them being what we have termed 'semi-Red'.

When one is viewing urban Bantu society from the angle of structure it is easier to distinguish changes which are specifically related to urbanization. The rural structure has, of course, been affected by westernizing influences. The emergence of the Red–School division and the relative weakening of patrilineal kinship ties and paternal authority on the School side illustrate the point. However, patrilineal kinship ties still dominate the rural structure, mobility within the rural community is restricted, status is largely ascriptive—in short the social network remains essentially close-knit.[4] Moreover, although the rural Xhosa have been drawn into the administrative and legal machinery of the South African state, the latter tends to be superimposed on a system of chiefs, headmen and councils reflecting traditional patterns.

In the urban situation, however, traditional patrilineal patterns have lost much of their significance for the structure and growth of domestic groups, and have largely had to make way for distinct matrifocal tendencies, to the extent of families becoming extended in the matriline much more commonly than in the patriline. Although kinship ties and clan membership are valued, larger kinship groups cannot be regarded as important categories of interaction in day-to-day relations. Group activity takes place according to the

[2] Mayer, *Townsmen or Tribesmen*, chapter 2.
[3] Op. cit., pp. 206–8.
[4] Op. cit., chapter 2.

principle of association rather than kinship. Seniority in terms of patrilineal descent is still significant when rites and ceremonies are performed, but is less important in the urban status system than the emerging distinctions in terms of education and wealth. Political authority is exercised by government and municipal officials appointed according to principles totally different from seniority in terms of patrilineal descent. In spite of the presence of a tribal council in town, and the connexion that some prominent townspeople have with this, it has little relevance for the daily life of the average townsman as compared to officials and police.

Immigration to town has had a direct effect on social networks, resulting in the loosening of individuals' networks. But with prolonged urban living of town-born persons, networks seem to be becoming less loose-knit for members of the lower social stratum. De-segregation of conjugal roles also seems to be related to urbanization, although other westernizing influences cannot be ruled out.

CHOICE OF TRADITIONAL PATTERNS

Of the urban Bantu culture in East London we may say, then, that its over-all orientation is to Western patterns, but in certain situations patterns oriented to traditional Xhosa culture emerge. This is in sharp contrast to the culture of the Red Xhosa migrants who, through force of circumstances, cannot avoid being involved in certain Western forms of behaviour, particularly in the economic field, but who, when they are free to choose, normally follow traditional patterns. It is also different from patterns of behaviour among African of the Rhodesian Copperbelt, where the African population is recruited from distinct tribes of varying languages and culture and where tribalism in the sense of 'persistent loyalties and values which stem from a particular form of social organization' constitutes 'a category of interaction in day-to-day social intercourse'.[5] Thus it would seem that there is a more continual switching backwards and forwards between Western and traditional (tribal) behaviour patterns according to the sets of relations involved. 'As industrial workers they sometimes unite and co-operate in terms of their common interests in opposition to their employers along trade union lines. But among themselves, when they are not involved in relationships with the employers, they see each other primarily as tribesmen.'[6]

If traditional patterns of behaviour among town-born Xhosa do not constitute part of an over-all conscious conservatism as in the case of Red Xhosa migrants, and are neither selected in terms of the differing sets of relations involved, why is it that in spite of the acceptance two generations back of church and school and many aspects of Western culture, and in spite of economic forces and administrative measures contributing towards westernization, urban Xhosa consistently choose to follow certain traditional patterns of behaviour? In the East London situation I find it difficult to connect the selection of traditional patterns with any purely sociological principle of the order of 'sets of relations'. But a comparison of the situations in which traditional patterns emerge suggests a common emotional background.

I suggest that traditional patterns of behaviour have a particular emotional appeal in situations of social insecurity. Take the examples of male initiation

[5] Epstein, *Politics in an Urban African Community*, pp. 231, 232.
[6] Mitchell, *Tribalism and the Plural Society*, p. 24.

and *lobolo*. They constitute the two most common instances of traditional customs observed by townspeople, and without doubt there is a particularly strong attachment to these customs. Compare with this the fact that male delinquencies as expressed in 'tsotsiism' and marital instability constitute two of the most acute social ills of urban Bantu society and are regarded as such by the urban Bantu themselves. The society feels uncertain and insecure over the socialization of its male youths and in this situation of insecurity there is particular emotional need for tradition, for something which is old and established. For the Bantu Western behaviour patterns are essentially new and stand for phenomenal change not for an established order, and therefore cannot satisfy the emotional needs arising from insecurity. When the future of every marriage tends to be uncertain, *lobolo*, traditional marriage negotiations and the *amabhaso* party and seclusion of the bride, as customs which have their roots in the distant past, meet the emotional needs arising from uncertainty and insecurity. Other traditional customs are observed in situations of individual or family insecurity: a ritual sacrifice may be made when there is anxiety over the behaviour of a son; a diviner may be consulted in the case of prolonged illness; traditional techniques are extensively used during the critical early stage of a baby's life.

It is not possible to relate every instance of traditional customs, values, or beliefs to a specific instance of social insecurity, particularly when we are dealing with values and beliefs. The emotional satisfaction deriving from tribal identity, clan or kinship ties, is of a more general nature. Kinship and descent and their putative extension through clan and tribe stand for continuity and enduringness, which new forms of social organization still lack. The novelty of Western patterns may act as an attraction on the one hand. On the other hand it implies risk and uncertainty and creates an emotional need for that which is traditional and enduring. Bantu nationalism and a high standard of Western education may fulfil the need for self-expression and self-assertion, but tribal and clan ties complement this by providing a sense of belonging. Traditional initiation and other forms of ceremonial and ritual help to preserve these ties, in spite of their having slackened considerably, and their being of little direct significance in the urban structure.

INTERRELATIONS

A final remark refers to the interrelation between change in different aspects of society. The concept of the interrelation between different aspects of society, and the logical concomitant that change in one aspect has repercussions in other aspects, is one of the major contributions of social anthropological studies to the understanding of society. Recent studies suggest, however, that the interrelation is of a less rigid nature than earlier anthropologists thought, and that the effects of change in one area do not spread out evenly over the whole of society. Thus Mitchell speaks of the social field as embracing 'the range of social relationships in which actions in one part are likely to spread. Within the field there are likely to be clusters of highly interconnected social relations in which actions in one part have a direct and immediate effect on other parts, while other parts of the field will be relatively unaffected by or isolated from these actions.'[7] In other words, the effects of change in one cluster do tend to spread over the social field, but these effects are not synchronized.

[7] Mitchell, op. cit., p. 32.

Our own material also illustrates how changes in different parts of the 'total social field' may be interrelated without being synchronized. We have seen that migration to town, which is primarily a change in spatial relations, radically changed the social network, and that this affected relations between husband and wife, but that the changes in network and conjugal relations respectively were not synchronized. An immigrant's network might change from the close-knit rural network to very loose-knit when he came to town, but prolonged urban residence seems to be producing a greater degree of connectedness in the network of persons in the lower social stratum. The looser urban network produces closer conjugal relations, but the change has been less profound, the process of de-segregration of conjugal roles being retarded by the patriarchal tradition. In other words, change in the internal (domestic) field (conjugal roles) is related to change in the external field (network) without being synchronized with it.[8]

The example cited above also points to another aspect of interrelation of changes without synchronization. I refer to structural change and cultural change. It is accepted that values, beliefs and symbols—the cultural aspect of social interaction—are related to the social structure, and that changes in the structure generate changes of a cultural nature. But structural change and cultural change are not necessarily synchronized.[9]

Take the example of patrilineal kinship. In rural Xhosa society it constitutes an important principle of social organization: the domestic group tends to become extended in the patriline, general social status derives in part from patrilineal descent and political status also. Members of the patrilineal kinship group often co-operate in economic activities and in ritual and ceremonial. Patrilineal kinship here is basic to the whole social structure. In urban society the continued existence of clan exogamy is about the only significant instance in which patrilineal patterns continue to regulate relationships decisively and more or less universally. Apart from this they have lost most of their structural significance as we have shown above (p. 169). But in spite of the insignificance of patrilineal kinship in the urban structure, patrilineal kinship ties, clan membership and patriarchal authority are generally still highly valued and this valuation is occasionally still expressed in ritual and ceremonies. We have seen that even in the case of an illegitimate child the baptismal dinner may be the occasion for stressing patrilineal kinship ties, the child being linked with a clan through its mother's father (pp. 85–6). It is also stressed in speeches in connexion with initiation ceremonies. The persistence of ancestor beliefs, again, results in an occasional ritual slaughtering for which the available patrilineal kinsmen are collected (p. 53). I argue that this gathering of kin is of little structural significance in the urban setting, and is rather the expression of adherence to values and beliefs relating to a form of social organization—still persisting in rural areas—in which kinship is a much more basic principle than it is in town.

It is probably a general feature of the urbanization of African peoples that

[8] I have some doubt about the usefulness of the term 'social field' in the sense it is applied by Mitchell, because the word 'field' lends itself to be used in so many different contexts. Mitchell himself speaks of 'differently but partially related fields of activity' which 'fit into a total social field'. (Op. cit., p. 33.)

[9] Vogt suggests that there is always a certain amount of discontinuity between the two dimensions of structure and culture, which creates constant pressure for change. Together with 'technological-environmental forms' and 'certain psychological adaptations' they constitute 'significant variables in the course of events'. (Vogt, Evon Z., 'On the Concepts of Structure and Process in Cultural Anthropology', *American Anthropologist*, 62, 1 (1960), pp. 18–33.)

customs, values and beliefs relating to certain principles of social structure change more slowly than the structure itself.[10] However, conditions in East London probably accentuate this tendency. Not only is there a very high degree of homogeneity of language and traditional culture, but rural communities in which traditional forms of social organization persist are close at hand. Between the town and these rural communities there is a great deal of interaction, and, as we have noted (p. 53), the presence of large numbers of 'country-rooted' migrants in town may considerably affect the atmosphere and behaviour on ritual or ceremonial occasions. This situation fosters the persistence of traditional beliefs and customs in spite of their loss of structural significance in town.

[10] This does not mean that change never follows the opposite course, namely that values and beliefs are first affected and that this results in structural changes. The direct effect of Christian teaching on ancestor beliefs, and through this, indirectly on the kinship structure, is a point in case. It should be remembered, however, that change is seldom as simple as this, and that other factors more directly responsible for the weakening of kinship ties, might through this again have an indirect effect on ancestor beliefs. (Cf. Pauw, *Religion in a Tswana Chiefdom*, pp. 238–42.)

11

Postscript - After Twelve Years

INTRODUCTION

The previous chapters, for which the fieldwork was concluded in 1960, were concerned with the family among Xhosa-speaking townspeople in East London, considered in a general socio-cultural context. We now seek to determine to what extent the major trends of 1960 are still discernable after an interval of twelve years during which many East London families have been resettled in a new township under conditions differing significantly from those obtaining during the earlier research.

Whereas the major East London residential areas for Bantu were within walking distance of the city's business centre, Mdantsane, the new township, is nearly twenty kilometres distant, just within the boundary of the largest of several spatially separated areas comprising a single Bantu homeland officially known as the Ciskei. The Bantu homelands are parts of the Republic of South Africa reserved for permanent occupation by the Bantu-speaking peoples, in which it is the Republican government's avowed policy to grant a large degree of political independence to the people concerned. The legal and political position of residents of homeland townships is therefore different from that in East London's old 'locations' and in urban concentrations like Soweto (Johannesburg), Langa (Cape Town) and New Brighton (Port Elizabeth).

Mayer has given an extensive description of Mdantsane[1] which sprawls over hilly country necessitating winding streets and curved rows of houses, which compensate for the monotony of the uniform design of the four-roomed cottages. The township is spacious in comparison with Duncan Village, even those parts of it that had municipal housing (p. 21). There is provision for a number of business and recreation areas and in different parts of the township blocks of larger residential plots have been set aside for 'self-building.' On some of these a number of more imposing dwellings have been erected and some of the most affluent residents who have bought plots are expected to build on a grand scale. In the two years since Mayer wrote, public amenities have improved considerably. A community hall is now in use, the number of shops is steadily increasing, several rugby fields are in use, soccer fields are available, work on a large central sports stadium is well-advanced and tenders have been called for the construction of a swimming bath of Olympic standards. Six all-weather public tennis courts are, however, deteriorating for lack of use. There are two beer halls and a distributing depot selling commercially produced beer of the same kind as the traditional brew of South African Bantu peoples ('kaffir beer'). A small hotel is soon to be opened, a high standard boarding house is already in business and building of a hospital for 1 700 patients is in progress.

In 1960 two basic family types were distinguished, the one developing from

[1] Mayer, Philip, *Townsmen or Tribesmen* (second edition), 1971, pp. 295–8.

an elementary family and the other centring on an unmarried mother, both having a tendency to develop a multi-generation span (p. 154). Although the father was not merely marginal in the first type (p. 159), it also had matrifocal features: it tended to become extended by the addition of the children of unmarried daughters and often lost the father at an early stage after which extra-maritally conceived children might still be born to the mother. In this chapter we shall see to what extent Mdantsane families still tend towards matrifocality and a multi-generation span. Further, in view of our associating matrifocality with the dispendability of the husband-father and our emphasis on the lack of effective participation in local, tribal or national government as an important aspect of the insignificance of the role of husband and father (p. 163), certain recent developments in the field of government have to be recorded.

I have sensed some scepticism about the significance of traditional Xhosa customs for urban Xhosa. The question of the continuing validity of our earlier conclusions about Xhosa tradition among townspeople must therefore also receive attention.

Before turning to these subjects we have to consider some general information about the present Bantu population of East London and Mdantsane and the process of resettlement.

REDISTRIBUTION OF POPULATION

The twelve years that have elapsed since the original fieldwork for this book was completed have been marked by extensive rehousing of East London's Bantu population, either in extensions of Duncan Village (the East Bank Location) or in Mdantsane.

Not only was the housing scheme in Eziphunzana (Fig. 1) completed and occupied in the early sixties, but in spite of the imminent development of Mdantsane by the central government, Duncan Village was still further extended. Alarm about increasing tension among residents in the extremely congested wood-and-iron housing areas gave rise to a crash programme of building 3 500 houses by inexpensive methods in 1961. This new neighbourhood, Juliwe, borders on Eziphunzana and the cemetery beyond the Amalinda stream.

By 1963-4 resettlement of the East London Bantu population in Mdantsane began with the inhabitants of the smaller West Bank Location. The whole of the West Bank Location and almost the whole of the wood-and-iron neighbourhoods of Duncan Village have now been evacuated and demolished, while coloured people have replaced the Bantu residents in most of the older municipal housing schemes.

The only parts of the Duncan Village of the nineteen-fifties still occupied by Bantu are the part of Rawutini bordering on Thulandivile, the remaining hundred wood-and-iron shacks in Thulandivile, and the Ezikhawunsileni neighbourhood. The majority of the present Bantu population of Duncan Village are therefore housed in Eziphunzana and the emergency houses of Juliwe, the two very recent housing schemes.

The East London Municipality's official figure for Bantu persons housed in the city's Bantu residential areas as at 30 September 1972 is 47 103. With the exception of less than one thousand in the Cambridge Location these are all in Duncan Village. In addition there are those in the white residential areas, mostly accommodated on employers' premises, of whom 9 482 were enumerated in the 1970 census.

The virtual disappearance of the wood-and-iron neighbourhoods of the East London locations with their congested slum conditions must be recorded as one of the major changes that have taken place. It is unlikely that the extreme conviviality that marked the relations between inhabitants of these neighbourhoods, as described in some of the preceding chapters, will be reproduced in the new houses and neighbourhoods to which they have been moved. Brandel-Syrier writes of the nostalgia with which some of the elite in a Bantu 'housing estate' on the Witwatersrand remember the 'old location' where they used to live, with its slum conditions of congestion, filth and social evils but where there was 'real life' and intense sociability.[1]

Municipal records give the number of persons moved from East London to Mdantsane up to 30 September 1972 as 64 870. With the exception of a few hundred individuals these belonged to 11 916 'family units'. Over seven thousand family units and some six thousand individuals still await removal. The figures do not seem to account fully for the large numbers of unattached migrants so typical of the East London of the nineteen-fifties. Mostly housed in the wood-and-iron shacks, their numbers fluctuated between 10 000 and 16 000 in 1955.[2]

In spite of the large numbers that have been moved to Mdantsane, East London's present Bantu population is not much smaller than it was in 1955.[3] Since natural growth cannot account for the maintenance of these numbers in spite of the exodus, the continuing influx into East London must have been considerable. Even now there are continual attempts to erect illegal shacks in the bushes and in yards of municipal houses.

Meanwhile resettlement is proceeding visibly and smoothly: once a week a number of households and their belongings are transported to Mdantsane on municipal lorries. 1 015 persons were moved in this way during the April-June quarter of 1972, and 1 155 in the following quarter. There are misgivings, however, that the pace of removal is too slow to beat the natural population increase and illegal influx into East London, and to realize the aim of the removal of the whole East London Bantu population to Mdantsane in the immediate future.

Of the 20 000 houses planned for Mdantsane 13 362 had been completed and occupied by September 1972. The following numbers were on the township administration's files at that stage:

	Males	Females	Total
Children	18 318	21 487	39 805
Adults (over 16)	17 655	24 623	42 278
Total	35 973	46 110	82 083

The final 1970 government census figure was 66 380. If allowance is made for probable under-enumeration the actual population could well be around 95 000. Obviously a substantial minority has not come into the township via

[1] Brandel-Syrier, M., *Reeftown Elite*, Routledge & Kegan Paul, London, 1971, pp. 55–6.
[2] Reader, *The Black Man's Portion*, p. 116.
[3] Cf. Reader, op. cit., p. 42.

the official channels of removal from East London. Persons entering by other official channels are mostly government officials, teachers and key employees in factories and other private concerns, who have come to East London on transfer, and a number of people who have had to leave the Western Cape and have been resettled in Mdantsane. These and the natural population increase can, however, only partly account for the discrepancy between the numbers officially brought in from East London and the total population.

The preponderance of females is somewhat less pronounced in the 1970 census figures than in the administration's figures. The trend is reminiscent of our finding in respect of the sample of families fully settled in East London (p. 150). When present Mdantsane figures are compared with the sample of the total East London population in 1955[1], in which females were slightly fewer than males, one must again conclude that the present figures do not reflect the presence of large numbers of unattached male migrants. They can hardly have disappeared from the population; the answer may lie in unregistered lodging of male Red migrants with Mdantsane tenants, who avoid enumerators during censuses since they rent rooms illegally.

FOLLOWING UP A CASE STUDY

In Mdantsane I managed to trace Manini whose extremely matrifocal, semi-Red multi-generation family is described on pp. 70-5, and who had moved to Mdantsane from their home in Duncan Village in 1968, exactly four years before I revisited them. A discussion of their present condition introduces some of the subjects that will concern us in the rest of this chapter.

Prior to the move from Duncan Village there was some moving of individual descendants out of, or back into, Manini's household. Now the large family has split into several units, but there is still a three-generation matrifocal core comprising Manini, one unmarried daughter, Nomanase, and six or seven grandchildren, most of them Nomanase's children born after our previous study of the family (see genealogy, p. 70). Nomanase is now expecting another baby.

Manini's eldest daughter, Nomvulo, still unmarried, is now living on her own with some of her children. Tembeka (daughter of Nomvulo) is also on her own as the registered tenant of half of a four-roomed house, and her brother, Newboy, is officially registered as her 'child' living with her. Nomazotshwa, another daughter of Nomvulo, is registered on Manini's certificate of occupation as her own child living with her, but stays in Eziphunzana in Duncan Village. Manini's middle-aged son, Makhwenkwe, and her granddaughter, Nomvuyo, are living in other houses in Mdantsane, each with a spouse, Nomvuyo having one child with her and one staying with Manini.

Nomvulo (eldest daughter) and Makhwenkwe (son) seem to have been on their own in Mdantsane from the start, and may already have separated from the main household in Duncan Village before the move. Tembeka (granddaughter) was originally registered with Manini in Mdantsane, but was given a house of her own within a month. Nomvuyo (granddaughter) was also on Manini's certificate at first but was later deleted with a note that she was married in December 1969. The process of splitting therefore began in East London but proceeded rapidly after the move to Mdantsane.

Manini's first comment after our meeting was that 'the rent is killing us'.

[1] Reader, op. cit., p. 151.

Whereas the family owned a house and had a regular income from letting a number of rooms in Duncan Village, they now have to pay rent. Manini and Nomanase no longer brew beer for sale and have a small income from sub-letting one or two rooms to 'lodgers' (not registered and therefore illegally accommodated), which supplements Manini's old-age pension and the maintenance fees Nomanase gets for some of her illegitimate children (cf. p. 120).Their furniture is simple as ever, but Manini is enthusiastic about the spinach and mealies in the irregular little patches she has cultivated around the house, and about laid-on water and waterborne sanitation inside the house, which contrast strikingly with the extremely congested living conditions, communal taps and communal ablution and sanitary facilities in Duncan Village. She voluntarily commented that she would never want to exchange their present condition for what it was in East London. I did not discuss compensation for their house; judging by general information it could well have been in the vicinity of R500, but Makhwenkwe possibly claimed at least part of it (cf. p. 71).

Manini and Nomanase were quite sure that they did not feel lonely in Mdantsane and spoke of old friends from their former neighbourhood who live near by.

They still distinctly conform to the semi-Red type distinguished in the earlier study (pp. 42, 59) and have friendly relations with their lodgers, one of whom wears the typical dress of Red women migrants in town.[1] It emerged that a visitor who joined the company during our visit, also a Red woman, was a diviner and that Nomanase herself was going through the extended ceremonial of initiation as a diviner after beginning to *thwasa*, as the condition of illness necessitating initiation is called. The *intlombe* (dance) of novices and the diviner supervising their initiation sometimes takes place in their house and Manini demonstrated how a large plastic container is used as a drum to beat the rhythm. The only other sign of Nomanase's initiation was a small necklace of white beads she was wearing.[2] Although these details are cited to emphasize Nomanase's semi-Redness, I must add that initiation as a diviner occurs also among School and church people, in the country as well as in towns.[3]

DIFFICULTIES OF RESETTLEMENT

Conditions in Mdantsane have in some respects improved considerably since Mayer's study two years ago and there is some appreciation for the positive side of resettlement. Manini was not the only informant who felt she was better off in Mdantsane. Some, however, were more fatalistic, accepting resettlement as inevitable, and some of the complaints Mayer recorded[4] are still common.

Rents and the high cost of transport are still the most serious problems, while unemployment is still in evidence. Although the rent for a four-roomed house is only R6,57, this is a good deal more than most people paid for their accomodation, often only one or two rooms, in Duncan Village. People who owned houses in Duncan Village now have to pay rent instead of receiving an income from rents, but they were of course compensated for the houses they had to evacuate.

[1] Cf. Mayer, op. cit., pp. 26, 299.

[2] Cf. Hunter, *Reaction to Conquest*, pp. 320–35; Hammond-Tooke, W. D., *Bhaca Society*, O.U.P., Cape Town, 1962, pp. 246–56.

[3] Pauw, B. A., *Christianity and Xhosa Tradition*, O.U.P., Cape Town, forthcoming.

[4] Mayer, op. cit., pp. 296–9.

A knowledgeable resident of Mdantsane, not partial to the East London Municipality, independently agreed with the view of a Municipality spokesman that there has been general satisfaction with the compensation. Most owners of wood-and-iron shacks received between R400 and R800. Two valuers, one representing the Municipality and the other the owners, jointly valued the properties, and very few owners availed themselves of the opportunity of appealing against the valuation. A four-roomed house in Mdantsane can be purchased for R750 to R820 but not many Duncan Village owners have used their compensation money to buy a house or a plot.

Transport is obviously much more important in Mdantsane than it was in East London where many people could walk to work. Only a small proportion of Mdantsane people can work for an income within the township. The majority of workers are still employed in East London. Even those working in 'border industries' nearer the township have to use transport to get to work. It is my impression that more people own cars in Mdantsane than used to be the case in East London locations. Some in fact used the money received as compensation for their East London houses to buy cars. The authorities estimate the number of privately owned motor vehicles in Mdantsane at about one thousand. In spite of the apparent increase in private transport the great majority of people have to use rail transport or buses.

The number of shops in Mdantsane is increasing but stock is generally limited to the more ordinary run of goods. The first fashion shop to cater for a wide range of tastes, including the more expensive and very modern, was opened early in October 1972. There are still complaints that shops are too few and prices not competitive, so that people feel the need to shop in East London, which again involves transport cost.

Wages and salaries have of course increased over the past years and further help is given by some East London employers who have introduced a special transport bonus for Mdantsane employees. It is felt, however, that such bonuses and increases have not been sufficient to counter the general increase in the cost of living as well as the additional expenses necessitated by living in Mdantsane instead of East London.

Paradoxically the 'torn social fabric' to which Mayer refers seems to be affecting the townspeople I spoke to less than migrants, but the time lapse between Mayer's study and my own might of course be the reason for the difference, since it has allowed for the improvement of amenities and a longer period of adaptation on the part of residents. None of my informants gave evidence of suffering from serious loneliness, and it was not unusual to hear of old East London friends whom they visited in Mdantsane. However, people who used to be within a few minutes' walking distance of each other are now often far apart, and people do lose contact with some of their former friends.

Some people have developed new interests in Mdantsane. In Duncan Village only a minority, for example, had space around their houses to do a little gardening, but in Mdantsane everybody has space and gardening has become a more common leisure time activity. The gardens vary from the irregular little patches of vegetables and mealies like Manini's to neatly laid out and well-cultivated lawns and flower beds. There are many more of the latter type than there were in East London and the township Manager has introduced an annual competition for the most attractive garden of this kind.

The musical companies which featured prominently in East London (p. 45) are gradually becoming active in Mdantsane, but more halls are needed if they are to flourish. Sporting activities are also increasing. The first attempt to offer regular film shows in the community hall has been abandoned, but a new tender has been accepted.

Violent lawlessness, however, is still a major public menace to which the Township Council is giving particular attention. A force of police reservists has been created to help check such thuggery.

Mayer suggested that drinking contributed to the violence people complained of and that there was probably more drinking in Mdantsane than there used to be in Duncan Village, especially among non-Reds. Some of them would have attended a show or watched a sporting event during the week-end, but for lack of such diversions now just drank. One would expect, then, that increasing opportunities for recreation would be leading to less drinking. There was no time to investigate this, nor to investigate drinking patterns in detail, but important policy changes regarding the supply of beer and liquor must be mentioned.

Legislation passed in 1961 removed the former restrictions on the purchase of liquor by persons classified as Bantu (Appendix IV); bottle stores and, in some cases, licensed hotels are doing a brisk trade in larger Bantu townships throughout South Africa. Further, whereas there was only home brewing of traditional Bantu beer—at that time commonly referred to as 'k.b.' or 'kaffir beer', even by Xhosa-speaking persons—and a great deal of illicit selling in East London of the fifties, commercial brewing and sale of such beer have been introduced in East London as well as Mdantsane. In both cases home brewing is still permitted, but private sale of beer remains illicit. The respective authorities say that illicit selling of beer leads to many prosecutions in Mdantsane but does not constitute a serious problem in Duncan Village. In both townships there are several briskly patronized beer halls and distribution points where beer can be bought for consumption off the premises.

Mr. W. R. Hart, Acting Manager of East London's Department of Bantu Administration, considers that consumption of liquor was initially 'rather excessive' after lifting of the restrictions, but that it has gradually diminished. Illicit sales through shebeens and other sources, where prices were higher than those charged by licensed distributors, continued for some time because they offered credit. But since obtaining the liquor no longer constituted a problem in itself, customers bought from the legal dealers at the lower prices when they had cash and from others only when they needed credit, so that illicit sellers were pushed out of business by amassing more and more debts. In Mdantsane, where bottle stores are still the only legal sources of liquor, shebeens and other forms of illicit liquor trade are still more common.

HOUSEHOLD AND FAMILY

A true comparison of families in Mdantsane with those studied in East London would have required extensive new fieldwork, but particulars available from Superintendents in Mdantsane concerning tenants in their respective 'zones' provided information that could be used to indicate certain trends. The main source of information in each case was the copy of a certificate of occupation, giving details about the tenant's wife, children and dependants. For former East London people this could usually be supplemented by information from forms filled in before the household moved to Mdantsane and the final application, mostly completed on the day of actual resettlement. Very few of the persons listed were not members of the tenants' families. The information did not refer to marital status explicitly but in the case of female tenants or males without wives there was usually a remark that the person was 'single', widowed, divorced, separated from a spouse or deserted. Thus the information was specific enough to allow for a classification of tenants' households in categories similar to those distinguished in our previous study.

At the time of this restudy seven zones in Mdantsane were fully occupied and an eighth partly occupied. The zones are numbered in order of occupation and numbers 4 and 7 were selected for sampling. Since the original research was mainly confined to Duncan Village (the East Bank Location) and the first three zones occupied in Mdantsane have many people from the smaller West Bank Location[1], Zone 4 was selected to include Duncan Village people who moved in earlier (mostly during 1967-8) and to exclude East Bank people as far as possible, and Zone 7 to include more recent arrivals from Duncan Village (1970-1).

From each of the two zones a 1 in 50 sample was drawn from a continuous series of plot numbers. In each zone the sample included a few houses divided between two tenants each, but no houses built by the owners themselves. In the following tables the information from the samples is summarized in terms of household type and marital status of the tenants who are presumably household heads in most cases. 'Single' is intended to mean 'unmarried' but it is possi-

ZONE 4

Tenant's Sex and Marital Status

Type of household	Male				Female			Total
	With wife	Widowed	'Single'	Other	Widowed	'Single'	Other	
Multi-generation, male tenant (presumably head)	1	–	3	–	–	–	–	4
Father-mother-children	16	–	–	1	–	–	–	17
Multi-generation, female tenant (presumably head)	–	–	–	–	1	–	–	1
Mother-children	–	–	–	–	4	7	2	13
Other:								
Father-mother-children plus son and wife	1	–	–	–	–	–	–	1
Mother-children plus son and wife	–	–	–	–	1	–	–	1
Male plus others attached	–	–	1	–	–	–	–	1
Female plus others attached	–	–	–	–	1	–	–	1
Single person	–	1	–	1	1	1	–	4
Total	18	1	4	2	8	8	2	43
	25				18			

[1] Cf. Reader, op. cit., pp. 42, 45.

ZONE 7

Tenant's Sex and Marital Status

Type of household	Male				Female			Total
	With wife	Widow-ed	'Single'	Other	Widow-ed	'Single'	Other	
Father-mother-children	20	–	–	1	–	–	–	21
Multi-generation, female tenant (presumably head)	–	–	–	–	–	–	1	1
Mother-children	–	–	–	–	2	5	2	9
Other:								
Father-children	–	–	–	1	–	–	–	1
Male plus others attached	–	–	–	1	–	–	–	1
Female plus others attached	–	–	–	–	1	–	–	1
Total	20	–	–	3	3	5	3	34
	23				11			

ble that a few mothers described as single were in fact married women deserted by, or separated from, their husbands. The category 'other' includes persons deserted by, or separated from, their spouses and those for whom no details of marital status were available. For two father-mother-children households of which the fathers' marital status has been left undefined there was information indicating temporary separation or desertion by the wives and in one of these another woman was said to have moved in to live with the man.

Further relevant information is that there were altogether 4 447 female tenants in Mdantsane at the end of September 1972. Since a limited number of houses are divided between two tenants, the total number of tenants is somewhat in excess of the 13 362 houses occupied, but it can safely be accepted that the female tenants account for close on thirty per cent of the total, if not more.

Subject to reservations which will be mentioned as we proceed, the figures suggest that most households are formed by father-mother-children families (presumably mostly elementary, but possibly including some compound families) or mother-children units, a considerable proportion of which are incomplete families of unmarried mothers. Multi-generation households appear to be less in evidence in the Mdantsane samples than in those studied in East London (pp. 144-5).

It should, however, be remembered that the latter were limited to households fully settled in town and that the Mdantsane information was not collected according to the very careful methods used with the Duncan Village sample. It is not surprising that a superficial check during visits to a small number of households included in the samples produced a few discrepancies between actual household composition and the official returns.

When interviewed, a female tenant registered as single and the mother of seven children living with her claimed that she was the second wife of a polygynist and that her husband was living with her in the house. Officially, however, he was the tenant of another house occupied by the children of his now deceased first wife. Since a person is not permitted to be the tenant of two houses simultaneously, but unmarried mothers can rent houses, the obvious solution for this polygynous family was for the second wife to apply for a house as an unmarried mother. She came to East London in 1940 and has adult children born in East London, while one of her grown-up daughters is being trained as a teacher. Jonas also records an instance of a polygynist and both his wives living in Mdantsane[1], but these are undoubtedly isolated cases.

According to official records another household consisted of a father, mother and children plus a married son and his wife. It emerged that the parents were not living in the Mdantsane house at all but were at a home in a reserve where the young couple's eldest child was living with them. Altogether this was a distinctly country-rooted family. Like the former irregularity, this kind is presumably not so common as to distort the general pattern seriously.

Discrepancies are probably more often due to incompleteness of the list of the tenant's children and dependants. Tenants are not particularly careful to have the names of young children registered on their certificates of occupation, especially those born after they were granted houses. To the extent that this applies to the children of unmarried daughters, as proved to be the case in one house visited, it would mean that an unknown number of three generation families figure as father-mother-children families in the official records. Further, in two father-mother-children households in Zone 7 having young children listed as dependants of the tenant without further details of the relation, it is highly probable that they were grandchildren, and that these were actually three-generation households. Multi-generation families are therefore not quite as uncommon in Mdantsane as would appear from the tables.

Discussions with officials and residents, and proceedings of the Township Council's Housing Committee confirm the conclusion from the samples that many unmarried mothers with children have become tenants in their own right. The regulations allow for the allocation of a house under stipulated conditions 'to any person who is the head of a family', 'family' being defined in relation to a person as, for example, including the wife and unmarried children 'of such a person' (R. 293 of 1962, Chapter I, sec. 1, Chapter II, sec. 8(1)). 'Head of a family' is not further defined and unmarried mothers are not explicitly excluded. The local authorities are in favour of granting separate houses to unmarried mothers and their children if they belong to households considered too large for one house. Even unmarried mothers who are quite young can become tenants: one in the samples who had children of her own was twenty-one when she took occupation; two others were under thirty. There are also unmarried mothers who have purchased houses of their own.

The process of splitting that took place in Manini's multi-generation family during, and after, the move to Mdantsane is therefore not unusual and it is likely that it has reduced some multi-generation families to a span of only two generations. Close links may of course be maintained between families living in different houses. A widowed mother and her mature daughter observed in the process of moving from Duncan Village to Mdantsane specially requested to be given neighbouring houses 'for health reasons', the mother in this case apparently needing the daughter's care. On the other hand a young unmarried mother living in her own house could also be so dependent on her family of origin that

[1] Jonas, P. J., *Die Veranderende Posisie van die Vrou in die Huwelik en Gesin by die Stedelike Xhosa van Oos-Londen, met Besondere Verwysing na die Dorp Mdantsane*, M. A. thesis, University of South Africa, 1972, p. 77.

she and her children merely constitute a spatially separated extension of the senior household.

Outside the samples I found several instances of young married men and their wives, some with children, initially living with the man's parents and then seeking houses of their own.

The male heads in the four multi-generation households in the samples all belonged to the second generation in their families, the first and third being accounted for by their mothers and their own or their sisters' children respectively. On the whole it has been the policy in Mdantsane to register adult sons rather than their mothers as tenants, even though the mothers regarded themselves as heads in East London and the sons were still young and unmarried. In some such cases the mother might still be the de facto head. That tension could arise from the registration policy is illustrated by the complaints the authorities received from a woman who was the head of a household in East London but was registered as a dependant of her step-son, the tenant, together with his sisters and their children in a Mdantsane house. She maintained that the authorities gave the certificate of occupation to her and that she was paying the rents and investing money in improving the house and garden. She cared for the step-son and he used to treat her as a mother but his attitude had changed and he was trying to get her out of the house. On the other hand a son's registration as tenant could accord with a change in the economic and authority structure of the household. In one three generation household visited, the mother explained that her son took over as head in Mdantsane because she was no longer working.

Sub-letting to 'lodgers' is common in Mdantsane though often illicit, as official permission has not been obtained.[1] This goes undetected since raids of the kind that used to take place in East London[2] are not made in Mdantsane. Very few of the tenants in the Mdantsane samples had lodgers holding permits. It is known that lodgers are sometimes related to the tenants with whom they live and form part of their households.

The difference between the Mdantsane samples and the earlier Duncan Village samples is no doubt partly due to the fact that the former include an unknown number of households that have not been settled in town as long, and to the same extent, as those in the Duncan Village samples. It is clear, however, that easing of the housing situation has led to the hiving-off of sub-families or mother-children units from multi-generation households. If the population increase continues to be provided for sufficiently by the continuing expansion of Mdantsane or other future developments, it is likely that multi-generation households, especially those with female heads, will in the long run be less conspicuous in Mdantsane than they were in Duncan Village.

The conclusion that a distinctly matrifocal type of incomplete family with an unmarried mother as head persists in Mdantsane is fully justified. Statistics showing the proportion of births in respect of which the mothers are unmarried are not available for Mdantsane, but it is obvious that there are still many young unmarried mothers. Casual information, including letters, advice columns and articles in publications with a predominantly Bantu readership suggest that the acceptance or tolerance of the extensive premarital sex experience described

[1] Mayer, op. cit., p. 301.

[2] Cf. Mayer, op. cit., p. 58.

elsewhere (pp. 115, 121-4) and the use of contraceptives by unmarried girls among South African urban Bantu are gradually increasing. This use of contraceptives could of course curb the matrifocal trend in future. Trends in connection with sex in the Western world in general may now have greater influence on urban Xhosa sex attitudes than they had twelve years ago (p. 121).

Some of the findings in a study of belief and ritual among Xhosa-speaking Christians are relevant to the matrifocal trend in urban family structure. In a comparison of rural and urban samples of persons on the registers of several churches in the Transkei and in Port Elizabeth a distinct difference emerged with regard to the ancestors supposed to have visited respondents in dreams or other forms of visitations: patrilineal ancestors predominated in the visitations reported by rural as well as urban informants, but in visitations of persons born in town mothers and matrikin (including matrikin of fathers and husbands) were distinctly more in evidence than in the visitations reported by rural respondents. With regard to such of these visitations as led to the performance of ritual the contrast between rural and town-born respondents was even more distinct.[1] Thus the matrifocal trend in family structure is parallelled by a shift in respect of kinsmen with whom belief and ritual are concerned.

The matrifocal trend in urban Bantu families has been explicitly documented in a study of illegitimacy in Watville, Benoni[2] and there are hints of it in a study of an urban elite on the Witwatersrand[3] and in studies of Atteridgeville (Pretoria)[4], Langa (Cape Town)[5] and Port Elizabeth Bantu townships.[6]

LOCAL AND REGIONAL GOVERNMENT

Twelve years ago we noted lack of interest in organizations concerned with local and national government (p. 184), and we argued that the urban father's negligible participation in local, tribal or national government was one facet of the insignificance of the father-role (p. 163). In 1970 Mayer still commented on the lack of opportunities for participation in administration and local government in Mdantsane[7] but important developments are now taking place at the local and regional level.

The key figure in the administration of Mdantsane is still a white Manager but like other white officials in the township he has been temporarily seconded to the Ciskeian government by the central government's Department of Bantu Administration and Development. The present Manager actively fosters communication and contact with the residents of Mdantsane and the public in general, and in the field I could observe his close co-operation with leading citizens. Further, four out of eight zones in the township now have Bantu Superintendents, compared to the one out of five in 1970.

A major development was the institution of a Township Council under the provisions of special regulations for the administration and control of townships

[1] Pauw, op. cit.

[2] Moeno, S. N., *The Urban African Family Disorganisation with Special Reference to the Problem of Illegitimacy*, M.A. thesis, University of South Africa, 1969, pp. 57–60, 112–13.

[3] Brandel-Syrier, op. cit., pp. 234–43.

[4] Coertze, R. D., 'Die Gesinslewe in Atteridgeville', in Eloff, J. F. and Coertze, R. D. (eds.), *Etnografiese Studies in Suidelike Afrika*, Van Schaik, Pretoria, 1972, pp. 319–21.

[5] Wilson, M. and Mafeje, A., *Langa*, O.U.P., Cape Town, 1963, pp. 78–9.

[6] Durand, J. J. F., *Swartman, Stad en Toekoms*, Tafelberg, Cape Town, 1970, pp. 36–7.

[7] Mayer, op. cit., pp. 298–9.

in Bantu homelands (Procl. R.293 of 1962). The first Council, elected for three years, took office towards the end of 1971. Three members were appointed by the Ciskeian government and the other seven elected by Mdantsane residents, one for each zone occupied at the time. The members include a medical doctor, a journalist who has visited the United States and several businessmen. One of the latter is a celebrated eulogizer (*imbongi*) of major chiefs among the Xhosa proper, whose performance has now been curtailed by the loss of his eyesight. The Council has elected the white Manager its secretary.

In five of the six constituencies contested in the elections there was a poll of between 30 and 35 per cent in each case, while it was 24,5 per cent in the remaining one, the total electorate varying between 3 000 and 5 000 in each zone. This reflects much greater interest than there was in the East London Advisory Board elections in the middle fifties.[1] Moreover, since the elections were held on a weekday and polling booths were small, many people were still waiting their turn to vote at the closing of the polls. The Manager and present Council members expect a marked increase in the polling at the next election; they maintain that the people are only now beginning to realize what powers the Council is able to exercise.

At present the Council's influence is most apparent in allocating houses, granting lodgers' permits, cancelling permits and certificates of occupation, and the steps taken in default of payment of rent. A certain number of the new houses that become available for occupation are reserved for allocation to people already in Mdantsane to provide for natural population increase. A Housing Committee of the Council attends to these matters in co-operation with the Manager at weekly sessions in each zone. Observations at a few sessions indicate that the Council members actively participate in decisions and do not merely endorse the Manager's ruling.

Refuse removal is the Council's responsibility and has been given out on contract. A Transport Committee is concerned with improving public transport facilities, none of which are, however, run by the Council. The Council has also given some attention to the problem of lawlessness and individual councillors sometimes assist Superintendents in resolving conflicts between neighbours or members of the same household. The regulations provide for levying a rate not exceeding R1 per annum on every grantee or holder in the township, but by September 1972 the Council had not yet imposed such a rate and its activities were restricted by limited funds.

Current regional developments affecting the people of Mdantsane flow from the Bantu Authorities Act of 1951. In spite of the very critical attitude of some Bantu (pp. 184-5) considerable progress has been made in implementing the Act and developing the principles it embodies. After Tribal and Regional Authorities had been instituted at the lower and the intermediate level respectively, the pyramid was completed by the institution of the Ciskeian Territorial Authority in 1961. In 1969 its powers were extended and it was reconstituted to include the Paramount Chief of the Rarabe tribes and his personal representative and a chief, headman or chairman and an additional representative of each of 38 Tribal and three Community Authorities. 'Rarabe' is now used to designate all the tribes in the Ciskei regarded as Xhosa proper, as distinct from Mfengu (Fingo) and Thembu tribes, which are also Xhosa-speaking. A

[1] Mayer, op. cit., p. 53.

few Sotho-speaking tribes of the Herschel district are also represented in the Territorial Authority. The Authority has six Executive Councillors, now called Ministers, forming a Cabinet, two representing the Rarabe tribes, two the Mfengu, one the Thembu and one the Sotho, each responsible for one of the following departments: Authority Affairs and Finance, Community Affairs, Works, Education and Culture, Agriculture, and Justice. A separate Ciskeian civil service in which seconded Whites are gradually to be replaced by Bantu civil servants has been instituted.[1] A further development came with the establishment of the Ciskeian Legislative Assembly under Proclamation R.118, 1971 (21 May, 1971). On 1 August 1972 the defined Bantu areas of the Ciskei became a 'self-governing territory within the Republic' (Procl. R.187, 1972) with the same kind of limited self-government granted earlier to the Transkei. The Ciskei is now preparing for its first Legislative Assembly elections in February 1973. In the new Assembly there will be twenty elected members representing nine electoral divisions, in addition to the Rarabe Paramount Chief or his representative and twenty-nine chiefs. The number of seats assigned to each division has been determined by the number of voters registered in each.

Mdantsane has thus far had no direct representation in any Territorial body, but the Mdantsane district which includes the area of one Tribal Authority in addition to the township, constitutes one of the nine electoral divisions. It appears, however, that whereas citizens under Tribal Authorities will have dual representation—through their chiefs as well as through elected representatives—those residents of the township who have no ties with a Tribal Authority will be represented by elected members only.

The people of Mdantsane and of the Ciskei in general are showing a lively interest in the elections. In the Mdantsane electoral division which includes the whole district and in which a total Bantu population of 103 963 was returned in the 1970 census, 77 023 voters have been registered, while the figure for the whole Ciskei is 480 801. It should be remembered, however, that large numbers of Bantu not domiciled in the Ciskei, for example in urban areas throughout South Africa, qualify for Ciskeian citizenship and that many of them have been registered as voters.[2] Sixty-three candidates have been nominated for the twenty seats in the Legislative Assembly; eight will contest the three seats assigned to the Mdantsane division.

No distinct major divisions based on differing policies had emerged among candidates by early January 1973. Extensive coverage given to Ciskeian politics in the East London *Daily Dispatch*[3] suggests that the principle of separate political development for the Ciskei and other Bantu homelands is accepted by most candidates but that criticism of particular aspects of South African government policy and that of the present Ciskeian government will be voiced in election campaigns. Members of the present Cabinet of the Ciskei have also been attacked for not being critical enough of the central government. It is unlikely that the brand of politics propagated by the banned African National Congress and the more radical Pan-African Congress (pp. 184-6) will play an overt role

[1] Holdt, C. C. S., 'Constitutional Development', in University of Fort Hare, *The Ciskei – a Bantu Homeland*, Fort Hare University Press, 1971, pp. 210–14.

[2] *Daily Dispatch*, November 16 and 17 and December 9, 1972.

[3] E.g. *Daily Dispatch*, September 27, November 23 and December 9, 1972 and January 6 and 8, 1973.

in the elections. There is not much enthusiasm for a 'super-state' of all South African Bantu peoples, but the amalgamation of the predominantly Xhosa-speaking Ciskei and Transkei has received general though cautious support.

The old Xhosa-Mfengu opposition (p. 183) may still prove to be a significant factor in Ciskeian politics. The registration of voters was the responsibility of the Ciskeian government, but certain chiefs and their representatives organized, especially in urban areas, to ensure that people affiliated to their tribes, were registered as voters. This gave rise to an attack by the Chief Minister of the Ciskei, Chief Justice Mabandla, who represents a Mfengu Tribal Authority in the Legislative Assembly, on a so-called 'Rarabe Group' for what he regarded as interference with the business of the Ciskeian government. The latter, he said, 'would keep a close watch on them' and he appealed for the elections to be conducted on the basis of merit, not tribal affiliation.[1] At the same time two of my informants maintained that Mfengu people were also organizing. A Mdantsane and East London journalist later openly wrote about the Rarabe-Mfengu rift in current politics, predicting that the election would be fought along 'tribal' lines.[2]

All the members of the Mdantsane Township Council are men and only one of the sixty-three candidates for the Legislative Assembly elections is a woman. Women can, however, play a significant role as voters and some have in the past been as active as the men in political organizations. It therefore remains to be seen whether all the new political activity will enhance the significance of the father in the family and thus counter the matrifocal trend.

CULTURAL TRENDS

Judging by women's fashions, the cultural variety in Mdantsane is no less than it was in East London twelve years ago. The same long-established dress of Red women from the country—large woollen turbans, long skirts, shawls around the shoulders, garments tied round the waists as a sign of respect, and rough bare feet—is still there, while Euro-American fashions of the last decade, like mini-skirts, slacks and modern shoes, have appeared at the other end. Black and brown wigs in 'Western' and 'Afro-' styles are another addition.

In view of the very obvious westernization and the non-traditional living conditions under which townspeople are permanently settled, there might be some scepticism about our earlier findings on the persistence of features of traditional Xhosa culture among townspeople. Recent studies in other South African urban centres, however, also illustrate the continuing significance of features of indigenous Bantu cultures for many townspeople. Wilson and Mafeje refer to the continuing significance of traditional initiation of males, reverence for the shades or ancestor spirits, and diviners for Xhosa-speaking townspeople in Langa, Cape Town.[3] Durand, a theologian who conducted research and worked as a minister in the Port Elizabeth Bantu townships, gives similar information, although he holds that the adherence to *ukulobola*, initiation and other features of Xhosa tradition are futile attempts at adaptation.[4] In an investigation of explanations of misfortune among the long-established and 'comparatively westernized and

[1] *Daily Dispatch*, September 27 and October 6 and 10, 1972.

[2] Qumza, G., 'Ciskei Tribal Rift', *Daily Dispatch*, October 28, 1972.

[3] Wilson and Mafeje, op. cit., pp. 105–12.

[4] Durand, op. cit., 38–42, 108–12.

sophisticated' Xhosa-speaking population of Grahamstown, Hammond-Tooke found that 52 per cent of his cases were ascribed to witchcraft, sorcery or the ancestors.[1] A forthcoming book on belief and ritual among Xhosa-speaking Christians contains extensive information on the persistence of traditional beliefs about the ancestors, magical medicines, witchcraft and sorcery among Xhosa-speaking Christians in Port Elizabeth.[2] Equally extensive material from the more heterogeneous Bantu population of Soweto, Johannesburg, is contained in a recent report by Möller,[3] while Coertze gives information on traditional beliefs among the predominantly Sotho-speaking population of Atteridgeville, Pretoria.[4]

For Mdantsane two examples of ancestor beliefs among well-educated and highly westernized townspeople will therefore suffice. In August 1972 a tenant wrote to the officials for permission to brew beer and slaughter an animal 'to shed a little blood as propitiation to my ancestors'. A visit to his well-furnished home revealed that he was a man of about fifty with a Senior Certificate and a teaching qualification, although no longer teaching, and that he held the office of Preacher in a historic or orthodox church. He was born in East London where his father owned two wood-and-iron houses, but inherited a home and arable land in a reserve, which his father had never relinquished. The reserve home is cared for by relatives; his widowed mother, who inherited and later received compensation for the town properties, lives in Mdantsane. He may be regarded as primarily a townsman although he has strong links with the country.

The second example involves a younger man, also well-educated, more completely a townsman, with several years of experience in business, who has applied very modern ideas by township standards in his venture in Mdantsane. The following notes are from my own account of his views recorded on tape from memory immediately after a conversation conducted with him in English. Questioned about his success in business he ascribed it to 'sheer hard work' and the support of his people, especially his widowed mother, younger brother and clients. When I enquired about 'the unseen'—referring to people who speak of help from God or help through prayer or a blessing from the priest or through *amawethu* ('our ancestors')—he said that God helps one if one helps others, mentioning his deliberate liberal contributions to bereaved customers. He continued without prompting: 'When I have problems I go to my Dad's grave and think about my problems there, and this always sort of makes me feel better.' Question: 'Is there anything in particular that you do in connection with visiting the grave?' Answer: 'I do not do anything there but our people have the belief that some time after a person's death one has to slaughter an ox, and the custom is referred to as "bringing back" the dead person [cf. pp. 52-3]. We have not done this for my father yet but we still intend doing it. When things go wrong I sometimes think it is because we still have not done that. Then I go to the grave and tell him we do intend doing it, but we have this and that problem preventing us.'

1 Hammond-Tooke, W. D., 'Urbanization and the Interpretation of Misfortune: a Quantitative Analysis', *Africa*, 40, 1 (1970), pp. 26, 29.

2 Pauw, op. cit.

3 Möller, H. J., *God en die Voorouergeeste in die Lewe van die Stedelike Bantoe*, Stedelike Bantoe en die Kerk, Part II, Report Submitted to the Human Sciences Research Council, Pretoria, 1972.

4 Coertze, R. D., 'Godsdiens in Atteridgeville', in Eloff, F. J. and Coertze, R. D. (eds.), *Etnografiese Studies in Suidelike Afrika*, Van Schaik, Pretoria, 1972, pp. 346-69.

This kind of visit to a grave to pray or pay respect to an ancestor is apparently an urban development. Among Xhosa-speaking and other Nguni peoples visits for ritual purposes to graves other than those of chiefs[1] were unusual. Among Sotho peoples sacrifices were commonly performed at the graves of certain ancestors,[2] but visits merely for prayer were not common. Among Soweto people, however, Möller found that praying at the graves was a common way of maintaining or effecting contact with the ancestors among Nguni as well as Sotho-speaking townspeople.[3] I suggest that the custom of white South Africans to visit the graves of close kinsmen and friends has served as an example and has been reinterpreted in terms of traditional ancestor beliefs. Some Xhosa regard such visits as sure proof that Whites render the same kind of worship to ancestors as the Xhosa do.[4]

It is interesting to note some of the other values our businessman holds. When asked what he would do with his money if he became 'really rich', he first mentioned providing a comfortable home for his family, which includes unmarried adult siblings. In addition he wanted to found a bursary fund. Questioned about the number and make of cars he would like to own, he replied that one for himself and one for his wife 'would be enough'—for himself a Jaguar XJ if he had enough money, otherwise 'any good car would do'.

On first impressions one could have expected this businessman to represent the materialistic and secularized type about which we speculated in an earlier chapter (p. 42). However, although his interest in material advancement is unmistakable, it is balanced by altruistic interests combined with explicitly religious beliefs partly continuous with Xhosa tradition. In discussing the beliefs of Xhosa townspeople in Port Elizabeth who have drifted away from the churches, Durand emphasizes that, although their values are those of Western materialism, they are not atheists or agnostics: they still adhere to traditional beliefs about ancestors and to magic.[5] In Soweto Möller also found that the great majority of people without church connections and 'inactive' church people still believe in the influence of the ancestors, while many claim experience of ritual or the intervention of the ancestors.[6]

Our own findings on the almost universal adherence to initiation of males in ceremonies that accord with Xhosa tradition (pp. 88-94) are parallelled by Mayer's findings based on more recent fieldwork (1967, 1970) in Port Elizabeth, a larger and more industrialized town which also has a predominently Xhosa-speaking Bantu population but in which Red traditionalists are much less in evidence than in East London. He further reports that educated young men do find much of the ceremonial procedure meaningless and expect that it will undergo modernization and that the division between boys and men should become less rigid, but that even they remain convinced of the value of initiation for Xhosa people in general. Mayer sees this general interest in traditional ini-

1 Krige, E. J., *The Social System of the Zulus*, Shuter & Shooter, Pietermaritzburg, 1950 (second edition), p. 252.

2 Eiselen, W. M. and Schapera, I., 'Religious Beliefs and Practices', in Schapera, I. (ed.), *The Bantu-speaking Tribes of South Africa*, Routledge & Kegan Paul, London, 1937, pp. 255–6.

3 Moller, op. cit., pp. 124–6.

4 Pauw, op. cit.

5 Durand, op. cit., pp. 108–10, 117.

6 Möller, op. cit., pp. 107–9.

tiation as evidence of a concern to retain something that is distinctly African (although not even all South African Bantu peoples observe initiation ceremonies) in some kind of synthesis with contemporary urban experiences.[1] My own fieldwork in Port Elizabeth produced evidence of Xhosa-speaking political leaders extolling traditional customs in an attempt to raise enthusiasm for a broad African political unity.[2] Among the Xhosa-speaking population of Langa there have been similar attempts to link traditional customs expressing respect for the ancestors with 'modern nationalism'.[3] Altogether the conscious concern with the indigenous traditions of Africa and their adaptation to modern conditions seems to have increased in recent years.

SOCIO-CULTURAL CHANGE

For the sake of undergraduate students using this book as a text on social and cultural change, the contents may be more explicitly related to relevant theoretical concepts.

First there is the distinction Mitchell draws between 'situational' and 'historic' or 'processive' change.[4] When migrants move back and forth between a rural 'tribal' area and a town, the changes in the urban context may be situational, that is lasting only while they are in the urban situation, since they revert to their 'tribal' ways back at the rural home. The changes in behaviour of Red migrants in East London (pp. 17-18, 176) to which Mayer has paid particular attention aptly illustrate situational change. When in town they are forced to adapt their social relations and behaviour to economic and administrative patterns that differ distinctly from rural Red patterns. However, not only do they shed these adaptations when back at their rural homes but in those fields of activity and social relations in town in which they are able to choose, they consciously strive to maintain and establish the kinds of relations, and keep up the tradition-oriented activities, that exhibit their continuing identification with the Red home community and its way of life.[5]

A Xhosa born and bred in town usually does not experience such radical change in the course of his own life, but his way of life at any given time is the outcome of a gradual process of change that can be traced through documented history from the first contact of literate Western Europeans with non-literate Xhosa-speaking peoples. Admittedly our original study of Xhosa townsmen was largely synchronic, but our first chapter took account of certain aspects of family history. Moreover, knowledge of the major details of the history of the Xhosa-speaking peoples since their earliest contacts with Whites is sufficiently disseminated to be taken for granted. To the extent that we consider the social relations and customary behaviour and ideas of Xhosa townspeople against this historical background (e.g. p. 195), we are concerned with processive or historical change.

Our interpretation of change has been partly in terms of culture contact or

[1] Mayer, Philip, ' "Traditional" Manhood Initiation in an Industrial City: the African View', in De Jager, E. J. (ed.), *Man: Anthropological Essays Presented to O. F. Raum*, Struik, Cape Town, 1971, pp. 17–18.

[2] Pauw, op. cit.

[3] Wilson and Mafeje, op. cit., p. 112.

[4] Mitchell, J. C., 'Theoretical Orientations in African Urban Studies', in Banton, M. (ed.), *The Social Anthropology of Complex Societies*, Tavistock, London, 1966, p. 44.

[5] Mayer, *Townsmen or Tribesmen* (second edition), pp. 286–93 et passim.

acculturation, that is culture change resulting from the contact of people with differing cultures. The total process of acculturation in South Africa is of course extremely complex, involving a number of Bantu peoples between some of whom there were significant cultural differences, the Khoikhoin (Hottentots) and the San (Bushmen), Whites—mostly of Dutch, French, British or German descent—and Islamic Malay slaves and Islamic and Hindu Indians and their descendants. It would probably be possible to demonstrate reciprocal transmission of cultural elements between almost any two of the groups mentioned and in some cases there has also been some physical coalescence. There can, however, be little doubt that in this total South African situation westernization of the respective Bantu peoples represents the most extensive transmission or taking over of culture between two groups. In its concern with culture change this study has been dealing with such change among the Xhosa.

Although westernization is evident in many parts of the world to-day, it is not a distinct *type* of acculturation by itself; there are similar processes involving non-Western cultures. The Islamization of large parts of Africa, Asia and Indonesia, for example, has resulted in broad cultural uniformities among many people who have nevertheless retained their own cultural identity to some degree. In India the spread of Hinduism has brought a degree of cultural uniformity among large parts of the population in which many groups nevertheless still retain a distinct cultural identity.

The process of acculturation, described as westernization in the present context, has resulted neither in complete substitution of Western forms for indigenous ones nor in a mere juxtaposition of elements from two cultural traditions, but in a new way of life in which continuity with both traditions is recognizable. For Xhosa townspeople the continuities with Western tradition are the more obvious (pp. 27-8, 194-5).

It is characteristic of this process that items from the initially foreign culture are adapted to the indigenous culture, and portions of the latter to what has been incorporated from the foreign culture. A simple example of the first kind of adaptation is drinking tea or coffee without milk after a death (pp. 102, 107). The Xhosa learnt to drink tea and coffee from the Whites, but there is no precedent in customs of the latter for taking these beverages black at funerals. Only after writing the first edition of this book did I realize that tea and coffee are taken black in deference to a traditional custom of discarding the supply of milk in the home and not drinking milk when a death has occurred.[1]

Ukulobola (giving marriage cattle called *ikhazi* in Xhosa) again represents a traditional custom that has been adapted in the context of a Western money economy, not only in that money has replaced cattle, but in that such money is now often spent on the wedding reception or the bride's trousseau or even on matters having no connection with the marriage (p. 129). This is a distinct deviation from tradition which required that the *ikhazi* normally be kept by the bride's father or his successor, and be returned should the marriage be dissolved without any children being born.

Seclusion of the bride before marriage (p. 94) is an adaptation of traditional girls' puberty ceremonies which included a period of seclusion for the girl. The complete ceremonies have been dropped by rural School people and towns-

[1] Cf., for example, Hunter, *Reaction to Conquest*, p. 229, and Soga, J. H., *The Ama-Xosa: Life and Customs*, Lovedale Press, 1932, p. 324.

people, largely on account of the opposition of missionaries who regarded some features of the ceremonial as immoral. The custom has, however, been adapted to this Western approach by retaining only the seclusion as a very attenuated form of the traditional ceremonial and linking it with the wedding ceremony.

The process of change can also be considered as one of increase in the scale of society.[1] When a tribe or a people is small in numbers and most of the relations between its members are of an intense and personal nature, when it lives in relative isolation from other groups, lacks writing and has limited technological control over its environment and little specialization of economic functions, it is regarded as small in scale. Further, in small-scale society the individual's status is largely ascribed—that is, determined by his position in a particular kinship network or by birth in a particular local group and by sex and age. He cannot do much to change his status by his own efforts and the degree of choice open to him in his social relations and behaviour is limited. Kinship and neighbourhood form the basis of co-operation in different kinds of activities so that relations are of a multiplex nature: the same relationships may function in social, political, economic and religious activities. Other characteristics of small-scale society are magical ideas of causation and particularistic beliefs and morality that show concern only with one's own tribe or people.

With due regard for the relativity of the concept and most of the criteria applied, we may say that most tribes or clusters of tribes in Southern Africa were small-scale societies before the advent of Whites, and that the changes that have since taken place represent a reversal of many of the characteristics mentioned and therefore an increase in the scale of society.

When Xhosa-speaking people began making their way to towns, increase in scale was already in evidence. Some tribes had been incorporated into a colony and an empire, while others had extensive dealings with these larger political units. Xhosa-speaking people were buying goods imported from Europe and conducting a general trade with Whites. Some of them had accepted the Christian gospel and joined churches linking them with Christians far outside their own tribes, and missions and their schools had already made an impact on magical and particularistic ways of thinking and introduced writing and other new skills which led to economic diversification. In all these activities the amount of contact with non-tribesmen and non-Xhosa had increased considerably, while the determining role of kinship and neighbourhood ties had become less pervasive for people who attended schools and joined church congregations and new voluntary associations. Professor Monica Wilson typifies the process as one in which the Xhosa-speaking tribes, especially the communities of School people in them, developed into a peasantry.[2] There has been much argument about the definition of peasant society, but communities of School Xhosa were certainly taking on the intermediate nature of peasant society: while unmistakably having become part of a larger society with which they shared certain cultural features associated with a 'great tradition' (in this case Western European tradition), they retained a degree of social, political and economic autonomy

[1] Mair, L., *New Nations*, Weidenfeld & Nicholson, London, 1963, p. 13; Wilson, G. and M., *The Analysis of Social Change*, Cambridge University Press, 1954, pp. 24–44 et passim; Wilson, M., *Religion and the Transformation of Society*, Cambridge University Press, 1971, pp. 12–25; cf. Evans-Pritchard, E. E., *Social Anthropology*, Cohen & West, London, 1951, p. 8.

[2] Wilson, M., 'The Growth of Peasant Communities', in Wilson, M. and Thompson, L. (eds.), *The Oxford History of South Africa*, Vol. II, Clarendon Press, Oxford, 1971, pp. 49–103.

and a cultural identity of their own showing continuity with Xhosa tradition, a 'little tradition' accepted as their own by a limited population.[1] It is this pattern as it developed further in the course of time and was duplicated in the case of other peoples, that has made the Republic of South Africa the kind of society that some scholars call a plural society.

Urbanization furthered the process of increase in scale, especially for those Xhosa who made a town their permanent home. For them kinship has become still less significant than for rural School people so that they are freer to choose with whom they associate or how they behave, and voluntary associations and clubs are particularly significant (pp. 169, 171-4). The townsman can significantly enhance his status by his own efforts, especially by education and economic effort (pp. 178-9). The loose-knit social network of many townspeople (pp. 188-91) makes for fewer intense and personal relationships of the kind associated with small-scale society. For townspeople different kinds of relationships —social, political, religious and economic—do not necessarily overlap between the same persons as in small-scale society: here the school teacher, the minister, the legal adviser, the superintendent and the boss are different persons, each with functions limited to the relevant kind of activity. Townspeople have a larger range of technological devices—motor transport, electrical devices, water taps and waterborne sanitation, for example—at their disposal, and they participate in a greater diversity of economic activities than people in rural Xhosa communities. All this goes with a large variety of groups and relationships between individuals resulting in a complexity that also distinguishes large-scale from small-scale society.

Although it is difficult to interpret the matrifocal trend in family structure as a direct concomitant of increase in scale, it is related to this to the extent that it is associated with the diminished significance of patrilineal kinship groups (p. 164).

In spite of the obvious increase in scale, features associated with small-scale society are not altogether absent among urban Xhosa. Kinship ties, for example, although less binding, are still of considerable importance and magical beliefs about causation are still in evidence. While there is general consciousness of being part of a larger South African society and some people want to be 'Africans and nothing else', narrower traditional loyalties still play a role as in the competition between Xhosa proper and Mfengu. The majority of townsmen pay allegiance to churches and subscribe to their universalistic beliefs— one God, one Saviour and one book of Scriptures for all men—but many still adhere to particularistic beliefs about ancestors and witches. Even among townsmen we therefore find something of the intermediateness characterizing rural Xhosa School communities.[2]

[1] Cf. Redfield, R., *The Little Community*, pp. 132–48 and *Peasant Society and Culture*, pp. 40–59, (reprinted and published in one volume), University of Chicago Press, 1960.

[2] This theme is extensively dealt with in a forthcoming book (Pauw, op. cit.).

APPENDIX I

ADDITIONAL TABLES

TABLE 23

Occupation by sex and age

Type of occupation	MALES 15–24	25–34	35–44	45+	Total	FEMALES 15–24	25–34	35–44	45+	Total
Employees:										
'White-collar'	—	3	—	2	5	2	—	—	—	2
Skilled	2	3	1	2	8	3	—	—	—	3
Semi-skilled	—	—	—	—	—	5	—	1	—	6
Unskilled:										
Factory workers	5	7	—	—	12	6	3	—	1	10
Messengers	6	2	1	—	9	—	—	—	—	—
Domestic servants and washerwomen	—	—	—	—	—	3	8	4	5	20
Office cleaners	—	—	—	2	2	—	2	2	1	5
Other unskilled	10	4	4	1	19	2	4	1	—	7
(*Total unskilled*)	(*21*)	(*13*)	(*5*)	(*3*)	(*42*)	(*11*)	(*17*)	(*7*)	(*7*)	(*42*)
Self-employed	—	1	1	4	6	2	2	3	4	11
Not employed	11	1	1	2	15	35	9	10	7	61
Unknown	—	—	—	—	—	1	—	—	—	1
Total	34	21	8	13	76	59	28	21	18	126

Note: The occupations recorded include the following:

MALES: *White-collar:* 1 teacher, 1 commercial traveller, 1 hospital clerk, 1 male orderly, and 1 insurance agent.

Skilled: 3 factory-workers, 3 motor-car or lorry drivers, 1 ambulance-attendant, and 1 presser (dry-cleaning).

Unskilled: 5 packers, 3 butchery or bakery employees, 1 night-watchman, 3 garden-boys, 1 golf-caddie, 1 service-station attendant, 1 workshop cleaner, 1 wool lorry 'guard' (railways), 1 store labourer, 1 railway labourer, 1 labourer employed by firm handling reinforced metal.

Self-employed: 1 cartage contractor, 2 painters, 1 used clothes pedlar, 1 singer, 1 milk pedlar.

Not gainfully employed: 5 scholars.

FEMALES: *White-collar:* 2 nurses.

Skilled: 3 factory workers.

Semi-skilled: 5 factory workers, 1 'receptionist' to a dealer in native medicines. (The latter was a trained and experienced nurse who was unable to find a nursing post.)

Unskilled: 1 shop-assistant, 3 nurse aids, 1 waitress, 1 office girl, 1 cook and searcher of female prisoners for the police.

Self-employed: 2 used clothes pedlars, 3 liquor traders, 3 vegetable hawkers, 1 firewood pedlar, and 1 seller of roast cakes.

Not gainfully employed: 10 scholars and a number who regard themselves as occupied in domestic duties at home. Some of these derive an income from the letting of rooms.

TABLE 24

Occupation by sex and education

Type of occupation	Males 0–4	5–6	7–8	9–11	12+	Total	Females 0–4	5–6	7–8	9–11	12+	Total
	EDUCATION IN YEARS											
Employees:												
'White-collar'	—	—	1	3	1	5	—	—	—	—	2	2
Skilled	—	—	4	4	—	8	—	—	3	—	—	3
Semi-skilled	—	—	—	—	—	—	—	—	4	1	1	6
Unskilled:												
Factory workers	—	3	8	1	—	12	—	5	5	—	—	10
Messengers	—	3	4	2	—	9	—	—	—	—	—	—
Domestic servants and washerwomen	—	—	—	—	—	—	4	5	8	3	—	20
Office cleaners	1	1	—	—	—	2	1	1	2	1	—	5
Other unskilled	5	6	6	1	1	19	—	1	—	6	—	7
(Total unskilled)	*(6)*	*(13)*	*(18)*	*(4)*	*(1)*	*(42)*	*(5)*	*(12)*	*(15)*	*(10)*	*(—)*	*(42)*
Self-employed	2	2	1	1	—	6	—	4	6	1	—	11
Not gainfully employed	5	—	7	3	—	15	6	17	22	15	1	61
Unknown	—	—	—	—	—	—	1	—	—	—	—	1
Total	13	15	31	15	2	76	12	33	50	27	4	126

TABLE 25

Economic category by rooms per household

Number of rooms	White-collar	Intermediate	Simple-A	Simple-B	Other	Total
	ECONOMIC CATEGORY					
1	4	4	26	11	5	51
2	5	7	7	4	3	26
3	—	6	4	4	3	17
4	4	4	4	—	3	15
Total number of households	13	22	41	19	14	109
Total number of rooms	30	53	68	31	32	214
Average rooms per household	2·3	2·4	1·7	1·6	2·3	1·9

TABLE 26

Economic category by persons per room

Persons per room	White-collar	Intermediate	Simple-A	Simple-B	Other	Total
	ECONOMIC CATEGORY					
0–1	3	2	3	1	1	10
1·1–2	4	5	10	2	2	23
2·1–3	5	7	5	6	5	28
3·1–4	—	3	10	2	1	16
4·1–5	1	1	3	3	—	8
5·1–6	—	2	6	2	4	14
6·1–7	—	1	2	1	—	4
7·1–8	—	—	2	1	—	3
8·1–9	—	—	—	—	—	—
9·1–10	—	—	—	1	—	1
10·1–11	—	1	—	—	1	2
Total number of households	13	22	41	19	14	109
Total number of persons (net)	58	134	231	111	96	630
Average persons per room	1·9	2·5	3·4	3·6	3·0	2·9

TABLE 27

Economic category by pictures in main room[1]

Types of pictures	White-collar	Intermediate	Simple-A	Simple-B	Other	Total
	ECONOMIC CATEGORY					
Nil	2	—	15	5	1	23
Calendar only	1	1	3	3	1	9
Religious pictures[2]	—	—	3	—	—	3
Religious pictures, photographs of people and other items	6	12	1	3	8	30
Religious pictures and photographs of people only	3	5	8	5	—	21
Photographs of people only	—	—	4	2	1	7
Photographs of people and other items	1	4	5	—	1	11
Other items only	—	—	2	1	2	5
Total	13	22	41	19	14	109

[1] The material refers to pictures, original prints and enlargements of people, calendars, religious and educational certificates displayed on the walls, and diverse pictures. Of the latter there were only a few. 'Other items' include calendars, certificates and the diverse types of pictures.

[2] In one household under this heading there was also a calendar.

TABLE 28

A. *Education by sex*

Education in years	Males	Females	Total
0–6	28	45	73
7–8	31	50	81
9+	17	31	48
Total	76	126	202

Chi-square test indicates table is not significant.

B. *Education by age*

Education in years	AGE 15–24 I	25–34 II	35–44 III	45+ IV	Total
0–6	30	12	17	14	73
7–8	37	23	8	13	81
9+	26	14	4	4	48
Total	93	49	29	31	202

Chi-square test indicates that the whole table is significant at a 5 per cent level; further that tables I, II and III, IV are not significant, but that table (I + II), (III + IV) is significant at a 1 per cent level.

TABLE 29

Degree of interest in church by sex and age

Age	DEGREE OF INTEREST IN CHURCH: High or steady M	F	Medium M	F	Low or nil M	F	Total M	F
15–24	10	22	11	17	13	20	34	59
25–34	13	15	4	4	4	9	21	28
35–44	4	7	2	6	2	8	8	21
45 +	11	15	1	2	1	1	13	18
Total males and females	38	59	18	29	20	38	76	126
Totals	97		47		58		202	

TABLE 30

Degree of interest in church by education

Degree of interest in church	EDUCATION IN YEARS 0–6 I	7–8 II	9+ III	Total
High or steady	25	45	27	97
Medium	17	15	15	47
Low or nil	31	21	6	58
Total	73	81	48	202

Table significant at a 1 per cent level.

TABLE 31

Some leisure activities by sex and age

Activity	AGE 15–24	25–34	35–44	45 +	Total
			MALES		
(Total in Sample)	*34*	*21*	*8*	*13*	*76*
Church activities	21	14	4	10	49
Sport	21	13	2	5	41
Film and concert	8	3	—	—	11
Visiting beach	5	3	—	—	8
Jiving and dancing	4	1	—	—	5
Band and vocal group	6	—	—	1	7
			FEMALES		
(Total in Sample)	*59*	*28*	*21*	*18*	*126*
Church activities	39	17	14	14	84
Sport	9	5	1	1	16
Film and concert	9	2	—	—	11
Visiting beach	9	—	1	—	10
Jiving and dancing	4	1	—	—	5

TABLE 32

Some leisure activities by sex and education

Activity	EDUCATION IN YEARS 0–4	5–6	7–8	9+	Total
			MALES		
(Total in Sample)	*13*	*15*	*31*	*17*	*76*
Church activities	7	7	19	16	49
Drinking	12	11	4	4	31
Sport	4	3	20	14	41
Film and concert	2	1	5	3	11
Visiting beach	—	2	3	3	8
Jiving and dancing	—	1	1	3	5
Band and vocal group	—	—	5	2	7
			FEMALES		
(Total in Sample)	*12*	*33*	*50*	*31*	*126*
Church activities	5	18	36	25	84
Drinking	6	8	8	3	25
Sport	—	2	7	7	16
Film and concert	—	2	3	6	11
Visiting beach	—	—	5	5	10
Jiving and dancing	—	2	—	3	5

TABLE 33

Attitude to witchcraft beliefs by interest in church

Attitude	DEGREE OF INTEREST IN CHURCH Nil or low	Medium	Steady or high	Total
Positive	42	13	36	91
Undecided	6	7	15	28
Negative	10	27	46	83
Total	58	47	97	202

TABLE 34

Unmarried mothers: age of mothers by number of pregnancies

Age	Number of pregnancies 1*	2	3	4	5	6	Total mothers	Total pregnancies	Average pregnancy per mother
15–19	15	1	—	—	—	—	16	17	1·1
20–24	7	3	2	—	—	—	12	19	1·6
25–29	3	2	1	3	1	—	10	27	2·7
30–34	—	—	2	1	—	—	3	10	3·3
35 +	—	2	1	—	—	2	5	19	3·8
Total	25	8	6	4	1	2	46	92	2·0

* Includes two girls each expecting her first baby.

TABLE 35

Attitude to pre-marital sex relations by degree of interest in church

Attitude	DEGREE OF INTEREST IN CHURCH Nil	Low	Medium	Steady or high	Total
A. Traditional	7	23	17	31	78
B. Christian	—	2	9	12	23
C. Sanction or condone present practices	3	2	—	14	19
D. Conflicting attitudes	8	8	12	21	49
E. All answers negative	—	—	3	3	6
Total	18	35	41	81	175

TABLE 36

Attitude to pre-marital sex relations by education

Attitude	YEARS EDUCATION 0–4	5–6	7–8	9–11	12 +	Total
A. Traditional	13	16	31	15	3	78
B. Christian	2	4	13	4	—	23
C. Sanction or condone present practices	1	3	10	3	2	19
D. Conflicting attitudes	8	14	14	12	1	49
E. All answers negative	1	2	1	2	—	6
Total	25	39	69	36	6	175

TABLE 37

Attitude to pre-marital sex relations by cultural category

Attitude	CULTURAL CATEGORY Non-Red White-collar	Intermediate	Simple	Other	Semi-Red	Total
A. Traditional	9	24	27	9	9	78
B. Christian	1	9	13	—	—	23
C. Sanction or condone present practices	2	6	6	2	3	19
D. Conflicting attitudes	4	7	24	7	7	49
E. All answers negative	1	1	3	1	—	6
Total	17	47	73	19	19	175

TABLE 38

Household composition

		I			II			III			IV			V			VI			VII			VIII			IX			X			XI		
Type of household	Number of house-holds	'Fathers'			'Mothers'			CHILDREN						GRANDCHILDREN						OTHER MEMBERS						TOTAL						GRAND TOTAL		
								Male			Female			Male			Female			Male			Female			Male			Female					
		15–29	30–39	40+	15–29	30–39	40+	0–14	15–29	30+	0–14	15–29	30+	0–9	10–14	15–29	0–9	10–14	15–29	0–14	15–29	30+	0–14	15–29	30+	0–14	15–29	30+	0–14	15–29	30+	M	F	T
Multi-generation: male head	18	1	—	17	1	5	10	22	6	0	20	21	1	18	1	1	12	1	2	1	4	3	1	1	10	42	12	20	34	25	26	74	85	159
Father-mother-children	35	4	12	19	11	15	9	33	8	0	43	5	0	—	—	—	—	—	—	—	8	4	2	2	1	33	20	35	45	18	25	88	88	176
Multi-generation: female head	21	—	—	—	2	—	19	13	11	3	11	17	8	22	7	2	20	3	8	4	—	1	4	5	4	46	13	4	38	32	31	63	101	164
Mother-children	17	—	—	—	1	5	11	17	10	0	15	10	0	—	—	—	—	—	—	5	3	1	6	4	1	22	13	1	21	15	17	36	53	89
Other	18	1	3	8	3	1	6	—	5	1	—	—	—	—	—	—	1	3	—	1	—	3	1	3	3	1	6	15	5	6	10	22	21	43
Total	109	6	15	44	18	26	55	85	40	4	89	53	9	40	8	3	33	7	10	11	15	12	14	15	19	144	64	75	143	96	109	283	348	631
		65			99			129			151			51			50			38			48											
		164						280						101						86														

TABLE 39

(Extracted from Table 38, Column II)

'Mothers' (female heads and male heads' spouses): age by household type

Age of mother	HOUSEHOLD TYPE Multi-generation (M or F head) or Mother-children	Father-mother-children	Total
15–29	4	11	15
30–39	10	15	25
40+	40	9	49
Total	54	35	89

Table significant at a 1 per cent level.

TABLE 40

(Extracted from Table 38, Column IV)

Daughters: age by household type

Age of daughter	HOUSEHOLD TYPE Multi-gen. female head	Multi-gen. male head	Mother-children	Father-mother-children	Total
0–14	11	20	15	43	89
15+	25	22	10	5	62
Total	36	42	25	48	151

Table significant at a 1 per cent level.

TABLE 41

Marital status of household members 15 years and older

Type of household	MOTHERS OF 'FATHERS' or 'MOTHERS'		'FATHERS'			'MOTHERS'				SONS		DAUGHTERS				GRAND-SONS	GRAND-DAUGH-TERS		OTHER MALES				OTHER FEMALES				Total
	Living together	Widowed/Divorced/Separated	Single	Married or Living together	Widowed/Divorced/Separated	Single	Unmarried mother	Married or Living together	Widowed/Divorced/Separated	Single	Married or Living together	Single	Unmarried mother	Married or Living together	Widowed/Divorced/Separated	Single	Single	Unmarried mother	Single	Married or Living together	Widowed/Divorced/Separated	Unknown	Single	Unmarried mother	Married or Living together	Widowed/Divorced/Separated	
Multi-generation: male head	—	5	—	16	2	—	—	16	—	2	1	7	11	2	1	1	2	—	8	1	1	—	1	2	2	2	83
Father-mother-children	—	—	—	35	—	—	—	35	—	8	—	5	—	—	—	—	—	—	8	1	—	3	2	—	—	1	98
Multi-generation: female head	1	1	—	—	—	—	4	—	17	11	3	3	18	—	4	2	2	6	1	1	—	—	—	2	3	1	80
Mother-children	—	—	—	—	—	—	5	—	12	10	—	7	3	—	—	—	—	—	4	—	—	—	—	3	1	1	46
Other	—	—	1	8	3	1	2	4	3	5	1	—	—	—	—	—	—	—	1	2	—	—	—	2	2	2	37
Total	1	6	1	59	5	1	11	55	32	36	5	22	32	2	5	3	4	6	22	5	1	3	3	9	8	7	344

TABLE 42
(Extracted from Table 21)

Family structure by cultural category

Table A

Type of family	CULTURAL CATEGORY White-collar	Inter-mediate	Simple	Total
Multi-generation (male or female head)	3	7	25	35
Father-mother-children or mother-children	8	13	23	44
Total	11	20	48	79

Table not significant.

Table B

Type of family	CULTURAL CATEGORY White-collar	Inter-mediate	Simple	Total
Male headed	10	13	25	48
Female headed	1	7	23	31
Total	11	20	48	79

NOTES ON FIELDWORK, SAMPLING AND ANALYSIS

The fieldwork for this volume commenced with a number of intensive pilot interviews, followed by the application of a major questionnaire (A) seeking information mainly on cultural characteristics dealt with in chapter 3, and on marriage, household, and family, to some two hundred adults (over 15 years). A second questionnaire (B) sought information about preceding generations in the country and migration to town. After preliminary analysis of the returns from questionnaire A, fourteen households, representative of different cultural and structural types were selected for periodic visits, mainly with a view to observation and questioning on family life. The original intention was also to study a few families within a single neighbourhood context, but it proved that families with adult East London-born members were too thinly distributed over the greater location population to make this practicable. A series of open-ended questionnaires was further applied to small samples which were usually selected by assistants from the people they knew, representative of different sexes, ages, and educational levels. A few ceremonies and rituals were also observed. Fieldwork commenced during August 1958 and proceeded until March 1960, although after July 1959 the author spent most of his own time analysing material and writing-up.

Liberal use was made of the services of Bantu research assistants, but the author made a point of taking part in different phases of fieldwork himself, so as to be able to evaluate properly the information collected by assistants. Mr. S. Campbell Mvalo must be mentioned for having the lion's share in collecting the raw material, and for his talent for establishing close rapport with informants. Mr. Enos L. Xotyeni also gave assistance at various stages, and his contribution of reports rich in detail was particularly valuable. The services of a few other male assistants were enlisted temporarily for applying questionnaire A, and a female assistant was employed for a few weeks to interview girls and women on sexual activities. Assistants were trained along the lines described by Reader.[1] Messrs. Mvalo and Xotyeni had already had considerable experience as research assistants when they joined the author on the present project. All assistants were paid a weekly wage, varying according to experience and ability.

There was no known method of drawing a truly random sample of the total town-born Bantu population of the East Bank Location—the major Bantu location in East London, on which this study was concentrated—but I was fortunate in being able to follow in Reader's footsteps, who in his main survey questionnaire applied to every inmate on every tenth site in the location, had inquired after every respondent's place of birth. It was hoped that by selecting the East London-born respondents in his sample, 392 in all, we would have what would approximate to a one-in-ten sample of the professedly East London-born Bantu. The problem was, however, that anonymity had been preserved in the previous survey, so that to find the potential members of our sample, we had no names, only the site numbers where these persons were residing, as well as a few details of sex, age and relationship to the household head, to guide us. The result was somewhat disappointing in that many people could not be traced,

[1] *The Black Man's Portion*, p. 169.

and we ended with about half the number we had expected. But the persons in our sample were spread over all parts of the location, and we are confident that the sample is broadly representative of the second generation of Bantu in East London. In spite of the smaller number than we had expected, it still seems to have been the most satisfactory method of drawing a representative sample of this particular category. Out of a number of 221 persons contacted, 202 were interviewed for questionnaire A, 18 refused, while 1 could not be interviewed because of mental deficiency. The persons interviewed belonged to 109 different households. It must be made clear that this sample of urban households did not consist of households of which all the heads were East London-born, but all of them included adult members who claimed to be born in town. Questionnaire B was applied to the same sample, but as it sought information on ascending generations, only one form was filled in where two or more persons were children of the same father and mother. This left us with information on 130 sets of parents and grandparents on which our first chapter is based. Answers to this questionnaire revealed that 30 respondents were not genuinely East London-born, and for one or two sets of information these persons' details were eliminated.

Quantitative material collected through questionnaires A and B was transferred to cards uniformly punched close to the edges, by clipping out the edge opposite the appropriate holes. The use of these cards, which could easily be sorted by hand, made it possible to try out different bases of classification in order to find the most appropriate one. This was particularly helpful for the identification of the cultural types in chapter 3.

The relatively small size of the sample made statistical testing impracticable in some cases, but an attempt was made to test for significance wherever suggested trends were important for the main argument of a chapter, as in chapters 3 and 8. For 2 × 2 tables Armsen's exact tables[2] have been used, or for larger N Yates's test, (Fisher and Yates,[3] table VIII). For tables larger than 2 × 2 chi-square tests have been carried out, cf., e.g., Fisher and Yates,[3] (table IV).

[2] Armsen, P., 'Tables for Significance Tests of 2 × 2 Contingency Tables', *Biometrika*, 42, 3 and 4, pp. 494–511 (1955).

[3] Fisher, Ronald A., and Yates, Frank, *Statistical Tables for Biological, Agricultural and Medical Research*, Oliver Boyd, London, 1953.

NETWORK OF A HOUSEWIFE (R)

R is a young mother of three children. Her husband makes a living for the family by selling 'soft goods', but has no shop in which he does business. They used to live in Maxambeni, but when the houses of their neighbourhood had to be demolished to provide for a new thoroughfare they moved to Mekeni, where they bought a house of their own. 'Most of the people staying here are our friends whom we knew before we came here.' They moved in as tenants after R's husband bought the house. Details of the more important persons in R's network are tabulated below.

Person No.	Sex	Kinship relation	Residing in E.L.: YES/NO	Frequency of contact	Nature of contact
1	F	Nil	YES	Daily	Met through no. 1's selling soft goods and her coming to R's *husband*, who is in the *same business*, for advice. Now stays in the *same 'yard'*. Since R came to their present home, no. 1 became one of the people she 'talked to daily'. When in difficulties R would turn to no. 1, 2 or 3 for assistance if no. 5 (Hm) could not help.
2	F	Nil	YES	Daily	Used to be a neighbour in Maxambeni before the houses were demolished. Followed R when they came to their present home, and is also staying *in the yard*. They fetch water together and no. 2 'likes to come and *help* me, even in scrubbing the floor'. When in difficulties R would appeal to no. 1, 2 or 3 for assistance if no. 5 (Hm) could not help.
3	F	Nil	YES	Daily	Childhood friend; attended *school together*; now living in the *same house*. They go to town and to market together. 'She is like my mother's child to me. I trust her to the extent that she knows all my personal affairs.' When in difficulties R would appeal to no. 1, 2 or 3 for assistance if no. 5 (Hm) could not help.
4	F	Fs	YES	About once a week	R usually *visits* her at the week-end and she also visits R.
5	F	Hm	YES	2–3 times a month	R *visits* no. 5 at the week-end when possible. She and her husband render his parents *financial assistance* when they are short of food or clothes, and R would first *appeal* to them *for help* when in difficulties.
6	F	H B w	YES	Occasionally	Mutual *visiting*.
7	F	msHBd	YES	Occasionally	Mutual *visiting*. Stays in the *same yard as no.* 8 who is *her FBS*.
8	M	m s S	YES	Occasionally	Mutual *visiting*. Stays in *same yard as no.* 7 who is *his FBd*. No. 13 is his *mother*.

Person No.	Sex	Kinship relation	Residing in E.L.: YES/NO	Frequency on contact	Nature of contact
9	F	F s d	YES	Seldom	Came to *assist in housekeeping, when R was confined* in hospital with a baby. No regular contact.
10	M	Father	NO	Very seldom	*Letters* exchanged about once a month or less often; also *greetings and enquiries* after health *through visitors* to or from E.L. R *visited* them about nine months ago. She would appeal to them for help when in difficulties, but since they are not in town, this is not always possible.
11	F	Mother	NO	Very seldom	
12 (& fam.)	M	H F B	NO	Very seldom	Occasional exchange of *letters and messages*. R *visited* them about six months ago.
13 (& fam.)	F	m s	NO	Very seldom	'They *wrote* to me about four months ago to inform me of their daughter's engagement. When she marries, we will surely be invited and will *attend the wedding*.' No. 8 is her *son*.
14	F	Nil	NO	Very seldom	The only close *friend* R could think of outside E.L. Born in King William's Town and now in Port Elizabeth with her husband, whose country home is the place where R's parents-in-law were born.

R's network appears to consist of a close-knit nucleus of neighbour-friends, nos. 1, 2 and 3, who obviously must know each other well. The chances are that they also know several of the other persons who visit R, although this was not ascertained. There are a number of kinsfolk and affines in East London with whom contacts are on the whole not so close; some are closely connected with each other, e.g. nos. 5 and 6, and 7 and 8. Outside East London contacts are confined to her parents—they were married and lived in East London until her father retired, then settled in the country—and two families closely related to herself and her husband respectively, and one personal friend with whom her present contacts seem tenuous but whose husband is known to her parents-in-law. She further knew of her H F B and family in Johannesburg, but had not had any contact with them. Church services are the only gatherings she attends and she does not belong to any association or club. She does not regularly speak to any Whites, Coloureds or Indians, since she does most of her shopping in the location and has never been employed.

NEW LIQUOR LEGISLATION

Before August 1962 Bantu were able to buy 'Western' liquor only by permit, for which a standard four certificate was required. This restriction was removed by Act no. 72 of 1961, which allows the sale of liquor to Bantu on the same basis as to Whites and Coloureds. It is still too early to dogmatize about the effects of the new legislation, but there is substantial evidence of a decrease in the illicit sale of Western liquor. Enquiries made in Port Elizabeth locations indicate that there has been a decrease in the demand for liquor through illicit channels, while licensed liquor-dealers in other parts of the town state that many Coloureds who acted as runners to illicit dealers have quitted and taken on regular employment. That some volume of illicit trade still persists is probably due to the fact that illicit dealers readily offer credit and do not restrict their hours of business, while their premises have an atmosphere of their own more appealing to some of the location inhabitants than that of public bars.

To what extent there has been an increase in the consumption of Western liquor is difficult to tell. Some dealers, in fact, state that their business with Bantu has decreased, but consider that the trade they have lost has gone to new dealers in and near the Bantu residential areas. In any case there does not seem to have been any spectacular over-all increase so far.

In the absence of beer halls the sale of 'kaffir beer' continues much as before.

BIBLIOGRAPHY OF WORKS CITED

Armsen, P., 'Tables for Significance Tests of 2 × 2 Contingency Tables', *Biometrika*, 42, 3 and 4 (1955), pp. 494–511.

Banton, Michael, *West African City*, O.U.P., 1957.

Banton, M. (Ed.), *The Social Anthropology of Complex Societies*, Tavistock, London, 1966.

Bothma, C. V., *'n Volkekundige Ondersoek na die Aard en Ontstaansoorsake van Tsotsigroepe en hulle Aktiwiteite soos gevind in die Stedelike Gebied van Pretoria*, unpublished M.A. thesis, University of Pretoria, 1951.

Bott, E., *Family and Social Network*, Tavistock, London, 1957.

Brandel, M., 'Urban Lobolo Attitudes', *African Studies*, 17, 1 (1958), pp. 34-50.

Brandel-Syrier, M., *Reeftown Elite*, Routledge & Kegan Paul, London, 1971.

De Jager, E. J. (Ed.), *Man: Anthropological Essays Presented to O.F. Raum*, Struik, Cape Town, 1971.

Dubb, A. A., *The Role of the Church in an Urban African Society*, unpublished M.A. thesis, Rhodes University, 1962.

Durand, J. J. F., *Swartman, Stad en Toekoms*, Tafelberg, Cape Town, 1970.

Eloff, J. F., and Coertze, R. D. (Eds.), *Etnografiese Studies in Suidelike Afrika*, Van Schaik, Pretoria, 1972.

Epstein, A. L., *Politics in an Urban African Community*, Manchester University Press, 1958.

Evans-Pritchard, E.E., *Social Anthropology*, Cohen & West, London, 1951.

Fisher, Ronald A., and Yates, Frank, *Statistical Tables for Biological, Agricultural and Medical Research*, Oliver & Boyd, London, 1953.

Fort Hare, University of, *The Ciskei—a Bantu Homeland*, Fort Hare University Press, Fort Hare, 1971.

Gist, Noel P., and Halbert, L. A., *Urban Society*, Crowell, New York, 1954.

Goody, Jack (Ed.), *The Developmental Cycle in Domestic Groups*, Cambridge Papers in Social Anthropology, No. 1, Cambridge University Press, 1958.

Hammond-Tooke, W. D., *Tribes of the Willowvale District*, Dept. of Native Affairs, Ethnological Publications No. 36, 1957.

Hammond-Tooke, W.D., *Bhaca Society*, O.U.P., Cape Town, 1962.

Hammond-Tooke, W.D., 'Urbanization and the Interpretation of Misfortune: a Quantitative Analysis', *Africa*, 40, 1 (1970), pp. 25-39.

Hellman, Ellen (Ed.), *Handbook on Race Relations in South Africa*, O.U.P., Cape Town, 1949.

Holleman, F. J., 'Die Bantoehuwelik op die Kruispad', *Journal of Racial Affairs*, 11, 2 (1960), pp. 82–117.

Houghton, D. H. (Ed.), *Economic Development in a Plural Society*, O.U.P., Cape Town, 1960.

Hunter (Wilson), Monica, *Reaction to Conquest*, O.U.P. 1961 (second edition).

Jonas, P.J., *Die Veranderende Posisie van die Vrou in die Huwelik en Gesin by die Stedelike Xhosa van Oos-Londen, met Besondere Verwysing na die Dorp Mdantsane*, M.A. thesis, University of South Africa, 1972.

Krige, E.J., *The Social System of the Zulus*, Shuter & Shooter, Pietermaritzburg, 1950 (second edition).

Levin, Ruth, *Marriage in Langa Native Location*, Communications from the School of African Studies, University of Cape Town, 1947.

Madge, John, *The Tools of Social Science*, Longmans Green, London, 1953.

Mair, L., *New Nations*, Weidenfeld & Nicholson, London, 1963.

Marwick, M. G., 'The Modern Family in Social Anthropological Perspective' (Inaugural Lecture), Witwatersrand University Press, Johannesburg (reprinted from *African Studies*, 17, 3), 1958.

Mathewson, J. E., 'Impact of Urbanization on Lobolo', *Journal of Racial Affairs*, 10, 3 (1959), pp. 72–6.

Mayer, Philip, *Townsmen or Tribesmen* (*Xhosa in Town*), O.U.P., Cape Town, 1961 (first edition), 1971 (second edition).

Mills, E. M. Elton, and Wilson, Monica, *Land Tenure*, Keiskammahoek Rural Survey, Vol. IV Shuter & Shooter, Pietermaritzburg, 1952.

Mitchell, J. C., *Tribalism and the Plural Society*, O.U.P., 1960.

Moeno, S.N., *The Urban African Family Disorganisation with Special Reference to Illegitemacy*, M.A. thesis, University of South Africa, 1969.

Möller, H.J., *God en die Voorouergeeste in die Lewe van die Stedelike Bantoe*, Stedelike Bantoe en die Kerk, Part II, Report Submitted to the Human Sciences Research Council, Pretoria, 1972.

Ogburn, W. F., and Nimkoff, M. F., *A Handbook of Sociology*, Routledge & Kegan Paul, revised edition, 1953.

Pauw, B. A., *Religion in a Tswana Chiefdom*, O.U.P., 1960.

Pauw, B.A., *Christianity and Xhosa Tradition*, O.U.P., Cape Town, forthcoming.

Philips, Arthur (Ed.), *Survey of African Marriage and Family Life*, O.U.P., 1953.

Qumza, G., 'Ciskei Tribal Rift', *Daily Dispatch*, October 28, 1972.

Radcliffe-Brown, A. R., and Forde, D. (Eds.), *African Systems of Kinship and Marriage*, O.U.P., 1950.

Reader, D. H., *The Black Man's Portion* (*Xhosa in Town*), O.U.P., Cape Town, 1961.

Redfield, R., *The Little Community* and *Peasant Society and Culture* (reprinted and published in one volume), University of Chicago Press, 1960.

Schapera, I. (Ed.), *The Bantu-speaking Tribes of South Africa*, Routledge & Kegan Paul, London, 1937.

Shepherd, Robert H. W., *Lovedale, South Africa*, Lovedale Press, 1940.

Smith, Raymond T., *The Negro Family in British Guiana*, Routledge & Kegan Paul, London, 1956.

Soga, J. H., *The South-Eastern Bantu*, Witwatersrand University Press, Johannesburg, 1930.

Soga, J.H., *The Ama-Xosa: Life and Customs*, Lovedale Press, 1932.

Southall, A. W., and Gutkind, P. C. W., *Townsmen in the Making*, East Africa Institute of Social Research, Kampala, 1957.

Southall, Aidan (Ed.), *Social Change in Modern Africa*, O.U.P., 1961.

UNESCO, *Social Implications of Industrialization and Urbanization in Africa South of the Sahara*, 1956.

Vogt, Evon Z., 'On the Concepts of Structure and Process in Cultural Anthropology', *American Anthropologist*, 62, 1 (1960), pp. 18–33.

Warner, W. Lloyd, and Lunt, Paul S., *The Social Life of a Modern Community*, Yankee City Series, Vol. I, New Haven, 1941.

Wilson, G. and M., *The Analysis of Social Change*, Cambridge University Press, 1954.

Wilson, M., *Religion and the Transformation of Society*, Cambridge University Press, 1971.

Wilson, M., and Mafeje, A., *Langa*, O.U.P., Cape Town, 1963.

Wilson, M., and Thompson, L. (Eds.), *The Oxford History of South Africa*, Vol. II, Clarendon Press, Oxford, 1971.

Wilson, Monica (and others), *Social Structure*, Keiskammahoek Rural Survey, Vol. III, Shuter & Shooter, Pietermaritzburg, 1952.

Young, M., and Wilmot, P., *Family and Kinship in East London*, Routledge & Kegan Paul, London, 1951.

INDEX

(not incorporating new chapter 11)

Date Due
